W9-CGL-838

America The Endless Quest

VOLUME 1

H.L. Ingle
University of Tennessee, Chattanooga

James A. Ward
University of Tennessee, Chattanooga

William B. Scott
Kenyon College

KENDALL/HUNT PUBLISHING COMPANY

4050 Westmark Drive   Dubuque, Iowa 52002

Cover design courtesy Stephen Le Winter

Stamp Designs © U.S. Postal Service. Reproduced with permission. All rights reserved.

Copyright © 2003 by H.L. Ingle, James A. Ward, and William B. Scott

ISBN 0-7872-9763-1

Kendall/Hunt Publishing Company has the exclusive rights to
reproduce this work, to prepare derivative works from this work,
to publicly distribute this work, to publicly perform this work and
to publicly display this work.

All rights reserved. No part of this publication may be reproduced,
stored in a retrieval system, or transmitted, in any form or by any
means, electronic, mechanical, photocopying, recording , or otherwise,
without the prior written permission of the copyright owner.

Printed in the United States of America
10 9 8 7 6 5 4 3 2 1

*Dedicated to our students who
have taught us so much.*

H.L.I.

J.A.W.

W.B.S.

CONTENTS

PREFACE

Woody Guthrie roamed the length and breadth of America during the dust bowl years of the 1930s talking and singing to the downtrodden and dispossessed. After years of hopping freight trains, eating from tin cans with other "knights of the road," and singing for his room, he became convinced that beneath the physical suffering and deprivation he saw lay a powerful belief in America's ongoing quest for greatness and unity. He put it to music:

> *This land is your land*
> *This land is my land*
> *From California*
> *To the New York Island*
> *From the red wood forests*
> *To the gulf stream waters;*
> *This land was made for you and me.*[1]

Guthrie's tune became a classic because it touched a responsive chord in the collective American psyche and echoed a firm belief that there was and is something intrinsically special about this land and its people.

It reflected the notion that Americans have been endowed with a high moral purpose to show the rest of the world how to be happy and prosperous—in short, that we believe in our own moral superiority. John Winthrop articulated this notion as early as 1630 when he told his fellow Puritans, bound for Massachusetts Bay, that "wee shall be as a city upon a Hill, the eies of all people are uppon us." We took his words seriously.

The Founding Fathers believed that Americans would need only a few broad rules to guide them because they believed, above all, that individuals have the right

---

1. "This Land Is Our Land," Words and Music by Woody Guthrie; Copyright 1956, 1958 and 1970 Ludlow Music, Inc., New York, New York. Used by Permission.

to determine their own destinies. This cult of individualism is the foundation on which we have built our form of capitalism. Just as surely, it has affected our exploitation of natural resources and the environment, our elective, supermarket system of education, even the way we rear our children. And, of course, American foreign policy has sought to internationalize and protect this central assumption.

Our strong belief in competitive individualism coexists with our contention that we are a nation of people holding common ideals. And that is what this book is all about: the story of our struggle of over three-and-one-half centuries to live with both our commitment to high ideals, which unites us, and our exaltation of the individual, which drives us apart and ultimately fosters class antagonisms, racial discord, sexual discrimination, and religious bigotry. It is this natural cleavage that divides Americans in crises. During the Revolution, throughout the process of writing and ratifying the Constitution, amid the struggle over states' rights and slavery, in the depths of depressions and two world wars, through racial unrest, prolonged conflict over Vietnam, the Watergate crimes, and defense spending, Americans fought among themselves. What made these struggles so terribly intense and divisive was that each side laid legitimate claim to being true to the country's basic ideals; the conflict is inherent in the ideals themselves. The continuing quest to bring our ideals into line with our actions is an important part of what makes American history so fascinating.

In *The Endless Quest* we have sought to portray, in as few words as possible, some of the high drama, color, pathos, and optimism that has molded America. The book is not an encyclopedic history in short form; history as a mass of data to be memorized and spewed back on exams is meaningless. Rather, we have selectively presented facts, topics, and interpretations that we feel are essential to some understanding of our heritage. Our organization, presentation, and interpretation are largely the result of our experiences in teaching American history to large classes of predominantly non-history majors. The book is directed to the student who quite likely is taking history because it fills an empty time slot in his schedule, because the instructor has a good reputation, or because the course is required. We believe that no substantial learning can take place in such classes if the instructor or the assigned readings do not in some degree generate student enthusiasm. So we have written a sprightly book filled with enthusiasm, humor, and verve. At the same time, we make no attempt to talk down to students. This book contains some words and phrases possibly unfamiliar to undergraduates. If the student looks them up, we have generated interest; we think this is what education is all about.

As an interpretative history, this book has a flow that is sometimes chronological and sometimes topical. For purposes of clarity and convenient reference we have inserted topical headings, but not so many as to chop up the narrative. To further help the student put American history into chronological perspective we have provided at the opening of each chapter a "time line," which lists important events and their dates. At the end of each chapter we have inserted a section "Historical Potpourri" that we hope gives something of the *flavor* of the period. We have also included maps where they will be useful. Because we cover no historical episodes in great depth, we have added at the end of each chapter a list of good books for further reading. The list is certainly not all-inclusive; it is merely a starting point for motivated readers who want to learn more about a specific topic. The books included are ones that our own undergraduates have told us they enjoyed and, to be frank, books that we like as well.

As all histories do, this one covers the "movers and shakers" in America, the people who made decisions that have affected us all. In addition, we have tried to give the flavor of what it has meant to be poor, black, Indian, female, Chicano, or Puerto Rican in a predominantly WASP, male-dominated society. After all, nobody can move and shake unless there are people to be moved and shaken. We have also woven economic and social discussions into the American fabric to give some idea of the complex nature of our nationhood. If we have slighted issues, periods, groups, or ideologies that an instructor believes are important, *The Endless Quest* is brief enough to allow leeway to assign outside works that emphasize particular interests.

The Endless Quest, then, is a concise, provocative, and interpretative book written for undergraduate non-history majors in the hope that it will motivate such students to at least reflect on their past and perhaps excite them enough to elect to take additional history courses.

CHAPTER ONE

GENESIS

Genesis

Had the earth remained as it was hundreds of millions of years ago this book would have been much longer, for the history of this land would encompass the entire history of man. At that time all dry land was a single mass scientists call "Pangaea." Fulfilling the biblical injunction in Genesis 1:9, "let the waters under the heaven be gathered together unto one place," a single ocean surrounded Pangaea. Some primeval force caused cracks to develop in the one huge land mass. Slowly the pieces drifted outward. Over the eons seven continents formed. As generations have noticed, the world map is like an unassembled puzzle whose pieces are permanently separated: if joined, the continents would fit roughly together.

In Medieval times the Western Hemisphere remained unknown to European civilizations. But there were hints that something lay to the west. In the classical period Plato had hypothesized that the mythical city of Atlantis lay somewhere in the Atlantic. Chinese tales related that Buddhist missionaries explored and mapped the west coast of North America. Later European legends told of an Irish Catholic monk, St. Brendan, who in the sixth century crossed the Atlantic in an open boat with seventeen followers.

More insistent are the sagas that tell of Leif Erikson, son of the Norwegian discoverer of Greenland, who explored the coastline of the new world and built a temporary settlement sometime around the year 1000. The legends relate that later Scandinavian adventurers named three areas of the Western Hemisphere Helluland or stone land, Markland meaning woodland, and Vinland land of grapes. Some sketchy

A Leif Erikson statue stands in front of the National Cathedral in Reykjavik, Iceland. The United States gave it to Iceland to commemorate the 1,000th anniversary of its Thing, the world's oldest parliament. (1968)

documentary evidence indicates that Greenlanders carried on a regular trade for centuries with the new world, primarily for lumber. As late as 1347 a small dismasted ship blew into an Icelandic port where the harbor master recorded that the vessel had come from Greenland and had traveled to Markland for a load of timber when a storm had swept it off course.

After years of searching for physical evidence of Scandinavian presence in the new world, archaeologists in the early 1960s located the remains of a small Norse settlement at the northern tip of Newfoundland at a site called L'Anse Aux Meadows. Years of excavation have unearthed eight buildings, including houses, perhaps a boathouse, and a smithy which carbon date to around the year 1000. That the area was a Norse site is unquestioned; whether it was the location of Leifs' Vinland is not known. Shortly after the archeological excavation of the Meadows site, a coin found earlier in an old Indian site in Maine was identified as an 11th century Norse piece. How it got there is a fascinating question that probably will never be satisfactorily answered, but the speculation that Scandinavians used it to trade with the Indians is certainly intriguing. Equally interesting are several artifacts unearthed in Greenland itself. Archaeologists working there in the 1920s found an Indian arrowhead of a type used by New England tribes and a lump of coal that seems to have come from a Rhode Island coal deposit. The new world, however, swallowed up the Scandinavians just as it later did thousands of other hardy Europeans. For the 145 years that intervened between the last documented contact with the western hemisphere by the Scandinavian wood gatherers who had washed up on the Icelandic coast and Columbus' "rediscovery" of the new world, America lived only in the dim mists of European legends.

The First Americans

In 1492 Columbus discovered America while searching for a western sea route to China. When he landed at the Caribbean island of San Salvador, he believed that he had reached the East Indies. Hence, he called the native inhabitants, whom Columbus found to be gentle and generous people, "Indians." It is not known when the first people arrived in the Americas, but it is estimated humans lived in the New World anywhere between 12,000 and 45,000 years before Europeans arrived. Most early Americans migrated from what is now Russian Siberia across a bridge of land that connected Asia with Alaska. Others might have sailed or paddled across the then-much-narrower Bering Straits or from the western horn of Africa to what is now

Brazil. From wherever they may have migrated, by 25,000 B.C., people lived throughout the New World from the Arctic Circle to Cape Horn. Most, however, concentrated in the warmer climates of Central America. At the time of Columbus' arrival, the Aztecs in Mexico were the largest and most influential New World people, dominating the Carribean much as the ancient Romans had dominated the Mediterranean Sea.

A romanticized depiction of Columbus, well armed and ceremonially clad, claiming San Salvador for Spain. No one knows whether Columbus landed on that island or one nearby. Whichever, the native Americans' lives were changed forever. (1893)

If the Indians had known Columbus was coming, nobody knows with any certainty how many could have been on hand to greet him. Estimates of the number of Indians in both North and South America range all the way from 8 to 75 million, with the best guesses centering around 10 million or roughly the same person to land ratio in Europe, Asia, and Africa. Of these about a million or more lived in what is now the United States. The history of New World people from the arrival of Columbus through the nineteenth century was an unmitigated tragedy. By the American Civil War only 340,000 native Americans lived in the continental United States. By 1910 that figure had shrunk to 220,000. Since then, their high birth rate has almost tripled their numbers in the United States. Today, there are more native Americans in the United States than in 1492, although they occupy less than 1% of the land their forbears claimed.

Both Indians and Europeans must have greeted each other with a mixture of curiosity and fear of the unknown. Certainly early colonists found the Indian culture most unfamiliar, and with few exceptions, notably William Penn and Roger Williams, they considered the native Americans hopelessly backward and inferior. Yet, the multitude of tribes scattered across the continent had adapted to widely different environments with a degree of success that allowed them to flourish. Depending on their native habitats, they hunted, gathered wild berries and nuts, fished, or farmed, and left the land very much as they found it. They cultivated an almost mystical relationship with the land and nature, believing that a special spirit infused both animate and inanimate objects that affected or acted on humans to determine individual destinies. Some tribes believed in one Great Spirit who was responsible for creation; others believed the sum of human spirits pervaded the world and determined the fate of individuals, and one Algonquian group identified its supreme being with the caribou. Almost all tribes counted intermediaries who mediated between earthlings and the various spirits, cured the sick, and petitioned the spirits for good crops, victory in war, or good luck. Most Indians conceived of a life after death, not the "happy hunting ground" attributed to them by whites, but another physical world where existence would be considerably easier.

Indian society revolved around the family and clan within the various tribal groups. They traced their tribal relations through bloodlines on the fathers' side or, among Siouan tribes, on the mothers'. The clans often assumed responsibilities and duties within the tribes that elsewhere would be the function of a family. Frequently clan activities were of such a cooperative nature that some clans assumed responsibility for the care, training, and discipline of all the tribe's children. In only a few tribes, such as the Natchez in the lower Mississippi valley, did a rigid class system exist. Most groups viewed land ownership as a tribal responsibility that precluded individual ownership or even tribal sale. They limited individual ownership to personal items such as weapons, clothes, and cooking utensils.

Contrary to Western beliefs, Indians did not spend all their time fighting. Indian conflict was frequent, often developing over territory, horses, women, pride, or for innumerable other reasons. The wars themselves did not last long, although tribal hatreds and feuds sometimes lingered for centuries. And often, killing the enemy was not the goal. The Iroquois confederation honed torture to a fine point; on the Plains, Indian warriors gained honor by "counting a coup"—physically touching their opponents and escaping alive.

Americans Confront Europeans

Early European settlers were fortunate in that the Indian groups that they first encountered were smaller and militarily weaker than many of the more powerful ones in the interior. Had the earliest English settlers encountered the powerful Southeastern Choctaw or the Iroquois Nation—an advanced league of five northern tribes, the Oneida, Mohawk, Onondaga, Seneca, and Cayuga, in which women had the power to depose sachems or chiefs—they might never have gotten a toehold in the new world. The coastal tribes, however, could never unite against the colonists. Indeed, many tribes took white settlers as allies against their traditional enemies. The Algonquians, the most widespread group along the coast, maintained relatively permanent villages that were easy to destroy. More serious, Native Americans possessed no immunity to Old World diseases, including influenza. When the

Pilgrims landed in Plymouth in 1619, they found an empty land that had been ravished by small pox acquired from Europeans who fished the offshore cod fish banks and dried their catch on the mainland.

The Indians faced distinct military disadvantages against the ever-encroaching colonists because of their almost anarchic forms of tribal government. In many tribes, especially in the middle Atlantic and southeastern areas, councils made decisions on the basis of consensus; even war chiefs were often elected. Such customs allowed great individual freedom to tribal members, and in times of battle warriors had the right to withdraw from the fighting if they so desired. Such informal procedures made long wars or protracted sieges difficult. Confronted with organized European armies and more centralized colonial militia units, the Indians, although man for man as tough and courageous as their white opponents, fought under obvious handicaps.

Despite the constant Indian wars, colonists often owed their survival to the Indians. The story of Squanto and his friends who helped the Pilgrims endure the first desperate winter in Massachusetts and who then taught the settlers to plant and fertilize crops the following spring shows that relations between native Americans and whites could be friendly, at least in the early days. To survive, European settlers adopted many Indian foods and words. Corn and potatoes, unfamiliar to the Europeans, became staples the world over. Other now commonplace foods—peanuts, sweet potatoes, squash, pumpkins, peppers, tomatoes, and baked beans—came to grace American tables from Indian gardens. Perhaps the most precocious of all agricultural people, Native Americans domesticated 45% of the agricultural crops currently grown in the United States, including maize, a mainstay of the American economy.

European colonists also adopted numerous Indian devices suited to the New World such as canoes, toboggans, moccasins, snowshoes, hammocks, kayaks, and ponchos. The Indian rubber ball made numerous popular American pastimes possible. Settlers also assimilated many Indian words, such as that mainstay of the southern diet, hominy, and others like chipmunk, moose, opossum, skunk, raccoon, and tomahawk. Europeans could not live in close proximity with native Americans without adopting some of their superior techniques.

The cultural exchange worked both ways. From Europeans, Native Americans acquired gunpowder and firearms, the horse, metal utensils from knives to pots, woolen clothing, blankets, in some cases the ability to read and write, facets of Christianity, liquor, and disease. Furs, trapped during the winter when coats were thick and sleek, paid for purchases and revolutionized clothing styles in Europe; beaver hats, for example, became a rage all across the continent. The fur trade introduced native peoples to the market economy. Before European contact, Native Americans had only traded for rare metals and prized flint. But having acquired a taste for European trade goods, they hunted fur-bearing animals, not for clothing or food, but to exchange for knives, glass, whiskey, and blankets. Such trade demanded intensive hunting, leading many to trespass on the traditional boundaries of other groups and fostered unprecedented hostility between Indian peoples as it destabilized their economies. In 1492 few native people would have understood the meaning of famine. By 1800 thousands of Native Americans lived on the edge of starvation because males devoted all of their time to fur trapping or fighting other groups over hunting grounds rather than growing and gathering food. Throughout the colonial period, fur trading remained a mainstay of the colonial economy, particularly in New York and the Carolinas, enriching traders and merchants while destroying native tribes.

The New Man

Columbus' arrival was immediately followed by a flood of adventurers, who within another century charted the entire eastern and a portion of the western coastlines of North and South America. The Spanish and the French quickly founded permanent settlements, established a vigorous trans-Atlantic trade, and whetted Europeans' interest in all things American. Europeans certainly had not ventured out with such enthusiasm after the earlier Scandinavian discoveries. Europe was in the throes of dramatic changes. Aggravated by the multitude of small warring principalities, the old society built on the ruins of the Roman Empire was in an advanced state of decay. Columbus' discovery opened the way for change in Europe, including the formation of nation-states, new religious beliefs, and bold ideas. Vitally for the Americas, the Renaissance—the intellectual revolution—created a "new man," one who, instead of concentrating on the life hereafter, expected his rewards now; a man with a newly found confidence in his own worth and abilities; a man always testing his own physical limitations; an acquisitive man. These new men chanced their lives on the world's uncharted oceans for the greater love of God, glory, and gold. The potential rewards were immense, but for the first two centuries the risks were even greater. The new world was a killer, yet inspired Europeans continued to pour across the Atlantic to test their mettle.

The Commercial Revolution

The changes convulsing Europe led directly to the discovery and settlement of the new world. These changes began as early as the Crusades when the luxuries of the East once again became popular in Europe. By 1100 Europeans imported high value articles such as steel, chinaware, carpets, perfumes, gems, drugs, spices, and even underwear, all of which had been scarce for centuries. This trade was handled by Italian middlemen who purchased goods from Arab traders in the eastern Mediterranean and resold them to western Europeans. Western merchants sold the products at the Atlantic coast ports where they were then transported to the interior for resale. Because of all the middle-men, prices were high, enabling a new rising class of merchants to acquire great wealth. After the Crusades, Europe faced the specter of over-population, probably due to better nutrition and an increased protein intake primarily caused by the introduction of the bean into people's diets. An agricultural society with limited land cannot absorb a sudden increase in population—farmers' plots either have to become smaller or the surplus people had to migrate to the towns and cities. In Europe the migration began and the cities grew. Individuals newly divorced from the land purchased or bartered for all their necessities, which led to a larger demand for goods and, in turn, to a heavier trade with the Italian middlemen.

Prosperous trade needs large, safe, markets and political protection. The merchants had to pay numerous feudal rulers to protect their trade and financially supported other leaders who were ambitious to expand their domains. Over several centuries, with help from the rising merchant class, a few monarchs conquered huge territories that eventually became modern nations; France was unified in 1453, Spain in 1492, and England during the course of the fifteenth century. Merchants increasingly demanded that these new national rulers protect their expanding trade, a policy that submerged individuals' interests to the larger requirements of the nation. The ability of these nations to defend themselves was measured by their financial resources.

In the interest of national strength, a body of economic doctrine called mercantilism emerged by the seventeenth century in Europe. Mercantilists believed that a nation was only as powerful as the amount of gold it held in its treasury plus the quantity of specie its citizens possessed; private gold was always available to the tax gatherers to help finance wars. To keep its gold at home a nation had to buy as little as possible from the outside and sell as much as possible to its neighbors, thus maintaining a "favorable" balance of trade. Because economic thinkers believed that there was only a limited quantity of gold in the world, mercantilism became a form of economic warfare, a "beggar thy neighbor" proposition. Each nation intervened in its economy and set up taxes on imports, called tariffs, to discourage the purchase of foreign products and to encourage domestic production, thus providing employment for the growing population. Also, ways were sought to avoid paying Italian and Arab middlemen. The theory was simple, but its effect on the new world was immense. After the rediscovery of the new world, Europeans sought colonies and trading stations to provide raw materials that otherwise would have to be purchased from others.

The quest for raw materials and new markets was made easier by a simultaneous scientific revolution. The invention of moveable type and the printing press, developed in the 1440s, enabled explorers to spread the news of their discoveries complete with maps, thereby sharpening the European fascination for the new world. Nautical inventions were even more important for exploration. In the early fifteenth century the compass was widely introduced into Europe, and the astrolabe, a forerunner of the sextant although it only determined latitude, was developed. A reliable mechanical clock allowed sailors to take more precise sightings, and new sail and hull configurations permitted the voyagers to sail more closely into the wind. Although none of these devices guaranteed a safe trip across the ocean, the sailors thought that they did, and in history what is thought is usually more important than what is real.

The Reformation

Scientific improvements, the search for trade routes, the need for greater national security, and for relief from overpopulation lured Europeans to the New World. A religious revolution, the Reformation, drove many people to it. In 1517, in the midst of all the other changes shaking the Western world, a German monk, Martin Luther, rebelled against his church. When the Catholic church failed to respond to Luther's challenge for reforms and excommunicated the errant monk, Luther unleashed a powerful imperative toward literacy. Luther fervently believed that all people were capable of finding Christian truths if they could have direct access to the Bible without priestly interpretation. This led to translations of the Bible from Latin into the national languages to allow more people to read the Holy Writ; Luther himself translated it into German. Thereafter Latin declined as the international language. Luther also believed that once a person experienced the truth he had achieved salvation by his personal faith alone. He did not need the outward signs of holiness demanded by Rome, such as indulgences, penance, pilgrimages, fasts, and relics.

Luther's Reformation had a profound influence on all aspects of European life. It soon became political as many German princes saw a chance to throw off the yoke of Rome, to confiscate rich Catholic properties, to head their own state churches, and to increase popular allegiance to themselves as sovereign rulers. In the 1520s religious revolutions in the German states and in Scandinavia pitted Catholics against those who now called themselves Protestants.

John Calvin, a Frenchman, took many of Luther's ideas, added the notions of predestination—that God willed in advance each person's destiny—and the theory that religion was not subordinate to the state, and internationalized the Reformation. Men from all over Europe came to the town of Geneva in Switzerland to imbibe Calvin's teachings and returned to their native countries to spread the new doctrines. Soon sizable numbers of Protestants appeared in most nations. Protestantism received an additional boost in 1534 when King Henry VIII declared himself head of the English church, independent of Rome, after the Pope had refused to annul his marriage to Catherine of Aragon.

The Reformation, started just after the discovery of the new world, had a massive effect on America. A sense of national identity, or nationalism, already encouraged by mercantilist policies, suddenly had religious undergirding. Protestant kings and princes, in addition to their political duties, abruptly acquired spiritual legitimacy as heads of their respective state churches. Capitalism, the quest for private profit, long fettered by the Catholic church's declaration that charging interest on loans was a sin, was encouraged by the Protestants' willingness to allow such transactions. Jews, the most prominent bankers in Medieval Catholic Europe, faced competition from wealthy Protestant merchants who performed banking functions. Many of the Protestant merchants risked their money in transatlantic voyages hoping to reap huge profits. Moreover, as the religious conflicts continued, the Catholic church mounted a Counter-Reformation, the Protestant sects began to squabble among themselves, and thousands of people's lives were endangered due to their religious beliefs. Many Huguenots or French Calvinists, Catholics in northern German states, Protestants in southern German states, Catholics, Puritans, and Quakers in England, all of whom were religious minorities in their native lands, welcomed the chance to flee to a new world.

Voyages of Discovery

The impulse for discovery of new lands had come from European kings' and merchants' efforts to eliminate the expensive Italian middlemen involved in the Eastern trade. The first nation seriously to attempt to bypass the Italian trade monopoly was tiny Portugal, itself a middleman between the Italians and the merchants of northern Europe. Portuguese ships began to venture down the west coast of Africa searching for a sea route to the Indies around its southern tip early in the fifteenth century. Although the Portuguese were primarily in pursuit of gold and glory, they did not neglect God. Prince Henry the Navigator, the sponsor of these voyages, hoped that his sailors would locate the kingdom of the legendary Christian monk, Prester John, supposedly located in central Africa, somewhere south of the Arab infidels. If true, the Arabs who had invaded Spain on a religious crusade to convert the Spaniards to the Muslim faith, would be surrounded by Christians and crushed. Prester John was never found of course, but his myth died hard. For years Europeans continued to hope that he was waiting for them deep in Africa.

In 1487 Bartholomew Diaz, a Portuguese explorer, sailed as far as the Cape of Good Hope, the southern tip of Africa. Twelve years later Vasco da Gama completed a round-trip voyage to India and brought back to Lisbon a valuable cargo. The Italian monopoly was broken, although Italy's economic importance only slowly diminished. The Mediterranean Sea eventually became a backwater as the Atlantic seaboard witnessed the growth of the great colonizing nations. Portugal, the first of these, wasted no time in establishing an eastern empire, parts of which she retained for over 450 years. The new routes caused prices on imported goods to fall as much as 80 percent. Ironically, the Portuguese replaced the Italians as the hated middlemen, thereby forcing other nations to search for their own shortcuts to the fabled East, to keep their gold at home.

The Spanish, enmeshed in these national rivalries, suddenly listened to the Italian, Columbus, who promised to locate a new trade route to the Far East. Educated men since ancient times had surmised that the world was round, and any sailor who watched a ship disappear over the horizon at least knew that the world was not flat. Columbus was the first man known to stake his life on the theory. The fact that he slightly miscalculated the size of the world made the risk seem much less. His own estimate of the distance from the Canary Islands to Japan was 2,400 miles, a 9,366 mile error. Confident that he could open a fresh route to the Indies, he pestered the Spanish monarchs for money. King Ferdinand and Queen Isabella denied his requests until 1492—not only did they need all their wealth to rid Spain of the Moors but also their advisors warned them that the Bible denied such a voyage was possible. Immediately after expelling the Moors, however, Isabella granted his request.

Columbus assembled a crew of ninety men and three ships. On October 12, 1492, when Columbus landed on the island of San Salvador he was about the same distance from the North American mainland as the Norwegians had been in Greenland. For a hero, Columbus had more than his share of grief. His royal employers had named him the Admiral of the Ocean Sea and had granted him 10 percent of all the wealth of the lands he discovered. He received nothing. Although he discovered the fastest route across the South Atlantic, made four voyages, and rediscovered the mainland, he was sent home in chains from his third voyage and on his last was stranded for a year on Jamaica after worms ate the bottom out of his ship. In 1506 he died in Spain, still mistakenly believing he had discovered the outlying islands of the East Indies. Even in death he found no peace; at least two churches now claim to have all or part of his body.

The new lands bore another's name, Amerigo Vespucci, who claimed to have sighted North America a year before Columbus' first voyage. Vespucci, however, was the first to publicize that the discovery was a "new world" and not the East. He published his claims in a pamphlet *Mundus Novis,* and a copy found its way into the hands of a German map maker in 1507. Looking for a name for the new world, he seized on America and it stuck.

Unfortunately, Columbus must take the responsibility for bringing syphilis to Europe. The debate over whether the Spanish gave it to the Indians or vice versa still rages. The first recorded outbreak of the disease in Europe occurred in 1494. A contemporary narrative recounts that French soldiers were infected by Spanish women who in turn contracted the disease from several male Indians whom Columbus had brought back to Spain on his first voyage. The Spanish crown paraded these native American curiosities on a grand tour of Spain. The Europeans reciprocated by introducing to the new world smallpox, measles, and other old world diseases that decimated the Indians.

New Spain

For 150 years following Columbus' historic voyages, Europeans became obsessed with finding a water route through the Western Hemisphere to the East. The start of permanent colonization was almost accidental. Small settlements developed in the sixteenth century around trading posts established to exploit local riches and to supply explorers. Not until the seventeenth century did permanent colonization become an end in itself, pursued by all the powerful mercantile nations of the West.

As the strongest European nation in the sixteenth century, Spain took the lead in exploration and colonization of the new world. The Spanish, however, proved better explorers than settlers. The names of Balboa, de Leon, Magellan, Cortes, Pizarro, De Soto, and Coronado conjure up the majesty and power of sixteenth-century Spain. Within fifty years of Columbus' first voyage, the Spanish had explored all the coastlines south of present-day Canada on the west and Labrador in the east. Portugal was the only other serious competitor in the new world. Because both nations were Catholic they asked the Pope to arbitrate their territorial disputes. In 1493 the Pontiff, using a faulty map, drew a line down what he thought was the middle of South America and awarded Spain everything to the west of that line. When the actual line was located, Portugal got only the eastern tip of Brazil, leaving that nation the only one speaking Portuguese in Latin America today.

Spain was the only European colonial power to gain immediate wealth from her possessions, but it did little to alter the Spanish economic and social structure. The gold and silver of the Aztec Empire, conquered in 1521 by Cortes with only 550 men, and of the Inca in Peru doubled the amount of gold circulating in Europe. But Spain received few long-range benefits from its colonies in "New Spain."

Actively engaged in the Catholic Counter-Reformation, the Spanish spent money lavishly to stem the Protestant tide. Spanish military expenditures were so great that the nation was perpetually in debt. The gold and silver from its colonies flowed through Spain to northern European bankers. Spanish society, virtually untouched by the commercial revolution, remained agrarian and backward, much to New Spain's detriment.

The Spanish established the most confining mercantile system in America. Because their colonies existed only for the enrichment of the mother country, the Spanish attempted to construct a "closed" trading system by forbidding its merchants from trading with other nations. All ships to and from New Spain had to pass through the Spanish port of Seville, which soon proved too small to handle all the business. Moreover, after many ships carrying gold and silver were lost to marauding pirates, Spain convoyed all vessels to Spanish America, sending two fleets each year. These were not enough to keep its colonies supplied with needed goods.

Politics and society in New Spain reflected conditions in the mother country. To ensure that the colonies served Spain, the Spanish government ruled directly from Madrid. Because Spain claimed a huge territory, ranging from the future Southwest United States down to the tip of South America, the Spanish government divided New Spain into districts and the king appointed viceroys, literally assistant kings, to rule each district. There was little opportunity for the colonists to participate in government. They were also discriminated against in the social system that evolved in New Spain. Only those born in Spain had full rights. Creoles, children born in New Spain of Spanish parents, suffered legal disabilities. This distinction led many Spanish males to leave their wives and daughters in Spain resulting in a disparity in numbers between Spanish males and females. Many Spanish men took Indian wives. Their children, called mestizos, assumed a position on the social scale below that of the pure-blood, New World-born Spanish creoles.

The lack of political opportunities and the rigid social system of New Spain discouraged permanent settlers. To make it more attractive to wealthy Spaniards, the government offered huge land grants running into millions of acres, along with the right to enslave Indians. This policy sparked an Indian uprising in the 1680s in Sante Fe and resulted in the Spanish being driven out for a time. To alleviate further its labor shortage, black slaves were brought into New Spain as early as 1502. Also Spain's policy of allowing only Catholics into New Spain did nothing to attract more settlers. Despite all its measures, Spanish America remained thinly populated by Europeans, leading to a much greater Indian presence in Spanish Central and South America than in British North America.

New France

After 1600 Spain's colonial superiority in the Western Hemisphere was seriously challenged for the first time. This colonial situation reflected Spain's decline in Europe after the defeat of her Armada by the English in 1588 and the squandering of her national wealth in the constant religious wars that sapped her resources. France and England, long at odds with each other, became the two most powerful European nations during the seventeenth century. Much of western history for the next 200 years on both sides of the Atlantic revolved around their constant warfare. Both nations sponsored new world explorations, but only France possessed the necessary resources in the seventeenth century to establish permanent settlements.

New France has been pictorially characterized by a musket, a rosary, and a pack of beaver skins. To this should be added a fish hook. French fishermen came over each spring as early as 1504 to fish the North Atlantic waters. They caught the fish, lightly salted them, and hung them on the shore to dry—the cheapest known method of preserving fish. The seasonal fishing cycle did little to promote permanent settlement. Occasionally a few fishermen wintered to trade with the Indians for furs, but most of them returned to France each autumn.

The basis for New France's economy for 250 years was the fur trade. This trade was carried on by private French companies that sent agents to the gulf of the St. Lawrence each spring to bargain for the Indians' winter catch. Like fishermen, with the advent of bad weather, the fur traders returned to France. As late as 1627 there were fewer than 100 permanent French settlers in North America. The intense competition between the companies for furs offered one advantage. The French probably had the best relations of all the colonial powers with the Indians. Each needed the other; the French needed the Indians to trap the animals and for colonial defense. The Indians desired the trade goods they received for their furs. Their relations grew more intimate through extensive intermarriage. The fact that the French did not push the Indians off their land helped maintain Indian good-will.

Much of France's claim to widespread territory in North America came from fur traders who ventured far inland in search of more pelts and from the zeal of the Jesuits who came to convert the Indians to Catholicism. Missionaries such as Father Marquette, who explored from Green Bay, Wisconsin, down to the Mississippi River and south to the Arkansas River, roamed across the American Midwest, claiming it all for France. When LaSalle reached the Gulf of Mexico in 1682 he named the region Louisiana after his King, Louis XIV. To the far north the French, who named almost everything after their king, established a fort at Louisbourg, on Cape Breton Island, that controlled the entrance to the St. Lawrence River. The chain of waterways from Louisbourg to Louisiana was the heart of New France.

The French colonies faced many of the same problems as New Spain: isolation, small population, and political dependency. The French attempted to lure settlers into the wilderness of New France when they advertised in 1670 for "strong and healthy" women "entirely free from any natural blemish or anything personally repulsive." Quebec, New France's largest city with about 1500 people in 1706, found itself cut off from the outside world for about five months a year when the St. Lawrence River froze over. New Orleans, founded in 1718, lay a continent away from Quebec, yet it was ruled by the same colonial government. Policies were dictated from France. The political history of New France can be summed up as constant bickering between the colonial officials, all appointed by the king. Most French colonists were either government officials, soldiers, fur traders, or priests. Almost none were farmers, merchants, or artisans. Most critically, almost all were transient males. Without French women or settled occupations, New France remained largely an Indian country. Dependent on the mother country for food, defense, and political decisions, despite the courageous efforts of its Jesuit missionaries, France failed to Europeanize New France, making it easy prey for its English neighbor to the south. Unlike the French and Spanish, the English brought with them both women and plows.

The English Colonies

England entered the race for colonial possessions late, primarily because the country had long been torn by domestic strife. Catholic against Protestant, religious dissenters against both, King against Parliament, yeomen farmers against the landed gentry, troubles with Scotland, Wales, and Ireland, and the tensions created by the commercial revolution, all diverted the nation's attention from North America.

When Englishmen finally caught the colonizing fever at the end of the sixteenth century, they committed many of the same mistakes as Spain and France. The earliest settlers at Roanoke and Jamestown searched in vain for gold and for a sea route to the Indies. The settlers were not self-sufficient, were governed from home, felt constantly threatened and outnumbered by the unfamiliar Indians, and failed to grow in number. And yet, from these hesitant starts, England created a colonial empire that after 1700 matured rapidly. It attracted settlers from all parts of Western Europe, soon fed itself and exported a surplus, became a strong trading rival of its mother country, achieved a measure of self-governance, assumed distinctive social characteristics apart from England, and prospered even within a mercantile system.

The English colonists differed from other colonial peoples. Spain and France allowed only Catholics into their empires; anyone could find a home in some English colony. The internal English conflicts also played their part. Whenever a faction found its cause suffering at home, it could emigrate to the colonies to escape the pressure to conform. The Pilgrims, Puritans, and Quakers all fled persecution at home and introduced a dynamic element into the new world.

The seventeenth-century English exhibited pronounced individualistic and even eccentric traits that served them well in the new world. They were less prone than their fellow Spanish and French colonials to look to their king or to their church officials for direction. They carried their personal convictions to America and acted on them. They were more adaptable and more quarrelsome than other colonists; they passed on to later generations of Americans many of these cultural traits.

English institutions appeared more adaptable to the colonial situation than did those of Spain and France. The tradition of parliamentary democracy, when introduced in 1619 in America, solved the problem of how to make daily political decisions 3000 miles removed from the mother country and simultaneously gave the colonists a sense of responsibility and self-importance. The English code of common law, based on precedents rather than on an abstract theory of absolute right and wrong, transferred well to the colonies. Confronted with a strange environment, the law adapted well—for example, to deal with problems with the Indians. England also had a long tradition of local law enforcement and local control of the churches, both desirable in a world where people were widely dispersed and transportation wretched.

Of great importance to the colonists was the English tradition of depending on local militia instead of standing armies. Colonial Englishmen did not expect regular English soldiers to defend them. They defended themselves—or else. Until the late 1760s one of the most noticeable differences between the English colonies and their rivals was the absence of regular soldiers in England's domain.

The diversity that characterized the English settlers plainly showed in the varied forms of their colonies. The English colonies were founded as private commercial undertakings. On the eve of the American Revolution, eight of the thirteen colonies had become "crown colonies"—directly ruled by the king—but had not been founded by the crown at all. The crown's chronic lack of money and the nation's domestic turmoil had led English sovereigns to use their claims in the new world to raise funds by issuing, for a fee, private charters to joint-stock companies, or to individual proprietors to found privately owned and governed colonies. Joint-stock companies, which sold shares to individual investors who hoped to share in any profits, founded three colonies: Virginia, Plymouth, and Massachusetts Bay. The most popular form of settlement was the proprietary colony. The monarch, for a fee or to repay a debt, granted charters to individuals or groups of men that permitted them to establish colonies at their own expense. The majority of the colonies were founded in this manner: Maryland, the Carolinas, New York, Pennsylvania, Delaware, New Jersey, and Georgia. The remaining English colonies—New Hamphsire, Connecticut, and Rhode Island—were founded by people who fled Massachusetts and later applied to the king for charter rights. English colonies reverted to crown possession only as a last resort, when the joint-stock companies failed, when the proprietors could not support their colonies, or when domestic difficulties threatened to destroy the colony. From the beginning, the English colonies were a bewildering mixture. This diversity led to the formation of distinct differences between the colonies that made later attempts at colonial unity difficult, but it also fostered local, self-government.

The Colony of Virginia

Comparisons among the colonies illustrate the depth of British North American diversity; politics, religion, class structure, economy, labor, and attitudes varied immensely. Virginia was named by Sir Walter Raleigh for Queen Elizabeth I, "The Virgin Queen," who encouraged his explorations on her behalf. In 1587, at his own expense, Raleigh outfitted an expedition of 117 colonists and started a settlement on Roanoke Island, just off the coast of North Carolina. There Virginia Dare became the first known English child born in North America. Raleigh intended to resupply the colony the following year, but on returning to England he was caught up in the preparations to repulse the Spanish Armada. When he finally returned to Roanoke, the settlement was deserted. Only the word "Croatan" carved on a tree remained as evidence of an English settlement. The fate of the colonists was never discovered, as the island was also deserted, but the best guess is that they were killed or captured by the Indians.

Raleigh assigned his colonization rights to a group of London merchants who formed the London Company. In 1606 the London Company received a charter from King James I and the following year it sent out about a hundred men to start a settlement in Virginia. They selected a low, swampy, heavily wooded site on the James River and named the first permanent English settlement in America Jamestown. The location proved to be a deadly choice. Most of the settlers considered themselves too highborn to work and instead spent much of their time searching for gold, exploring, and looking for a route to the East. Their problems mounted: the drinking water was bad, they ran out of beer, they failed to plant enough crops, and they fought with the Indians. The death toll was frightful. Of the 105 people at Jamestown who had arrived in the spring 1607, only thirty-eight were alive a year later. During the "starving time" desperate settlers even dug up a recently buried Indian and ate the corpse while another colonist became so hungry that he murdered his wife "and had eaten part of her before it was known; for which he was executed." The colony survived only through the abilities of John Smith, an Elizabethan swashbuckler who ruled with a strong and sometimes brutal hand, forcing peace on the Indians and punishing malingering colonists.

The settlement survived its first decade largely due to the timely arrival of ships from London that brought new settlers and needed food. The London Company, later renamed the Virginia Company, poured men and money into the settlement. Profits, however, were elusive. When nothing of value was discovered in the immediate area, the settlers searched desperately for a profitable commodity to sell. About 1612 they found it in the "noxious weed" tobacco, imported from the Caribbean Island, Trinidad. The Virginia climate was ideal for its cultivation, and within fifteen years the colony was shipping out a half a million pounds each year, securing its future.

Corporate Virginia

Until 1619 Jamestown was an experiment in corporate socialism. The company owned all the land, buildings, and tools; the settlers brought their produce to communal storehouses and drew on their stocks according to individual needs. Some

The Mayflower brought the Pilgrims to the new world seeking religious freedom. Contrary to common belief the Pilgrims did not build log houses at Plymouth Rock. In the 1930s historians found the pilgrims had constructed small dwellings of wood and stucco, like the homes they had left behind. (1920)

colonists refused to contribute, however, and the system proved unpopular. In 1619 the company introduced reforms to attract new settlers. The reforms of that year were crucial for all the English colonies because they established a form of colonial governance that was later imitated up and down the Atlantic seaboard. All company laws were abolished and the colonists were given all the legal rights of Englishmen; they were not to be second-class citizens, as were the Spanish colonists. The same English common law applied on both sides of the Atlantic. Company lands were distributed to the settlers and provisions were made for "headrights," originally a grant of fifty acres for each newcomer with an additional fifty acres for each member of the family and each servant brought over. The small size of the headrights ensured, at least at first, a colonial society made up of small farms, unlike the great land grants in Spanish America, those along the St. Lawrence in New France, and those up the Hudson River north of New Amsterdam, capital of the New Netherlands. The small headrights did not prevent the rise of great estates in Virginia and elsewhere, as many enterprising men legally and illegally put together vast tracts of land. Attempting to improve colonial government, the company granted the settlers the right to elect an assembly to meet starting in July 1619. To oversee the colony, the company appointed a governor and a group of local councillors; later the governor and his council sat with the Burgess as the law-making body. This political organization suited the isolated new world and became a model for the other English colonies.

In spite of these reforms, the Virginia Company could not make its colony pay. The company failed to win a monopoly for its tobacco in England, the company's directors squabbled over policies, and in 1622 the Indians launched a surprise attack on the Virginia settlers killing many of them. By 1623 Virginia had an unsavory reputation as an unhealthy place to live, and with the company on the verge of bankruptcy, King James ordered an investigation into its affairs. His inquiry discovered that 4000 out of the 6000 settlers had perished during the sixteen years. Unlike in the Massachusetts Bay Colony to the north, there had been no natural increase. In the first three decades of settlement Virginia's colonists died nearly as fast as they arrived. The king concluded that the colony had been mismanaged; in 1624 Virginia became the first crown colony.

Virginia Political Institutions

The king's takeover did little to change the political process in Virginia. The monarch now appointed the governor, who was sometimes chosen from among the colonists. The governor then appointed his councillors, usually drawn from among wealthy Virginians; this group functioned much as the English House of Lords. The House of Burgess, the assembly, elected at first by all white males over seventeen years of age, and later only by property holders, met every year after 1639. For a time in Virginia, women could vote if they were widows whose husbands had left them enough property to qualify for the franchise. Legally, the women cast their dead husbands' ballots.

On the local or county level governing institutions arose quickly to deal with daily problems. The county court judge, the highest local official, who did everything from trying minor cases to chasing stray hogs off the roads, the sheriff, who enforced the county court's decrees, and the justice of the peace, were all offices brought over from England. These were changed, however, by the new world's environment. These offices offered the colonists a large number of political jobs that carried responsibility. It became a badge of honor among the more wealthy and influential families to hold these positions. A large cross-section of the colonial elite, including almost all of the Founding Fathers, gained political experience that proved invaluable when the colonies later revolted. These men understood not only political theory but also the practical problems of operating a government. Over the course of the next 150 years these officeholders became jealous of their political rights and increasingly resented any outside interference, particularly from London imperial bureaucrats.

Anglican Church

Aside from government, the most influential institution in Virginia and many other colonies was the established church. Where colonies had an established church, everyone of whatever faith had to pay taxes to support that church. In Virginia it was the Anglican church. The huge institutional Church of England, however, was drastically altered in the colonies. Virginia's white population dispersed itself widely and was too poor to support an elaborate church hierarchy. The Anglican church in Virginia and elsewhere in the colonies became congregational with nearby elites controlling church affairs. Local vestries hired and fired ministers and, within limits, determined church doctrine. Ministers were always in short supply in Virginia because they were paid in tobacco, whose value fluctuated wildly, and because they had to be ordained in England as there was no American bishop. The colonists, with unlimited western lands, saw no need to send their second sons into the church to keep family estates intact for their firstborn male heirs, as was the case in England; colonial sons simply moved on and cleared new land. Throughout the colonial period about one-half of the Anglican churches were often without a minister.

Such a haphazard church structure could not be as powerful in the colonies as the church was in the mother country. Nevertheless, the Anglican church was influential in colonial affairs. Church and state relations in the colonial period were much closer than now. Colonists believed that a close relationship between religion and politics was the essence of good government. In Virginia, as elsewhere, ministers did not take an active part in government, but colonial politicians frequently passed civil laws to enforce religious practices. Colonial citizens were often punished for church crimes. The colonists strongly believed in the biblical dictum of being "thy brother's keeper" with the result that everyone's activities were closely scrutinized by neighbors. Surviving colonial court records indicate that Virginians were frequently hauled into court for violating the Sabbath, for drunkenness and adultery, for profanity and bastardy.

Morals

The Virginia colonists did what they could to stamp out such moral lapses. At its very first meeting, the House of Burgess passed a law requiring every citizen to attend church on Sunday under penalty of a fine to be paid to the church. The Sabbath, however, could be violated in other ways. Colonists were punished for fishing, carrying tools, taking a long journey, loading a boat, delivering a writ, and watering tobacco on Sunday. After Parliament passed the Toleration Act late in the seventeenth century, Virginians could attend the church of their choice—but they were still required to be present at some service; their taxes supported the Anglican state-church and its ministry; and only Anglicans could hold public office.

One of the biggest problems in Virginia was drunkenness. Drinking was perhaps more common because of the bad drinking water and lingering European habits. The seriousness of the problem became evident as early as 1619 when the House of

Burgess passed a law penalizing drunkenness. Too poor to build jails and maintain prisoners, the courts handed down sentences that were intended to benefit society. Common punishments were to sentence the convict to construct bridges across local creeks, or build ferryboats. Sometimes, stocks were erected in which the offender was condemned to sit. Drunks became such a problem that the lower house in 1658 decreed that anyone convicted of the crime three times or more lost his right to hold public office—a serious penalty.

Profanity in colonial Virginia was considered a crime against God. Penalties for it were levied as early as 1619, and after 1631 an offender was fined one shilling for each oath—presumably someone had to keep count. The most common and offensive oaths were to "swear by God's wounds," the origin of the English term "bloody." The vice was widespread and not confined only to men; in 1692 John Huddlesey was indicted for "oaths innumerable," and Ann Stop, who obviously could not, was convicted sixty-five times for profanity.

Breaking the Sabbath, drunkenness, and profanity were serious moral and religious offences. But bastardy had additional economic undertones. The number of illegitimate children born, particularly to servant women, rose rapidly. Because most masters refused to support these unwanted babies, the expense for their upkeep fell upon the county courts. The illegitimacy rate was high for several reasons: the severe lack of housing forced masters to house servants, regardless of sex, together in barns, cellars, and attics; most of the servants came from lower class English backgrounds where premarital sex was more common. And there were some masters who took sexual advantage of their female servants. To avoid losing the services of servant women and to escape the cost of maintaining their children, masters forbade their servants, most of whom were young, to marry. Penalties for illegitimacy were severe, usually public humiliation at the front of the church on Sunday followed by a severe whipping. The mother was normally punished more severely than the father. Even as the Empire failed to enforce its will on Virginia, so Virginia's elite failed to enforce its moral strictures on the people of Virginia. Unlike New England, public drunkenness, profanity, sexual promiscuity, and Sabbath breaking went largely unpunished in Virginia through the colonial era. Indeed, in the 1740s, in Richmond County, prostitution virtually became a "right of English women."

Social Structure

By the end of the seventeenth century, a colonial elite had emerged to dominate the Virginia government and the established church, the two institutions that determined the laws. The appearance of this elite in Virginia was typical of the same process that took place in other colonies. Basically, Virginia went through three distinct social phases. In the first, from 1607 to 1624, a person's position within the Virginia Company largely determined his social status. After the crown's takeover in 1624, however, these social distinctions disappeared, and in their place a society of white farmers appeared. The period from 1624 to about 1670 saw few men of great wealth or distinction arise. The headright system worked to keep most farms small enough so that their owners still tilled them. Society was relatively crude and illiterate; most people lacked a sense of social responsibility. By the middle of the seventeenth century, however, economic pressures created a third social phase symbolized by the large plantation. Low tobacco prices forced many farmers to expand their acreage to grow more of the weed or to switch to new crops. Over the last half of the century headrights dramatically increased in size, up to 670 acres per person, large numbers of servants and slaves were imported, and many farmers amassed large estates. After 1650 a so-called Virginia aristocracy emerged that aped the living style of the English gentry and gained control of colonial affairs.

An excellent example of this new breed was William Byrd. Byrd's father inherited a large farm and by dealing in Indian, white, and black servants, he collected enough headrights to put together a great estate. His son, born in 1674, was educated in England, studied commerce in Holland, and graduated from Middle Temple, then considered the best English law school. In his first year back in Virginia, 1696, he was elected to the House of Burgess, an indication of what the voters looked for in an officeholder. By the early eighteenth century Byrd owned over 23,000 acres, 220 slaves, and numerous servants. In addition to being a planter and a politician, he built, bought, and sold ships and practiced law. His house, Westover, still stands as a monument to his good taste and opulence. Before Byrd died in 1744 he held every colonial political office available to him, except the royal governorship, a post he eagerly sought most of his mature life. Byrd was remarkable because he kept a personal diary that provides an excellent glimpse into the life of the colonial elite. His diary reveals a well-educated man who read at least five languages and who frequently "rose at 3 o'clock and read two chapters in Hebrew and five leaves in Lucian (Greek and French)." Ambitious and powerful, he lived a comfortable life, yet was always deeply in debt to London merchants, as were many others of his class. He entertained lavishly, which helped to keep him in debt, because those of his social station were expected to maintain such appearances. He set a plentiful table, although some of his food would be foreign to modern tastes: boiled milk for breakfast, boiled beef, boiled and hashed mutton, white wine and toast, bacon and fowl, broiled pork, cherries scalded in hot water, and roast pigeon and asparagus. He drank heavily with his friends, fancied himself something of a ladies' man, and described his most intimate relations with his two wives. He certainly was not a modest man for he often noted with pride, "I gave my wife a powerful flourish and gave her great ecstasy and refreshment." What stands out, however, is the routine and boredom of the plantation life. One of the wealthiest and busiest men in the colonies, Byrd still spent most days doing nothing, hoping for a visitor with fresh news.

Indentured Servants

If life was boring at the very top of the colonial social pyramid, it was suffocating for the servants and the slaves at the bottom. These two classes developed because the colonies had more land than labor. Land was the colonies' principal wealth, but to make it pay in the form of forest products, crops, minerals, and furs, the colonies desperately needed a source of cheap labor. To supply these workers, the English colonies resorted to two systems of bondage: slaves and indentured servants. Indentured servants served for only a specified time whereas slaves and their children served for life. A color line also separated the two. Although a few Indians and blacks served indentures, most servants were white. Slaves were never white, almost always Africans, except in a few cases when Indians were enslaved.

Indentured servants served in the colonies until long after the revolution. In exchange for their passage to the new world, they sold their labor for a specified number of years, usually between four and seven. Such contracts were usually signed with a ship's captain before the voyage. The captain then brought the servants over and sold their contracts in the colonial port cities. It was not uncommon for entire families to sign such agreements and then find themselves sold in different ports, never to see one another again. At least one-half of all white immigrants to the English colonies came over as indentured servants.

The system had its evils. Many people were lured to the colonies under the false impression that streets in America were paved with gold. The transatlantic passage on the "White Guineamen," as the servant ships were called, was often a nightmare, with their human cargoes crowded into holds where a death rate of 50 percent was common. Since children brought higher prices because of their longer indenture periods, a thriving industry, "kid-nabbing" grew up in England. English convicts often had a choice of prison terms or servitude in the colonies. Those who chose to emigrate drove personal and property crime rates up drastically, particularly in the middle colonies. Interestingly, many criminals preferred prison to the colonies. The hope of most indentured servants was a clause in their contracts promising "freedom dues" at the end of their service, usually land, and perhaps some tools, money, or clothing. Probably only about 20 percent of the ex-servants collected, kept, and used their "dues" to reach positions of even moderate comfort. Most servants either died prematurely or became public charges. Their lot remained always a hard one, their rewards meager, but their contribution to American development was of immense value.

Slavery

Of at least equal value to America was slave labor. The origins of colonial slavery are surrounded by mystery and the early evidence is contradictory. The first Africans brought to Virginia arrived without fanfare before 1619—at least one will probated in the colony prior to 1619, matter of factly, included an African as part of the estate. John Rolfe observed a better known, larger arrival of Africans and remarked simply, "about the last of August came in a dutch man of warre that sold us twenty Negars." There was no evidence of slavery before 1639 and no definition of slavery existed in Virginia law until 1661—although following Spanish and Portuguese experiences, Englishmen assumed blacks to be prime material for enslavement. Rolfe's group was probably sold as servants, and at least one of them, Anthony Johnson, later purchased his freedom and owned slaves himself. They were not treated equally to white servants, however, for by 1640 some blacks served for life, some were indentured, and a few who had secured their freedom had accumulated property of their own. By the 1640s distinctions had arisen between blacks and whites on both racial and legal grounds. For example, black women, but not white, could be worked in the fields, blacks could not bear arms, and interracial sex was discouraged by heavy penalties. Distinctions such as these slowly pushed blacks to the bottom of the social scale. In 1661 the Virginia legislature indirectly recognized black slavery when it held that "in case any English servant shall run away in company with any negroes who are incapable of makeing satisfaction by addition of time," the white had to serve the slave's lost time as well as his own. The blacks reaction to these evolving developments remains hopelessly lost.

Slavery evolved over the forty-year period for a number of reasons. There was an obvious need for cheap labor in the colonies, and lifetime servitude helped stabilize its supply; the Africans were black, a readily apparent difference that automatically led whites to react differently to the newcomers; blacks were considered heathens, and hence did not have the legal protections afforded Christian whites; the blacks had few members of their own race who could offer protection; Africans came from societies that practiced slavery; and the colonists reasoned that since blacks were forced to come to the colonies it did not make any difference how they were treated once here. Even after 1661, however, Virginians did not rush to buy slaves. The institution grew slowly. As late as 1670 there were about 8000 indentured servants in the colony and only about 2000 slaves. But for Virginia and the rest of the South slavery represented the wave of the future, especially after 1698 when England opened the American slave trade to all countries and the number of imported slaves rose phenomenally. Although the northern colonies passed slave laws, starting with Massachusetts in 1641, the institution never really took root in the middle and northern colonies.

The New England Way

Similar changes took place further north where two settlements, Plymouth and her sister colony, Massachusetts Bay, had been settled a half-century before Philadelphia. Both of these settlements originated when these Protestant groups sought an asylum from the established English church. By the first two decades of the seventeenth century, England resembled a seething vortex of contending religious and social groups and the Pilgrims and the Puritans seemed especially prone to splintering.

They also possessed an almost uncontrollable urge to purify and correct what they regarded as the existing evils of the Anglican church. Often representing the newly developed middle and urban classes, these people thought that true religion required each individual to demonstrate a personal encounter with God; only those thus redeemed, called "saints" or "the elect," qualified to hold membership in the church. The dissenting sects could not get along with the dominant Anglican faithful, so in exasperation they departed England.

The Pilgrims who settled Plymouth represented one of the more extreme wings among such dissenters. Realizing their inability

Peter Stuyvesant, fondly remembered as "Peg-Leg Pete" by generations of New York schoolchildren' was the new world's earliest fireman and the last director general of the New Netherlands which he surrendered in 1664 to the English (1948)

to convert many Englishmen to their severe faith, these separatists migrated to Holland in 1608 in a vain search for a place to start afresh. But the low country across the North Sea proved a disappointment because the newcomers could not practice their trades. Consequently, they decided to go to the new world, though they had neither legal authority nor a charter. And neither did they have money. Thus, in order to pay for their passage, about 100 Pilgrims had to indenture themselves as a group to a company of London merchants. They were supposed to settle within the Virginia Company's land grant, but the captain of the *Mayflower* sailed slightly off course and landed just south of Boston. Before disembarking most of the men signed a compact that formally unified them to face the challenges of the unknown. This agreement established "a civil body politic" that would bind them to "just and equal laws" in which all male church members had an equal voice. This compact eased some of the leaders' fears that the separatists would separate once again. As the number of settlers and settlements grew and spread out, they finally had to resort to a representative form of government.

Plymouth was never as important as her sister colony to the north, Massachusetts Bay, with which it merged in 1691. In Massachusetts more moderate, but no less committed to their faith, Puritans predominated. Unlike their brothers the separatists, they hoped to win control of the Anglican church, free it of altar, priest, and images—the very symbols of popery, they said—and institute a new holy order. Unfortunately for them, the accession of Charles I to the throne in 1624 brought intense pressures on them to conform to Anglican ritual. Moreover, Englishmen struggled through a long economic depression, so in 1629, a number of well-to-do Puritans resolved to put their religious and social ideas to the demanding test of the untried new world. They organized a Puritan joint-stock company, procured a charter from the king, and organized the first mass exodus to America.

The Puritans learned from other colonies' mistakes. They sent advance expeditions across the Atlantic to scout the best location, report on the Indians, and advise on agricultural possibilities. Before the first 1000 colonists came over in 1630 the advance group had selected Boston because it had an excellent natural harbor and had even laid out its first streets. When the settlers arrived they knew what to expect and were prepared for it. As a consequence the Puritans did not endure the early hardships that faced pioneers at Jamestown and even at Plymouth. They also had another advantage: their charter did not specify the company's official residence, so the crafty Puritans brought the document with them giving Massachusetts Bay its independence—except for England's commercial restrictions—for almost sixty years.

The Puritans wanted to establish a society in harmony with biblical truths as they understood them. This meant a close union, much closer than in Virginia, between the church and the state. They believed that God extended a covenant, literally a contract, that permitted man to create a government if he made his laws to conform to God's word. As long as the laws were godly, man was bound to obey his earthly rulers. There were two compacts, one between God and man, a covenant of grace, and the other between the government and the governed, a social covenant. The notion of a social covenant gave the Puritan government its moral legitimacy; God's permission to govern according to his will as directed by Holy Scripture.

Work Ethic

In seventeen-century Massachusetts, religious status, rather than wealth, determined the governing elite. But as religious intensity declined by the second and third generations and as the gap between the rich and the poor widened, the Puritan elite, as Virginia's Anglican elite, increasingly judged itself by wealth and manners. Paradoxically, in Massachusetts spiritual commitment led to materialism. Puritanism required those people not yet certain of their salvation to live godly lives to prepare themselves to receive God's grace. Their Protestant ethnic required hard work, as God considered all "callings" equally holy. Moreover, good Puritans lived simply, saved the fruits of their labors, and avoided display. In the New World such behavior almost guaranteed material well-being. As New Englanders became richer each new shilling became a sign of God's favor. By the third generation, wealth in itself had come to denote holiness. By 1700 the Puritan colony of devout believers had become the land of thrifty and materialistic Yankees.

In the early years of the Puritan experiment the close union between religion and the state created great pressures for conformity. Puritans did not tolerate dissenters because any deviation in religious belief endangered both the state and the religious community. Those who disputed accepted beliefs, such as Roger Williams and Anne Hutchinson, who dared to call for freedom of worship and for separation of church and state or a personal vision of God, were banished from the colony, or worse, executed. Driven out of Massachusetts, Williams founded Rhode Island as a haven for dissenters and unbelievers. The Quakers, however, were the bane of the Puritans' existence. Quakers came to the Bay Colony to spread their truths, sometimes by running naked through Boston's streets to flaunt their theological freedom. The Puritans banished, flogged, imprisoned, and finally executed four Friends in an attempt to maintain the purity of their utopia. The Salem witch trials in 1692 marked the Puritans' moment of truth when several teenage girls accused fellow villagers of bewitching them. The victims' primary offence had been their refusal to conform to Puritan norms enforced by the village minister. Following the execution of twenty accused witches, villagers viewed their behavior as unChristian. The Massachusetts legislature later censored the village and ordered that the victims' families be compensated. After the Salem witch trials Massachusetts authorities no longer possessed the will to forcefully impose their religious beliefs on all members of the community. Earlier the colony had legalized Anglican worship and in 1691 it removed the religious requirement for voting, replacing it with a property qualification.

Puritan Society

Most colonists in Massachusetts farmed, but their settlement patterns differed strikingly from those in Virginia. The Puritans expanded outward from Boston in an orderly pattern. When a township became overcrowded, those wishing to migrate obtained enough unoccupied land from the General Court to start a new township according to need. These towns lent the whole region its peculiar social values and culture and imprinted a communal legacy that has endured to modern times. As the colonists pushed westward they made conscious efforts to create closed Christian communities, the better to serve God. The typical New England colonial town closely identified with its local church. Indeed, membership in church and town was almost synonymous. The towns could refuse permission to settle within their bounds to anyone who did not meet whatever religious, social, or other tests the town councils imposed. Citizenship was anything but voluntary. Until late in the seventeenth century, selectmen, the most important local officials, exercised strong control over their towns; they enforced the ever-present religious and social consensus. They maintained the desired order and kept change to a minimum to preserve the community's saintly values and its sense of social responsibility.

Life in the small towns was routine and revolved around the church and family. Families included parents and children under one roof, but few other kin. High infant mortality rates and the toll of childhood diseases required ten to twelve births per woman for six to survive to maturity. About one in three women died in childbirth. Widowers quickly remarried, sometimes two to three times in their lifetimes.

The active participation of women in Puritan churches led to expanded legal and social rights, more so than other Western women at the time. In Plymouth, widows received a larger portion of their deceased husband's property than in Virginia, they managed inns and held liquor licenses, received divorces, and obtained redress for physical violence on their persons. While strict parents, Puritans allowed their children frequent play time, games such as tag, blind man's bluff, and hop-scotch. Most importantly, virtually all New England children learned to read and write, even girls. Universal literacy, combined with material success, undercut the power of political authorities, whether Puritan or imperial.

Houses in colonial Massachusetts were small, dark, and dank. A shortage of glass dictated small windows, some so poorly crafted that it was impossible to see through them. These houses were heated by fireplaces in which all the cooking was done and had no indoor water or sanitation, all of which made the long New England winters seem unduly harsh. The log cabin was unknown to the early colonists. They were found only in New Sweden, a small colony located near Philadelphia. The Swedes and the Finns had long built such cabins in northern Scandinavia and brought this knowledge with them. English colonists also brought their native architecture and at first built stuccoed houses, halftimbered in the Elizabethan fashion. Later they used native resources and built their houses of clapboard, shingles, stone, or brick.

Few opportunities existed for gaining great wealth in these small villages and towns, but that lack was balanced by the close-knit family and neighborly ties that ensured that nobody starved. The gap between a town's wealthy and poor was not great. There were prosperous farmers and less prosperous farmers, but nobody lived in luxurious ease. Isolated from metropolitan markets, towns became nearly self-sufficient, filling as many of their own needs as they could, and bartering for or purchasing only those goods they could not provide themselves. Early New England towns offered security and social cohesion, but not personal freedom. Bolstered by Puritan religious beliefs, town fathers enforced their own codes of authority, threatening to expel anyone who dissented. Most remained silent and "kept up appearances."

Society Fragmented

By the turn of the eighteenth century, even the appearance of consensus in these towns began to break down. The problems came from within. Earlier, in response to the shrinking numbers of elect, the church admitted children of the elect even if they could not demonstrate a religious conversion. In 1662 through the Half-Way Covenant, non-elect had been admitted to church membership, although they were denied communion and a voice in determining church affairs. Eventually these distinctions between full and halfway church membership were forgotten as religion became less exclusive. The decline of religious zealotry meant that by the last quarter of the seventeenth century only about one-half a typical town's adult males belonged to the church and the theological consensus suffered accordingly. The shortage of land broke down many of the towns' enforced isolation. Every new township, when chartered, set aside unused land for newcomers and children and reserved certain land for use in common, hence the "commons" still evident in many New England towns. As population grew, however, the village parceled land to the founders' children and grandchildren. Within two generations many towns ran out of unused lands and had to divide up the commons into private plots. In Massachusetts most parents at death divided their estates among the surviving children equally. Over the years individual land holdings became smaller and more scattered. Moreover, the unused lands lay on the outer fringes of town. With the allotment of these distant parcels the population moved outward from the town center and its church. In time, most New Englanders lived on scattered farms, much as in Virginia, diminishing the intimacy created by village life. Isolated farmsteads pushed people outward rather than brought them into a close social union.

As the leaders of the first generation—the men who had been elected time and again to important local posts—died off and the population dispersed outward, the hold of selectmen over their towns' affairs weakened. The second and third generations challenged their elders and each other for leadership. Town meetings became longer and more heated; selectmen were voted in and out of office with more regularity; a surplus of potential leaders appeared; and many towns divided into geographic factions with specific concerns. By the eighteenth century most New England towns no longer tried to enforce a consensus. Instead, villagers worked out compromises. New Englanders learned to tolerate differences of opinion and belief. Liberty and social peace became as important as religious devoutness and social conformity.

In the eighteenth century the gap between rich and poor in New England towns increased. Although everyone became somewhat poorer as the size of the average farm decreased, some plunged faster than others. A growing number of citizens in every town were landless, living a precarious existence at or below subsistence level and dependent on their own sweat for a livelihood. Many farmers held barely enough land to feed themselves and their families, and their land's fertility had often been leeched away. Dire poverty crept into the New England towns, but it took an act of great courage for people living at minimal levels to strike off on their own. Most preferred to stay with the familiar and, even if uncomfortable, to eke out a living. By the time of the revolution New England towns no longer seemed so different from those in other British colonies.

Literacy Levels

The early religious emphasis in these closed communities gave literacy a great impetus. With the colonists living in compact settlements, education was easier. As early as the mid-seventeenth century the Puritans made schooling compulsory for all males, and to ensure an adequate supply of trained ministers, started Harvard in 1636, the first college in the English colonies. Generally, however, literacy in colonial America was highest where an intense Protestantism existed. It was also highest among the wealthier people in all colonies. By the revolution, the male literacy rate in New England approached 85 percent, while for Pennsylvania and Virginia, it hovered around 60 percent; both of these figures were higher than the 55 to 60 percent estimated male literacy rate in England for the same period. For wealthy males, however, literacy was almost universal. While significantly lower than male literacy, a higher percentage of British North American women could read and write than males in England. About half the females could read and write by the time of the revolution in New England and fewer in Virginia. Literacy rates among the bulk of the colonial population, small farmers, laborers, and artisans, fell below that of the elite but far above European levels. By the middle of the eighteenth century most British North Americans, male and female, had access to books, political and religious tracts, and newspapers, making them participants in the Enlightenment discourse. In the years leading up to American independence, the leaders of the revolution exploited this literacy to formulate a distinctly American political culture.

The Puritan Legacy

The Puritans left a legacy that went far beyond literacy. Faced with organizing and operating a biblical commonwealth in the wilderness, their belief in the sinfulness of humankind made them distrustful of granting too much power to any official or to any branch of government. Moreover, the Puritans pioneered self-government. They reasoned that because all people were capable of receiving God's grace, all were competent to determine their own destiny, although most limited such rights to white, adult, propertied males. To protect individual rights the Puritans erected a federalized society. With no central church authority, each congregation made its own policies within the limits of Calvinist theology. In Massachusetts town meetings all voiced their opinions, even women, and each town sent representatives to sit in the General Court to protect and to advance the town's interests. The colony divided government between the executive—a royal governor after 1691—and the legislative. All this resulted in a political balance of power in which authority shifted to Boston as local communities increasingly found themselves unable to solve their own problems, including Indian conflict and an aggressive French colony to their north and west.

A Middle Way

One of the striking features of British North America was its uniformity and the overwhelming presence of English culture. Both seventeenth-century Virginia and New England, the two most populous regions, were self-consciously English and Protestant. New England had been settled by radical religious dissenters and Virginia by ner-do-well Anglican gentry, but each group spoke English, each looked with reverence on the English legal tradition, each modeled its government on England, each required its inhabitants to conform to Protestantism, and the population of each was almost exclusively English in origin. Throughout both regions little diversity existed. One Virginian or Yankee looked, believed, and spoke pretty much like every other Virginian or Yankee.

In this manner both regions conformed to a traditional social model in which all free persons were of the same race, worshiped the same religion, and spoke in one voice on most issues. Once a decision had been reached, everyone conformed to the communal decision. Open, vocal dissent was not just discouraged; it was considered subversive, punishable as a crime. In seventeenth century Virginia the aristocratic planter oligarchy set the standard and enforced the consensus; in seventeenth-century New England the democratically elected town meeting did so. But the result was the same—uniformity, consensus, and communalism. Both regions discouraged individualism and, at times, violently suppressed it. The whole was considered greater than the sum of the parts; and individuals existed to serve the whole. The source of authority differed in each region, but the result was the same—authoritarian conformity.

This seems curious, given that after 1776 the United States cherished individualism, diversity, and political and religious dissent. These were not values that derived from either the Old Dominion nor New England. American individualism and cultural diversity arose in the Middle Colonies and the port cities of New York, Philadelphia, and Charleston. Here, even in the colonial period, immigrants from a variety of nations and religions were welcomed. Here, freedom did not mean the freedom of the aristocratic elite or the democratic majority to act autonomously, free from imperial control. In the Middle Colonies and, especially in New York, Philadelphia, and Charleston, freedom meant the individual's right to criticize political authorities, local as well as imperial, to organize opposition political parties, to worship or not worship as he chose, and quite often, to behave in an unruly, even lewd manner. Here, society placed a higher value on individual freedom than on social conformity, on cultural diversity than on racial purity. By the first third of the eighteenth century, the democratic pluralism of the middle colonies and colonial port cities had become the American norm. The way of the middle colonies became the American way.

New York

New York was the oldest and, in the long-run, the most influential of the middle colonies. In 1608 Henry Hudson discovered New York harbor while sailing under the Dutch flag in search of a Northwest Passage to Asia. Although disappointed when he found that the Hudson River petered out north of Albany, Hudson claimed the territory for the Dutch. The Dutch postponed settlement until 1626 when Peter Minuit (Minniwit) bought Manhattan Island, at the mouth of the Hudson from the Manhatt tribe for 60 guilders, the famous $24 for Manhattan. Contrary to legend, the Dutch did not swindle the Manhatts. Rather, the visiting Manhatts sold the Dutch an island to which they had no tribal claim.

Unlike the English in Virginia and the Puritans in Massachusetts, the Dutch viewed New Amsterdam as a trading post, not a settlement, very much as the French viewed New France. For this reason, the Dutch cared little about New Amsterdam's culture or the moral life of its inhabitants. The Dutch Reform Church enjoyed the status of a state church, but the Dutch tolerated other religions. And while Dutch families monopolized the political and social life of New Amsterdam, the overwhelming majority of the population was not of Dutch birth. New Netherlands was a polyglot colony. Its people spoke 18 different languages. It also differed from the English colonies in its authoritarian political system. The Dutch considered New Netherlands a commercial enterprise created to foster trade with the Indians. As such, representative government seemed out of place. Not only the governor, but the court officers ·and lawmakers were Dutch appointees. The citizens of New Netherlands enjoyed religious liberty, property rights, and the right to legal due process, but not the right to representation nor to approve or disapprove tax levies.

UNITED STATES POSTAGE

1682 1932

3 WILLIAM PENN 3
CENTS

The Quaker, William Penn, was the son of a British admiral to whom King Charles II owed money. The king repaid the admiral's son with a grant of land in the wilderness of North America, Penn's Sylvania, that made Penn the largest landholder in the world. (1932)

Dutch rule came to an end in 1664 when the English captured New Netherlands, making it an English colony with the Duke of York as its proprietor. The English brought many changes to the colony including a new name. Still, the Dutch influence remained. From the Dutch, New Yorkers, and later Americans, acquired the customs of sleigh riding, ice skating, and Easter eggs, Santa Claus, and New Years. The Dutch also contributed to the American language such words as spook, boss, stoop, yacht, and the place names of Staten Island, Hoboken, Hakensack, Yonkers Brooklyn, the Bronx, and Harlem as well as the names of three presidents—Martin Van Buren and Theodore and Franklin Roosevelt. More important, New York continued to be the most diverse and least democratic North American colony.

Until the early nineteenth century, New York City remained little more than a trading center for farmers in adjoining New Jersey and on Long Island, for the large estates located along the Hudson River, and for western fur traders. Compared to Philadelphia, Boston, and Charleston, colonial New York lacked a populated and prosperous hinterland. Even though the Hudson was one of the most extensive rivers in Eastern North America, the Dutch policy, which the English continued, of granting enormous tracts of land to a handful of aristocratic favorites, known as patroons, stunted the growth of small farming. To the north, the powerful Iroquois blocked western settlement into the Mohawk Valley. Until the 1760s, immigrants to the English colonies avoided New York in preference for Pennsylvania, New England, Maryland, and Virginia which offered inexpensive farm land and few Indians. Consequently, colonial New York lacked the large free-holding middle class characteristic of most of the other British North American colonies. Instead, New York found itself divided between the large Hudson River landlords with their tenant-run estates, subsistence Scot-Irish back-country farmers who had settled around Albany, and the polyglot and largely disenfranchised population of New York City.

These divisions led to a factionalism unrivaled in the other British colonies. By the mid-eighteenth century New York already possessed the beginnings of a two-party political system—the Delanceys and the Livingstons. New York's politics recognized no simple divisions as neither political party stood for any clear-cut program or ideology. It was neither the country versus the city, nor poor versus the rich, nor English versus Dutch, nor Republicans versus Monarchists. Rather, the two parties were coalitions of various factions that made up New York. In any given election, one coalition would consist of any number of factions, some of whom had participated in the opposing party in the previous election. By the mid-nineteenth century in the United States, the non-ideological, group interest, and highly vocal political behavior of New York had replaced the genteel and conformist politics of New England and Virginia. Two of America's favorite past-times, politics and baseball, were products of boisterous and diverse New York.

Pennsylvania

At the time of the American Revolution, Philadelphia was the largest and most important British colonial city, indeed, the second largest English-speaking city in the world, second only to London. In one way Philadelphia resembled New England. It too was established as a refuge for religious dissenters. In 1682 William Penn founded Pennsylvania to provide a sanctuary for Quakers, envisioning the colony as a living example of a Christian community. Penn, a close friend of King Charles II, received his proprietary charter in 1681. To encourage settlement, Penn drew up a liberal Frame of Government that granted to prospective settlers religious liberty, the right to vote, the promise of no taxation without representation, immunity from arbitrary arrest, trial by jury, and a representative legislature. Penn retained the right to appoint the governor, who could veto all legislation. All in all, Penn's Frame of Government represented the freest and most generous system of government in British North America. To make Pennsylvania even more attractive, Penn at first offered each settler free land. As late as the mid-eighteenth century prospective settlers could acquire 100 acres of land from Penn for £5. If that were not enough, for those who could only afford passage to Pennsylvania, Penn offered free farmsteads and lent settlers the money for tools and seeds to be paid back in five years. Determined to profit from other colonies' mistakes, Penn carefully planned Pennsylvania's settlement. He recognized the vast potential of the Delaware River Valley, locating Philadelphia so that it served as a market center for the Delaware and Schuykill rivers. Such generosity, coupled with Penn's invitation to all religious faiths, quickly made Pennsylvania the most attractive and fastest growing British colony known widely in the colonial period as the "Best Poor Man's Country."

In two respects Pennsylvania resembled New York. It was diverse and it developed a complex two-party political system. Pennsylvania attracted a wide variety of people. Penn openly recruited from throughout Europe settlers of all religious persuasions including Catholics, Jews, and Amish. People suffering religious persecution in their native countries found Pennsylvania a welcome haven. Not only did Philadelphia acquire a diverse population, so did Pennsylvania. Throughout the Delaware Valley various religious and national groups arose. With easy access to the Delaware and Skuykill Rivers, Pennsylvania, New Jersey, and Delaware farmers grew wheat, corn, barley, rye, and fabricated virtually everything imaginable, including iron. Philadelphia served as the hub of this pre-industrial agricultural empire, making Pennsylvania and the Delaware Valley the "bread basket" of the British empire and the manufacturing and trade center of British North America.

William Penn, the colony's proprietor, was the Quaker son of Sir William Penn, an admiral in the royal navy. Penn the younger had been converted to the teachings of George Fox, founder of the Religious Society of Friends, who believed that every human being possessed an infinitesimal spark of God within him and could best serve God by being kind and just to his fellow men. Disdaining a highly organized church and ministry, the Quakers held that all true believers were ministers and hence equal before the eyes of God. The Quakers put their beliefs into everyday practice—they refrained from observing class distinctions such as doffing their hats to superiors; they would not sign oaths because they insisted that they always told the truth; and of course, they refused to fight in wars and kill others.

For their dissenting beliefs, the Quakers suffered intense persecution in England and on the continent as their ranks swelled. Like other hounded religious minorities they naturally looked to the new world as a place to practice their creed without running afoul of the established political or religious authorities. Penn had early been active in behalf of Quaker interests in West Jersey, later to become part of New Jersey, and a large number of Friends moved to that colony. In 1681, King Charles II, who owed Penn's father a large debt he was unable to pay, rewarded the son with a massive land grant located between New York and Maryland which Penn named Sylvania. Charles II, to honor his deceased friend the admiral, renamed it Pennsylvania. Penn became the world's largest landholder.

To attract settlers Penn decreed religious freedom in Pennsylvania and invited dissenters of all varieties to settle without fear of persecution. He set up a republican form of government with a two-house legislature and voting qualifications so low that almost all freed men possessed the ballot. For several generations, however, the Quakers controlled the colony's government. Penn personally visited his Sylvania in 1682 and selected a spot between the Delaware and Schuylkill rivers where he had laid out in a squared grid pattern, a city for his commonwealth which he called Philadelphia, the city of brotherly love.

Of all the English colonies, Pennsylvania probably enjoyed the best relations with the Indians, at least in its early stages. Firm in his belief that the Indians owned the land that the king granted to him, Penn purchased it from several tribes and negotiated treaties of peace which he unfailingly kept. Because Quakers refused to fight for any reason and believed that native Americans possessed a full measure of divinity,

Penn had little choice in his Indian relations. The Indians came to trust Penn, and during his lifetime the colony remained amazingly free of conflict with them.

The prolonged peace was even more astonishing because Pennsylvania, with its religious and political toleration, attracted a diverse group of settlers. Pennsylvania originally included Swedish, Dutch, Finnish, and English settlers already living in the vicinity. Religious minorities hailing from all over the Western world soon increased this ethnic mix; Scottish Presbyterians, French Huguenots, and German Mennonites and Lutherans settled the fertile lands around Philadelphia and with their thrifty husbandry established renowned and prosperous farms. Penn encouraged all such immigrants, the stuff of which good colonists were made, by widely advertising the lures of the new commonwealth, by selling small parcels of his land at reasonable prices, and by tolerating the claims of squatters who came and settled without thought of paying. The success of his policies can be measured; in 1681 there were 500 settlers in Penn's domain but only eight years later its inhabitants numbered almost 12,000.

Philadelphia

In the eighteenth century Philadelphia thrived by dealing in the wheat, flour, pork, and beef produced on the surrounding farms. Lively artisan and mercantile classes appeared in the little city, and its increasing foreign trade lent it a cosmopolitan air. By the revolution the city of brotherly love boasted about 20,000 souls.

For at least the first generation of its existence, Philadelphia differed from its competitors-Boston and New York to the north and Charles Town to the south— because of its Quaker influence. The Friends initially refused ostentatious display of their persons or their possessions as an affront to God and evidence of a false inequality. Above all, the Friends were always practical. Prosperous Quakers in the city built substantial, but severely plain, brick houses fronting right on the streets. Philadelphia's streets were built with depressions in the middle to allow for water runoff, rather than gutters on both sides as in most other urban areas. Building costs seem to have been cheaper in Philadelphia than elsewhere and enabled middle class artisans and small merchants to own their own homes.

By the 1730s, however, the plain Quakers had succumbed to worldly temptation. Among the wealthy, dress grew more ornate, they used costly materials and velvets of drab hues and later adopted the lively colors characteristic of the colonial upper class. They added exterior ornamentation to their houses, purchased larger, more costly carriages and covered them with decorations. Now the lower classes became identified by their plain dress and living styles. The poorer tradesmen, artisans, and unskilled laborers became resentful of the upper class pretensions that emerged and separated the classes, as indicated by this 1727 ditty from the city of brotherly love:

Now the Pleasant time approaches
Gentlemen do ride in coaches
But poor men they don't regard
That to maintain them labor hard.

As Philadelphia grew it also attracted drifters, day laborers, and sailors who were largely transients. By 1700 numerous taverns and dram houses, licensed and unlicensed, had opened along the waterfront to cater to these people's prodigious thirsts and other needs. Frequent brawls and melees and a rising crime rate in the area served only to alienate the classes further.

Philadelphia, like other colonial cities, had a sizable population of "bonded" people who were not legally free. Boys and girls of all classes were frequently apprenticed to master tradesmen for a period of years, normally seven, to learn a trade. Such apprentices, of whom Benjamin Franklin from Boston was the most famous, lived with their masters and provided labor in exchange for room and board. Young girls usually were indentured to learn the mysteries and techniques of "housewifery," which really meant that they were servant girls in prosperous artisans' homes. Young boys also performed household duties; indeed, conflict between the masters' haughty wives and the apprentices was commonplace. At the end of their contracts, the apprentices became journeymen and could offer their skills on the open market. Once they had become master craftsmen, they could take apprentices of their own. Although actually a period of bondage, apprenticeship carried with it no social stigma because successful trainees would enter the artisan middle class as printers, candle-makers, tinsmiths, or whatever, and eventually become employers.

Benjamin Franklin was an early advocate of colonial independence and became something of a backwoods sage and philosopher. Ironically, when the revolutionary war broke out Franklin's illegitimate son was the royal governor of New Jersey and sided with the British. (1908)

By 1720 the system of apprenticeship was not as secure as it once had been. Although the Philadelphia city council still forbade non-freedmen from opening their own shops or becoming masters, immigrants could set up businesses and practice their professed trades without going through apprenticeship. The trades were losing their complete control over who could enter their crafts, thus no longer enjoying a monopoly. Still, the system remained important as a means of preserving and passing down vital skills from generation to generation.

Philadelphia was also home to black slaves and a few free black artisans who together comprised perhaps 5 to 10 percent of the city's population. As in other colonial cities, they usually worked as household servants and encountered as much racial prejudice in the North as enslaved blacks did in the South. By the 1730s it was common for Philadelphia slaves to work in livery—fancy clothes which befit their stations as servants of the rich. When such well-dressed slaves circulated among poorer free workers after working hours and tossed their money around, jealousy often manifested itself in racial sneers and even at times fisticuffs. Undoubtedly, however, the plight of the urban slave was less harsh than for his brethren working the southern tobacco fields.

By mid-seventeenth century, Philadelphia exhibited the diversity and tensions that mark modern cities. Class distinctions, ethnic and racial tensions, crime and drunkenness, combined with an international culture, material affluence, good manners and learning, to create a city that became increasingly stratified and hierarchical. The strains of a more virulent individualism, evident elsewhere in the western world, were breaking down the bonds of deference that had once held the interdependent classes and groups together. By the revolution, ethnic and economic tensions were no longer subtle and subdued but formed the basis of Philadelphia's society.

Charleston

South Carolina stood in glaring contrast to egalitarian Pennsylvania. At the time of Charles II's restoration to the throne of England in 1660 a group of powerful English lords approached Charles for a proprietary charter to all the land between Virginia and Spanish Florida. Precariously situated on his throne and heavily in debt, Charles granted a charter to this proprietary group led by the leader of the Whig Party, Lord Anthony Ashley-Cooper, John Locke's patron. At Ashley-Cooper's request, Locke wrote the Carolina constitution, called the Fundamental Constitution. A curious effort to create in the New World a system of feudal baronies, Locke's Fundamental Constitution was completely at odds with the colonial reality of enormous expanses of inexpensive land. The Constitution was quickly and mercifully forgotten, giving way to American practicality. Still, it reflected the aristocratic intentions of Carolina's founders, intentions its white settlers never forsook.

In 1670 settlers established a colony at the confluence of the Ashley and Cooper Rivers, naming the settlement Charles Town in honor of the king. Like Jamestown, the Charles Town colony suffered immense problems. An unhealthy, snake and mosquito ridden region with no obvious economic assets, Charles Town attracted ne'er-do-wells from the British empire, religious dissenters from Europe, pirates from throughout the Atlantic, and prostitutes from everywhere. In time, Carolina managed to lure three somewhat respectable groups—French Huguenots, Sephardic Jews, and Scottish Presbyterians. These groups provided the colony with ambitious and resourceful leadership that transformed Charles Town into a thriving trade center for the Caribbean and a market for the Carolina backcountry. Charles Town merchants financed traders who hunted for deer skins and captured Indians, both of which, along with lumber, were traded to West Indian sugar planters in exchange for African slaves and sugar which, in turn, were marketed in the other British North American colonies. The West Indian trade justified Charles Town's existence, but it failed to make it a major Atlantic seaport.

Then, in the 1690s, Carolina planters discovered their magic crop—rice. Along the low-lying, humid, and warm coastline, rice thrived. By the early eighteenth century, Charles Town virtually monopolized rice production outside of Asia. Cheaper than wheat and other traditional food grains, rice became the staple food for Europe's rapidly expanding urban, working classes. Carolina planters could sell all the rice at high prices they could grow. But rice cultivation required enormous capital investment and labor. Rice grew in swamp land that had to be drained and irrigated by a complex system of ditches, dikes, and flood gates. It was nearly impossible to find laborers willing to do such work at affordable wages. Moreover, those who were foolish enough to work in the rice fields, in almost all cases, quickly succumbed to malarial mosquitoes. With fortunes to be made, Carolina planters unhesitantly turned to slave labor. By the mid-eighteenth century over 40% of the slaves imported into British North America entered the colonies through Charles Town, making it, in effect, the Ellis Island of African-Americans. Forty percent of black Americans' ancestral roots go back to colonial South Carolina.

The sickle-cell anemia trait, so common among African Americans, flourished among those who worked in Carolina rice fields. The sickle-cell trait carries with it an immunity to malaria. Those Africans who came to South Carolina without the trait died; those with the sickle-cell trait survived, passing it on to their children. Within several generations, the sickle-cell trait became highly concentrated in South Carolina's slave population from whom so many African-Americans descended.

The Carolina climate, the lucrative rice culture, and the adoption of slavery made South Carolina the most distinct colony in British North America. The climate meant that no sane person voluntarily lived in the country-side during the mosquito season that lasted from April to September. Instead, the white population clustered together in Charles Town, leaving slaves alone with their overseers on the rice plantations. Carolina became a city-state ruled by absentee rice planters who lived in Charles Town and who only occasionally visited their plantations. South Carolina was both more centralized and more urbanized than any other colony. Nearly every free person lived in Charles Town which ruled the remainder of the colony as if it were a conquered territory. The only court in the entire colony was located in Charles Town.

Rice created a large class of extremely wealthy families. About 300 families—Pinkney, Middleton, Managault, Huger, and Ravenel—monopolized the colony's political and social life, conducting themselves like Old World aristocracy. They built beautiful mansions, purchased fine furniture, hired French music and dance teachers for their children, patronized the finest theater in the colonies, and all in all, engaged in the most high powered social life outside London, Paris, and Vienna. Horse racing, gambling, drinking, dancing, and fornicating became municipal traits, thoroughly scandalizing visitors from puritanical New England while fascinating everyone else.

This festive, unrestrained hedonism took place amid unrivaled poverty and misery. Outside Charles Town lived a slave population from whose labor and suffering the rice planters' leisure and wealth derived. Only in South Carolina was a majority of the population slaves. In South Carolina African slave outnumbered free whites by 3 to 1. Outside Charles Town, African slaves outnumbered free whites by 9 to 1. While Charles Town might resemble Paris and London, the South Carolina low country resembled West Africa. Isolated from whites and European culture, South Carolina slaves preserved many West African customs and much of their West African language, creating in the Carolina Low Country a distinct culture that provided the foundation for an African-American culture that subsequently spread throughout the South. Even today, in the South Carolina and Georgia Low Country West African ways persist, not just among black Carolinians but whites as well. Because of the radical contrast between the black, impoverished, and enslaved countryside and white, affluent, and libertine Charles Town, South Carolina whites jealously guarded their political power, becoming highly sensitive, even paranoid, towards all criticisms of their slave economy. The egalitarianism that had emerged in New England and Middle Colonies had little in common with the nouveau riche aristocracy of Charles Town, except that Charles Town, too, consisted of a highly diverse white population that placed personal freedom of white males above all other values. The residents of New York, Pennsylvania, New Jersey, Delaware, South Carolina, and later Maryland, all looked to and depended on cosmopolitan port cities. Even New Englanders looked to Boston, Providence, and Newport. These seaports provided British North Americans intimate links with Europe. Ocean-going ships, along with their cargoes, brought into the colonies people and ideas from all over Europe. Each American seaport became a microcosm of the North Atlantic Community with enclaves of Africans, Sephardic Jews, Greeks, Germans, Scots, Swedes, French, Italians, and Dutch. And because the only limitation on political participation was property, a remarkably large percentage of these people participated in colonial politics, including Jews and Catholics. Toleration, in time, became the rule in every city, permeating the countryside. Only in Virginia, South Carolina, and to some extent in New York, did wealthy families monopolize political power. Even in these colonies, wealthy families, at least publicly, played down social and religious differences among whites out of fear for servile insurrections. The result was a tolerant and diverse urban culture that accepted religious differences, thrived on political controversy and dissent, ignored ethnic and national backgrounds, and judged individuals on accomplishment and wealth.

The Great Awakening

In the 1720s, as the religious zeal of the early generations subsided and worldliness increased, a wave of revivalism swept through the colonies. In the hundred years since the founding of the first British colony, settlers had moved westward where they often found themselves far from an organized church. Such isolation fed fears that without the social controls supplied by the churches, frontier people would throw off civilized restraints and revert to savagery. Also, for increasing numbers of colonists, the theological quibbling among the various sects obscured whatever religious truth the churches claimed.

The revivalism of the Great Awakening attracted colonists of all Protestant denominations because the ministers preached a basic, easily understood "fire and brimstone" message that plainly defined right and wrong and entreated all sinners to acknowledge the reality of their condition and accept the freely offered salvation. Jonathan Edwards, Puritan pastor in Northampton, Massachusetts, was the most famous of these ministers. Edward's plea was simple: return to the religious convictions of our forebears. More than simply an emotional fiery preacher, Edwards ranks as one of America's greatest theologians. Yet, his pious enthusiasm sparked masses of conversions wherever he spoke.

The Great Awakening reached its zenith in 1739-41, during the two-year visit of English evangelist, George Whitefield. An Anglican priest, Whitefield had become awakened by John and Charles Wesley. Whitefield became famous in England by addressing his message to the English working class in large, outdoor meetings, apart from the bounds of Anglican authority. Shunned by the Anglicans, Whitefield continued his out-of-doors ministry in the colonies. "Open air" revivals only added to his appeal, allowing him to speak to thousands of listeners at one time and freeing him from any dependency on the hospitality of colonial religious leaders. He traveled where he wished; he preached how he wished. The "open-air" meetings also meant that anyone who wished to hear Whitefield could. People of all religious denominations, all classes, and races listened attentively to his message of spiritual salvation. Benjamin Franklin expressed his admiration for Whitefield as a performer:

> *His delivery . . . was so improved by frequent repetitions, that every accent, every emphasis, every modulation of voice, was so perfectly well turned and well placed that without being interested in the subject, one could not help being pleased with the discourse, a pleasure of much the same kind with that received from an excellent piece of music.*

During his two-year stay, Whitefield traveled to every British North American colony, spending most of his time in Boston, New York, Philadelphia, and Charleston, but also traveling through the hinterland as well. Tens of thousands of colonials heard him first hand, and by the time he left in 1741, he was the best known personality in the colonies. After his departure, the most dramatic phase of the Great Awakening ended, but the message that he, Edwards, and other Awakeners preached continued to spread throughout the colonies. Awakeners, discontented with their established churches, organized congregations of their own and formed colleges and seminaries, including Dartmouth, Princeton, Brown, and Andover, to train an evangelical ministry. Annually, scores of newly trained "New Light" ministers left these seminaries to form churches of their own and to spread the revitalized Calvinism of Jonathan Edwards.

Meanwhile in England, the Wesleys formed a radical sect within the Anglican church, training their own cadre of ministers to preach throughout Britain and the colonies. These "methodists," so called because they followed faithfully the "methods" laid down by the Wesleys, broke from the Anglican Church, forming the Methodist Church, which in the years immediately following the revolution became the second largest church in the United States.

While the pietistic message of the Great Awakening appealed to a broad spectrum of people, it appealed especially to the uneducated, to middle class Protestants, to women, to young people, to servants, and to slaves. The New Light congregations cut across race, gender, and class lines. Blacks were eagerly recruited; servants treated with regard; women played much more important roles in evangelical congregations than in the established churches; and neither wealth nor education conferred on individuals special status. Democratic in character and organization, evangelical congregations treated all persons equally. They simply asked: "Are you saved?"

The egalitarian message of Awakeners caused the most difficulty in the planter dominated, southern slave colonies, especially Virginia. By the 1750s Virginia's Anglican elite faced a rising tide of evangelicalism that openly challenged the planters' moral authority to govern. Evangelical ministers—largely Presbyterian and Baptist—offered Virginians a choice between a state church, run by Virginia's planter class, and administered by a corrupt, incompetent, immoral ministry or a dissenting church, controlled by the congregation itself which insisted that all sinners were equal in the eyes of God. Not surprisingly, Virginia's poorly educated, small freeholders found irresistible an evangelical religion that treated the non-planter class with respect. The radical implications of evangelicalism went further. The dissenting ministers also taught that the planters lived decadent, immoral lives, and were an abomination in the eyes of God. They were unworthy leaders. Evangelical ministers did not stop there, they also openly violated the racial code that separated poor whites from slaves, inviting all believers, regardless of class or race, to their churches.

The evangelical tide that swept Virginia after the 1740s threatened to topple the planter class from political power as well as undercut the racial order that undergirded black slavery. Outraged, the Virginia elite responded by outlawing dissenting churches, whipping dissenting ministers, tearing down their churches, and fining dissenters for failure to attend Anglican services. Their heavy-handed approach failed. Evangelical ministers were treated as sainted martyrs, their modest churches rapidly rebuilt, juries dominated by dissenters refused to punish persons for failing to attend Anglican services, membership in the evangelical churches swelled, and in a few cases, evangelicals desecrated Anglican sanctuaries by covering altars with human excrement and filling the planters' boxed pews with horse manure. Virginia's planters, realizing that they had initiated a religious war that they could not win, conceded to the dissenters' demands for religious freedom, but with qualifications.

The House of Burgess and the county courts allowed dissenting ministers to preach freely in their own meeting houses, and they concurred that Virginians could attend the church of their choice without legal penalty. But the Anglican establishment insisted that blacks attend separate services overseen by their masters and that evangelical ministers cease converting slaves. This compromise satisfied no one, but given the planter class' support by English law, the evangelicals accepted it. Despite the radical social implications of their message, they were primarily interested in their own salvation, not social and political revolution. Nonetheless, during the American Revolution, evangelicals demanded the complete disestablishment of the Anglican Church and the formal recognition in the Virginia Constitution of religious liberty, a demand to which the planter class reluctantly concurred with an exchange of evangelical support for the revolution.

The Great Awakening's consequences are difficult to document but were, nonetheless, substantial. Beginning in the 1730s and persisting in the South and back country until the 1760s, the Great Awakening touched and changed every colony in British North America. First and most obviously, it ended forever the medieval pattern of a single, established church. After the Great Awakening, in virtually every town and village in British North America, at least two churches existed—the established church, Congregational in New England, Anglican elsewhere, except in Pennsylvania, and a "New Light" evangelical church. Having broken the monopoly of state churches, most communities witnessed a proliferation of Protestant churches—Presbyterian, Quaker, Baptist, and Lutheran—but also, in the cities, colonials accepted the right of Catholic and Jewish congregations to worship freely also. Religious freedom, once granted to some, became nearly impossible to deny to all. Moreover, even though initially evangelicals had been the primary exponents of religious freedom, by the 1760s Anglicans, facing the prospect of an evangelical majority, in self-defense, became themselves converts to religious freedom. By the American Revolution, religious toleration and freedom had become enshrined as a principle of American life.

The Great Awakening, by emphasizing personal salvation and appealing to all believers, also diminished the differences between Protestant faiths. After 1760, all Protestant churches, to some extent, were evangelical. Church services became less formal, the singing of hymns became commonplace, and emotional expression became an accepted part of American religion—all of which enriched the musical life of the colonies even as it encouraged Americans to act less formal, more spontaneous. American Protestants discarded the order, decorum, and restraint that had characterized seventeenth-century Protestantism. That is, the freedom that had first manifested itself in the removal of communal restraints on property, in time, led to both a liberalization of politics and of religion.

Finally, the Great Awakening altered colonial Americans' sense of themselves. As God's saved, they imagined themselves free of sin. Collectively, they came to view themselves as morally superior to Europeans. Free to worship as they wished, free from the worldly concerns and aristocratic influence of state churches, American colonials thought of themselves as an uniquely moral and free people. Having undergone a religious awakening, they believed that they enjoyed God's special blessing. They, like the ancient Hebrews, were God's chosen, elect people. Earlier, when colonials had compared themselves to Europe, they judged the differences between Europe and America as indexes of American provincialism, of American inferiority. After the Great Awakening, increasingly, they believed that the differences were, instead, signs of American superiority. Self-government, the absence of aristocratic classes and large cities, the disintegration of established churches, the emergence of individualism, and the relative equality—all signified American superiority. Believing themselves a special and blessed people, British colonials developed an identity as Americans, a people determined to resist all efforts to make them more like Europeans, a people who would fight to preserve those differences, believing that God stood at their side.

Growth and Development

By the 1750s the English colonies had become complex, self-sustaining societies. With an estimated population of 1,200,000 at mid-century, they enjoyed a phenomenal growth rate. Benjamin Franklin, the new world's most famous sage and wit, estimated that the colonial population doubled every twenty to twenty-five years. The statistics bore him out. The crush of newly arrived English, German, Scottish, Irish, and African people contributed to this increase. By the Revolution about thirty percent of British North America was non-English. The heavy concentration of non-English peoples in colonies south of New York complicated the efforts to achieve inter-colonial unity by such men as Franklin. But as much as immigration, the colonies' astronomical birth rate, reflected in the average of eight children per family, coupled with a low death rate, fed the unprecedented population growth.

Indeed, the demographic revolution that led to a twenty fold increase in the human population since 1700, first manifested itself in seventeenth-century New England. There are several explanations. The colonial diet was probably better, especially in fresh milk, fruits, and vegetables. Due to almost unlimited wood supplies, British North American housing was larger, better ventilated, and better heated than European housing. Finally, viral diseases were less rampant in North America. While Old World diseases and influences traveled to North America on ships, often the length of the passage exceeded the longevity of the disease. Even those diseases that reached eastern ports, rarely went beyond the ports due to the colonies primitive transportation networks. And since 96% of the population lived in the relatively disease-free countryside, most North Americans did not have to confront the plethora of diseases that annually plagued Europeans and other Old World people. In 1776, Boston, New York, and Charleston all had fewer than 10,000 inhabitants, and the largest colonial city, Philadelphia only about 20,000, compared to a million people who lived in London. And unlike Native Americans, European and African Americans enjoyed the acquired immunity to colds, measles, chicken pox, and other childhood diseases of their Old World ancestors. Due to immigration and high birth rates, the colonial population was also relatively young. A Maryland census in 1775 showed that over one-half the population was under sixteen years of age, and the first United States Census in 1790 confirmed this was true in the other states.

As Thomas Malthus pointed out in the early nineteenth century, population growth was a two edged sword. Without an equivalent increase in food supplies, over population led to famine such as occurred in Ireland in the 1840s. This meant that the colonies had to double their production of food, clothing, and houses every twenty-five years just to maintain their standard of living. Rapid population growth and readily available Indian land provided the colonies with a food surplus that freed people to work in nonagricultural jobs, leading to a much more diversified and specialized economy. By 1775 the colonists had started a number of important industries such as lumbering, shipbuilding (which constructed about one-third of all the merchant vessels flying the English flag), fishing and whaling, flour milling, furs, and iron manufacturing. By the revolution the colonies produced more iron than England. At least two colonial ironworks were capitalized at over £100,000 and each employed above 100 men.

Colonial Trade

The mainstay of colonial prosperity, however, was trade. The great colonial fortunes, including those of John Hancock in Massachusetts and Henry Laurens in

England's American Colonies

South Carolina, reputedly the two richest men in the colonies, were made in commerce. The settlers exported raw materials, flour, meat, livestock, rum, fish, lumber, furs, tobacco, indigo (a blue dye), and rice while they imported slaves and manufactured products. As the colonies matured their economies became increasingly interdependent. Most of the direct trade with England originated in the southern colonies which grew the important staple crops of tobacco, indigo, and rice. The middle colonies, New York, Pennsylvania, and New Jersey, became England's bread basket as well as helping feed the plantation colonies. New Englanders, lacking fertile land and a long growing season, fished and transported the other colonies' products between colonial ports and to England. In addition, a slave trade flourished with the slavers carrying iron, rum, and trade goods to Africa and bringing the slaves to the West Indies where they were broken in or "seasoned" before being brought into the mainland colonies.

These trade patterns fit English mercantilist theory. The colonies existed to export needed raw materials to the mother country and to import finished goods. To ensure this trade pattern, Parliament passed a series of Navigation Acts starting in 1650. These acts, particularly those of 1663 and 1696, required much of the colonial trade to go through England, where it was taxed. Parliament's Board of Trade drew up a list of enumerated goods, or items that could only be traded with England, which at various times included tobacco, indigo, sugar, molasses, rice, and naval supplies. English merchants resold many of these products to English buyers and to other European countries, enabling English merchants to take a lion's share of the colonists' profits.

The Navigation Acts, however, also worked for the colonists' benefit. The English paid bounties for certain goods such as indigo and naval stores and granted the colonists a tobacco monopoly in the mother country. The English mercantile system was not as strict as those of other colonial nations, and it certainly was not enforced closely. Americans mastered the art of smuggling, and they carried on a flourishing, if illegal trade, with the French and Spanish West Indies and with parts of Europe. On the whole, however, the Navigation Acts favored the mother country, as they were designed to do, but judging from the lack of colonial resistance to them prior to 1763 and from the rapid growth and development of the colonies, they did not create a great hardship in America. Moreover, they were only selectively enforced, and colonial merchants had little trouble bribing underpaid and corrupt British custom agents. The two most serious problems caused by the navigation laws were that they drained gold from the colonies to England and restricted colonial manufactures. Always short of specie, the colonists experimented with paper money, which England quickly outlawed. England's prohibition of the colonial export of wool, hats, and finished iron products, however, indicated colonial economic strength. These American manufactures successfully competed with comparable English-made goods. The Navigation Acts symbolized that the colonies existed within a much larger empire. From an imperial point of view they were but a contributing part of the English Empire, whose value was measured in the extent the colonies benefitted powerful imperial interests in England. Regarding the empire's income, the British West Indian sugar islands and India were more valuable than the more economically autonomous North American colonies.

The French and Indian War

In this larger context, the American colonies found themselves as pawns in a worldwide struggle between the English, French, and Spanish empires over control of the world's resources. Americans lacked an identity of their own, were quite diverse in makeup, and maintained no well-defined border. The colonies were but imperial assets in European diplomacy. Each empire worked to offset the power of another, shifting alliances as their imperial interests dictated. Prior to the American Revolution, New France, New Spain, and England shared a regional balance in North America. No single empire dominated. The extensive territorial holdings, the allegiance of the Indians, the radically different population sizes, armaments, local military skills, and transportation all made the three-way American diplomatic balance unique. Tied to England, the North American colonies found themselves entangled in wars that had started in Europe for reasons that colonials often did not understand.

In the eighteenth century the European balance of power had become dangerously simple with England opposed to France and Spain. King William's War from 1689 to 1697 had no great effect on the colonies. In Queen Anne's War from 1702 to 1713, however, the English won extensive territory from New France. The War of Jenkins' Ear started in 1739 when an English captain, Jenkins, presented his shriveled ear in a box to King George II claiming that the Spanish had cut it off while he was trading legally with New Spain. King George's War, 1744 to 1748, largely took place in the West Indies and had little effect on the North American balance of power.

By 1748, however, France embarked on an aggressive campaign to expand both on the European continent and overseas—a policy that required France to maintain both a powerful army and a strong navy. In opposition, England wanted to maintain the existing situation in Europe and to improve its position in the New World by picking up additional colonies.

Starting in the 1740s, France expanded its land claims in the New World by fortifying the Ohio River Valley. Some of this land, already claimed by several English colonies, had been purchased by colonists for speculation. In 1753 Governor Dinwiddie of Virginia, himself a speculator in Ohio Valley lands, sent young Colonel George Washington into the wilderness to ask the French to leave the Pittsburgh area. They refused. The following year Washington was sent to throw the French out of the newly constructed Fort Duquesne, but the French defeated him. The fight was the opening

The young George Washington attired in the uniform of a Virginia colonial militia officer. The planter and land speculator would soon make a military reputation in the French and Indian war that would later catapult him into command of the new nation's continental army. (1932)

salvo of the next European war. For the first time, the regional balance of power in the New World upset the balance of European power, setting off a general European war, called the Seven Years' War in Europe because it did not break out there until 1756, and the French and Indian War in the British colonies.

The first battle took place when General Braddock, resplendent in a bright red uniform, was ambushed on his way to Fort Duquesne. The colonists failed to budge the French from Fort Niagara, Lake Champlain, or the Ohio valley. Things went no better for the English in Europe. In 1758, however, William Pitt became England's prime minister, and immediately negotiated a new coalition altering the balance of power. He allied England with Prussia, which had the largest land army in Europe. Against France, Spain, Austria, Russia, Sweden, and many of the German states, the Prussians held their own while Pitt concentrated on controlling the seas and winning in America. Pitt ordered the successful assault against Fort Louisbourg in 1758, and the following year, sent General James Wolfe's expedition down the St. Lawrence to assault Quebec. On the Plains of Abraham, Wolfe and General Louis Montcalm fought in a classic battle in which both lost their lives, and France lost her North American colonies. For all practical purposes the war was over in America by 1759.

Peace

The war dragged on around the world, however, until 1763 when the victors exacted peace terms in Paris. The treaty dictated the first turnover of North American colonies. England received Canada and all the French territory east of the Mississippi River, except New Orleans. Spain gave England East and West Florida. France, to repay Spain for aiding a losing cause, gave it the French territory west of the Mississippi River and New Orleans. France now had no territorial claims on the North American continent. The most important consequence of the 1763 peace treaty, however, left the continent largely in the hands of a relatively weak Spanish Empire and the British North American colonies. After 1763, American colonials no longer viewed the British as their guardian against the French, but as an over-bearing, imperial overlord.

Flush with wartime prosperity, the colonists at first behaved as if they expected to continue their loyal allegiance to England and continued to date their legal papers with "the _____ day of the year of the Reign of our Sovereign Lord . . . King of Great Britain." The ties that bound them to their "Sovereign Lord" remained strong. American colonists boasted of being members of the great British empire that continued its global expansion. The colonists enjoyed the naval protection afforded them by the British Union Jack. They considered themselves as free as any peoples known to history. British redcoats were rarely seen, the crown only infrequently intervened in colonial affairs, and even the English customs officials charged with enforcing the Navigation Acts were usually easy to get along with. For over a century and a half, the British had governed the colonies with a glorious inefficiency some historians have called "salutary neglect." The colonists took advantage of British neglect to develop illegal trade—for example, in French molasses—which in turn contributed to colonial prosperity. Prior to 1763 American colonists did not complain much about British mercantile restrictions; they realized that they were a small price to pay, even when it had to be paid on occasion, for the benefits of belonging to the British Empire. When the Paris peace treaty was initialed, there was no hint of the stormy conflict with the mother country that loomed just ahead.

Historical Potpourri

A stroll through any cemetery dating back to the colonial era is a good way to acquire a feel for living conditions in the period. The tombstone of Mary Buell in Litchfield, Connecticut, for example, graphically illustrates the new world's rapid population growth:

> *She died Nov 4th*
> *1768, at age 90*
> *Having had 13 Children*
> *101 Grand Children*
> *274 Great G. Children*
> *22 Great G. G. Children*
> *410 Total*
> *336 survived her.*

At the other end of the spectrum many women died in childbirth leaving poignant reminders of lives suddenly cut short. On a headstone in Harvard, Massachusetts, a loved one had the following engraved for a lost wife and child:

> *In memory of Mrs. Nancy Worster.*
> *who Died in Childbirth Sept ye 21.*
> *1776, Aged 24 years 8 months & 21 days.*
> *Though she was fair while she had breath,*
> *And on her cheeks the Rose did bloom,*
> *Yet her Dear Babe became her Death,*
> *While she became the Infants Tomb.*

Equally sad are the numerous stones dedicated to the dead infants found in almost any old cemetery. In Salem, Massachusetts, someone raised a monument to little Thomas Smith who died in 1771 at the age of four:

> *Now in my childhood I must die*
> *And hasten to eternity*
> *Leave all my playmates and my toys*
> *Hoping to inherit eternal joys.*

Occasionally a memorial tells a brief history of a family's trials and tribulations in the colonial world. Such a stone is in Vineyard Haven, Massachusetts:

> *Lydia, the Wife of John Claghorn*
> *She died in Child bed December 31st 1770, in ye 2nd year of her Age*
> *John and Lydia, That lovely pair A whale killed him, Her body lies here.*
> *There souls we hope, with Christ now reign,*
> *So our great Loss is there great gain.*

In New Bern, North Carolina, relatives of Charles Elliot, a local member of the bar, had these simple sentiments engraved; perhaps to rebut contrary views:

> *An Honest Lawyer Indeed.*

Mortal man in the colonial period was always threatened by the specter of natural disasters and less than talented epitaph writers. Marcy Hale, who died in 1709 and was buried in Glastonbury, Connecticut, was the victim of both:

> *Here lies one whose life stands cut asunder she was strucke dead by a*
> *clap of thunder.*

A few tombstones raise more questions than they answer. Mary Brooks' monument, raised after her death in 1736 in Concord, Massachusetts, says simply:

> *She was very Excellent for Reading & Soberness.*
> *Mary was 11 when she died.*

Source: Charles L. Wallis, *Stories on Stone: A Book of American Epitaphs* (New York: Oxford University Press, 1954)

Good Books

Samuel Eliot Morison's two books, *The European Discovery of America: The Northern Voyages* (1971) and his *Southern Voyages* (1974) along with his older *Admiral of the Ocean Sea: A Life of Christopher Columbus* (1942) are excellent studies of the daring "new men" and the challenges they faced in the new world. Else Roesdahl, *The Vikings* (1987) presents a view of Norse contributions to the New World; William D. Phillips, Jr. and Carla Rahn Phillips, *The World of Christopher Columbus* (1992). Kirkpatrick Sale's *The Conquest of Paradise: Christopher Columbus and the Columbian Legacy* (1990) raises troubling questions about relations between Europeans and Native Americans. For the ecological impact see William Cronon, *Changes in the Land: Indians, Colonists, and the Ecology of New England* (1983).

William McNeil in his *The Rise of the West* (1963) presents absorbing insights into the massive European changes that produced the modern world. Charles Gipson's *Spain in America* (1966) presents a good overall picture of New Spain. J. A. Caruso does the same for French colonial expansion in his book *The Mississippi Valley Frontier: The Age of French Exploration and Settlement* (1966). Also see Reuben Gold Thwaites, *The Jesuit Relations and Allied Documents* (1896-1900) and W.J. Eccles, *France in America* (1992) and David J. Weber, *The Spanish Frontier* (1992).

See Alden T. Vaughn, *American Genesis: Captain John Smith and the Founding of Virginia* (1975) for a realistic portrayal of the colonists' early suffering at Jamestown and Wallace Notestein's *The English People on the Eve of Colonization; 1603-1630* (1954) for an idea of how English institutions were adaptable to the new world. Ivor Noel Hume's *Martin's Hundred* (1982) artfully depicts an archeologist's reconstruction of an early Virginia settlement at the moment of an Indian massacre; Edmund S. Morgan, *American Slavery: American Freedom: The Ordeal of Colonial Virginia* (1975);

Philip A. Bruce, *Social Life in Old Virginia* (1910) is absorbing, and *The Secret Diary of William Byrd of Westover. 1709-1712* (1963) presents a superb glimpse of the life of Virginia's colonial upper crust. Winthrop Jordan explores the origin of slavery in his book *White Over Black: American Attitudes Toward the Negro. 1550-1812* (1968). Abbot Emerson Smith, *Colonists in Bondage: White Servitude and Convict Labor in America. 1607-1776* (1947) and Richard B. Morris' *Government and Labor in Early America* (1946) survey the whole colonial labor problem, including indentured servants.

Alan Simpson, *Puritanism in Old and New England* (1955) is excellent. Daniel Boorstin, *The Americans: The Colonial Experience* (1958) takes a close look at the Puritans' utopia as well as their treatment of the Quakers. Kenneth Lockridge, *A New England Town: The First*

Hundred Years (1970) and *Michael Zuckerman, Peaceable Kingdoms* (1970) examine New England towns carefully and find political oligarchies and great pressures for conformity everywhere. Bryan F. LeBeau, *The Story of the Salem Witch Trials* (1997) is a good introduction to the witch trials. Also see Paul Boyer and Stephen Nissenbaum, *Salem Possessed* (1974).

Kenneth Lockridge, *Literacy in Colonial New England* (1974) compares the literacy rates of England, Pennsylvania, and Virginia. David S. Lovejoy, *Religious Enthusiasm in the New World* (1985) is the broadest study of colonial religious dissent. For the Great Awakening in Virginia see Rhys Isaac's pathbreaking *The Transformation of Virginia. 1740-1790* (1982). The racial implications of the Great Awakening are addressed in Mechal Sobel, *The World They Made Together: Black and White Values in Eighteenth-century Virginia* (1987) and Gary B. Nash, *Red, White, and Black: The Peoples of Early America* (1974).

Carl Bridenbaugh's *Cities in the Wilderness: The First Century of Urban Life in America 1625-1742* (1938) is the standard work on colonial cities but also see Gary B. Nash, *The Urban Crucible: The Northern Seaports and the Origins of the American Revolution* (1979). H. H. Peckham takes a good look at *The Colonial Wars 1689-1762* (1964) and Richard Hofstadter presents a thumbnail sketch of *America at 1750: A Social Portrait* (1971). For changes in women and family see Barry Levy, *Quakers and the American Family* (1988) and Laurel Thatcher Ulrich's *A Midwife's Tale* (1990).

For slavery and African American culture see Peter H. Wood, *Black Majority* (1974); Michael Gomez, *Exchanging Our Country Marks: The Transformation of African Identities in the Colonial and Antebellum South* (1998); and Betty Wood, *The Origins of American Slavey* (1997).

Alvin Josephy, Jr. details Indian contributions and culture in *The Indians' Heritage of America* (1971). For North American Indians in the colonial period see James Axtell, *The European and the Indian* (1981) and *After Columbus* (1988); James H. Merrell, *The Indians' New World* (1989); Daniel H. Usner, Jr. *Indians, Settlers, & Slaves in a Frontier Exchange Economy* (1992).

CHAPTER TWO

REVOLUTIONARY FERMENT

1763	Proclamation Line
1764	Sugar Act
1765	Stamp Act
	Stamp Act Congress
1766	Stamp Act repealed
1767	Townsend Duties
1770	Townsend Duties repealed
	Boston Massacre
1773	Tea Act
	Tea Party
1774	Coercive or Intolerable Acts
	Quebec Act
	Quartering Act
	First Continental Congress
1775	Battles of Concord and Lexington
	Second Continental Congress
	George Washington elected to command Continental army
	Continentals captured Fort Ticonderoga and Boston
1776	Thomas Paine wrote *Common Sense*
	Declaration of Independence
	Continentals lost New York City and surprised Trenton
1778	France recognized American independence, signed defense treaty
1780	Benedict Arnold committed treason
1781	Cornwallis surrendered at Yorktown
	Articles of Confederation ratified
1783	Paris Peace Treaty
1787	Northwest Ordinance
	Shays' Rebellion
	Constitutional Convention
1790	Constitution ratified by last of original thirteen states

The American Republic

The Treaty of Paris in 1763, which ended the Seven Years' War, radically changed British North America. A hostile French empire no longer menaced the borders and slowed westward expansion. For the first time the English colonists possessed a confidence and security that made the mother country's protection seem unnecessary. The altered diplomatic situation underscored important changes within the colonies. Even as the colonists celebrated their victory and their common ties to the mother country, they also discovered a sense of growing colonial identity and tensions between themselves and English Empire.

Toward Unity

From the colonies' founding, the settlers held many common values. Overwhelming numbers of colonists were English, and even after the influx of non-English immigrants in the eighteenth century they shared a common language and a western European culture. A southern planter, a Philadelphia merchant, and a well-read Boston Yankee discussed the same books, debated familiar points of English law, played whist, savored the same wines, dressed similarly, and held similar religious beliefs. Although they might argue interminably over fine theological points, most British colonists agreed on such Protestant principles as individual responsibility for salvation. Moreover, these convivial men represented the vast majority of colonists who owned property. To an amazing degree, the colonists owned a stake in the future of the North American English colonies. As a group they were not a desperate, downtrodden mass of dispossessed humanity. Most farmed and wrestled with problems of weather, insects, transportation, and markets no matter where they lived. They tended to look to the world in similar ways. The widespread ownership of property, especially land, allowed the colonists a degree of political representation unique to the West. Almost all male property holders, and even a few females, exercised political responsibilities on some level and took them seriously.

The colonists did not necessarily recognize the growth of this "Americanism." Benjamin Franklin considered himself a foreigner in Philadelphia after he had left Boston—but the similarities pulled them together, especially in the face of outside pressure. Prior to 1763, their affinities had reinforced the strong ties the colonists felt toward the mother country. In that year the English government reorganized its empire in North America to make it pay its own way and moved to tighten its trade regulations. Colonial resistance to such policies was at times ferocious, and over the next decade the colonists' sense of their American identity slowly diverged from their English heritage. By the Revolution, many colonists thought of themselves as Americans first and Englishmen second.

Rise of the Spirit of Independence

By post their objections to the crown's policies. Such proclamations brought the colonists together and helped to create the spirit that led to independence. (1973)

The growing sense of colonial identity explains why the revolution remained primarily a struggle for independence from outside control. The colonists in 1775 wanted to regain the political rights that they had enjoyed in the British empire before 1763. The revolution's leaders had no desire to stand society on its head, to uplift and catapult the lower classes to power or even to positions of equality. In social and political terms it was conservative. Revolutionary leaders wished to regain the political rights that they had enjoyed before 1763 and at the same time preserve the social status quo. They fought a war for independence, and they established two postwar governments intended to preserve as much of the colonial world as they could. To ensure that their basic rights as Englishmen would never again be abridged and unwilling to rely on oral traditions, the American founders wrote these rights into the Articles of Confederation, the federal Constitution, the Bill of Rights, and their various state constitutions.

Colonial Economic Changes

Until 1763 British colonists had experienced a measure of economic autonomy. Under the English imperial system they had prospered, their per capita incomes, already higher than those on the continent, nearly doubling after 1700. The Navigation Acts that controlled American trade had worked to the colonists' advantage.

At mid-century, however, the colonies' relationship to the empire had become less profitable. By 1750 the colonists had used their entrepreneurial talents, organizational and technological abilities, natural resources, high levels of education, and political stability to advance their own interests. After 1750 the imperial balance of trade turned against the colonists. In all but two years between 1745 and 1776, they bought more from England than they sold, a sign of increasing colonial prosperity and of the colonists' rising economic expectations. But the trade deficit also drained the colonies of currency and led many to suspect the English of taking advantage of them. Parliament had designed the British mercantile system to serve England's long-term interests, not colonists' welfare. Colonials, like John Hancock and Henry Laurens, had acquired their legendary fortunes outside the law, by smuggling. After 1763, colonists came to see the entire imperial system as contrary to their economic and political interests.

The Rise of Colonial Legislatures

Colonial politics paralleled these economic changes. Colonial legislatures, more than anything else, wanted home rule. For years colonial assemblies had chipped away at the power of the royal governor. After 1763, as Parliament sought to reassert its control over the colonies, it clashed head-on with stubborn colonial assemblies. By the mid-18th century, the royal governors found their positions almost impossible. Theoretically representing the king while serving the colonists represented in the legislatures, the governors were caught in the middle. In most disputes the governors had to side with the crown to hold their jobs, but they did so at the price of losing American colonials' confidence. Frustrated by colonial resistance and isolated from English court politics, many governors simply resigned. As the revolution approached the turnover of high British colonial officials increased.

The colonial legislatures, composed of ambitious and prosperous politicians, had gained great power through the gradual accumulation of small rights. By 1763 their most important prerogative was control over the purse that included the assembly's right to draft financial legislation, audit all public accounts including the governors', print paper money, appoint officials to spend the money, and in some cases even pay the salaries of the royal governor. The legislators usually appointed their own speaker as treasurer to insure control over public spending during legislative recesses. If, in the assembly's absence, the treasurer sided with the governor, he was not often reelected speaker. Moreover, the legislatures gained the right to regulate their own membership, to determine the frequency of elections, and importantly, to elect a colonial agent to lobby for the colony's interests in London. These agents, including the well-known Benjamin Franklin, gave colonial legislatures a voice in royal circles that could undercut an unpopular royal governor. The assemblies also lessened English influence in the colonies by controlling the press. They passed out public printing contracts only to editors who shared their political viewpoint.

Colonial Leaders

The power of the colonial assemblies demonstrated the colonists' political skills. Astute men, well versed in English law and political thought, dominated the colonial legislative councils. In the 1760s a brilliant generation of Americans emerged that included John Adams, Thomas Paine, George Washington, Patrick Henry, Robert Morris, John Hancock, Thomas Jefferson, John Jay, James Madison, and Alexander Hamilton together with two elder statesmen, Samuel Adams and Benjamin Franklin. These men combined rare traits of thought and action. They influenced colonial attitudes toward the mother country and planned and executed the daily developments that led to independence and the formation of the American nation. They were not without flaws. The two Adams, Washington, Jay, and Hamilton were sharp-tongued, cold, aloof, and difficult to know intimately. Jefferson was an erratic genius; Madison had severe emotional problems; Morris was greedy, dying a fugitive from his numerous creditors; Paine, ever the lonely revolutionary, drank himself to death; Henry was incredibly impetuous while, even at an advanced age, Franklin was a sexual libertine. Well known for his commonplace sayings in *Poor Richard's Almanac*, Franklin elsewhere observed, "She that paints her face, thinks of her tail" and advised a young man on selecting the proper mistress to choose an older woman because she would be "so grateful."

Revolutionary Thought

American revolutionaries ably articulated the political and philosophical justifications for revolt. John Adams explained that "the Revolution was effected before the war commenced. The Revolution was in the minds and hearts of the people." Adams saw the revolution as an intellectual revolt built upon the twin pillars of the Bible and the works of English political philosopher John Locke. The biblical interpretation derived from the Puritans' conception of godly rulers who, as long as they followed biblical teaching, merited the people's support. If, however, rulers departed from God's word, then the populace had no moral duty to support the government. The writings of John Locke secularized these biblical truths. Locke contended that free people first established governments through "compacts" while living in a state of nature. In the compacts rulers agreed to protect all citizens' "natural rights," particularly the ownership of private property. Natural rights were defined within the context of natural law, an Enlightenment concept that asserted everything in the world, including human beings, operated under a set of knowable laws. Under the political compact agreed to by the rulers and the ruled, government did not have the right to take property without the consent of its owners. If the government persisted in defiance of the agreement and the natural laws regarding basic rights, the compact became void, the rulers ungodly, and the people free to negotiate another compact. During the 1760s this new political generation became convinced that Parliament, through its tax policies, had broken both God's and nature's laws. By 1776, armed with the Bible and their John Locke, American colonial leaders concluded that it was their right and duty to shake off the English yoke and to draw up a new compact of government that conformed to natural law and respected all men's natural rights to life, liberty, and property.

The Seeds of Revolt

Imperial officials provoked the revolution by their efforts to reorganize the mercantile system without the consent of the colonial assemblies. Strapped for revenues following the Seven Years' War, the British government searched for ways to raise additional revenues from its overseas possessions.

The war had been costly, almost doubling the English debt. To service the debt, in 1763 English tax payers paid almost one-third of their income in taxes, creating enormous complaints in England. In addition, English political officials believed that Americans had not paid their fair share of the war's cost. During the war colonial legislatures had denied that England had the right to demand money from them and insisted that they had "donated" funds to the cause. Some colonial militia had refused to fight outside their own colonial borders, making the prosecution of the war difficult. To add insult to injury, some colonists had traded with the French during the war. Not only was this trade treasonable, but colonial merchants prospered while their English counterparts paid increased taxes to support a war that they believed the colonies had started.

The English cabinet heeded demands of the heavily taxed landowners represented in Parliament that the colonies pay their fair share of the war debt. But the government did not thoroughly consider the situation in the colonies or its own lack of power. The crown did not control the influential molders of colonial public opinion—newspaper editors, preachers, teachers, and lawyers. Its policies eventually offended every influential class of colonists except royal officeholders and Anglican clergy. Because most colonial political leaders belonged to the wealthy and influential colonial upper classes, the long succession of these acts explained why propertied, normally conservative men, such as Jefferson the slaveholder, Hancock the wealthy merchant, Jay the prosperous New York lawyer, Washington the planter, and Franklin the international dilettante, chose to lead the colonies into revolt. The Revolution's leaders had interests to protect. Moreover, Parliament had no means to enforce its policies because the English government kept no standing troops in the colonies and because Parliament lacked the will to force unpopular measures down the colonists' gullets. Often, after the colonists protested strongly against an act, Parliament backed down and withdrew the offending legislation. Such behavior only encouraged colonial resistance. The revolution was caused less by English imperial tyranny than by English weakness and vacillation.

Origins of the Struggle

The colonists' long struggle with Parliament began with Pontiac's Rebellion in the spring of 1763, during which the Ottawa chief laid siege to Detroit for five months. London officials searched for a solution to end colonial Indian problems once and for all. A British general suggested sending blankets infected with smallpox to all rebellious tribes, an idea finally rejected because no way could be found to insure that English soldiers would not also contract the dreaded disease. Just before Pontiac lifted his siege in November, King George III signed the Proclamation of 1763 that forbade white settlement beyond the crest of the Allegheny and Appalachian mountains. All settlers already located west of the line were ordered back east.

The act sought to end hostilities with the Indians and to save the costs of garrisoning a British army in the West. Crown officials realized that white pressure on Indian lands caused Indian hostility. The colonists, however, viewed the act otherwise. Colonies with sea-to-sea charters saw their claims evaporate. Wealthy colonial land speculators such as Washington, who had invested in 200,000 acres of land along the Ohio River, were enraged at the crown's infringement on their property rights. At the stroke of a pen, great tracts of land held for future price appreciation by colonists became worthless. Small farmers lured West by the promise of free land were also disappointed by the proclamation, although many remained in the forbidden areas and new settlers such as Daniel Boone arrived daily. Even colonists who had no interests in western lands feared the act would hem them along the coast where the mother country could more easily control them. The proclamation line also restricted the prospects of young males to acquire farms or plantations of their own at a time when the price of land in the East had escalated due to increased population.

Sugar Act

In 1764 Parliament passed the Sugar Act to raise colonial revenue for the crown. This bill lowered the tariff, or import fees, on molasses by one-half, although it raised some other tariffs. The chancellor of the exchequer, George Grenville, also attached to the bill a plan to reform the American customs service. In short, the crown now intended to collect the lower and, they hoped, more acceptable duties. Prior to 1764 British custom agents collected only one-quarter of the costs of running the customs houses. In a tight financial bind, Grenville wanted to make the customs service self-supporting. During the parliamentary debates over the bill the chancellor estimated that the Sugar Act would add £45,000 annually to the crown revenues. To ensure that the colonists paid their tariff fees in "good" money, Parliament enacted the Currency Act that outlawed all colonial issues of paper money after September 1.

Parliament reaped more colonial ill will than the additional income was worth. It passed the Sugar Act at the start of a five year depression in the colonies caused by worldwide, postwar economic dislocations. As economic distress spread, Parliament responded to domestic pressures, increased taxes, and outlawed paper currencies in the colonies, creating a severe shortage of money there. Colonial reaction, led by New England merchants, on whom the tariffs fell the hardest, was swift. They decided on a selective form of nonimportation. Even Boston's upper classes supported the boycott by doing without imported laces and ruffles. The town's artisans followed suit and quit wearing leather clothes of English manufacture. Such colonial resistance was light and futile, but it marked the first halting step toward colonial unity.

Stamp Act

The Stamp Act (1765) aroused the colonists' wrath and increased their sense of unity. The act, which required a tax stamp on all colonial legal documents, licenses, newspapers, insurance policies, and even on playing cards and dice, was the first direct tax levied on them. To make the measure more palatable, colonists themselves were selected to collect the duties and the revenue was specifically earmarked for colonial defense. Nevertheless, the act outraged many colonists on economic

News traveled quickly through the colonies as the arrival of this messenger shows. Note the mixture of Georgian and Federal architectural styles in the background; urban colonists were more sophisticated than their British cousins thought. (1973)

and philosophical grounds. Unlike the Sugar Act, which bore most heavily on New England merchants, the Stamp Act affected all of the colonies. Moreover, it reached into the pockets of all classes—tavern owners, gamblers, land speculators, shipowners, lawyers, and newspaper editors, all struggling in the midst of a depression. Many did not think that Parliament had the right to levy such a direct internal tax. Almost all colonists agreed that England could collect external taxes on foreign trade; it had long done so under the Navigation Acts. Some colonists even believed England had the right to use trade regulations to raise taxes indirectly. But direct taxes, levied by a Parliament without colonial consent, violated ancient English principles. Patrick Henry, in a fiery speech before the House of Burgess, declared it "taxation without representation." Worse, if allowed to stand, the act set a dangerous precedent that would allow Parliament to levy any direct tax it chose. The colonists argued that Parliament was treating them as a subject people not as English citizens.

To coordinate opposition to the stamp tax a secret organization, the Sons of Liberty, was organized throughout the colonies in the summer of 1765. Lower class mobs, often led by wealthy colonists, resorted to violence to force colonial stamp agents to resign their positions. In August 1765 a Boston mob sacked Governor Hutchinson's house and wrecked all "but the bare walls and floors." Passions everywhere ran high. Some married couples in Connecticut publicly vowed early in 1776 "to suspend their usual endeavor to contribute toward the population of North America, 'till the Stamp Act is suspended or finally repealed." By the end of the year not one stamp agent still held his post in the colonies.

Stamp Act Congress

In direct response to the Stamp Act, the Massachusetts legislature called a general colonial congress to meet in New York City. Nine of the thirteen colonies sent delegates to the Stamp Act Congress, which met in October 1765. The representatives passed a "Declaration of Rights and Grievances" contending that taxes could be levied only by the colonial legislatures in which the colonists were represented, and that the Stamp Act was unconstitutional because the colonists enjoyed all the rights of Englishmen. The Congress called for its repeal and for the annulment of the Sugar Act as well. The colonists' anger led to the revival of nonimportation and in all colonial port cities nonimportation associations were organized. Trade soon came to a standstill, with those merchants opposed to the resistance forced to close their businesses and sometimes even to flee. Sympathetic judges halted court proceedings, putting lawyers out of work. Now idle, attorneys wrote pamphlets attacking the stamp tax.

Nonimportation worked. English sales in the colonies fell in 1765. Stung by their losses, British merchants petitioned Parliament to repeal the tax. Parliament, prodded by pro-colonial Whig members such as William Pitt, heard testimony from colonial agents early in 1766. Franklin delivered a memorable address describing colonial sacrifices during the recent war. He explained that the colonists could not afford the taxes and asserted that Parliament had no constitutional right to levy direct taxes. On March 18, Parliament repealed the obnoxious legislation. When word reached the colonies in April, there were celebrations up and down the seaboard. The colonists overlooked the ominous warning contained in the Declaratory Act passed the same day that said Parliament had the authority to "bind" the colonists "in all cases whatsoever." By 1766, many colonists, especially the influential upper classes, were convinced that a show of colonial force and an exposition of political principles were enough to back Parliament down on any unpopular measure. They were confident they had demonstrated their rights to govern themselves within the empire.

Townshend Duties

Such convictions were strengthened the following year when a change of cabinet brought Charles Townshend in as chancellor of the exchequer. Townshend was determined to raise revenues in the colonies to offset a popular reduction in land taxes at home. He designed his colonial taxes as external levies to conform with the colonists' professed distinctions between indirect and direct taxes in the hope of thwarting opposition on the other side of the Atlantic. The 1767 Townshend duties increased import taxes on lead, paint, glass, tea, and paper and pledged the revenues to offset colonial administration and defense costs. His strategy failed. The colonists ignored their own earlier distinctions and resorted once more to nonimportation.

The Townshend duties pushed the colonists a step closer toward denying Parliament's authority over them in any guise. In a series of "Farmer's Letters," John Dickinson from Pennsylvania maintained that although Parliament had the right to regulate colonial trade, it did not have the authority to raise revenues. That is, it lacked the authority to tax the colonials. Only their elected representatives had that right. Buoyed by this new tactic, resistance to the duties escalated early in 1768 when the Massachusetts Assembly passed, over the royal governor's strenuous objections, a circular letter written by Sam Adams for distribution to all the colonial assemblies. The circular denied Parliament's right to tax the colonists and asked for suggestions for united action against the duties. Adams' action placed him in the forefront of resistance to English policies. After bankrupting his father's brewery and serving for a time as a tax collector, Adams became a professional revolutionary. Like his second cousin John Adams, he was prominent in all the resistance movements from the Stamp Act Congress through the Continental Congresses.

First Outbreaks of Violence

Adams and the Boston resistance so frightened British customs officials that they asked the armed forces for protection. English authorities dispatched a warship to Boston, followed by two regiments of infantry, marking the first military occupation of a British colony. Although British troops had always been stationed in the colonies, they had only been used to protect frontier outposts, to fight in colonial wars, or to defend fortified positions. Rather than stabilizing the situation in Boston, the redcoats acted as an irritant, particularly to the Sons of Liberty.

The nonimportation movement was strengthened by popular feeling against the Townshend duties. At the end of 1769 only New Hampshire merchants had not joined the boycott. Colonial imports from England fell forty percent from 1768 to 1769. In May 1769 the English government indicated it would consider "modifications" of the Townshend duties. After a new English cabinet, headed by Frederick North, took office in January 1770, Parliament voted to rescind the hated taxes, but, to reaffirm its right to tax, it left the levy on tea. Additionally, North promised that he would place no new taxes on the colonists. Most colonial merchants quickly capitulated and resumed normal trade. Only the Boston merchants held out until the end of the year. To save face, they agreed not to import the taxed tea.

Boston "Massacre"

On the day that Lord North's cabinet repealed the Townshend duties, violence erupted between Bostonians and English troops stationed there. Relations between the two groups had been strained since the redcoats arrived. Local youths found the guards tempting targets for snowballs and iceballs in the winter and for verbal abuse in all seasons. The English troops displayed remarkable patience in the face of such taunts, although in October 1769 several soldiers had fired a volley over the heads of a threatening crowd, narrowly averting a disaster. Friction between Boston's laborers and English soldiers, who sought off-duty jobs in competition with local workers, was a special irritant. On March 5, 1770, a fistfight involving civilians and soldiers broke out at a local rope walk, and tensions in the town continued to rise throughout the day. By evening a crowd had assembled before hapless British sentries near the State House. Thoroughly frightened, the sentries called for aid and a detachment of soldiers under Captain Preston arrived. The events were confusing, but someone gave the order to fire. When the melee ended, five colonists lay dead. The captain and six of his men were arrested and charged with murder.

Sam Adams immediately dubbed the incident the "Boston Massacre" and engaged his friend Paul Revere to make an engraving of the scene for posterity. The popular illustration showed Preston ordering his sneering soldiers to fire on unarmed civilians. Underneath, Revere listed the dead, one of whom, Crispus Attucks, was later immortalized as the first African American to die for the revolutionary cause. Passions were so inflamed in Massachusetts that all the soldiers had to be withdrawn to islands in Boston's harbor for their safety. Sam Adams hastily published an account of the incident entitled "Innocent Blood Crying to God from the Streets of Boston." Meanwhile, his cousin John agreed to defend the prisoners. John Adams and his co-counsel, Josiah Quincy, did a remarkable job before a local jury. They succeeded in getting Preston and four of his men acquitted; the other two, convicted of manslaughter, were branded on their hands and released. Even with justice done, many colonials remained convinced that the English were simply murderers.

The withdrawal of the Townshend duties immediately after the Boston Massacre cooled colonial tensions. For the next two and one-half years calm prevailed in the colonies. However, some serious, but unrelated, incidents occurred. In 1771 a civil war broke out in North Carolina, pitting small farmers from western areas, known as "Regulators," against eastern plantation owners, over representation in the colony's assembly. The following year, another group of colonists—led by wealthy merchant John Brown—burned the English revenue cutter *Gaspee* off the coast of Rhode Island. Sam Adams' followers established Committees of Correspondence in all but two colonies to keep the flames of resistance burning. But great popular outcries against the mother country were not heard, primarily because the depression of the 1760s had lifted and the colonists enjoyed unparalleled prosperity. Starved for English goods after two years of nonimportation, colonists purchased twice the value of goods in 1771 as they had in 1770, setting an all-time colonial record. Exports also increased, doubling over the next five years. Lord North's pledge not to impose additional taxes helped to preserve domestic tranquility, leading many colonists to believe that Parliament now agreed that it did not have the right to intervene in their domestic affairs.

The Boston Tea Party

The calm ended abruptly in May 1773 over the tea trade. The East India Tea Company, a government monopoly with about seventeen million pounds of tea stored in England, hovered on the verge of bankruptcy. To assist the company, Parliament passed the Tea Act, which permitted the company to ship its surplus tea to the American colonies and to pay a much lower import tax than colonial merchants. Parliament also gave the company authority to sell its tea directly in the colonies, enabling it to cut out middlemen. With this advantage, the East India Tea Company, not only undersold honest colonial merchants who had paid the full legal taxes, they even competed with colonial smugglers. The company made immediate plans to ship 500,000 pounds of tea to the colonies. They argued that if Parliament could grant a monopoly to the East India Tea Company nothing would prevent it from granting a similar privilege to any other, well-connected concern. Mass meetings in colonial coastal cities demanded the resignations of any American agents who agreed to receive the tea. The Sons of Liberty used strong-arm methods to persuade such people to relinquish their commissions. Parliament had thought that the colonists would applaud lower prices on their favorite drink. As it transpired, however, tea drinkers stood squarely behind the local merchants whose businesses were threatened by the act.

When ships laden with East India tea arrived in Boston at the end of November, angry colonists greeted them with demands to return to England. Governor Hutchinson refused to comply, whereupon Sam Adams staged a dramatic protest. On December 16, 1773, about 150 men, poorly disguised as Mohawk Indians, boarded the ships and dumped 342 chests of tea into the harbor. The Boston Tea Party was an instant popular success. Almost everyone in town knew who had organized it and who had taken part, but when the royal authorities investigated, not a single citizen stepped forward to testify against the "Indians." Other tea parties along the Atlantic Coast prevented the unloading of tea in every harbor except Charleston, where it was stored until the revolutionary government auctioned it off to raise money for the cause.

Parliament Reacts

Parliament—along with many colonists—was enraged by such wanton destruction of private property. The House of Commons passed three acts in 1774 that put the empire on a collision course with its colonies. Called the Coercive Acts in England and the Intolerable Acts in the colonies, the new laws ordered the port of Boston closed until the colonists repaid the East India Company for its losses, stipulated that crown officials could be tried in England for crimes committed in the colonies, and revised the Massachusetts government, making many formerly-elected officials royal appointees. Moreover, future town meetings could be held only with the royal governor's express permission. Governor Hutchinson, a native son of Massachusetts, was replaced by a British General, Thomas Gage.

At the same time Parliament also voted to establish a colonial government in Quebec, the ex-French colony England had won in 1763. Although the Quebec Act had been under consideration for eleven years, to the British colonists it seemed part of the Intolerable Acts. The Quebec Act allowed trial without jury, confirmed the established position of the Catholic church in Quebec, reaffirmed parliament's right to tax the colony, and extended Quebec's southern border to the Ohio River, including lands claimed by other English colonies. Colonists to the south reacted in horror to the suspension of the traditional English rights in Quebec. Parliament had clearly expressed its right to suspend liberties in any colony whenever it wished.

The shock produced by these two acts had hardly died away when news arrived that Parliament had approved a new Quartering Act. In 1765, Parliament had demanded that local officials provide barracks and supplies for English troops. The following year an amendment required the colonists to house troops in inns and unoccupied buildings. Citizens, particularly in New York, had reacted against these regulations, but in June 1774 Parliament went even further by providing that soldiers be quartered in occupied houses—and left it to local officials to enforce the act. Home owners had to bear the expenses of hosting their unwanted guests. No elected official wanted the task of apportioning soldiers among local householders.

First Continental Congress

Colonial protest against Parliament's 1774 actions took two forms: a call from Boston for a revival of nonimportation and a request to convene a colonial congress to consider this increasingly critical situation. Although the Coercive Acts applied only to Massachusetts, they threatened every other colony's charter. On

September 5, delegates from all colonies except Georgia assembled in Philadelphia to open the First Continental Congress. This congress was no revolutionary body. Many of those who came were conservatives who sought accommodation with England and guarantees for American rights. A bare majority took the radical position that the congress should force England, even at the point of a bayonet, to recognize colonial prerogatives.

The radicals, led by John and Sam Adams, persuaded their colleagues to pass the "Suffolk Resolves," drawn up by Joseph Warren, whose wife Mercy Otis Warren was one of Massachusetts' ardent militants. The strongly worded declaration proclaimed the Coercive Acts unconstitutional and called for Massachusetts to organize a government apart from the colony's royal government, to form its own militia, and to cease trade with England. Conservatives countered with Joseph Galloway's plan to unite the colonies under a president-general appointed by the king, but this proposal failed by a narrow margin. After endorsing the Suffolk Resolves, congress approved a series of resolutions explaining colonial rights, attacking English policy since 1763, and pledging economic sanctions against the mother country until such rights were restored.

Before adjourning, the congress created the Continental Association to organize and enforce nonimportation. It was to prove a convenient instrument for local radicals to coerce their opponents. Only Georgia refused to be bound by the congress' actions. Having taken a strong stand against Parliament and encouraged by colonial unity, the congress adjourned in October and promised to meet six months later if England still had done nothing to redress colonial grievances.

When the resolutions of the Continental Congress arrived in London in January 1775, the British government split over how to deal with them. Lord North favored conciliation, but his proposal, which included recognition of the Continental Congress' legality, lost in Parliament. Instead, both houses accepted resolutions that declared Massachusetts in a state of rebellion and afterward, by narrow margins, passed a weak act promising to levy only regulatory taxes on any colony that taxed itself for defense and administration. Parliament followed this conciliatory measure, however, with a resolution that prohibited Massachusetts from trading with any nation except England and the British West Indian islands. In April Parliament extended the trade prohibitions to other colonies that formally adhered to the Continental Association.

The War for Independence

From the fall of 1774 through the spring of 1775, as the pamphlet war continued, feverish preparations for war began on both sides. Several near conflicts occurred in the fall, but violence became inevitable in January 1775 when the Privy Council ordered General Gage to use troops, if needed, to enforce the Coercive Acts. Gage struck the village of Concord, twenty-one miles from Boston, because the Massachusetts provisional government used the town as a supply depot for its militia. On April 18, 1775, about 700 redcoats left Boston just behind Paul Revere, William Dawes, and Dr. Samuel Prescott, three riders sent to warn the villagers. Revere never reached Concord. The British captured him just outside of Lexington and later released him. Dawes turned back, but Prescott outwitted the British to warn the militia leaders.

On the Lexington green the English found seventy armed minutemen drawn up to block their advance. When they failed to disperse, someone fired a shot. The English responded, killing eight. The redcoats pushed on to Concord where they destroyed some military supplies but failed to capture Sam Adams, John Hancock, or any other colonial leader. As the British lingered in Concord, colo-

On April 19, 1775, armed colonists drew up on Lexington's common facing the British troops. Somebody fired, and when the smoke cleared eight patriots lay dead. The Revolutionary War had begun. (1925)

nial militiamen attacked, killing fourteen redcoats at Concord's North Bridge. The trip back to Boston was a nightmare for the British. As their columns filed down the narrow colonial roads, militiamen sniped from behind trees and stone fences. By the time they arrived in Boston, the English had lost 273—killed, wounded, or missing. Of the estimated 4000 colonists engaged in the battle, ninety-three were lost. The Revolutionary War had begun.

Second Continental Congress

The Second Continental Congress assembled the following month in Philadelphia where for the next six years it coordinated the war effort against the world's most powerful empire. The Continental Congress included the first three presidents of the future United States. It divided sharply, however, over what course colonial policy should take. Wealthy conservatives, especially those from New York and Pennsylvania, hoped for an immediate end to hostilities and a quick reconciliation with Britain. A larger group of moderates favored a show of force to convince Parliament the colonists were serious about protecting their rights. Moderates believed that Parliament would reverse itself again and recognize the justice of the colonists' complaints. By May 1775 radicals called for independence.

Congress' first major business was to organize a continental army and select a commander to oversee the troops who besieged the British in Boston. The congressional delegates chose George Washington who had worn his Virginia militia colonel's uniform to the assembly. Congress chose Washington because he had commanded troops during the French and Indian War and it wanted to appoint a commander from outside New England to make it a genuinely continental war. Washington accepted the position and offered to serve for nothing except his personal expenses, which were often padded. Although Washington never decisively beat the British in the open field, he possessed an unusual measure of common sense, keeping his rag-tag army intact and always in front of the British. A cold and sometimes disdainful man, he won the admiration of his men, who respected his dogged persistence when he had nothing to offer them but danger and hardship. Over the eight years of war, Washington became to many people the symbol of the revolutionary cause.

After selecting a commander in chief, the Second Continental Congress drew up the Olive Branch Petition, which absolved King George III of any blame for the recent troubles and placed responsibility for the conflict squarely on his ministers and Parliament. The petition asked the king to restrain Parliament from further tyranny until some plan of reconciliation could be worked out. While congress awaited the English reaction, the colonists maintained that they only struggled for a greater measure of home rule within the empire.

The Split Widens

The war proved unpopular in England. Still deeply in debt from the last conflict, Britons could not work up much enthusiasm to fight fellow Englishmen. Moreover, an influential Whig minority in Parliament openly supported reconciliation with the colonists and spoke against war preparations. By November 1775, however, George III believed that it was too late to draw back. To falter, he feared, would encourage his other colonies to raise the flag of rebellion. To lessen the effect of the war at home, George III hired troops from tiny German principalities that frequently leased young men for foreign wars. Thirty thousand Hessians, from German states such as Hesse-Hanau and Hesse-Kassel, headed across the Atlantic. Radicals, like Franklin, exploited the king's action, explaining to fellow colonists that the king did not think enough of them to send Englishmen over to die.

In 1776 the king represented the last link that tied the colonies to the empire. In the heated and crude colonial protest literature from 1763 to 1776, the crown had enjoyed a sovereign's immunity. Colonial radicals blamed unpopular English policies on the king's ministers, Parliament, or the royal governors. By spring, however, the first attacks against George III signaled the beginning of a serious move toward independence.

The revolutionary momentum received a powerful impetus from a recent English immigrant, Thomas Paine, who wrote an influential little pamphlet entitled *Common Sense*. In this widely read polemic, Paine attacked the institution of the monarchy and King George III by name, calling him the "Royal Brute." In simple terms the pamphlet outlined the advantages of independence. Its clear, urgent prose and its timing gave it widespread appeal. Soon it became required reading in all colonial taverns where, if patrons could not read, some patriot willingly read it aloud to all. *Common Sense* seemed to have pushed the Continental Congress toward independence.

Congress took the first step on April 6, 1776, when it opened American ports to trade with all nations—except Britain. The measure amounted to a de facto declaration of independence. Two months later, Virginian Richard Henry Lee introduced a motion stating that the colonies "are and of right ought to be, free and independent states." A committee composed of Jefferson, Franklin, John Adams, and two others was empowered to prepare a suitable declaration. On July 2, 1776, twelve delegations, with New York abstaining, endorsed Lee's motion for independence. Two days later, by an identical tally, Congress approved Jefferson's declaration.

The Declaration of Independence

The Declaration of Independence with its ringing phrases has become a sacred American document, but the men who drew it up had more practical hopes. They wanted to win public support at home and in Europe. John Adams estimated that when the declaration was signed no more than one-third of the colonists favored independence while another third was undecided, and the final third remained loyal to the empire. Adams and the other signers wanted to attract that undecided third to their cause by justifying their right to revolt and their right to establish a new government. To achieve this goal, they drew on the principles of John Locke

The Boston "Tea Party" in December 1773 involved the destruction of private property by a gang of disguised ruffians, but it dramatically demonstrated how far the colonists were willing to go to achieve their goals. (1973)

and emphasized that governments derived "their just powers from the consent of the governed." When a government violated that consent and jeopardized the people's right to "life, liberty, and the pursuit of happiness," they explained, the people had the right and duty to withdraw their consent and to form a new, more congenial government. These rights, wrote Jefferson, were based on "the laws of nature and nature's God." The declaration listed twenty-eight specific grievances against King George III. It blamed no one else. If Americans had continued to condemn Parliament and the cabinet instead of George III, potential allies would have correctly concluded that the colonists were still holding out the olive branch and would have withheld their aid. The Declaration of Independence was a masterpiece of propaganda, combining philosophical depth with a popular and universal appeal.

By 1776 American revolutionary leaders had had enough. When royal officials forbade them to buy land from the Indians or levied a tariff on imported goods, Americans chafed under what they boldly called "repeated injuries and usurpations." All the revolting colonists wanted, they claimed, were their rights as freeborn English citizens, rights demanded by their forbears stretching back to the Magna Carta. Given such a conception of empire, the declaration and the revolution seemed as inevitable as Parliament's determination "to bind in all cases whatsoever."

The explanation for the Revolution, as contained in the declaration, implied more than the continental congressmen intended. These leaders desired no social revolution, no upheaval from below, no elevation of the lower orders. They believed, after all, in an ordered and orderly society. As members of the colonial elite, they expected to govern after the colonies achieved independence. But the words they used to rally popular support—"all men are created equal," "The Rights of the People to alter or to abolish" government justified the revolution on moral principles that could be applied to all governments, including the Continental

Congress. The Declaration of Independence inspired countless other disaffected groups. Already Abigail Adams had complained to her husband about Congress' neglect of true equality. Following her lead, other women, African Americans, Latinos, Indians, Haitians, even Vietnamese found in the eloquent phrases of the Declaration of Independence justification for their own liberation. Ironically, Jefferson the slave holder, in defending the property and political power of a colonial elite from imperial encroachments, justified the revolt with a revolutionary theory based on universal human freedom and justice.

The Loyalists

Not all Americans applauded independence or its revolutionary justification. Those aware of such implications drew back lest radicals like the Sons of Liberty go too far. Removal of royal authority, many feared, would feed further agitation and could easily undermine all established order. As many as one-third of the 2.5 million colonists remained loyal to their king. Nearly 100,000 fled to Canada or England while others hid their true feelings and made the best of a situation that grew progressively worse. Up to 30,000 colonists fought in the British army and at one point during 1780, the British army had 8000 Americans in its ranks while Washington's army numbered only 9000. Areas around New York, Philadelphia and Charleston, and the up-country regions of North and South Carolina where the Regulators had been strong, were centers of loyalist, or "Tory," strength. Some groups such as the Anglican clergy and royal officeholders had a vested interest in British control. Others, such as great landowners, particularly those in New York's Hudson Valley, wealthy merchants, many of whom at first resisted English policies but drew back because of the civil disorder, and the Quakers, who refused to countenance any war, continued to support the crown despite great personal risks.

Tories faced a variety of disabilities, ranging from mob action to official proscription. The term "lynch law" originated because of the vigilante activities of Virginian William Lynch against pro-British elements. Adherents to the Revolution required oaths of allegiance to the cause. The simple refusal to accept continental money singled out those who opposed independence and opened them to boycotts and mob violence, as well as tarring and feathering. State laws denied them the vote, levied taxes up to three times as high as those on the patriots, and expelled them from occupations like medicine and teaching. Following Congress' 1777 recommendation, most states enacted legislation confiscating loyalist property and, in a few instances, sold it to poor patriot farmers. The struggle on the home front verged on civil war in which no one's home or life was safe.

Diplomatic Efforts

The patriots' success depended on their ability to maintain a strong army in the field and to convince a major European power to aid the fledgling nation with money and material. France, still smarting from its losses in the French and Indian War, was potentially Americans' best chance for a European ally. But the calculating French foreign minister, Count Vergennes, as much as he wanted revenge against the hated British, did not want to back a loser. With a cold, calculating eye, he assessed America's chances.

Vergennes realized that the most important factor in the war was that the Americans had a cause after July 4, 1776. They knew exactly what they were fighting for—independence—and that knowledge dictated their overall strategy of wearing the enemy down. Moreover, they fought on familiar terrain, a hilly, forested region of the colonies where precise European military formations were often impossible. But America's lack of a strong centralized army and navy dismayed Vergennes. To a great extent Washington's army, never more than 10,000 troops, depended on unreliable and poorly trained state militias. British loyalists provided spies, necessary provisions, and recruits in the colonies. Vergennes held the Second Continental Congress in contempt, a mere semblance of centralized government that lacked even the authority to levy tax for war purposes. Finally, Vergennes doubted that the Americans could equip an army in the field for a long war. Vergennes approached the Spanish who had never been sympathetic to the American cause; they worried that their own colonies might follow suit and feared later boundary disputes with a new nation. Faced with this balance sheet, Vergennes waited before deciding whether to openly support the American cause. To keep his options open, however, in May 1776 he agreed to aid the Americans secretly with a dummy private company, Roderique Hortalez et Cie., through which the French government funneled badly needed arms and munitions to the Americans.

The War for Independence

Washington welcomed French aid. On May 10 the year before, Benedict Arnold and Ethan Allen with a force of 83 men had overwhelmed a British force half its size at Fort Ticonderoga. And General Henry Knox had laboriously hauled the captured cannon to the heights overlooking Boston and forced the British troops to evacuate the city in March 1776. Elsewhere, the Continentals suffered setbacks. A two-pronged offensive against Quebec under generals Richard Montgomery and Benedict Arnold was repulsed on the last day of 1775 and ended with heavy losses. With Montgomery dead and Arnold wounded, Americans laid siege to the city through the dead of a bitter winter. The frigid assault ended in May 1776 when the British troops routed the American army that straggled home to the safety of Fort Ticonderoga a month later.

For the several thousand troops stationed at Fort Ticonderoga, located at the choke-point on the vital waterway between Canada and New England, life in the Continental Army was exceedingly dull. Soldiers rose at first light, spending little of their time fighting. They devoted many hours to "fatigue" duty, drilling, parading, and simply finding ways to pass time. Fatigue duty involved digging trenches and fortifications, felling trees or clearing brush, hauling cannon, and building and maintaining boats. Disease and infection posed constant problems, accounting for more deaths than combat. To counter the threat of disease, soldiers infected with smallpox were moved from the main garrison to outposts on Lake George, 35 miles to the south. General orders from July 1776 states: "To preserve the new camp perfectly clean, & free from infection," officers should "have their necessarys fix'd upon the brink of the precipices, or in such places as are least obnoxious." Soldiers who "shall commit any nastiness in any other place" faced punishments up to forty lashes. The orderly book of Colonel Anthony Wayne's 4th Pennsylvania regiment tells of disciplinary procedures for sleeping on duty, public drunkenness, desertion, disobeying orders, cooking in the streets between tents, stealing boats to go fishing, using the oars as carrying poles for baggage, and enlisting in multiple regiments to receive extra bonuses. A soldier's diet consisted of salt pork or beef, flour or, more often, an indigestible bread known as hardtack, dried peas, and whatever the sutlers who followed the arm sold. Perhaps only the daily ration of a half gill of rum (the equivalent to a modern half pint), which was doubled in cold, rainy weather or just before battle, kept the soldiers going.

Washington did not soon win another important victory. In August British general Sir William Howe and his brother Admiral Lord Richard Howe combined forces to push Washington off Long Island, New York, after a series of bitterly fought battles. The British kept up a relentless pressure as they pursued the continentals across the East River and up Manhattan Island culminating in the October 28th battle at White Plains. New York City, with its superb harbor facilities, became a British base of operations that they held until the peace treaty was signed. Weakened but not despairing, Washington eluded the British and kept his army intact as he retreated into New Jersey and finally Pennsylvania. Congress, fearing the fall of Philadelphia, fled to Baltimore.

After Washington's reversals in 1776, both armies settled into winter quarters. Washington, still capable of the bold stroke, took his army on a freezing Christmas night march across the Delaware River to attack Trenton, New Jersey. His army occupied the town, captured nearly a thousand Hessians, and killed another three hundred while he lost only 5 men. While strategically unimportant, Trenton boosted patriot morale and contributed to Washington's reputation as a skilled fighter.

Over the winter the British carefully laid plans to deliver a telling blow at rebellious colonials. They devised a three pronged attack to split New England away from the rest of the colonies that called for an invasion from Canada along Lake Champlain. The British planned to send a second army to wreack havoc from Oswego down the Mohawk Valley while a third force under Howe would move up the Hudson River to join General John Burgoyne's army arriving from Lake Champlain. It all went awry, however, when Howe decided instead to capture Philadelphia. He set that plan in motion in late July when he confronted Washington's 10,000 men with half again that number and after a grueling series of battles, flanking movements, and Continental retreats, took the Patriot capitol on September 26, 1777. Congress again scurried away, first to Lancaster and then to York, Pennsylvania, where it hastily reconvened.

Howe's change of plans left "Gentleman Johnny" Burgoyne slogging southward from Canada with about 7700 British troops and a huge baggage train that included his mistress, a selection of fine wines, and 138 pieces of artillery. Nothing went right for the British general. Left by Howe to fend for himself in the wilderness of upstate New York, Burgoyne watched as General Nicholas Herkimer with 800 men soundly defeated his western force at Oriskany, New York; his troops on his eastern flank were defeated at Bennington, Vermont. When Burgoyne encamped at Saratoga, New York, General Horatio Gates and his patriots surrounded him. Cut off from help, Burgoyne surrendered his entire army of about 5000 men on October 17, 1777.

The battle of Saratoga was the turning point of the war. Count Vergennes now had to make his decision. As soon as Lord North received the news of Saratoga he drafted an order of reconciliation. While Washington and his army starved and shivered for lack of supplies at Valley Forge, Franklin, Silas Deane, and Richard Henry Lee played on Vergennes' fears that they would negotiate a peace treaty with England and deprive France of the chance to strike at the British.

American diplomatic efforts were singularly successful. On February 6, 1778, France formally recognized American independence and signed a permanent treaty of mutual defense should France and England go to war, which occurred on June 17. American diplomats had transformed their colonial revolt into an international war that allied the United States with France and, in 1779, with Spain which entered the war to regain Gibraltar from England. Britain, now fighting a general

European war, found it more difficult to continue the conflict in the American wilderness. The outcome of America's Revolutionary War was sealed by the French-American pact in 1778. To honor the treaty, France dispatched advisors, war material, money, and naval support to the struggling former English colonists.

After Saratoga, the fighting in the Northeast stalemated. For two years Washington took up positions from which he kept a wary eye on the British, who had retreated from Philadelphia to New York. In the meantime, Captain John Paul Jones raided towns on the English coast and in 1779, while commanding a French ship, the *Bonhomme Richard*, engaged the forty-four-gun British warship *Serapis* in a classic sea battle. After pounding Jones' ship with devastating fire, the British captain demanded his surrender. Jones replied, "I have not yet begun to fight." After a grenade set off the *Serapis'* powder supply, shattering the ship's mainmast, the British captain struck his colors and surrendered. When Jones' ship, riddled with shot, sank the following day, the Americans transferred to their British prize and sailed it triumphantly into port.

On the mainland the focus of the war shifted in 1778 to the South. Sir Henry Clinton, who had replaced Howe, hoped that an invasion of the southern colonies region would attract the loyalists to the royal standard and that the British could split the southern slave states away from the rest of the United States. Clinton placed Lord Cornwallis in charge of the southern operation. After initial success in capturing Savannah and Charleston, Cornwallis invaded the interior of the Carolinas where he gained some loyalist support. He stretched his supply lines thin, however, becoming increasingly vulnerable to the hit and run tactics of the American southern commander, a former Quaker blacksmith, Nathanael Greene. A series of inconclusive, yet exhausting battles persuaded Cornwallis to march northward into Virginia where he could join forces with Benedict Arnold and try to capture that state. In 1780, as an American commander, Arnold had given detailed plans of his fort at West Point to a British agent, Major André, who was later captured. Arnold fled to a British ship when the captured documents revealed his participation in the plot. Major André was executed. The British rewarded Arnold for his treachery with a commission as brigadier general, over £6,000 cash, and healthy pensions for his wife and five children.

Together, Cornwallis and Arnold led raids across Virginia, at one point almost capturing Thomas Jefferson, Virginia's war-time governor, before they fell back to the Yorktown peninsula for protection and supply by the British fleet. Sensing a golden opportunity, Washington joined forces with the French and blocked any British landward retreat from Yorktown peninsula. Unknown to Cornwallis, a

The Declaration of Independence, 4 July 1776 at Philadelphia
From a Painting by John Trumbull

One imaginary scene from John Trumbull's painting of the Declaration of Independence depicts the five members of the drafting committee (John Adams, Roger Sherman, Robert R. Livingstone, Thomas Jefferson, and BenJamin Franklin) presenting the document to the seated congressional secretary, labor leader Charles Thomson. John Hancock watches beside Thomson. (1976)

French fleet commanded by Admiral de Grasse drove back to New York the British ships that had been sent to rescue Cornwallis. Trapped between Washington's army and the French fleet, after a six weeks' siege, Cornwallis surrendered his entire force of 8000 men on October 19, 1781. At the ceremonial surrender the Yankee bands played "The World Turned Upside Down." When Prime Minister Lord North heard the news he was reputed to have exclaimed, "Oh God, it's all over." In fact, the war dragged on for two more years, but the United States simply fought for better peace terms. At Yorktown Americans had won their independence. The British army remained ensconced in New York City, and Washington again took up defensive positions as the important actions shifted to the diplomatic front.

Negotiating the Peace

The American peace commissioners sent to Paris discovered that the peace negotiations were a complicated game of cat-and-mouse. American friendship with France had soured because Vergennes did not want to see a strong, unified nation emerge in North America. Complicating everything was a secret treaty France had signed with Spain in which both agreed not to make peace with England until Spain had recaptured Gibraltar from the British. In its 1778 treaty the United States had pledged France not to make a separate peace. Consequently, the Americans were constrained from talking to the British until Spain had recaptured Gibralter, an unlikely development. American peace commissioners chose to ignore the treaty with France and initiated secret negotiations with the British. A preliminary agreement gave the United States almost everything it desired: British recognition of their independence, ownership of all territory east of the Mississippi River, a hazy northern boundary with Canada, and an equally unclear border with Florida (which Britain returned to Spain in the treaty), the right to dry fish caught in Canadian waters, an agreement that the Mississippi River should be open to all nations—though Spain, who controlled the river, was not a party to this agreement. In return, the United States promised not to block British attempts to collect debts in the United States and to "earnestly recommend" to the states

that they return confiscated loyalist property. Of the major American desires, only a trade agreement with Great Britain was missing in the treaty.

The 1783 peace treaty was the most favorable pact the United States ever negotiated. This occurred even though the rebels did not decisively win the war; they simply avoided losing it. The careful diplomacy of envoys John Adams, John Jay, and Ben Franklin succeeded in securing for a weak, insignificant country a major victory.

Social Consequences of the Revolution

The American Revolution, capped by the Paris peace treaty signed September 3, 1783, successfully ended an eight-year revolt. The American experiment was not a starry-eyed adventure to create a political and social utopia in the wilderness. Rather, it was a conservative effort, first to preserve and later to regain the rights and legal privileges of Englishmen that Americans thought that they had lost. Americans used radical means to achieve their ends that included confrontation, violence, and international war, but at all times their ultimate aims remained conservative. The unintended results of those means, however, proved more radical than the revolution's leaders had intended.

Militarily, Americans created a modern, disciplined army. Used to fighting in a hilly, forested region where precise European military formations were often impossible, the patriots took advantage of natural obstructions to hide and shoot at the British, a tactic European soldiers believed unfair. Washington's troops were notoriously unruly men who had enlisted for a short, specified time and served under officers elected by popular vote. But in the end, Americans' adoption of European models of combat and the organization of a disciplined regular army enabled Americans to defeat the English. Washington recruited valuable foreign talent to reorganize and train his army: The Marquis de Lafayette, a glamorous young French nobleman who became almost a son to Washington; Thaddeus Kosciusko, a talented Polish engineer; the Prussian Baron Friedrich von Steuben, who as inspector general of the army drilled Washington's troops even though von Steuben spoke no English. The men taught farmers, sailors, and laborers to march, fight, and accept discipline like British regulars, lessons that enabled Americans to win set piece battles, like Yorktown, that defeated the British army and secured American independence.

Similar social transformation took place in the lives of African Americans and women. Although neither group realized full equality, they experienced a significant loosening of their bonds during the revolution. Black soldiers and sailors took part in almost every major engagement during the war, actions that earned some slaves their freedom. In the South, British troops promised emancipation to any slaves who fled to their lines. Tens of thousands answered the call. As a consequence of the revolution, every state except Georgia abolished the slave trade, and Pennsylvania enacted the first gradual emancipation law in 1780 that was soon followed by similar laws by all the states north of New Jersey.

Women also enjoyed new freedoms during the revolution, in part, because so many men were off fighting. Left in charge of farms and businesses, women headed many households. In the absence of their husbands and adult sons, these women constantly faced violence at the hands of British soldiers or irregular loyalists, including beatings, rape, and murder. Women also supported the war in their traditional roles, leading the non-importation movement, offering emotional support to their husbands and sons, raising loyal and patriotic children, and maintaining their households during the war.

Native Americans paid the greatest price during the revolution. Their repeated attempts to play both sides of colonial rivalries, whether between France or England, or England and the United States, failed miserably. No matter which side of the revolution they chose, Native Americans lost. American troops destroyed Iroquois villages in New York and Cherokee settlements in the Carolinas, showing little mercy to women and children. Frontier settlers took advantage of the war to kill Indians in their midst, regardless of whether or not they supported the revolution. In the West, American victories forced the English to abandon their support of those tribes loyal to the empire who came under American control, leading to their annihilation.

Articles of Confederation

The most significant changes brought about by the revolution were political. After declaring independence, the colonists were free to establish any government they wished. During the Revolution all but two states wrote new constitutions, incorporating the revolutionary ideals for which they fought. In general, the constitutions differed little from the old colonial charters. Except for Pennsylvania and Georgia, which experimented with unicameral assemblies, the states kept their two-house legislatures but increased their powers. They weakened the powers of governors and in Pennsylvania eliminated the executive branch altogether. Most assemblies retained the right to initiate money bills and, in eight states, the legislatures chose the governor. Despite the protests of a few doctrinaire patriots, colonial property qualifications for office holding remained in place, as high as £10,000 in South Carolina for the governorship. In all states the property qualifications for voting remained in place while judges were appointed and served with tenure for good behavior. The authors of the new constitutions were not interested in political experimentation. New Jersey unintentionally allowed women to vote, but quickly corrected the law. Most states wrote a bill of rights into their constitutions, disestablished the Episcopal Church in the middle and southern states and the Congregational Church in New England. All but Georgia prohibited the importation of slaves, a few northern states abolished slavery, a few granted married women property rights, and some wrote a more lenient penal code into their laws. The most striking change was the American departure from the English notion of an unwritten constitution. Having fought with the empire over the meaning of their liberties, every state and the new central government carefully put their fundamental law into writing, assuring that Americans would remain a litigious people. Even so, the colonial governments largely survived the Revolution with only the minor modifications derived from Americans' experience with the English political system.

Most revolutions bring in their wake a massive social upheaval. American society was changed by the revolt, but in almost imperceptible ways. Some conservative patriots complained that the "lower orders" deferred less to their betters than before the conflict. The class of former royal office holders had lost its power with the British exodus, but a new American elite, many of whom made fortunes during the war, took their place. The new state governments confiscated almost 100,000 loyalist estates, most of which found their way into the hands of wealthy Americans and speculators. No fundamental land redistribution took place, however. The war ended primogeniture and entail, feudal laws that required estates to pass intact to the eldest son. As a result a few of the largest land holdings were broken up, but most represented uninhabited western land claims worth less than their tax liabilities.

Freedom from the English mercantile system and the Navigation Acts created new commercial opportunities because all the trading markets of the world, except

North America after the Treaty of Paris, 1783

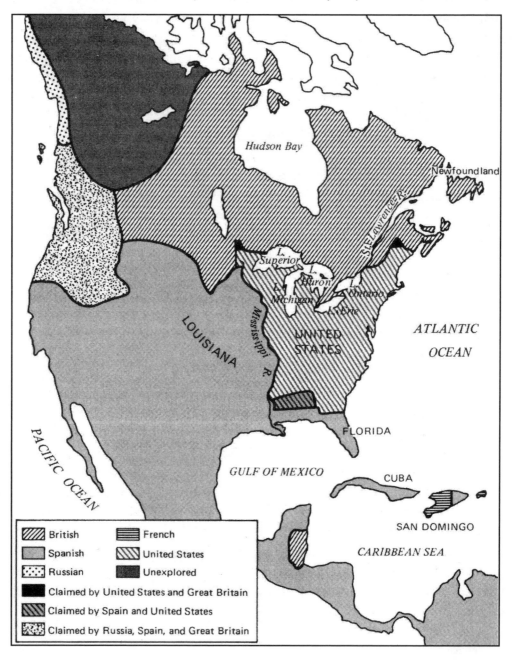

Hudson Bay

Newfoundland

St. Lawrence R.

L. Superior

L. Huron

L. Michigan

L. Ontario

L. Erie

UNITED STATES

LOUISIANA

Mississippi R.

ATLANTIC OCEAN

PACIFIC OCEAN

FLORIDA

GULF OF MEXICO

CUBA

SAN DOMINGO

CARIBBEAN SEA

British		French
Spanish		United States
Russian		Unexplored

Claimed by United States and Great Britain

Claimed by Spain and United States

Claimed by Russia, Spain, and Great Britain

Britain's, were opened to United States citizens. Only Americans with money and resources, however, could exploit them. American merchants who had depended on close English commercial ties before the war, and those who were involved in the raising and the distribution of bountied articles such as indigo and rice, suffered financially from their new commercial freedom. And the war itself, disrupted the economy. Not until the mid-1780s did American exports regain their pre-independence level.

American Political Theory

Independence came so suddenly that the new leaders had no firm ideas about what kind of new government they wanted to unify the states. Even before the Declaration of Independence, the Second Continental Congress confronted the problem and appointed a committee to draft a proposal for a central government. The committee faced the impossible task of creating a central government that did not weaken the powers of the states. The Articles of Confederation recognized state sovereignty and proposed a weak central government. Congress did not ratify the committee's Articles of Confederation until 1781, at the very end of the war. Until 1781 the unelected Continental Congress, unhampered by a written constitution, exercised much more power than the later Articles of Confederation allowed.

The Articles of Confederation embodied Americans' fear of allotting too much power to any one person or group. It specified that every state would elect and pay the expenses of its delegates to the Congress, where each state regardless of its size had one vote. The central government had no executive. Instead, a thirteen-man council acted when Congress was in recess. Despite its unwieldy organization and lack of executive authority, the Confederation Congress could make war and peace, fix state quotas for men and money (a legacy of the French and Indian War), make treaties, decide interstate disputes, limit state boundaries, admit new states, borrow money, and regulate the post office. Its greatest structural weakness lay in its lack of taxing powers, the absence of a national judiciary, and the requirement that all thirteen states had to agree before the Articles could be amended. Moreover, it lacked prestige. The government had no head and no permanent capital, and in a world of monarchies and lavish palaces, these were important. When the Dutch representative arrived in the United States in 1783 he could not find the government, for in June 1783 it had fled to Princeton, New Jersey, to avoid a confrontation with angry, unpaid Revolutionary War veterans. It took the Dutchman ten days to locate even one member of Congress.

By far its most serious flaw, however, was that it had not been approved by the people. After fighting a revolution against English tyranny for the ideals of popular sovereignty, the Articles of Confederation had been ratified by the thirteen state legislatures, not popularly elected constituent assemblies nor by popular plebiscite. It had failed to acknowledge the fundamental difference that distinguished American notions of constitutional law from English, between legislative law and constitutional law, between legislatures and and constituent assemblies. This made the Articles of Confederation vulnerable to reformers and one of the first victims of Americans' literal rendering of ancient western ideas of government.

Financial Problems

The weak and hobbled Confederation government's most important postwar tasks were to survive, keep the thirteen states united, and ease the inevitable postwar dislocations. As the revolutionaries had intended, the central government had far less effect on the daily lives of Americans than did state and local governments. The Confederation often struggled with its problems in unfunded, grand isolation. Without the power to levy direct taxes, the government relied on the states' goodwill in meeting their assigned financial quotas. The Confederation treasurer, the wealthy Robert Morris, was so dismayed by the government's poverty that for almost five years he resigned daily. Morris tried desperately to persuade the states to levy a national tariff, but Rhode Island would not assent. The government limped along by borrowing money overseas and issuing certificates of indebtedness to pay bills. In 1784 it owed 39 million dollars, five years later 79 million dollars at a time when its total income was only 4.6 million dollars, and one-half of that came from Dutch loans. It could not even pay the interest on the national debt.

To increase Morris' misery, the wartime economic boom, fueled in part by the high inflation, came to an abrupt end in the fall of 1783 when a mass of British goods flooded American markets and depressed prices. What began as a commercial depression spread rapidly into the rural areas, and by 1785 farmers found themselves in financial trouble. The economic slump made it all but impossible for the Confederation government to raise needed revenues.

Diplomatic Perils

While wrestling with its money problems, the government also faced continuous crises at home and abroad. Waiting for the new nation to fall apart and defying their treaty obligations, the British occupied posts on American soil near the ill-defined Canadian border. From their posts, the British also controlled the American trade and aroused the Indians against the settlers who flooded into the West. In the Southwest, Spain closed the Mississippi River to American navigation and even invaded American territory to capture the town of Natchez. The Mississippi grew in importance as more people moved into the Ohio valley. Western settlers transported their crops down the Ohio River and the Mississippi to New Orleans more easily than carrying them overland across the mountains. Congressional efforts to deal with Spain only aggravated the situation. In 1786, John Jay negotiated a treaty with the Spanish Ambassador, Don Diego de Gardoqui, in which the United States surrendered navigation rights on the Mississippi River in return for a trade treaty with Spain. Westerners screamed that their interests had been sold out for the benefit of eastern merchants. The treaty, however, died in Congress, and the Mississippi River remained closed.

Domestic Unrest

On the domestic front the Confederation government faced serious problems with the American army and western lands. At the end of the war the soldiers grew rebellious because Congress failed to pay them or give them their lifetime pensions of one-half pay as promised in 1780. In March 1783 an unsigned address that circulated in Washington's encampment near Newburgh, New York, threatened a march on Congress if the army's demands were not met immediately. Washington, who believed in civilian control over the military, dissuaded the soldiers from threatening the legislative body.

The army was not the only group in a rebellious mood. Conflicts arose between and in the states because Congress was powerless to mediate. Vermont, claimed by New York, Massachusetts, and New Hampshire was convulsed by sporadic disorders through the period as each claimant sought to establish its control over the area. In 1784, the Pennsylvania militia invaded its Wyoming Valley region to oust Connecticut settlers who claimed the area for their native state; violence continued in the Wyoming Valley through 1787. The most politically dangerous outbreaks, however, occurred in rural New England. With the British army gone and Americans denied access to many foreign ports, New England farmers found little demand for their foodstuffs. The state governments increased their taxes to pay off their debts and required that the taxes be paid in specie that farmers rarely saw. The state legislatures that levied these taxes were dominated by eastern interests who shifted their states' tax burden onto underrepresented, distant farmers. Smarting under heavy taxes, western farmers demanded the printing of paper money to relieve the shortage of gold coin as well as the passage of stay-laws to postpone mortgage foreclosures. Several states issued paper money, and in New York and Pennsylvania it held its value quite well because the little that was issued made it more acceptable as legal tender. Rhode Island and Georgia, however, printed so much unbacked paper currency that it lost all value. In desperation, Rhode Island passed a law that required creditors to accept its worthless money as legal tender with fines of £100 and loss of citizenship for noncompliance. A toothless law, the fines could be paid in the worthless, but legal tender.

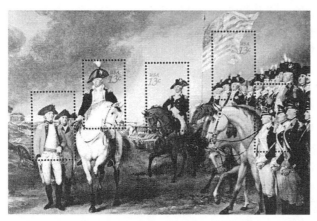

The Surrender of Lord Cornwallis at Yorktown
A souvenir sheet to commemorate Lord Cornwallis' surrender at Yorktown, this detail from John Trumbull's painting shows leading American officers preparing to receive the surrender. Washington, of course, occupies center stage with Alexander Hamilton on foot to the commander's right. (1976)

Northwest Ordinance

Just as the situation became acute in the states, Congress resolved its financial problems by insuring itself a steady income through the sale of western lands. In 1781 the thirteen states ceded to Congress their western land as a precondition for the ratification of the Articles of Confederation, leaving Congress with the task of organizing and disposing of the western territories. After several false starts, Congress passed the Land Ordinance of 1785, which became the model for the future organization of all western territories. It provided for surveys and division of the land into townships. Each township contained thirty-six sections, and each section comprised 640 acres, or one square mile. Congress set aside four of the thirty-six sections in each township for the government and one section for public education. The central government auctioned off the remainder, starting at a dollar an acre for a minimum purchase of 640 acres. Later, smaller land parcels became available and prices rose. The act permitted a systematic survey, greater security for land titleholders, regular government income, and for those with money, a fair and equitable distribution of unused land which, in truth, usually meant Indian land.

In 1787 Congress passed the landmark Northwest Ordinance that provided for the orderly political expansion of the new nation into the Ohio and Mississippi valleys. North of the Ohio River it established the Northwest Territory, with a governor and three judges, all appointed by Congress. When the territory reached

5000 inhabitants it could elect a territorial legislature, subject to the governor's veto, and send observers to Congress. When 60,000 settlers had settled in the territory, the territorial legislature could draw up a constitution and petition Congress for statehood. Ultimately, the Northwest Territory was split into five states, ensuring that new states would be approximately the size of the existing states. In a gesture that reflected the lingering effects of revolutionary sentiment, Congress also outlawed slavery throughout the territory. The township and territorial concepts worked so well that they were applied across the continent as Americans relentlessly pushed westward; the ordinance's prohibition of slavery in the Midwest, in the long term, insured its destruction. Few statutes have had a greater impact on American life.

Shays' Rebellion

Expansion was slowed, however, by the postwar agricultural depression. Farmers, faced with numerous foreclosures and an inability to meet their tax burdens, protested in the American revolutionary fashion, voting with their guns. In 1786 a mob surrounded the state house in Concord, New Hampshire, requiring the state militia to disperse it. Serious violence erupted in Massachusetts after the state legislature hurriedly adjourned in June 1786 to avoid farmers' petitions for help. The initial violence in western Massachusetts spontaneously grew from disruptions of foreclosure auctions and the breakup of legal proceedings against defaulting debtors. But Daniel Shays, an ex-army captain, quickly assumed leadership of the disgruntled farmers and pressed for more paper money laws to delay foreclosures, abolishment of debt imprisonment, and the relocation of the Massachusetts state capital to the interior. One of Shays' loudest critics was the old radical, Sam Adams, a member of the state legislature. When Shays' rebels attacked the Springfield armory in the winter of 1786, the state called out the militia with wealthy Boston merchants supplying the money on loan to pay its expenses. Defeated by the state militia, Shays fled to Vermont, in February 1787, to avoid capture.

In the wake of Shay's unsuccessful rebellion, the Massachusetts legislature levied no further direct taxes on the farmers and relaxed debt collection laws. Many Americans, however, saw Shays' Rebellion as a frightening portent of things to come. Individuals, such as George Washington and James Madison, already predisposed toward a more centralized and powerful general government, were particularly upset. Dismayed that Congress could not suppress these internal uprisings, many feared the eventual disintegration of the United States unless the central government gained additional powers. Washington described the

Continental Congress as "a half-starved, limping government, always moving on crutches and tottering at every step."

The Constitutional Foundation

Powerful political leaders cast about for ways to revise the Articles of Confederation. In January 1786, Virginia issued a call for a convention to settle commercial problems vexing the states, particularly navigation and trade on the Potomac River. Nine states responded, but when the conference convened at Annapolis, only five had sent representatives. The delegates realized that interstate commercial questions could never be resolved in so small a conclave. Alexander Hamilton, a delegate from New York, offered a successful resolution that asked the states to send representatives to a general convention to be held in Philadelphia in May 1787. His resolution directed the Philadelphia gathering to take up commercial problems and all other topics necessary "to render the Constitution of the Federal Government adequate to the exigencies of the Union." Congress did not act until February, and then it specified that the convention should meet for the sole and express purpose of "revising" the Articles. By May, all states, except New Hampshire and Rhode Island, had selected delegates to the new convention. New Hampshire finally sent representatives in June, but Rhode Island, always wary of compromising its sovereignty, ignored the proceedings altogether.

Independence Hall

Most of the fifty-five men chosen to attend the Philadelphia convention represented America's wealthy elite. Two of the delegates, Washington and Franklin, had international reputations, another ten were well known throughout the English-speaking world. Only Jacob Broome of Delaware was unknown—even in his home state. Most of the men had respectable family connections; sixteen had been born into the colonial aristocracy and only four representatives could boast that they had worked their way up from the bottom of the social ladder. Because the convention promised to keep the delegates away from their home and jobs for a long period of time, they had to be men of means. At least forty-six of them fell into the category of being between "comfortable" or "very rich." Only nine were of modest means.

With few exceptions the delegates were the same individuals who had precipitated the revolution, guided its destinies, and established the Confederation. In a nation that boasted a fifty percent literacy rate, these men were uncommonly well educated. Twenty-six held college degrees and, when those who had read and studied law and medicine are included, thirty-six had the equivalent of a college education. The oldest man at the convention was the eighty-one-year-old Franklin. The youngest man was twenty-six-year-old Jonathan Dayton from New Jersey. The delegates' average age was forty-three. Well-traveled, well-read, and well-educated, the delegates to the Federal Constitutional Convention thought in national, even global terms. The only major revolutionary figures who missed the conclave were John Adams and Thomas Jefferson, who were serving as ambassadors overseas; Patrick Henry, who said he "smelled a rat"; and Sam Adams, who was not invited.

Over that extraordinary long, oppressive, hot summer in Philadelphia the delegates got along with each other amazingly well—in part because they knew one another, and in part because they agreed on broad goals for the country. Despite the delegates' congeniality, the convention was a grueling affair that maintained an exhausting schedule, meeting six days a week, five hours a day, inside the locked and shuttered Independence Hall. Even though over forty delegates attended on an average day and most took their meals and drink at the Indian Queen Tavern every evening, not one word of the convention's proceedings leaked to the public. At the outset, the delegates decided on secrecy because they did not intend simply to revise the existing government. Boldly, they ignored their instructions to revise the Articles of Confederation and, instead, designed a wholly new government.

The Great Compromises

For the first month the convention considered various plans put forward by different states and sought grounds for a working consensus. They soon discovered that a basic conflict loomed between the bigger states that wanted their larger populations recognized in any new government and the smaller states that feared they would be overwhelmed and ignored in a government based on population. The larger states favored the Virginia plan introduced by Edmund Randolph that called for a bicameral national legislature with both houses based on proportional representation. The lower house would be popularly elected and the upper house would be chosen by the lower from a list of nominees submitted by the state legislatures. The nation's executive was to be chosen by the national legislature. Along with members of the judiciary, the executive would have a veto over all legislative acts. The small states countered with the New Jersey plan, which was basically a modification of the Articles. It sought to keep equal state representation as under the Confederation, to increase the central government's taxing powers and control over interstate commerce, and to establish a plural executive.

The crucial question was whether the government should be based on population that threatened the interests of the smaller states. The convention voted down the New Jersey plan overwhelmingly, suggesting a broad agreement on the need for extensive revision of the Articles. Despite this setback, the small states' delegates did not walk out. After that crucial vote, the provisions of a new document fell rapidly into place.

J.B. Sterns' famous painting showing George Washington addressing the Constitutional Convention depicts a scene that probably never took place as portrayed, but it suggests how Americans would like to remember this important gathering. (1937)

Between June 21 and August 5, the convention arrived at several compromises. The thorny problem of representation was resolved by basing representation in the House of Representatives on state population—the total white population and three-fifths of the slave population of each state. The Senate would safeguard the smaller states' interests by granting each state, regardless of its size, two seats. Another problem was how to ensure local liberties under a powerful central government. The framers of the Constitution were wary of vesting too much power in any person or office. They knew from experience that power in the wrong hands was dangerous. To prevent any part of the new government from usurping the authority of other parts, the delegates balanced off the powers of the separate branches of government—the legislative, the judiciary, and the executive. They relied on checks and balances, such as the presidential veto and staggered congressional terms of office, to prevent too strong a government and to make the document more acceptable to people who favored states' rights.

A great debate emerged at the convention over the nature of the executive. The delegates, who had spent most of their adult lives in opposition to royal governors and to the king, were leery of a strong executive. Much sentiment existed for divided executive who would represent different sections of the country to minimize the power any one man would hold. Delegates also disagreed over how long an executive should serve and how to elect him. The discussions soon degenerated into a dispute between the large and small states. The small states feared that a popularly elected executive would not have to win votes in the small states and would ignore them. An unwieldy compromise was finally worked out that established an electoral college, in which each state had as many members as it had representatives in the House and in the Senate. This scheme favored the larger states, but the framers decreed that a candidate must get a majority of the electoral votes to win because they thought that each state would probably run a candidate and that nobody would ever receive a majority in the electoral college. In such an event, the House of Representatives would decide the election where each state had but one vote on this issue, a solution that favored the smaller states. This electoral procedure has long bedeviled presidential politics especially after the unforeseen emergence of political parties.

After August 6 when the delegates received printed copies of a rough draft of the Constitution, the convention turned to details. It gave Representatives two-year terms, Senators six years, the President four years. To reduce state control over trade, Congress gained exclusive control over foreign and interstate commerce. And to foreclose the possibility of Shays-like rebellions, the convention gave the national government the power to print money and forbade the states from passing laws that impaired the obligations of contracts. Finally, on September 17, 1787, thirty-nine of the forty-two delegates present signed the new Constitution of the United States. The convention adjourned to await ratification by the voters. In a radical departure, Article VII stipulated that the new Constitution would become law after nine of the thirteen states conducted special elections for constituent assemblies to discuss and vote on the proposed constitution. While this explicitly violated the Articles' requirement for state unanimity, it submitted the document directly to the people, which the framers underlined by beginning the Constitution with the momentous phrase, "We the People of the United States of America . . . "

Ratification of Constitution

From the first the framers had debated how to present the Constitution to the people. Because they had exceeded their instructions, they were uncertain of the public's reaction to their summer labors. They rejected outright the idea of a popular vote on the document as too risky and feared that if it were presented to the state legislatures those bodies, upset at their loss of power to the central government, would never approve. The framers took the less risky course of submitting their work to specially elected constitutional conventions in each state, hoping that such conventions would be composed of like-minded men or at least men who could be persuaded of the document's merits.

From the fall of 1787 through the following summer, the constituent assemblies met in each state, except Rhode Island. Of the first four states to ratify the document, three of the more rural states, Delaware, Georgia, and New Jersey, ratified unanimously. In the large mercantile states of Massachusetts and New York, and in Virginia, the largest state to enter the new union, the ratifying conventions were nearly evenly divided. The big advantage of those favoring the Constitution, who called themselves Federalists, was that they had a positive program. They knew exactly what they wanted, were well organized, and faced dispirited opponents. Hamilton, Madison, and Jay published a series of essays, collectively known as "The Federalist Papers," during the ratification controversies setting out in positive terms the philosophical basis on which the Constitution rested. Opponents of the document, dubbed anti-Federalists, could only point to the weaknesses in their opponents' arguments, the probability of higher taxes, loss of states' rights, and the absence of guarantees for personal liberties; they supported the Articles of Confederation and had no positive program of their own to offer as an alternative.

Although New Hampshire became the ninth state to ratify in June 1788, the Federalists had some uneasy moments over the next month, as they nervously awaited favorable decisions from the two large and pivotal states of New York and Virginia. After a heated debate, Virginia ratified by a close vote in late June. New York elected an anti-Federal majority to its convention. It took all of the persuasive powers of Alexander Hamilton to sway the delegates to reverse themselves and to support the Constitution. Hamilton's most compelling argument was self-interest. New Yorkers believed that their state's commercial interests would be destroyed if they tried to go it alone. In July the state convention finally ratified the Constitution by a thin margin of thirty to twenty-seven. Both the Virginia and New York state conventions voted for the Constitution but only after its opponents were assured that a bill of rights would be attached to the Constitution that spelled out protections for individual liberties and state rights. North Carolina and Rhode Island, each controlled by anti-Federalist factions content with the Articles of Confederation, lagged behind and did not join the new experiment until November 1789 and May 1790, respectively.

Goals of the Document

The Constitution of 1787 succeeded and has endured, hallowed by time. Its success did not rest on its democratic features, for most of the framers harbored a deep mistrust of popular rule. The Founders compromised the revolutionary principle that government should flow from the people by instituting checks on popular participation. As heirs of the struggle for independence, politic men such as Alexander Hamilton and Gouverneur Morris could not openly repudiate popular sovereignty—they merely had to find some way to limit its operation. They submitted a document that would garner enough popular support to be ratified, yet would divide and balance potential majorities. Jeremy Belknap, a Congregational clergyman and Federalist writer, summed it up well; "Let it stand as a principle that government originates from the people." But let them learn, he went on, "that they are not able to govern themselves."

The men who wrote the Constitution did not write in a vacuum. During the Confederation period, they had seen where unchecked democracy could lead, and they determined that such an accident should not be repeated. Their intricate system of checks and balances, a bicameral legislature, an executive armed with a veto, and a supreme court, offered a formidable gauntlet for any proposed legislation to run and ensured that legislation which passed commanded wide support. The new government offered a way, as Madison rejoiced in the Federalist, to make it difficult for members of one faction "to discover their own strength and to act in unison with each other." Moreover, the Constitution, in specifying what people in the states might not do—issue paper money, abridge contracts, levy tariffs on imported goods-ensured that local factions could not place propertied interests under a disadvantage. Finally, the new document's guarantee of a republican form of government to each state would see to it that frightening uprisings like Shays' Rebellion could be met by the full force of national authority.

The Federalists did their job well. They wrote and won ratification of a basic law that produced stable political unity. They drew one salient lesson from their study of the past: that humans would inevitably pursue their own interests and would just as inevitably defeat the goals of living in a secure and ordered society. The Constitution formulated and enshrined a set of ideas around which they believed a majority of Americans would rally. At the same time, the charter controlled the human passions and interests that threatened to break these bonds. The document rested on the largely unstated aristocratic assumptions of pre-revolutionary America that the upper classes should govern. John Jay, New York delegate and later the first chief justice of the Supreme Court, stated it more baldly than most: "The people who own the country ought to govern it." It fell to such men, the first generation of American political leaders under the Constitution, to prove the validity of republican, if not democratic, government.

Historical Potpourri

Revolutionary era leaders were most adept with a pen and practiced at turning the felicitous phrase. Many of their comments were memorable and provide vivid insights into their world. Below is a sampling.

Benjamin Franklin:
"There never was a good war or a bad peace."
Letter to Josiah Quincy, September 11, 1773.

"I wish the Bald Eagle had not been chosen as the Representative of our Country; he is a Bird of bad moral Character; like those among Men who live by Sharping and Robbing, he is generally poor, and often very lousy. The Turkey is a much more respectable Bird, and withthal a true original Native of America."
Letter to Sarah Bach, January 26, 1784.

Eliza Wilkerson, South Carolina:
"Never were [there] greater politicians than the several knots of ladies who met together.
All trifling discourse of fashions, and such low chat was thrown by, and we commenced perfect statesmen."
Letter to Miss M—— P——, 1779

John Adams:
"The second day of July, 1776, will be the most memorable epoch in the history of America . . . . It will be solemnized with pomp and parade, with shows, games, sports, guns, bells, bonfires, and laminations, from one end of this continent to the other, from this time forward and evermore."
Letter to Mrs. Adams, July 3, 1776

Patrick Henry:
"I have but one lamp by which my feet are guided, and that is the lamp of experience. I know of no way of judging the future but by the past."
Speech in the House of Burgess, March 23, 1775.

Thomas Paine:
"War involves in its progress such a train of unforeseen and unsupposed circumstances that no human wisdom can calculate the end. It has but one thing certain, and that is to increase taxes."
Prospects on the Rubicon, 1787.

Thomas Jefferson:
"What country before ever existed a century and a half without a rebellion? . . . The tree of liberty must be refreshed from time to time with the blood of patriots and tyrants. It is its natural manure."
Letter to William Smith, November 13, 1787.

Abigail Adams:
"I long to hear that you have declared an independency—and by the way in the new Code of Laws which I suppose it will be necessary for you to make I desire you would Remember the Ladies, and be more generous and favorable to them than your ancestors. . . . Remember all Men would be tyrants if they could."
Letter to John Adams, March 31, 1776.

Iroquois, Shawnee, Cherokee, Chickasaw,
Choctaw, and Loup Indian Chiefs:
"That event was for us the greatest blow that could have been dealt us, unless it had been our total destruction."
On war, to Spanish governor of St. Louis,
Francisco Cruzat, August 23, 1784.

Good Books

The best short discussion of the social and political events of the American Revolution is Edward Countryman, *The American Revolution* (1985). Robert Middlekauff, *The Glorious Cause* (1982), and Don Higginbotham, *The War of American Independence* (1971). John Shy, *A People Numerous and Armed* (1990) and Charles Royster, *A Revolutionary People at War* (1979) offer insightful discussions of the war's social and political impact on the men who served. The loyalist experience is covered by Robert M. Calhoun, *The Loyalists in Revolutionary America* (1973), while Jonathan R. Dull's *A Diplomatic History of the American Revolution* (1985) covers foreign affairs.

The political theory of the Revolution and the Constitution are thoroughly discussed in Gordon S. Wood's *The Creation of the American Republic* (1969). The political theory of the Revolution is discussed in Bernard Bailyn's *The Ideological Origins of the American Revolution* (1967), which outlines the intellectual underpinnings of the revolt while the political philosophy that undergirded the new American governments is covered by Paul S. Conkin, *Self Evident Truths* (1976), Jack P. Green's *The Quest for Power: The Lower Houses of Assembly in the Southern Royal Colonies, 1689-1776* (1963), details the political changes that made the position of the royal governors untenable by 1775; Carl Becker, *The Declaration of Independence* (1942), thoughtfully essays the ideological background of that document. For a recent thought-provoking work, see Garry Wills, *Inventing America* (1979).

Charles A. Beard, *An Economic Interpretation of the Constitution* (1913), remains a book that must be read by all students of the Constitution, although Beard's interpretation has been frontally challenged, most notably by Forrest McDonald, *We the People: The Economic Origins of the Constitution* (1958). McDonald also looks at the document's intellectual origins in *Novus Ordom Seclorum* (1985). Despite its age, Merrill Jensen, *The New Nation* (1950) remains the most thorough discussion on the 1780s. David P. Szatmary, *Shays' Rebellion* (1980) provides a general overview of farm debt as well as the rebellion itself.

The groundbreaking work on women, Indians, and African Americans is Alfred F. Young ed., *The American Revolution: Explorations in American Radicalism* (1976). More recent works that have filled out the field include Mary Beth Norton, *Liberty's Daughters* (1980), Linda Kerber, *Women of the Republic* (1980), Colin G. Calloway, *The American Revolution in Indian Country* (1995); Richard White, *The Middle Ground: Indians, Empires, and Republics on the Great Lakes* (1991); Sylvia Frey, *Water from Rock: Black Resistance in a Revolutionary War* (1991), and Gary B. Nash, *Forging Freedom: The Formation of Philadelphia's Black Community* (1988).

The most provocative discussion of the Revolution and its transformative effect on society is Gordon S. Wood, *The Radicalism of the American Revolution* (1991) while Jay Fliegelman's *Prodigals and Pilgrims: The American Revolution Against Patriarchal Authority* (1982) is also provocative.

CHAPTER THREE

THE NEW REPUBLIC

1789	George Washington inaugurated first president French Revolution
1790	First United States census Hamilton funded United States debts
1791	First Bank of the United States
1792	Washington reelected
1793	Citizen Genêt affair United States broke 1778 treaty with France Eli Whitney invented cotton gin
1794	Whisky Rebellion Battle of Fallen Timbers
1795	Jay's Treaty
1796	John Adams elected second president Political party strife rampant
1798	XYZ Affair Two-year undeclared war with France Alien and Sedition Acts Kentucky and Virginia Resolves
1800	Thomas Jefferson third president
1801	Five-year war with Barbary states
1803	Louisiana purchased Marbury vs. Madison
1804	Aaron Burr killed Alexander Hamilton Lewis and Clark expedition Jefferson reelected
1807	Burr tried for treason Robert Fulton tested first successful steamboat *Clermont*
1808	Embargo Acts (1807-1808) James Madison fourth president

1812	War of 1812
	Madison reelected
1814	Washington, D.C. captured and burned
	Hartford Convention
1815	Treaty of Ghent
1816	Second Bank of the United States chartered
1817	Erie Canal construction started

The New Republic

The new nation in 1789 had form but no substance. An experiment on a grand scale, it faced the herculean task of binding together commercial interests in the North, slaveholders in the South, and small farmers scattered over a half a continent. Dedicated to the proposition that all white men were inherently capable of directing their own destinies, the new government had to tread warily in its attempts to solve pressing national problems lest its centralizing tendencies alienate large numbers of Americans. Moreover, faced with the crucial problems of establishing a small nation on the edge of a wilderness, the new federal government also had to deal with a world at war. The ever-present external dangers unified Americans and promoted loyalty to the new government and in large measure set the tone of the early administrations. America never had the luxury of isolating itself from world affairs in order to conduct its then unique experiment. Social, political, and economic conditions in the nation's first years were largely molded and defined in reaction to rapidly changing events in Western Europe dictated by the French Revolution and subsequent Napoleonic Wars.

The men elected to guide the new nation's destinies faced formidable problems. They were members of a government with little precedent and no structure. Their job was to give content to the Constitution. Washington had no firm sense of the limits on his executive power, no ground rules for his relations with other branches of government, not even a formal title. One of the sharpest controversies in the nation's first days concerned how the president should be addressed. Many officials favored "your elective highness" to give the president prestige. Vice President John Adams favored either "your highness" or "your excellency." For such aristocratic notions, Adams, who ran to portliness, won from his political opponents "your rotundity."

For the first inauguration on March 4, 1789, New York City, the temporary national capital sported patriotic bunting, cannons boomed, bells pealed, and the

The new government got off to an inauspicious start when congress and the new president arrived late to the new capital of New York City. Nonetheless, the city was festive at Washington's inauguration. (1939)

people celebrated—but members of the new government had not yet arrived. The house of representatives could not raise a quorum until April, and the senate required another six days before it mustered enough members to meet. President-elect Washington, chosen unanimously by the electoral college, did not take his oath until April 30. It seemed an inauspicious start for the new government.

Congress was simply a rowdy group of men assembled to make laws. It had no operating rules. Congressmen did not even know how to introduce bills. There was no committee system, of course, but also no voting procedures, no one to say how to determine the constitutionality of congressional legislation or how to enforce the laws once they had passed.

The supreme court did not even know how many members it would have. No one expressed surprise when congress decreed that the first court would have six judges. Until congress established federal circuit courts no system of federal courts existed below the supreme court, and the nation's highest justices remained uncertain of the questions they could review. With very light case loads, the justices spent most of the year out of the capital, riding circuit.

Members of the new government enjoyed a number of advantages, not the least the freedom from precedents. Most had supported ratification of the Constitution and were committed to making it work. Very few sought to undermine the new compact. Also, many of those who had spent the hot summer of 1787 in Philadelphia won seats in the new government, giving them firsthand knowledge of the framers' intent. They had also staked their reputations on the success of the experiment.

Outstanding Leaders Mold the Nation

The Constitutional Convention had designed the office of the presidency with George Washington in mind. The framers had argued over limiting the powers of the executive, but because they believed that Washington would be the first to hold the title president, they boldly delegated great authority to the chief executive. They simply trusted Washington not to misuse those powers. Washington proved a happy choice for first president. He embodied what Americans wanted to believe was their character. Almost six feet two inches tall, he was physically imposing, was seemingly oblivious to fear as his well-publicized feats in two wars attested, had an inborn habit of command, and attracted respect and deference. He also enjoyed a reputation as a ladies' man, at least before he married the widow Martha Custis. A man of independent means, he had no reason to pretend to be intellectual. His slowness to act moderated his thunderous temper.

The new president deliberately took his time putting together his government. It took five months for Congress to authorize executive departments and to approve his appointment of his wartime aide, Alexander Hamilton of New York, as the secretary of the treasury. For the war department he turned to Massachusetts and another trusted military companion, General Henry Knox, whose ample girth and 280 pounds added bulk to the cabinet. The attorney general's post fell to fellow Virginia Edmund Randolph, an active participant in the Constitutional Convention. Thomas Jefferson, also from Virginia, was Washington's choice for secretary of state. Sensitive to the republic's division between slave and free states, Washington's cabinet, including himself and Vice President Adams, consisted of three northerners and three southerners. Washington appointed men whom he could trust and with whom he could work harmoniously. He wanted his administration run on the basis of a consensus. He did not view his cabinet as a consultive body, although he sometimes asked for its opinions.

Congress moved with more speed than Washington. In its first year, 1789, it approved adding the Bill of Rights to the Constitution as promised during the ratification campaigns. The amendments engendered little debate; only James Madison seemed very interested in them. That year congress also passed the Judiciary Act, which spelled out procedures for the federal courts to hear appeals involving state laws and state court decisions; established the supreme court; and created United States marshals and United States attorneys. In 1790 congress also authorized the first national census, a pet project of Madison's and necessary for the determination of state representatives to congress. Since the first census in 1790, which recorded 3,929,000 inhabitants, the federal government has taken a general census at the end of every decade. The first congress also approved a tariff bill to provide the new government with income until the secretary of the treasury could formulate a national fiscal policy.

Hamilton to the Fore

It fell to Alexander Hamilton to wrestle with the problem of the nation's lack of money. Born outside wedlock in the West Indies, Hamilton had been a precocious child. He went to New York City as an adolescent, ingratiated himself with men of influence and power—something he did all his life—and attended King's College, renamed Columbia University after the revolution. Leaving school to join the army, Hamilton distinguished himself in battle and caught Washington's eye. The commanding general appointed Hamilton his aide-de-camp where he became indispensable. After the war he established a law practice in New York City, married the daughter of a member of the Hudson River aristocracy, dabbled in various business ventures, and pursued a growing interest in politics.

Hamilton's views resembled those of many well-to-do Americans. He believed fervently that the republic should be ruled by its "best people"—the rich, the wise, and the well-born. Hostile to democracy, which he equated with mob rule, Hamilton opposed expanding the franchise or eliminating property requirements for office holding. An admirer of the British system of government, he was often accused of acting as the prime minister in Washington's government and relegating the "old man" to ceremonial functions. Although such charges were political exaggerations, Hamilton sought to keep the American experiment well within the British political tradition, and he consistently favored a pro-British foreign policy. The secretary hoped that his adopted country would create a strong central government based on a "loose" interpretation of the constitution that would allow the

Alexander Hamilton, the first secretary of the treasury, performed a minor miracle when he placed the United States on a firm financial footing that within a decade gave it the highest credit in the world. Despite his undeniable talent and ambition, Hamilton had not risen to the heights he thought he deserved when Aaron Burr fatally shot him in a duel of honor on July 11, 1804. (1957)

federal government to exercise "implied" powers not specifically delegated in the document. He wanted the national government to use its resources to aid American businessmen, to promote industry and trade, to maintain a strong defense, and to keep order at home. Hamilton looked with favor on the national debt, banks, government bureaucracy, promotion of sectional aims—particularly those of the Northeast—and aid to urban interests. His outlook was an extension of his own personality—an urbane, educated, professional, upper-class American of talent and connections.

The secretary was in an unusual position to put his personal beliefs into practice. Through the manipulation of national fiscal policies he could help those social and economic classes, especially the wealthy supporters of the Constitution, who looked to the new government to rebuild its disordered finances and improve the prospects for national prosperity. These were the people, Hamilton reasoned, whose favor the government desperately needed if it were to survive. He attempted to gain their support with a fiscal program that long remained basic American policy and that had such widespread political repercussions that it drastically shaped the political patterns of the entire country.

Hamilton's Financial Plans

In 1789 the national debt stood at about 79 million dollars—54 million in foreign and domestic obligations owed by the federal government and an additional 25 million in state debt. In 1790, Hamilton proposed a new, low-interest federal loan to fund both of these debts. He wanted these new bonds funded, however, with continuing appropriations, not simply whenever the money became available as had been the case in the past. The secretary personally took his plan right into congress, argued in committees, circulated on the floor during debates, and discussed legislative tactics with the leaders of both houses. He had no trouble securing approval for the funding of the foreign debt. All agreed that it must be paid to establish national credit. Funding the domestic debt, however, proved controversial. Word of Hamilton's plans to fund it had leaked, leading speculators to hire agents who fanned out over the countryside and bought up the depreciated revolutionary and Confederation securities at depreciated prices before the public heard about the refunding. Some Congressmen, following Madison's lead, cried corruption although no evidence indicated that Hamilton had leaked the information or personally profited from his official position. Still, Madison demanded that the original holders, not the subsequent owners, of such securities be reimbursed at par by the government. Hamilton retorted that to do so would be a breach of contract, a violation of the right of fair purchase, and besides it would be impossible to track down the original owners as the securities had passed through many hands. Congress upheld Hamilton's position.

The proposal to fund the states' debt likewise encountered a storm of protest. Some states, such as Virginia, had paid their debts. Others, including Georgia, had not assumed many debts. Both resented being taxed to retire the obligations of other states. The debate uncovered sectional antagonisms since most southern states either had few debts or had paid them by 1790. Southern congressional delegations, again led by Madison, argued against an unwarranted extension of federal authority over the states. Congress defeated Hamilton's state funding proposal by a narrow margin.

Undaunted, Hamilton sought out Jefferson and made a classic political deal. Asserting that sectionalism would tear the new nation apart, Hamilton suggested that northern interests might accede to moving the national capital further south in return for southern agreement on the federal goverment's assumption of the state debt. As finally worked out, the understanding promised to shift the capital to Philadelphia in 1790 for ten years, after which it would be located at some spot on the Potomac River. In return, Jefferson twisted enough political arms in the Virginia congressional delegation—observers claimed one senator from Virginia sobbed as he cast his vote—to ensure passage of the debt bill. The capital was moved southward as promised, helping to secure southern slaveholder control over the federal government until the Civil War.

Results of Hamilton's Programs

To pay the interest on the new federal bond offering, Hamilton convinced congress to place new taxes on tea, coffee, wines, and whisky. Americans were understandably touchy on the subject of taxes, especially the whisky tax. Farmers in western Pennsylvania, who distilled their grain to transport it to market, refused to pay the tax. When they forcibly prevented tax officials from collecting the duties in 1794, Washington issued an executive proclamation ordering them back to their homes and called for 15,000 state militia from four states to put down the rebellion. Under Henry Lee and with Hamilton as second in command, federal forces invaded western Pennsylvania and the rioters scattered. Despite the continued fall in tax collections as the farmers persisted in their boycott, the federal government had demonstrated its determination to suppress internal revolt. Unlike Shays' Rebellion, the Whisky Rebellion attested to the new goverment's decisiveness.

Hamilton's refunding program proved highly successful. By 1794 the United States boasted a higher credit rating than any nation in Europe. Foreign investors bought an increasing number of United States bonds throughout the decade. More-over, Hamilton's program particularly benefitted those wealthy Americans whose support he sought. Wealthy Americans invested heavily in United States bonds and received regular interest payments from the government. The secretary had no intention of paying off the national debt of $20 per capita. In a country short of hard currency, United States bonds circulated as money. In this fashion the exis-tence of a regularly funded debt expanded the nation's credit. If the goverment's interest payments went into the hands of a few men, Hamilton knew they would reinvest it in productive enterprises; it was an indirect way of providing govern-ment aid to business and commerce.

Bank of the United States

Hamilton was unfazed by the public furor over his debt program. Soon after he sent to congress a second controversial report in December 1790 that requested establishment of a national bank. The proposal grew out of his frustrations in try-ing to administer the goverment's finances in a country with few banks. His expe-rience as a founder of the Bank of New York and his admiration for the Bank of England, a private institution that handled the English goverment's finances, led him to propose a bank that would be a partnership between public and private enterprise, capitalized at ten million dollars, eight million dollars of it private money. He had permited bank investors to pay three-fourths of their subscription in federal bonds, which immediately raised their value. The bank would serve as the country's financial agent, be available to private depositors, and make loans to the government. Its notes would also serve as a national currency, further expanding the republic's liquid capital.

Vehement opposition to Hamilton's bank bill arose in congress. Representatives from the South and from rural constituencies argued that the United States Bank, located in Philadelphia, favored northern mercantile interests. More ominously, the bill raised serious constitutional questions concerning the powers of the central government. Madison deemed the proposal unconstitutional since the Constitu-tion did not mention banks. Hamilton countered that the Constitution permitted the government to regulate the currency and that the United States Bank was a log-ical extension of that implied power. The question turned on whether the Consti-tution should be interpreted narrowly or broadly. Congress' passage of the bank bill placed the decision in Washington's hands. The president asked his cabinet mem-bers for advice, and they divided narrowly over the question. Washington finally sided with Hamilton and initialed the bill granting the bank a twenty-year charter.

In doing so, Washington endorsed Hamilton's notion of a strong, national government as well as his constitutional argument of "implied powers." The bank was a huge success. Over its lifetime it paid the government and its private stockholders an annual interest averaging eight percent, making it second only to Hamilton's funding scheme in attracting to the new government the support of private investors which in most cases meant the country's wealthiest classes.

Hamilton's successes encouraged him to present to congress in December 1791 a third report on the status of manufacturing in the republic. The document embodied Hamilton's dreams for the country's future. He saw that world power was passing to the industrializing nations, and he wanted the United States aligned with that trend. Lamenting the unbalanced national economy with its heavy reliance on agriculture, he recommended a system of tariffs to protect domestic industries, a network of federal internal improvements, and federal encouragement of manufacturing. The secretary himself invested heavily in a private venture, the Society for Useful Manufactures, capitalized at the astronomical sum of one million dollars, that proposed to construct an industrial complex at Paterson, New Jersey. Unfortunately, Hamilton did not have the time to oversee his investment, and the Society for Useful Manufacturers went bankrupt in 1795. Similarly, Hamilton's dreams for an industrial economy proved premature. Congress, representing a rural America, took no action on his suggestions.

During Washington's first administration the secretary of the treasury served as a lightning rod, drawing the unrelenting hostility and opposition of all who opposed the administration and its policies. Hamilton's controversial programs sparked the growing antagonisms that marked the new republic's early years. Many merchants angrily opposed paying his tariff. Farmers were doubly annoyed. They resented the taxes they paid to service the national debt, especially because the profits lined others' pockets. They also blamed the president and his advisors for falling crop prices, due in large part to agricultural surpluses in Europe. Opponents of the administration attempted to discredit Hamilton personally when his friend and confidant, William Duer, went bankrupt and ended up in debtors' prison. Although Hamilton had nothing to do with Duer's financial indiscretions, many regarded him guilty by association.

Thomas Jefferson

Thomas Jefferson led the public opposition to Hamilton and a strong federal government. Out of the personal conflict two distinct political parties developed around the two men. Two more opposite men than Hamilton and Jefferson could hardly be imagined. The low-born Hamilton gloried in his aristocratic pretensions. Jefferson, a descendant of Virginia's slave-owning aristocracy, championed the common man. Graduate of William and Mary College, lawyer, planter, and slave owner, Jefferson hailed from the upper reaches of American society. A tall, sandy-haired, gangling man, Jefferson was always very visible yet remained an intensely private individual. So reserved, he seldom looked another straight in the eye. Jefferson's wife died young, leaving him two daughters. He never courted another white woman—although strong circumstantial evidence suggests that he loved a black slave, Sally Hemmings, who bore in his household five mulatto children. Financially inept and self-indulgent, Jefferson accumulated enormous debts. At the time of

Thomas Jefferson thought so little of his two terms in the White House that he omitted mention of them on his tombstone. A erratic and eclectic genius, Jefferson was a bundle of paradoxes, lived far beyond his means, and died deeply in debt. (1938)

his death his estate was so encumbered that, unlike Washington, Jefferson failed to follow his conscience and free his slaves, not even his alleged children. Few individuals have lived such a contradictory life, even fewer have so personally embodied their society's loftiest virtues and meanest faults.

Jefferson's Views

Jefferson's social and political views put him in direct opposition to Hamilton. The secretary of state had no fear of mob rule, nor did he underestimate the collective intelligence of the masses. He favored the extension of political rights to all adult white males. What Jefferson most feared, based on his experiences during the colonial period and especially as governor of Virginia during the revolution, was an excess of power vested in a strong central government insulated from the people. "The government that governs best is the government that governs least," he often quoted Thomas Paine. Except when president, Jefferson advocated limiting the power of the central government by interpreting the powers of the Constitution strictly. Jefferson dreamed of an expanding republic of yeomen farmers who worked God's fertile soil, paid low taxes, and lived happily with an excellent chance of raising their social status. His self-sufficient, agrarian republic of farmers, artisans, and shopkeepers would contain no large cities, no dependent class of wage earners, only minimal government, no national banks, free speech and press, and secure personal liberties. In foreign affairs he remained consistently pro-French and a strong supporter of America's 1778 French alliance.

Jefferson had a loyal political following among those who feared a strong central government—many of his supporters had opposed the ratification of the Constitution and most opposed Hamilton's fiscal policies. Socially, Jefferson attracted a following among the poorer classes, debtors rather than creditors, small farmers rather than merchants, residents of rural areas rather than city dwellers, southerners and westerners rather than northeasterners. His supporters were usually younger, more ambitious, more energetic than Hamilton's. They aspired to wealth while Hamilton drew on established wealth.

At odds as early as 1791, Jefferson and Hamilton vied for influence with the president. Jefferson attempted to infiltrate the Treasury Department by having his supporter, Tench Cox, appointed assistant secretary. Failing at that ploy, he unsuccessfully tried to have the treasury department divided in two, removing the post office, a valuable source of federal patronage, from Hamilton's control. Hamilton kept Washington's ear on most domestic issues, but Jefferson made headway outside the government. He and Hamilton attacked each other with fury in a long newspaper dispute. Each man controlled his own newspaper in Philadelphia. Hamilton hired John Fenno to publish the *United States Gazette;* Jefferson followed suit by engaging the poet, Philip Freneau, to edit his *National Gazette.* Each frequently contributed pseudonymous articles to his own paper viciously slashing his opponent's policies.

Jefferson proved more adroit than Hamilton in soliciting support in the states. He numbered among his followers Governor George Clinton, who controlled upstate New York politics; Aaron Burr, who was influential in New York City politics through Tammany Hall, a drinking club and benevolent association; the old John Hancock of Massachusetts; James Madison, Jefferson's spokesman in congress; Pennsylvanians David Rittenhouse and Albert Gallatin; James Monroe and John Taylor of Jefferson's own state, and many others. By 1792 Jefferson's followers, sneered at as anti-Federalists by pro-Hamilton forces, held their own caucus in congress to plot legislative strategy. These pro and anti-administration congressional caucuses, in time, formed national political factions that became formal political parties—the Jeffersonian Republicans and the Hamiltonian Federalists.

Committed to consensus, Washington was dismayed by the split in his cabinet and the rising political factionalism. The president tried to remain neutral.

Seriously concerned that such political divisions might tear the country apart, he responded to pleas that only he could hold the nation together and in 1792 reluctantly agreed to stand for another term. Because even Jefferson and his followers accepted Washington as the best unifying candidate, he again won every electoral vote. Supporters of Jefferson's viewpoint flexed their muscle by running George Clinton against John Adams for vice president and carrying four states. Although Adams won reelection, the results foreshadowed the growing strength of the anti-Federalist Jeffersonians.

Washington and Foreign Affairs

In addition to the challenge of holding the new country together, Washington faced the difficult task of protecting the United States against external enemies. The Mississippi River and Spanish Florida remained closed to Americans, and British redcoats still occupied American soil along the Canadian border. In the Northwest Territory Indian groups refused to surrender their lands to the United States. In 1790 Washington sent General Joseph Harmar into the area to drive the Indians out, but he was roundly defeated by a confederation of northwestern Indians. Harmar returned the following year; again the Indians forced him to retreat. Washington changed generals, and finally under the leadership of General "Mad Anthony" Wayne, American forces defeated the tribes in 1794 at the Battle of Fallen Timbers along the Maumee River. The following year representatives from thirteen tribes signed away most of their Ohio lands in the Treaty of Grenville, opening the way for white settlement.

The French Revolution

The French Revolution posed dangerous foreign policy problems for Washington's second administration. Most Americans applauded the revolution when it broke out in 1789 for they relished the thought that American republicanism had spread into the very heart of monarchical Europe. The revolution turned unexpectedly violent in 1793, however, when Louis XVI and his wife Marie Antoinette were executed, followed by a "reign of terror"—a bloodbath in which reactionaries and revolutionaries alike lost their lives. This news divided American public opinion. The pro-British Hamiltonian Federalists, who disliked anything French, gained support by their opposition to the revolution. The Republicans supported the French Republic despite its violent and later dictatorial outcome.

The turmoil in France presented the United States with major problems. The United States had pledged in its 1778 treaty to defend the French West Indies and to open its ports to French privateers in the event that France went to war with Britain. When war erupted between the two countries in February 1, 1793, Washington's cabinet split over whether to honor the treaty. Hamilton argued against it because it had been made with the deposed French government. Jefferson retorted that the treaty was a pledge to the French people, not the French government, and should be honored. Washington vacillated.

The new French government maintained that the treaty was valid and dispatched an unconventional envoy, Edmond Genêt, to the United States. Before Genêt presented his credentials to President Washington, he commissioned privateers in Charleston to prey on British shipping. He also organized an American expedition to invade Spanish and British territories in the new world. Only then did Genêt journey northward to Philadelphia, receiving a warm public welcome along the way. Washington eyed Genêt's antics with alarm. On April 22, 1793, the president issued a Neutrality Proclamation which broke the 1778 treaty. Washington gave Genêt an icy reception and informed the envoy in writing that his capers infringed on United States' sovereignty. Moreover, Washington ordered all American privateers out of their ports and forbade them to return with any prizes. When Genêt threatened to take his case to the American public even Jefferson was appalled by Genêt's high-handed actions. On August 2 Jefferson voted, with other cabinet members, to expel the envoy. The French government that had sent Genêt had fallen in the meantime, and the new revolutionary government ordered Genêt's arrest. Washington refused to expatriate Genêt, and in a fairy tale ending, he became a United States citizen, married Governor Henry Clinton's daughter, and lived out the reminder of his life among the Hudson River aristocracy. Jefferson, upset because Washington had disregarded the 1778 treaty, resigned as secretary of state in December 1793, ending all hope of a faction-free republic. His resignation marked the beginning of the American two-party system.

Jay's Treaty

Soon, however, Britain, not France, became the nettlesome problem. Late in 1793, the British issued new rules regulating commerce that interfered with America's rights as a neutral party, particularly its right to trade with the French West Indies. British vessels stopped American ships, harassed passengers, impressed seamen into the British navy, and in some cases imprisoned private citizens. Moreover, westerners charged that the British still paid the Indians bounties for American scalps at their illegal outposts. By 1794 the two countries teetered on the brink of war.

Washington decided to negotiate a treaty that settled all outstanding disputes and selected Chief Justice John Jay of the supreme court for the delicate task. Jay's negotiating position was difficult. His only bargaining chip was the threat of war. After he departed for England, Hamilton undercut Jay by secretly informing the British minister to the United States that Washington would not go to war under any circumstances. With this confidential information the British government handled Jay roughly. His only triumph was renewal of a previously unfulfilled British promise to vacate their northwestern posts. Jay made no headway on matters such as impressment, payment for slaves removed by the British during the revolution, respect for American neutral rights, or British payment for captured American vessels.

When Washington read the treaty, he hesitated to send it to congress. When he finally did so, a storm of protest ensued, especially from Republicans. Jay was so unpopular that he admitted he could travel at night from one end of the country to the other by the light of his burning effigies. Despite popular reservations, after long debate, the senate ratified the treaty in June 1795. The British abandoned their posts on schedule. Although the agreement failed to solve any of the burning issues between the two countries, it did prevent a war and resolved the boundary disputes between the United States and British Canada left over from the revolution.

The treaty also resulted in better relations with Spain. The Spanish believed secret clauses lurked in Jay's treaty, and distrusting their English ally, they feared that the clauses were aimed at Spain. To avoid possible conflict with the new nation, Spain suddenly became amenable to settling its outstanding differences with the United States. In October 1795, Spain signed the Pinckney Treaty, recognizing America's southern and western boundary claims, granting Americans navigation rights on the Mississippi River for three years, and permitting Americans to deposit their goods at New Orleans. The pact proved popular in the United States and calmed much of the discontent aroused by Jay's treaty.

As a small weak nation, America could not afford to become embroiled in European wars. With its large merchant marine, however, the United States found it difficult to avoid entangling itself in overseas conflicts. Patiently, Washington waited, hoping not to alienate any warring powers. When foreign policy problems became critical, he struck the best deal he could get. Such a conciliatory foreign policy placed peace above national pride but risked domestic turmoil. Because Americans disagreed furiously over questions of foreign policy, events in Europe continued to divide them.

The First Two-Party System

As the election of 1796 approached, Washington refused to run again. His administration was in shambles, its principal figures gone—Hamilton had left in January 1795—and the replacements, all Federalists, lacked the status of his first cabinet. Washington even had a case of suspected treason in his official family when allegations surfaced in 1795 that his new secretary of state, Edmund Randolph, was in the pay of the French. Washington's evidence convinced him that Randolph had schemed with the French to block ratification of Jay's treaty. The president painfully confronted his secretary with the evidence, and Randolph resigned, protesting his innocence. His guilt or innocence has never been determined.

Party strife reached a peak by 1796. The Republican press heaped abuse on Washington, much of it unfair and untrue. He was called a tyrant, an impostor, and a dictator. Thomas Paine even charged that he had acted as a secret agent for the British throughout the revolution. Moreover, by 1796, Washington's health was failing. He complained of a wandering memory, poor hearing, and painful, ill-fitting, wooden dentures. He longed to return to Mt. Vernon to live out his remaining days. Before retiring, Washington took out the farewell address Madison had written for him in 1792, had Hamilton polish it up, and simply handed it to the newspapers. Washington explained why he did not want a third term, warned against a party spirit, and expressed his fears about future sectional divisions. Factionalism "agitates the community with ill-founded jealousies and false alarms" and "kindles the animosity of one part against another," he cautioned. His most famous parting admonition grew out of the foreign policy travails of his second term. Ominously, he warned against ever entering into "entangling" foreign alliances, another permanent foreign alliance, and called on his countrymen to maintain "a respectable defensive posture," and "trust to temporary alliances for extraordinary emergencies."

Washington retired confident that his judicious domestic and foreign policies had held the nation together through its first eight years. But he had done a great deal more. The hero of the revolution had represented a personal symbol of American unity. His administrations had harnessed individual passions and desires to the new national order, and although significant numbers of Americans disagreed with his policies, his opponents did not wish to change the constitutional system, only to exercise power themselves. Without Washington's steady hand, it is unlikely that the American experiment in republican government would have succeeded. Having sired no children of his own, Washington became the "father of his country," the "indispensable man." Lacking a natural heir, Americans had no choice but to elect his successor, squelching all hopes of an American monarchy.

The Adams' Administration

With Washington's departure, the Federalist caucus nominated Vice President Adams for president and diplomat Thomas Pinckney from South Carolina as his vice-presidential running mate. The Republicans nominated Jefferson for president and New Yorker Aaron Burr for vice president. Both tickets were carefully balanced sectionally. The always politically ambitious Hamilton broke with rival Adams and schemed to elect Pinckney president. Hamilton failed, but when

Following Washington into the presidency was a difficult task for John Adams. In an earlier age Adams, brilliant, driven, and self-sacrificing, would probably have been a Calvinist minister. A better revolutionary and diplomat than president, he was the only president between 1789 and 1828 to serve only one term. (1938)

the electoral votes were counted, Adams had won, and Jefferson, who had garnered the second highest number of votes, became the new vice president.

John Adams, a native of Massachusetts and Harvard graduate, lawyer, and brilliant political philosopher, had been an early colonial protester, a tireless worker for the radical cause, and an important figure in leading Americans toward independence. He wrote the new Massachusetts Constitution in 1780, helped negotiate the Treaty of Paris of 1783, and held the thankless job as first American minister to Britain after the war. A short, round man with a rapier-like tongue, Adams was quick to anger, argumentative, prompt to perceive a slight, and like his Puritan forebears, a man of deeply held principles. He was married to a remarkable woman, Abigail Smith, who frequently twitted her husband about his lack of sympathy for the rights of women. She once complained that while he was busy "emancipating all nations" he persisted in "retaining an absolute power over wives." Philosophically Abigail and John were close to Hamilton. They feared unrestrained popular rule and preferred a restrained, balanced government, managed by an educated, wealthy elite, although Adams himself enjoyed only modest wealth. Distressed by the rise of organized political factionalism, Adams was the most intellectual and best read of the revolutionary generation. Only Jefferson and Franklin approached Adams in intellect and education. Adams assumed the presidency at the age of sixty-one-probably a little past his prime, even though he lived to the ripe age of ninety-one.

Adams' administration, although not without success, ultimately disappointed him. He was the only president, between 1789 and 1824, to serve just one term. His first mistake was to retain his predecessor's cabinet, which remained loyal to Washington and in some cases to Adams' personal enemy, Hamilton. By 1798 Oliver Wolcott, secretary of the treasury, and Benjamin Stoddert, secretary of the navy, a post created in that year, dominated the cabinet. Under Adams the secretaries exercised more power than previously because Adams was absent from the capital during one-fourth of his administration. While he was away, usually with Abigail at his farm in Quincy, Massachusetts, his cabinet performed his executive duties.

Undeclared War with France

Adams' great boast in his later years was that he kept the United States out of war, and he did so under the most trying circumstances. The French interpreted Jay's treaty as a British diplomatic victory and sought to neutralize America's power on the seas. By Adams' inauguration, the French had captured over 300 American ships. Moreover, Washington had recalled James Monroe, his minister to France, for being pro-French. When Washington had sent Charles C. Pinckney as a replacement, the French government refused to accept him, and later expelled him from the country. The seizures of American ships and the French diplomatic insult enraged many Federalists, who followed Hamilton in clamoring for war. Adams believed the new republic was unprepared for war. Resisting his party's urging, he sought compromise and sent Federalists Pinckney and John Marshall and Republican Elbridge Gerry to negotiate with the French Foreign Minister Talleyrand. The French minister kept the delegation waiting for ten days and then offered to talk to them only after they paid a bribe of $240,000. Thoroughly insulted, the Americans refused, sent a report to Adams, and all but Gerry left France in a huff.

When Adams received the papers early in 1798 they placed him in a quandary. If he made the information public, the nation would certainly be aroused for war, but if he kept it a secret, he could make no headway toward negotiating a peace. Finally in March, under Republican pressures to make the information public, he relented and released the documents to Congress but omitted the names of Talleyrand's go-betweens, simply calling them X, Y, and Z. The predictable public outcry, in the wake of the "X, Y, Z Affair," nearly precipitated war. Congress hurried to put the country on a war footing, called Washington out of retirement to lead the army, named Hamilton his second in command, established the Navy Department, and abruptly terminated all treaties with France. But Adams stopped short of formal war. Instead, the United States conducted an "undeclared war" against France on the world's oceans between 1798 and 1800.

Adams eventually achieved the peace he so desired, but at high personal and political cost. Against the wishes of his party, he sent more commissioners to France to negotiate the Convention of 1800 that formally ended the 1778 treaty. The United States government agreed to reimburse American shipowners who had suffered losses to French raiders. With characteristic speed, the American government finally settled these French "spoilation" claims 115 years later. Adams' insistence on peace angered members of his own party who demanded a declared war. The division was so serious that he had to shake up his cabinet in 1800, removing his secretary of war and secretary of state. In his last year in office Adams went through four secretaries of war. Adams' determination to avoid war with France, ultimately, cost him reelection.

Domestic Problems

Adams also suffered much vilification in the press. Washington, at least, had a heroic reputation to shield him from the more vicious personal criticism. Adams lacked such protection. The Republican press delighted in attacking the "blind, bald, toothless" Adams whom it described as "a ruffian deserving the curses of mankind," and even more uncharitably, "foremost in whatever is detestable." The irate Adams and other Federalists quickly noted that many of these editors had come as refugees from France and joined the political opposition. Because of the undeclared war, public sentiment against France presented the Federalists with a golden opportunity to muzzle some of their worst critics.

In 1798 the Federalist majority in Congress united and pushed through a series of resolutions designed to destroy the Republican Party. Adams, the old revolutionary, supported these Alien and Sedition Acts. The Naturalization Act, the first of the four resolutions, raised the residency requirement from five to fourteen years for citizenship, the two alien acts authorized the president to deport any dangerous aliens and in time of war to arrest, imprison, or expel any alien suspected of working for the enemy. The Sedition Act was a catch-all, providing fines and imprisonment for persons convicted of "any false, scandalous, and malicious writing," that brought the United States government, congress, or the president into disrepute. After its passage federal marshals arrested about seventy people, almost all Republican newspaper editors. In front of kangaroo courts presided over by federal judges—

some of whom harangued juries with the Federalist Party line—the editors were denied even the semblance of a fair hearing. Even elected federal officeholders were not immune. Congressman Matthew Lyon, a Republican from Vermont, received a four-month jail term under the Sedition Act. While behind bars, Lyon won reelection to Congress.

Adams allowed his temper and his sensitivity to criticism to overrule his better instincts. It cost him his political career and his party's future. Jefferson and Madison used the acts as an election issue in 1800. Jefferson penned an essay, later adopted by the Kentucky state legislature, that upheld the idea that the states retained all powers not specifically delegated to the federal government. Madison wrote a similar resolve passed by the Virginia legislature. Denouncing the Alien and Sedition Acts, the "Kentucky and Virginia Resolves" argued that the states possessed the authority to judge the constitutionality of federal legislation and nullify it within state borders if they deemed it unconstitutional. An extreme statement of states' rights principles, the Kentucky and Virginia Resolves became the constitutional cornerstones of subsequent states' rights theories including John C. Calhoun's theory of nullification and southern secession in 1860-61.

The Election of 1800

Using the Kentucky and Virginia resolutions as a political rallying cry, Republicans renominated Jefferson and Burr in 1800. The Federalists were so badly split over policy and personality differences between Hamilton and Adams, they failed to muster a caucus to select nominees. By default Adams and Charles C. Pinckney carried the party's colors. Hamilton's private attacks on Adams, however, became public knowledge during the campaigning when Burr intercepted one of Hamilton's circular letters that attacked the president and published it. Hamilton's pique resulted from his own political decline and his anger that Adams did not uphold the national honor by striking harder at the hated French. In the background Hamilton again schemed to make Pinckney president, this time by persuading an elector to destroy an Adams' ballot to give Pinckney one more vote than the president. Hamilton's intrigues went for naught, however, as Jefferson and Burr won with seventy-three electoral votes each. The tie vote between the Republican candidates sent the election into the Federalist controlled house of representatives. The Federalists in the house opted for Burr. Hamilton, however, had long been Burr's bitter political enemy in New York and considered Jefferson the lesser of two evils. Ironically, after a long wrangle and thirty-six ballots Hamilton used his influence to break the deadlock and elect his arch-antagonist Thomas Jefferson as the third president of the United States. To prevent a repetition of such a tie, an amendment to the Constitution ratified in 1804 required electors to cast their votes specifically for a presidential and vice presidential candidate.

The election of 1800 was a milestone in the republic's odyssey. It marked the first time that the reins of power passed from the party in power to its political opposition, an accomplishment achieved under the strain of a deadlocked election, and in a congress controlled by the losing party. Most critically, it had all taken place without violence, setting an unbreakable precedent for the future. Since Washington's first election in 1788, every four years, without fail, in peace and in war, American voters have cast their presidential ballots. Even during the Civil War, Abraham Lincoln faced American voters. In retrospect, the peaceful transfer of power might be the American founders' greatest legacy to subsequent generations.

Federalists' Decline

Bitter over his defeat, Adams, in his last official act, filled a host of newly created federal judgeships with faithful Federalists. These "midnight appointments" were so called because he signed the appointments until midnight on his last day in office. The most important was Adams' selection of his secretary of state, John Marshall, as chief justice of the United States. Marshall, a die-hard Federalist and Jefferson's cousin, held his seat for over thirty-four years, and although his party never regained the presidency—indeed it was extinct at his death—Marshall interpreted the Constitution according to Federalist notions of centralized government, economic development, and implied powers.

The Federalist Party, though short-lived, served the young nation well. It laid a firm foundation for the republican experiment. When their country was weakest, party leaders wisely steered a neutral course through the warring European nations, never risking its existence over questions of national pride. It was a difficult task, especially because American ships were vulnerable at sea. These diplomatic successes, however, were offset by domestic blunders. Out of touch with the mood and desires of most voters, the party tore itself apart with internal power struggles after Washington retired in 1797. Neither the Adams faction nor the Hamiltonians fully understood Americans' aspirations for a better life nor their bitter hatred of the British empire and aristocratic rule. The Jeffersonians were much better attuned to those feelings. Moreover, the Federalists, mainly a party of established wealth, mercantile interests, and northeastern sectional interests, lost political power in the early nineteenth century when the country's population and wealth shifted south and west due to the cotton revolution made possible by Eli Whitney's invention of the cotton gin. The Federalists' insistence on a strong central government hurt the party in a time of rapid western expansion when new states demanded control over their own affairs. After the Federalists lost power on the national level, however, they became the champions of states' rights and regional interests. Conversely, the Republicans, once in control of the central government, abandoned their extreme states' rights position. By 1815 the Federalist Party had all but disappeared, and all political factions belonged to a single party. Washington would have been pleased. Unfortunately, from his perspective, it was not his party.

The Revolution of 1800

Jefferson described his election in 1800 as the second American Revolution. "The revolution of 1800," he said later "was as real a revolution in the principles of government as that of 1776 was in its form." He was wrong. In his inaugural speech he proudly proclaimed that "We are all Republicans, we are all Federalists," but Jefferson had spent a decade in opposition to the Federalists, during which time he had put forth a political philosophy at variance with Federalist principles. When he assumed power in March 1801, he amended his strict constructionist, states' rights constitutional principles. The only Federalist legislation he repealed was the Naturalization Act. The Alien and Sedition Acts merely expired.

When Jefferson could finally do something about them, he hardly touched Hamilton's fiscal programs. Jefferson's secretary of the treasury, Albert Gallatin, a more extreme states' rights man than the president, contented himself with abolishing Hamilton's excise taxes, paring government expenditures, and reducing the national debt. Gallatin even strengthened the detested Bank of the United States by establishing branches throughout the country. Still, Jefferson smarted under his inability to dismantle Hamilton's programs. He lamented to a friend, "It mortifies me to be strengthening principles which I deem radically vicious, but this vice is entailed on us by the first error. What is practicable must often control what is pure theory." Hamilton's programs had proven most practical. Jefferson did little more than tinker with the existing federal financial structure. He did, however, try to undo Federalist control of the federal courts, guaranteed by Adams' "midnight appointments," none more annoying to Jefferson than John Marshall's.

"Marbury vs. Madison"

Just before he left office, Adams had tried to ensure that Jefferson would have little leeway by appointing Marshall, the new president's cousin, as chief justice. Marshall, determined to check what he considered his kinsman's erroneous political principles, soon came into conflict with Jefferson. In 1803, in the case of *Marbury vs. Madison*, the chief justice revealed a political shrewdness that enabled him to shape the constitutional system nearly as much as the constitutional convention had done. The case arose after congress repealed the Federal Judiciary Act of 1801 under which Adams had made his midnight appointments. The Federalists howled that the repeal was unconstitutional because judges served for life and claimed that the supreme court had the right to review all congressional acts. A chance to settle this issue arose when one of Adams' appointees, William Marbury, failed to receive his com-

John Marshall was appointed by President John Adams as chief justice of the supreme court where he sat for thirty-four years, long after his Federalist Party had disappeared. Marshall made his court the equal of the other two branches of government. (1990)

mission from Madison, the new secretary of state. Marbury asked the supreme court for a writ of mandamus that ordered Madison to deliver the document. If the court held against the new administration by ordering the writ, Marshall feared that Jefferson would ignore the ruling and publicize the court's lack of enforcement powers. To avoid a confrontation, Marshall's court ruled that it had no power to issue the writ, although paragraph 13 of the Judiciary Act of 1789 had expressly given the court such authority, a paragraph that Marshall declared was unconstitutional. This was the first time that the court had declared an act of congress unconstitutional, and it did not do so again for fifty-four years until the controversial Dred Scott decision. But in *Marbury v. Madison* the Marshall court established an unequivocal precedent for judicial review in federal case law.

While the court reviewed Marbury's case, Jefferson intensified his attacks on the Federalist judiciary by invoking the Constitution's impeachment clause against obnoxiously partisan judges. The administration gathered evidence against John Pickering, a federal district judge in New Hampshire, and the house of representatives voted impeachment. The senate convicted Pickering, an insane alcoholic, removing him from the federal bench in March 1804. Encouraged by this success, Jefferson went after Samuel Chase on the supreme court. The house, at Jefferson's suggestion, set up a committee to investigate Chase's conduct on the bench and, on the committee's recommendation, voted impeachment. A competent, if wildly partisan judge, Chase had sentenced a number of Republicans to jail under the Alien and Sedition acts. The senate tried and narrowly acquitted Chase. After the trial many Republicans concluded that further attempts to purge the judiciary would not succeed. Marshall, the main Republican target, could breath more easily. The federal judiciary survived the first serious of attacks on its integrity and emerged from the ordeal strengthened. After Pickering, congress impeached no more federal judges, assuring in the future a strong and independent federal judiciary.

Foreign Affairs

Like earlier presidents, Jefferson devoted an inordinate amount of his time to foreign affairs. His initial problems came from a new quarter—the Barbary Coast where in 1801 the Pasha of Tripoli demanded large tribute payments for trading privileges. The president refused and the North African potentate declared war on the United States. Jefferson, who had slashed naval appropriations in 1802, found himself engaged in a naval war a quarter of the way around the world. He increased American strength in the Mediterranean Sea so that by 1803 the American fleet was strong enough to take offensive action. Lieutenant Stephan Decatur led a daring raid on Tripoli in which he boarded the captured American frigate, *Philadelphia*, and burned it. The war ended in a stalemate in 1805 when the Pasha threatened to kill all his American captives unless the United States paid a $60,000 ransom. Commodore Samuel Barron paid the ransom and negotiated a peace treaty in which the United States agreed to resume paying tribute for the privilege of trading in the area. The bribes continued until 1816 when Decatur and his fleet sailed back to the Mediterranean and forced the Barbary states to renounce the practice.

Louisiana Purchase

A similar expansionist effort, this one destined for greater success, involved the purchase of the territory of Louisiana. The origins of the Louisiana Purchase were deeply embedded in European power politics. This huge territory, deeded to Spain in 1762, reverted to France in 1800 in two secret treaties. Napoleon, the First Consul of France, dreamed of reestablishing the French empire in North America. When Jefferson learned of the secret treaties in 1801 he became alarmed. Fearful of a powerful

French empire at America's back door, he warned that if Napoleon took New Orleans, "We must marry ourselves to the British fleet and nation." To avoid that eventuality, Jefferson offered to purchase a tract of land on the lower Mississippi River or to nego-

tiate for permanent American use of the river. These deliberations dragged on for almost a year until Jefferson boldly offered to buy New Orleans and West Florida for up to ten million dollars. The president dispatched James Monroe to Paris with the new offer.

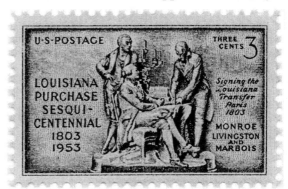

Before Monroe arrived, however, French plans for the new world had changed. Slaves in French Haiti, led by Toussaint L'Overture, had successfully revolted in 1794, and by 1803 France had lost all chance of suppressing the revolution. Without a safe French port in

To purchase Louisiana, President Thomas Jefferson had to violate his major political principles of minimal government and strict interpretation of the constitution. His two representatives, James Monroe, later president and Robert R. Livingston, American Ambassador to France in 1803, exceeded their instructions from Jefferson when they signed the transfer with Barbe-Marbois, Napoleon's finance minister. (1953)

the Caribbean and faced with a resumption of the war with Britain, Napoleon decided to sell all of Louisiana to raise sorely needed money. He sent foreign minister Talleyrand to ask the astonished American minister, Robert Livingston, how much the United States would pay for the whole territory. On his arrival, Monroe agreed to buy the parcel for about fifteen million dollars. For that small sum, the United States doubled its territory, added almost 828,000 square miles, and pushed its borders across the Mississippi River and up to the Rocky Mountains and to the Canadian border.

Jefferson had no constitutional right to purchase new territories. The president, who always had insisted that the constitution should be strictly interpreted, was embarrassed by his predicament. He toyed with amending the constitution to allow the purchase, but feared that it would take too long and that Napoleon might change his mind. Choosing practicality over principle, Jefferson adopted the Hamiltonian concept of implied powers and argued that the constitution allowed him to make treaties and thus, implicitly, gave him authority to acquire territories. When Jefferson called congress into special session in 1803 to ratify his purchase, the Federalists took the unaccustomed position that the Constitution should be interpreted strictly. The senate approved the purchase on October 20, leaving Jefferson the lifelong task of rationalizing his actions.

Exploring the West

Long before the "noble bargain," as Jefferson called it, the president had supported plans for exploring the West. The president, who had a scientific bent of mind, was fascinated by the Indians and the flora and fauna of the American wilderness. In fact, he was captivated by the exotic everywhere. Back in 1786 he had supported "Mad John" Ledyard, an American who planned to start in Moscow and walk around the world. Unfortunately, the Cossack police picked up Mad John at the start of his journey and shipped him home. Later Jefferson had helped finance André Michaux's planned walk across the American continent. Michaux started out, but fell in with Edmond Genêt, and never made it even to the Mississippi River.

Jefferson's abiding interest in exploration persisted, and in 1803 he asked congress for a secret appropriation to fund a western expedition to cultivate the friendship of the Indians and to expand trade. Congress complied, and with the Louisiana Purchase the expedition provided an opportunity to survey what the president had bought. To lead the party, Jefferson chose his personal secretary and fellow Virginian, Meriwether Lewis, who selected William Clark, the younger brother of the famous Indian fighter George Rogers Clark, as his co-leader. In the spring of 1804, with less than fifty men, the party set out along the Missouri River. They followed the Missouri northward and crossed the Rocky Mountains, guided by Sacajawea, the Indian wife of a French fur trader. After descending the Snake and Columbia rivers, on October 7, 1805, Lewis and Clark reached the Pacific Ocean. It took the party another year to return with their wealth of information on the Indians and resources of the region. Lewis and Clark whetted American curiosity about the West and proved that an overland route to the Pacific was feasible and relatively safe. In 1806 Jefferson sent explorer Zebulon Pike to explore the Arkansas River. Pike traveled as far west as the peak that bears his name, but he failed to climb it. More than any other explorer, Pike convinced Americans that the Southwest was a "Great American Desert," an American Mongolia, best left to the Indians.

Hamilton and Burr

Many eastern politicians feared that new states carved from the Louisiana Purchase would dilute the political power of the coastal states. To avoid that eventuality Federalist Senator Timonthy Pickering led a coalition of New England leaders, the Essex Junto, in calling for the formation of a new independent confederation. If their confederation was to survive, Junto leaders realized, they needed New York. In 1804 they approached Hamilton for his support, but he turned them down. They then turned to Hamilton's old adversary, Vice President Aaron Burr, who had

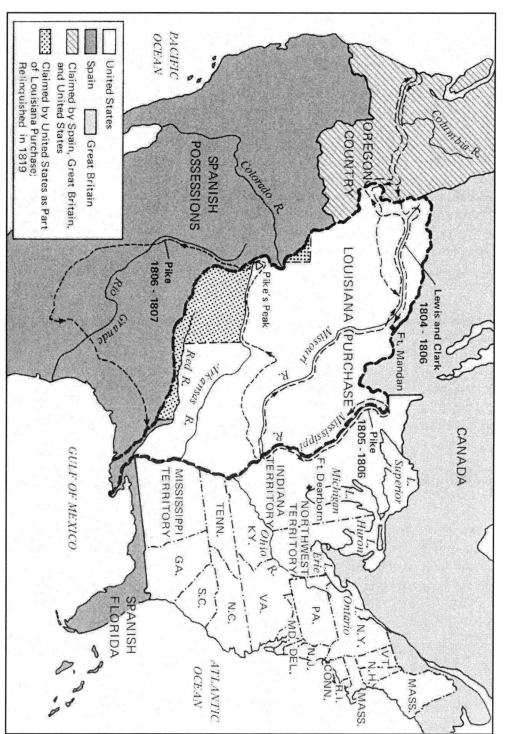

The Louisiana Purchase, 1803

broken with Jefferson and who was running for the governorship of New York. Burr needed Federalist support in the state and apparently agreed to support secession in return for their aid. Hamilton canvassed against Burr in the campaign, accused him of treason, and called his moral character into doubt. Burr lost by a wide margin and challenged Hamilton to a duel to avenge his honor. Hamilton accepted. His political career had waned for a decade, especially after he publicly had admitted to an affair with a married woman. On the morning of July 11, 1804, Hamilton and Burr met on Weehawken Island across the Hudson River from New York City. There Burr shot Hamilton who died the next day from loss of blood.

When Hamilton died, Burr had returned to the capitol to preside over the senate. After New Jersey and New York both indicted Burr for murder, he could not return home. His career destroyed, the brilliant but erratic Burr became involved in a series of mysterious plots in the American Southwest. Before leaving Washington, he approached the British minister with a plan to detach western territory from the United States in return for a half a million dollars. The British spurned the offer. Burr then befriended General James Wilkinson, Jefferson's military governor of the Louisiana Territory, a man in the pay of the Spanish. Burr's intentions remain unclear. Some thought Burr wanted to separate the Southwest from the United States and establish himself as the new country 's leader, although evidence also existed that he plotted to invade Spanish territory and claim it for the United States. Whatever his plans, on February 19, 1807, Burr was captured near Wakefield, Alabama, and returned to Richmond to await trial for treason.

Crowds in the Virginia capital greeted Burr as a hero. His jail cell was left unlocked, and he received many admirers, including numerous women. Burr's trial in Richmond developed into a struggle between the presiding chief justice John Marshall and the president. Jefferson badly wanted Burr convicted, but Marshall interpreted the constitution's treason clause in a manner that made it almost impossible to secure a conviction. Marshall ruled that there had to have been two eyewitnesses to Burr's alleged treasonous act. No one had seen him commit anything so he won his freedom. After a lifetime of adventures, Burr died peacefully in bed at age eighty.

Jefferson Fights to Stay Out of War

With Burr off the national ticket in 1804, Jefferson handily won over his Federalist opponent, Charles C. Pinckney. During his second term, Jefferson had to contend with threatening conditions in Europe. The Napoleonic Wars had resumed in 1803, and the United States became embroiled again in conflicts on the high seas.

European power had slipped into a simple, two-way wartime struggle that pitted France and her reluctant continental allies against England. Napoleon commanded Europe's most powerful land army and dominated the continent while England, with its huge navy, controlled the seas. By 1806 the two giants glared at one another across the English Channel.

As a neutral power, the United States had the right under international law to trade with both belligerents, but neither Britain nor France would willingly allow non-belligerents to supply their enemy. So, both violated American neutral rights. Initially, American vessels suffered greater indignities at the hands of the English. In 1805 Britain invoked the "continuous voyage" doctrine, which declared that unless an American captain could show that he intended to end his voyage in an American port and not reship to a belligerent country, his ship and cargo would be confiscated. This was almost impossible to prove, enabling British ships promiscuously to seize American ships engaged in the French West Indies trade. Jefferson retaliated with a mild form of economic warfare. In 1806 congress passed the first Nonimportation Act that specified a long list of goods which Americans could not import from Britain.

The United States' position became increasingly difficult when Britain declared a blockade of Europe and Napoleon placed the British Isle under a similar blockade and authorized French ships to stop and seize all vessels and cargo bound for the islands. Jefferson tried desperately to protect American rights short of war. In late 1806 he unsuccessfully negotiated with Britain to end ship seizures and the impressment of American seamen into the royal navy. The following year the war of the blockades intensified. The British retaliated against the French blockade with orders-in-council that prohibited all trade to any continental port where the British Union Jack was excluded unless such vessels had first passed through British ports, paid English customs duties, and obtained new clearances to sail. In short, contrary to international law, the British sought to control and tax the continental trade of all neutral nations. Napoleon countered by warning all neutral vessels that complied with the British orders-in-council that they would be subject to French seizure as British property.

As the war of words raged, in 1807, the British stepped up their campaign against American vessels. His Majesty's frigate, *Leopard*, hailed the United States ship *Chesapeake* off Norfolk Roads, a few miles outside of American territorial waters. The *Leopard* demanded to search the *Chesapeake* for four suspected British deserters. The American captain refused, and the British ship raked the American vessel with broadsides which killed or wounded about twenty sailors. The *Leopard* then boarded the *Chesapeake* and took off the four alleged deserters. When the *Chesapeake* limped back to port, public reaction was violent. Jefferson ordered all British warships out of American waters and started negotiations with the British demanding an indemnity for damages and national humiliation.

The Embargo

Jefferson had few options. He could declare war against one of the world's two major powers, accept the illegal violations of American neutrality, or retaliate in some nonbelligerent manner. He chose the latter course. At his request, Congress passed the 1807 Embargo Act that prohibited all United States vessels, except for coastal ships, to leave port. Because foreign ships could not carry cargoes out of American ports, international trade ceased.

Many Americans smuggled goods to the British, particularly through Canada, undercutting the embargo. Moreover, Britain imported most of its needs from elsewhere while some Englishmen even applauded an act that ended American shipping competition. The French were not hurt either. They simply declared all American vessels that appeared in continental ports illegal and seized them. The United States was the only country hurt by the embargo. Federal customs revenues plummeted. Merchants, shipping interests, and seamen all protested against a policy that brought widespread economic distress to the coastal cities. Commerce was prostrate, ships rotted in the harbors, thousands were imprisoned for debts, and the nation teetered on the brink of an economic breakdown. Jefferson's own popularity sank. An angry citizen wrote the president, "You infernal villain. . . How much longer are you going to keep this damned Embargo on to starve us poor people?"

Protest against the embargo rapidly became political and sectional. Angry Republicans in New England joined forces with the Federalists in the state elections of 1808, giving the Federalists a new voice in local politics. State legislatures, especially in the coastal areas, debated the rights of states to "interdict" or deny the authority of the federal government when it acted against the people's interest. Although a federal judge upheld the constitutionality of the embargo in 1808, Jefferson belatedly relented. During the last week of his administration he signed the Non-Intercourse Act that repealed the embargo against all nations except Britain and France and stipulated that the president could resume trade with those two powers when they agreed to respect American neutral rights.

In 1808 Jefferson's loss of popularity was severe, but not enough to prevent the election of his hand-picked successor. James Madison and James Monroe both sought the president's endorsement for the nomination. Jefferson finally chose secretary of state Madison, the elder of the two, telling Monroe it would be his turn eight years later. Madison was nominated by the Republican caucus and easily defeated his Federalist opponent Charles C. Pinckney. By 1808 a line of succession for the presidency had developed. The office of secretary of state had become the stepping stone to the executive office. Jefferson had served as Secretary of State under Washington and Madison under Jefferson.

The departing president returned to his mountain top estate "Monticello" where, until his death sixteen years later, he played the role of an elder statesman for the young republic. Jefferson's presidency had been anti-climatic. Always at his best in the role of an ideologue, especially in opposition, Jefferson's most important accomplishments—the Declaration of Independence, his foreign service, and terms as secretary of state—occurred before he had reached the White House. Once there he discovered that precedents and circumstances circumscribed his actions. As a consequence, his policies differed little from those of Washington and Adams. The narrow issues of political partisanship, in which Jefferson excelled, paled before the importance of avoiding European entanglements.

The War of 1812

James Madison, little "Jemmy," brought to the White House his small and impressive credentials. A brilliant political philosopher and legislator, Madison had been the most active delegate to the Constitutional Convention and wrote twenty-nine of *The Federalist Papers*. An inordinately shy man, and a hypochondriac, he was afflicted with epilepsy-like attacks from a nervous disorder. Like other founding fathers, Madison took an active interest in western land speculations, sometimes clouding the distinction between his public and private affairs.

Madison was not a president of the caliber of his predecessors. Unlike Jefferson, he could not withstand the strong forces that impelled the United States toward European conflicts. Madison even walked blindly into a diplomatic trap cleverly laid by Napoleon. Jefferson's Non-Intercourse Act was scheduled to expire in 1811, and congress had passed Macon's Bill Number Two a year earlier. It empowered the president to reopen trade with Britain or France if either ceased harassing American vessels. Napoleon led Madison to believe that he had withdrawn his blockade, although he had not. Madison opened trade with France and continued the embargo against Britain. The British responded with a blockade of New York City and increased their impressment of American seamen.

A New Political Generation

As a tide of indignation against Britain rose in the United States, a political revolution occurred that pushed the United States into war. The old revolutionary generation of politicians was aging, and in the elections of 1810 and 1812, new men appeared who led the nation for the next forty years. Two of the new generation's most important figures, Henry Clay of Kentucky and John Calhoun of South Carolina, took their seats in the 1810 Congress. Their colleagues elected young Clay speaker while Calhoun garnered the recognition his ego demanded and his razor-sharp mind deserved. Two years later Daniel Webster of Massachusetts joined them. The three men became the spokesmen for their respective regions.

But in 1810 they were all nationalists and in a belligerent mood. Dubbed the "war hawks," Clay, Calhoun, and their new colleagues dominated the congressional committees and prodded Madison to war. Many of the young war hawks hailed from rural western and southern areas not directly affected by impressment or the embargo, although, many farmers blamed low crop prices on the loss of British and French markets. What excited the political novices most was the prospect for American territorial expansion into Canada and Spanish Florida if hostilities broke out. To prepare for the coming conflict, congress passed a spate of bills in 1811 and 1812 that expanded the army and the navy, putting the country on a war footing.

Madison Asks for War

Madison responded to the rising clamor for war with a message to congress on June 1, 1812, that asked for war with Great Britain. His timing seemed odd. America's international position in 1812, if anything, had improved. But Madison was no Jefferson; facing reelection, he had little control over congress or his own party and his personal popularity had plummeted. Madison responded to the public's demand to vindicate America's honor and to political pressure in his own party, ignoring the enormous risks that a war with Britain entailed. The militant house quickly passed the resolution seventy-nine to forty-nine, but the senate debated for several weeks. Federalist senators accused Madison of pro-French tendencies and even offered an amendment to include France in the declaration of war, a proposal that failed by the surprisingly close vote of eighteen to fourteen. Finally on June 17, the upper house voted war with Britain by nineteen to thirteen.

Not only was the timing of Madison's war message odd, his argument and the subsequent congressional vote raised intriguing questions about the war. In hindsight, the justifications for war appeared contrived. Madison listed four reasons for war: British impressment of American seamen; British raids into American territorial waters to seize ships, cargoes, and men; the orders-in-council that prevented American goods from entering continental markets, ignoring similar action by France; and British manipulation of Indians on America's frontiers. Madison overlooked more active Indians along the Spanish border. As an afterthought, Madison observed that the United States might just as well go to war with France, except that an American minister was in France at the time seeking redress. The arguments in favor of war in Congress were loudest among representatives from the South, Southwest, and West and rural areas in all the states. The anti-war votes came from the maritime sections of the Northeast and the commercial centers in the Middle Atlantic states. These areas had suffered most from the British depredations that Madison had cited in his war message—impressment, blockade, and commercial war—yet they voted against the war. Representatives from these areas realized that their regions would suffer directly if war with Britain occurred. The rural areas, though nearly untouched by the British violations of American neutral rights, longed for territorial expansion into Canada and exhibited a growing sense of national honor. Moreover they were angry and frustrated over the agricultural depression that they erroneously blamed on the British rather than Jefferson's disastrous embargo. And, the war offered them an opportunity to destroy the remaining Indian groups in the Northwest and Louisiana Territories. Having secured congressional approval, on June 19, Madison declared war on Britain. Three days earlier England had announced the suspension of its orders-in-council. Had it come sooner, it might have answered many of Americans' professed grievances against Britain and, perhaps forestalled war.

Preparedness for War

Despite the swaggering congressional speeches, the United States was woefully unprepared for the war of 1812. Congress had allowed the charter for the Bank of the United States to lapse in 1811, leaving the country without central banking facilities and making it difficult for the government to raise funds. To finance the war, secretary of

Abraham Alfonse Albert Gallatin served as secretary of the treasury from 1801 until 1814. Although he attacked Hamilton's fiscal programs, when in the treasury he did nothing to end them. His adroit financial accounting during the War of 1812 and the British capture of Washington, D.C. in 1814 left the United States bankrupt for the only time in its history. (1967)

the treasury Gallatin kept two sets of books. He funded normal government expenses from tariff income and borrowed to pay for the war. Gallatin issued eighty-six million dollars in notes, but they sold at heavy discounts because, until 1813, he refused to raise taxes to fund the obligations. A postwar investigation revealed that the $86 million in loans netted only thirty-four million dollars in specie, a discount of over sixty percent. By 1814 the government found itself bankrupt and without credit. Moreover, when the war broke out, congress had not yet appropriated money to expand the army and navy, and few rushed to enlist when it did. Madison issued a call for 50,000 one-year volunteers. Only 5,000 responded. The regular peacetime army was in miserable shape and badly led. Many officers were Revolutionary War veterans, whom General Winfield Scott described as having "very generally sunk into either sloth, ignorance, or habits of intemperate drinking." Worse, the country was badly divided over the war. New Englanders were hostile toward "Mr. Madison's war," and on occasion even sold supplies to the enemy.

The British also evinced little enthusiasm for the war. The continental struggles had taxed their resources. Fortunately, for the United States, the war in the Western Hemisphere remained only a secondary theater for the English. Moreover, the British did not want to fight 3,000 miles away on terrain unsuited to European military tactics. And Canada, with its small population and long border, was difficult to defend from an American invasion.

The War

The United States, uncertain of its war aims, had trouble devising a sound military strategy. Madison's message had not mentioned Canada, and yet, despite serious domestic objections, the United States struck there first. The Canadian venture only served to increase sectional antagonisms. Westerners supported the invasion but did not want troops withdrawn from the western Indian frontier to fight in Canada. New England was the logical base of operations for such an invasion, but its citizens refused to cooperate and withheld militia support. The southerners wanted to concentrate only on assaulting Spanish Florida. Nevertheless, the army mounted a clumsy, three-pronged invasion of British Canada that petered out because of inept leadership, defeats, and refusals by militia men to leave home.

At sea, American success was mixed. The forty-four-gun frigate *Constitution* defeated the British ship *Java* in December 1812, earning the name "Old Ironsides" when its stout oak planking repelled the *Java*'s shot. American privateers roamed the oceans harassing British merchantmen, sometimes within sight of the English coast. By 1813, however, the British had confined the United States navy to its home ports. After 1813 American naval successes were on the Great Lakes. In the fall of 1813 Oliver Hazard Perry with a homemade fleet constructed at Erie, Pennsylvania, soundly defeated the British lake fleet at Put in Bay, Ohio.

Control of the Great Lakes made possible another invasion of Canada from Detroit to rout the British and break Indian resistance in the area. Just before the war broke out, the Shawnee chief Tecumseh and his brother, the Prophet, had attempted to create a tribal confederation, sweeping down from Canada into the Southeast, to stop the encroachment of American settlers onto their ancestral lands. Tecumseh, a great native political talent, and his brother, a religious mystic, almost succeeded. In 1811, however, General William Henry Harrison, governor of the Indiana Territory, led about 1,000 men against Tecumseh, surprising the Indians at Tippecanoe near Lafayette, Indiana. The results were inconclusive; both Harrison and the Indians withdrew. Americans, however, proclaimed the battle of Tippecanoe a great victory. When the War of 1812 started, Tecumseh allied with the British in the hope that the peace treaty would recognize three North American nations, British Canada, the United States, and an Indian Nation.

In 1813 Harrison again led American troops out of Detroit to battle Tecumseh and the British. In October Harrison met them on the banks of the Thames River where he decisively defeated the British and killed Tecumseh. With Tecumseh's death, the dream of a great western Indian confederation died. The Indian and British allies fared little better in the South, where an American army under Andrew Jackson, a famed Indian fighter, defeated the Creeks. The southern Indian campaign culminated in March 1814 at Horseshoe Bend, Tennessee, where Jackson's men exterminated a Creek encampment of men, women, and children. At Horseshoe Bend 557 Creek died, most in their sleep. Jackson lost only 55 soldiers. During the War of 1812, Harrison and Jackson swept the Mississippi Valley clean of Indian peoples.

In 1814 the British took the offensive following Napoleon's abdication and the end of fighting in Europe. Britain's major success occurred in the Chesapeake Bay region. Disembarking on August 19, the British forces pushed the American defenders back on Washington. After an American defeat on August 24, the government fled, and the British army entered the capital unopposed. Madison's wife, Dolly, was reported to have courageously saved the paintings in the White House from British marauders. For two days the British burned everything in sight—the Capitol, the White House, and all the government buildings except the patent office—then withdrew and pushed on to Baltimore. The capital's loss was a bitter psychological blow to the American cause, but because it lacked strategic value, its capture signified little. Washington was not a commercial, financial, or manufacturing center, and the small American government could perform adequately enough almost anywhere, even on horseback. And in the long term, Americans turned the Chesapeake invasion into a proud historical moment. Watching the burning of Baltimore from a distance, "At the dawn's early light," Francis Scott Key, noted "how proudly" the Star Spangled Banner "yet waved," inspiring his composition that later became the national anthem.

The last battle of the war was the most famous. The British wanted to control the lower Mississippi River up to New Orleans to choke off American western trade. When Jackson learned the British intentions, he rushed his army of about 5,000 men to New Orleans and threw up breastworks in a dry canal bed. Behind them he positioned his army composed of frontiersmen, blacks, creoles, and a few pirates, to await the redcoats behind piled up bales of cotton. On January 8, 1815, after a furious artillery barrage, General Edward Pakenham twice led his massed troops against Jackson's well protected defensive positions. The British suffered a humiliating defeat, leaving 2,000 dead and wounded, including Pakenham. Jackson lost only twenty-one men, killed or wounded, in one of the most lopsided victories in military history. Neither general realized, however, that the war had ended two weeks earlier and thus the battle had no impact on the Treaty of Ghent. Still, in American minds, Jackson and brave frontiersmen had mauled the mighty British once again, demonstrating the United States' unquestioned superiority, and in a stroke transforming a confused and humiliating war into a great patriotic moment for the young nation.

Treaty of Ghent

At the instigation of Czarist Russia, appalled by the war between two allies, peace negotiations were underway in Ghent, Belgium. The American delegation, made up of John Quincy Adams, Henry Clay, and two lessor lights, demanded satisfaction on the issues of impressment, blockades, ship seizures, and other infringements on American maritime neutrality. The British delegation, headed by Lord James Gambier, demanded territorial concessions along the Canadian border and the establishment of a neutral Indian buffer state south of the Great Lakes. The talks progressed and then stalemated as the military situation in the United States fluctuated. The turning-point came when the Duke of Wellington refused command of British forces in America. He advised his government that the loss of the Great Lakes made it almost impossible to win the war and undercut its demand for American territorial concessions. Foreign Minister Lord Robert Castlereagh, noting British war weariness, pressed by a mounting national debt and more important, diplomatic problems at the Congress of Vienna, moved to conclude peace with the Americans.

Initialed on Christmas Eve 1814, the Treaty of Ghent simply ended hostilities, exchanged prisoners, restored all occupied territory, and approved a commission to arbitrate the boundary dispute between the United States and Canada. Madison had asked for war to end impressment. It was not mentioned in the treaty, neither were his three other war aims, ship seizures, blockades, or peace with the Indians. The treaty simply restored the *status quo ante bellum*. The United States did not win the War of 1812, and by 1814 had lost all hope that it could. Given that the Battle of New Orleans lay in the future, American diplomats felt fortunate to have done so well. But England also had failed to win, and following the Battle of New Orleans, also felt fortunate to have done so well. Despite enormous provocation, the English never again risked war with the United States or challenged its domination of North America. The great losers of the War of 1812 were the native American peoples who could no longer play one white nation off against another. The Battles of Tippecanoe and Horseshoe Bend were but preludes to their systematic subjugation by white Americans. Within seventy-five years, every Indian group between Canada and Mexico would be soundly defeated and relegated to tribal reservations under federal supervision—step children of the federal government.

Repercussions of War

Even as the War of 1812 ended, new storms were brewing in the United States. Sectional unity, always fragile, had weakened during the war, particularly in New England. Not only did New England oppose the war, it had grown wealthy from the conflict. To encourage disloyalty, the British had not blockaded the region. Yankee traders took advantage of the opportunity to charge customers all over the country high prices for imported goods. While banks elsewhere suffered from a severe shortage of specie, New England banks quadrupled their deposits during the conflict. Yet, even in the face of war-time prosperity, New Englanders subscribed only paltry sums for Gallatin's war loans.

The sectional controversy became intensely political. As the last Federalist stronghold, New England forced the Federalists to take the blame for the region's antiwar sentiment. And if being tainted with treason were not enough, at the lowest point in American fortunes, Federalist-dominated legislatures in New England had elected delegates to a secret convention to revise the Constitution. Convened at Hartford, Connecticut, in December 1814, the Hartford Convention resolved to weaken the authority of the federal government, including the recognition of the right of states to deny any federal acts that infringed on the state's constitutional rights as determined by the state. The Hartford Convention created deep resentments outside New England. Moreover, the convention adjourned just as news of Jackson's great victory at New Orleans and of the treaty of Ghent spread across the country, undercutting the Federalist protest and hastening the party's demise.

Immediately following the war, the rest of the United States shared New England's economic boom. Poor European harvests and Britain's growing need for imported foodstuffs as it industrialized gave American farmers large and profitable European markets, particularly for wheat, corn, rice, and tobacco. High farm prices encouraged farmers to buy more land and drew droves of new settlers to the West and Southwest. Government land sales rose dramatically—3.5 million acres were sold in 1818—and brought desperately needed revenue into the national treasury. Even banks recovered quickly, especially in rural states where they offered loans to farmers and settlers buying new lands. Specie remained scarce in the rural areas, but paper bank scrip won ready acceptance even though most of it was backed only by a vault full of farm mortgages. Paper money expanded the currency and fueled the growing economy. As long as farm prices stayed up and farmers could meet their debts, scrip was a useful medium of exchange.

The South and the newly settled Southwest prospered more than other sections, thanks to cotton. Eli Whitney's cotton gin and its rapid adoption across the South enabled southern farmers profitably to grow short staple cotton, easily adapted to the climate of the Lower South. Cotton also fastened the institution of slavery securely on the South. The developing textile industry in the Northeast and in Britain created an insatiable demand for the "white gold," driving up its price as much as fifty percent during the immediate postwar years.

New England was further isolated when political leaders from the South and West allied to support the reestablishment of the national bank. The Republican Madison, who had bitterly opposed Hamilton's first bank charter, by 1816, had become an active supporter of the Bank of the United States. When Calhoun proposed a second bank in 1816, Clay supported it even though in 1811 he had argued that the bank was unconstitutional. Webster, however, came out against the new charter, thereby exactly reversing the sectional positions of 1791. Congress passed the bill, Madison signed it, and the Second Bank of the United States, operating under a twenty-year cherter, opened its doors January 1, 1817.

At first, New England merchants and manufacturers failed to share in the postwar boom. New England commercial interests faced renewed competition from British and French concerns, and the surplus of ships drove shipping rates and profits down. Budding manufacturing concerns suffered similar disabilities. The Embargo and Non-Importation acts had encouraged manufacturing in the United States as did the British blockade. Capital was diverted into manufacturing, especially the textile industry as production grew rapidly. At the war's end, however, cheap European goods flooded American markets driving many American manufacturers out of business. Such problems, however, proved short lived. Almost unnoticed at the time, Jefferson's embargo and the War of 1812 had provided American manufacturers and banks a protected economic environment in which they thrived and matured. By 1820 American manufacturers, merchants, and banks, still largely in New England and the Middle Atlantic states, stood second only to England in resources and expertise. Equally important, the nearly two decades of Napoleonic Wars had led to significant urbanization in the United States. In 1790 only about four percent of Americans lived in cities larger than 1500 people. By 1820 that had doubled in a country three times larger. This meant that, although the United States lacked a single, large city such as London, Paris, or Rome, when added together the populations of Baltimore, Philadelphia, New York, and Boston exceeded the population of Paris and Rome and approached London's. The cotton revolution in the slave states fueled northern urbanization which, in turn, transformed the Northeast and, in time, the Midwest, accentuating the already growing political division between the slave South and the free labor North.

Such momentous changes, however, had no noticeable effect on the 1816 presidential election. Upholding tradition, Madison declined to serve a third term and supported his secretary of state, James Monroe, in the party's nominating caucus. Within the party, opposition to Monroe arose from a faction of younger Republicans led by William H. Crawford of Georgia, a rising political figure. Monroe, however, won the caucus' nomination and easily defeated the Federalist nominee, Rufus King of New York. King carried only three states. He was the last presidential candidate fielded by the Federalists. After the election, a Boston newspaper editor celebrated the apparent end to party conflict by announcing that the "Era of Good Feelings" had arrived. The expression became a popular description for the one-party era of 1816 to 1824.

National Identity

The postwar boom and the growing sense of "good feelings" symbolized to many people the success of the American experiment in building and unifying a nation that only recently had been but a loose confederation of jealous states. Even as the Napoleonic Wars had isolated the United States economically, it also curtailed European immigration and the African slave trade. As a consequence, in the formative period following independence, the United States lost much of its ethnic and racial diversity. The English language became almost universally used, virtually all Americans were children of native-born Americans, Native Americans had disappeared from the eastern states, and the percentage of persons of African ancestry had declined. By 1820 an identifiable American ethnicity had formed that defined Americans as being of European ancestry, English in culture and language, and evangelical Protestant in religion. The new American nation was not simply a "white man's country," it had became white, Anglo-Saxon, and Protestant.

The fourth census, taken in 1820, revealed to everyone's amazement that the nation had tripled in population to 9.6 million people in just thirty years. And Americans lived longer. A male child born at Washington's first inauguration could expect to live 34.5 years. If he survived until age twenty, the odds then favored his living until fifty-four. Women lived longer by an average of a year and a half. Even slaves in the South lived longer and saw more of their children live to adulthood than was true of Europeans.

At the time, the medical profession claimed credit for the increased longevity. After the Revolution the practice of medicine evolved from a folk art into an academically-trained and certified profession. By the 1820s most of the larger cities across the country operated general hospitals staffed by male M.D.s, imitating the pattern set by Philadelphia in 1752. Formal medical education increasingly became the rule, starting at the College of Philadelphia in 1765. By 1810 at least seven other universities had opened medical schools, although, most doctors still learned the rudiments of healing by observing practicing physicians. Paradoxically, however, the professionalization of medicine led to higher, not lower, mortality rates, especially in child birth. Lacking a germ theory, physicians conducted surgery in unsanitary conditions, often not even washing their hands or instruments. Confident in their scientific training, they intervened when traditional practitioners, often midwives, wisely let nature take its course. As male doctors with medical degrees drove non-certified midwives out of American delivery rooms, maternity-related deaths increased substantially. Not until World War II, with the introduction of penicillin, did maternity-related deaths return to the lower pre-revolutionary rates when midwives delivered most infants.

There were a few beneficial medically-related advances, however. Small pox inoculations, which infected a patient with a mild case of the deadly disease, became common in the early nineteenth century and reduced the number of small pox deaths. Such techniques did not address the causes of the periodic epidemics, however, that swept the country prior to the Civil War; disease was brought in by ships from Europe and Asia and nurtured in the filthy conditions of American cities. In 1800 most American cities relied on pigs to eat the garbage, human waste, and horse manure left in the streets. Though pigs were effective, they also befouled the roads and sidewalks and occasionally ate small children. By mid-century city authorities had removed pigs and other free-running livestock from their streets. The most deadly disease that Americans faced following the revolution was cholera. In the antebellum years two cholera epidemics each killed nearly 25% of the people in the nation's eastern seaports. The severity of the epidemics led city authorities to improve the water supply and sewage disposal. Primarily, they carefully separated human sewage from the water supply, insuring clean and safe drinking water. This simple remedy ended the cholera epidemics and also reduced deaths caused by typhus and typhoid.

The vast majority of Americans in 1820 lived on farms in the older settled areas or rushed pellmell into the West to take advantage of cheap new land. By the fourth census, the number of states had swollen to twenty-three and part of the state of Louisiana, admitted in 1812, was west of the Mississippi River. Moreover, large numbers of Americans had already entered the new territories of Missouri and Arkansas across the river. The drive westward derived from two sources. By the end of the eighteenth century most land in the eastern states had been taken up by farmers in the Middle Atlantic and New England states and plantation agriculture in the South. With most American families bearing eight to ten children, each subsequent generation required twice as much land simply to maintain their parents' standard of living. The Ohio and Mississippi valleys enabled young white Americans to acquire enough land to sustain themselves and their offspring. At the same time, the expansion of cotton provided young, southwesterners a valuable money crop, opening the doors to the planter class. These new cotton plantations purchased much of their food and necessities from midwestern farmers and manufacturers, underwriting much of the cost of opening up the Midwest. Cotton, slavery, Indian removal, and westward expansion were integrally related. In a single generation the Northwest and Louisiana Territories made the transition from Indian country to settled agricultural communities, fueling the demand for further westward expansion.

Transportation

Vast transportation improvements aided the surging westward migration. Travel did not become a great deal easier or more comfortable, but for the first time it was at least possible. A "turnpike craze" that had begun during Washington's first term continued until superseded by a mania for canals about 1820. Most of the early turnpikes, such as the one completed between Philadelphia and Lancaster in 1794, were private corporate ventures that required travelers to pay tolls at gates along the way. The success of the Lancaster road led to the building of numerous other private roads in the eastern part of the country, but access to the more sparsely settled west had to await state or federal action. It came in 1807 when Albert Gallatin proposed a national transportation system that included a national road connecting the Potomac and the Ohio rivers. Construction on the national road began in 1811 at Cumberland, Maryland and ran to Wheeling, Virginia. Covered with crushed stone for most of the way—although some dishonest contractors even left the stumps in the road—the artery proved immediately popular. Small settlements grew up about twelve miles apart along the road, the distance a team could pull a heavy load, and many of them eventually grew into prosperous towns. Huge conestoga wagons, their high axle clearances perfect for passing over the stumps, plied the route with light freight of high value, because heavy, low-cost, bulk goods could still not be profitably shipped overland. Stagecoach lines, with colorfully attired drivers, vied to offer the fastest scheduled services; highway robbers also appeared and regularly separated passengers from their valuables. The great national road, completed to St. Louis by the Civil War, was routed forty miles south of the strategically located town of Pittsburgh to run across land owned by Gallatin. When the road later became U.S. Highway 40, travelers still had to detour to reach Pittsburgh.

Even as turnpike construction boomed, a radically new technology appeared. Improvements to the steam engine, especially Oliver Evan's development of the high pressure steam engine, created machines light enough for use in public transportation. One of the earliest promoters of a steamboat in the United States was John Fitch, who demonstrated a prototype of a steam powered paddle-boat at the Constitutional Convention. Robert Fulton, however, proved the practicality of such a vessel. In 1807 Fulton's boat, the *Clermont*, powered by a paddle wheel, raced up the Hudson from New York City and back at an average speed of five miles per hour. By 1811 a steamboat regularly worked the lower Mississippi River, and nine years later scheduled steamboat service existed on all the nation's major waterways. Speeds quickly increased to as high as twenty-five miles per hour downstream, and passenger fares dropped by one-half. Moreover, the steamboat helped to create new and important inland cities: Cincinnati, St. Louis, Louisville, Buffalo, and Cleveland. In 1824 the supreme court, in *Gibbons v. Ogden*, declared all navigable water fell under the federal government's exclusive authority to regulate interstate commerce, guaranteeing that this new technology would foster the national economy, unfettered by state regulation or private monopolies.

Canals

The ease and economy of water transportation encouraged landlocked cities and towns to construct their own waterways. Even during the height of the turnpike craze, a few small canals were dug; as early as 1793 a canal joined Boston with the Merrimack River, three years later a short waterway was opened to detour Little Falls in New York's Mohawk River. The Erie Canal, however, was the first large-

A 364 mile ditch, only forty feet wide and four feet deep, that connected Albany with Buffalo, New York, on Lake Erie, was designed, surveyed, and superintended by lawyers and dug mostly by Irishmen, and made New York City the foremost port in the new nation by 1825. (1967)

scale attempt to construct such a water course. Chartered as a state enterprise in 1817, when there were less than 100 miles of canal in the entire nation, it represented a dream of New York's Governor DeWitt Clinton to build a 364-mile canal from Albany to Buffalo and connect the Hudson River with Lake Erie. There were no civil engineers, so lawyers designed and superintended the project. From the first it had the sweet smell of success; construction began on July 4, 1817, and when the first seventy-five mile section opened, it was immediately overcrowded. Tolls from the opened sections paid for the rest.

The waterway tapped the valuable upstate and midwestern trade for New York City, and that port soon eclipsed its rivals, Boston and Philadelphia, in size and importance. Between 1820 and 1860, New York City grew tenfold, to more than a million residents, making it the second largest city in the world. The canal also tied western expansion to the rapidly growing cities of the Northeast, economically binding the Midwest to the Northeast. Even railroads did not make the Erie Canal obsolete; its tonnage peaked in the 1880s. Today, as the Barge Canal, it still does a brisk business. By 1820, then, the nation was tied more closely together, even as it spread outward at an explosive rate.

Republican Art

Growing wealth and urbanization also fostered cultural growth. In the colonial period religious tracts had dominated American writing along with such popular favorites as *Poor Richard*. During the revolution Paine's *Common Sense* and other essays collected in the *The American Crisis* captured people's attention, followed soon after by *The Federalist Papers*. In 1793 Noah Webster's *American Spelling Book* became the authority for spelling and pronunciation in a country whose elite feared democratic exuberance and creativity. Other readers preferred "sinful" novels, not to mention biography, history, philosophy, and local color tales. Franklin's *Autobiography*, published in 1794, became an instant hit and remains in print. Parson Weems' turn-of-the-century biography of Washington immortalized the myth of the cherry tree. The most important new group of writers to appear, the New York Knickerbocker School, was distinctly American. Washington Irving's *Sketch Book* of 1819 included the famous story of Rip Van Winkle and the "Legend of Sleepy Hollow." Another Knickerbocker, James Fenimore Cooper, started his career with the *Leatherstocking Tales*, in 1823, in which he romanticized the clash between civilized and primitive values on the frontier. He was best remembered for his later works, *The Last of the Mohicans, The Pathfinder*, and *The Deerslayer*. Irving, Cooper, and their colleague William Cullen Bryant, author of the poem, "Thanatopsis" and later editor of the New York *Evening Post*, discovered a wide audience for American topics and settings. All of these writings dwelt on American subjects, giving the young country its own literature, culturally validating its educated elite.

The era also produced numerous artists of distraction, principally portraitists. Gilbert Stuart spent much of his career abroad, but painted many famous portraits of Washington and other leading personalities of his day. Charles Wilson Peale studied under the renowned American artist, John Singleton Copley, and like Stuart painted likenesses of the rich and influential founding fathers. Samuel F. B. Morse succeeded as a painter before he invented the telegraph; his most noted portrait, of Lafayette, hangs in New York's City hall. At least one major American painter, John Trumbull, painted huge pictorial panoramas such as *The Declaration of Independence*, and the *Battle of Bunker's Hill* and other scenes depicting the great revolutionary battles. Paralleling the Knickerbocker writers, New York City's bourgeoning economy supported a growing group of portrait and landscape painters, collectively known as the "Hudson River School," led by Thomas Cole and his famous allegorical paintings that tied the American experience to republican Rome.

In the nation's first three decades American artists created a distinctive body of American painting and adopted explicitly American themes. But their work went well beyond art. These early national painters also built a pantheon of American heroes that included historical events, important individuals, and distinctive American panoramas such as the Hudson River, the Adirondack and White mountains, and Niagara Falls. These paintings, which often were exhibited in well-attended public shows or in public spaces such as the Capitol Rotunda, shaped Americans' vision of themselves and their country. Worth far more than a thousand words, to a people who had to "see to believe," these paintings became America.

American architects acted more timidly, largely copying well-accepted European styles. Still, builders in the new nation selected architectural forms that exhibited republican virtues. Charles Bullfinch of Boston brought back from Europe what became known as the "Federal" or "late Georgian" style—simple, elegant, severe forms with a minimum of ornamental detail and an emphasis on the rectangular. The shape became popular for houses, and many fine examples of Federal buildings still stand in the northeastern states.

The Federal style seemed too simple, however, for public buildings. The country's founders wanted such buildings to instill national pride and to impress skeptical European visitors. American designers used Greek and Roman temple styles, with their high arched domes, rotundas, pediments, and columns, for the new empire in the West. The United States Capitol and the University of Virginia, among others, served as excellent examples of this "republican" form. Jefferson's own home, Monticello, illustrated how the style could be reduced in scale and still maintain graceful proportions. The rage for temple architecture soon spread and dominated the nation between 1820 and 1850 from Maine to the southern plantation houses and on into the West. The fashion fit the American temper well. Even Baptist and Presbyterian churches found it irresistible as they simply placed Gothic steeples on the roofs of their white clapboard Greek and Roman temples. Neoclassical architecture associated the United States with the ancient Greek and Roman republics, making Americans' radical political departure seem conservative. Seemingly, republicanism had stood the test of time; it was well ordered and symmetrical, yet it also affirmed American republican beliefs and virtues as honor, beauty, truth, and hierarchical order.

Religion and Prisons

More than architecture, art, and literature, religion assumed a distinctly American coloration. At the end of the revolutionary war, the Congregationalists were the largest denomination in the country, but rapid westward expansion soon changed that. In the 1790s a reawakened interest in religion swept the East Coast, and when the evangelical fervor crossed the Appalachian Mountains it was transformed. Frontier Americans were not interested in theological quibbling. They demanded a simple explanation of right and wrong. The older denominations, Congregationalists,

Episcopalians, and to a lesser extent the Presbyterians, depended on a learned ministry and formal ceremonies, making them unattractive to westerners. The smaller, more spontaneous sects, such as the Baptists and the Methodists, swept the West. Sending out circuit-riding preachers, often qualified only by an "inner call" to serve, these denominations reached an astounding number of isolated people. With "fire and brimstone" revivalist oratory such preachers often worked their audiences into an emotional fervor, in which they responded by rolling, dancing, jerking, and speaking in tongues. Turnouts were large. In 1801 a Presbyterian revival held at Cane Ridge, Kentucky, attracted between 10,000 and 20,000 people, many of African ancestry. They offered isolated country folk opportunities to gossip, campaign for political office, find and woo a mate, trade horses, exchange news, and worship. The spontaneity of the Methodists and Baptists, the two largest Protestant denominations in the country by the 1840s, exemplified the growing American disdain for rigid, hierarchical systems. The camp meetings brought together people of diverse backgrounds and races who formed a distinctive American Protestantism and style of worship, melding European folk music with Protestant hymns and African work songs to create a vibrant, often spontaneous music, driven by African-derived rhythms that formed the basis of American popular music.

Americans also experimented with changes in their penal laws to fit their peculiar environment. Such laws had always been less well enforced in the United States than in Europe, but Pennsylvania, for example, in the last decades of the eighteenth century required the death penalty for sixteen crimes. As late as Washington's administrations, criminals everywhere were still brutally flogged, mutilated, branded, publicly executed, and exposed to ridicule in stocks. In a nation dedicated to the principles that most people know the difference between right and wrong and the state should constrict personal liberties as little as possible, brutal public punishments, and frequent executions—the latter an absolute denial of liberty—made little sense. Rehabilitation and a trust in the rational abilities of every man to learn to do what was right, seemed more reasonable. Such reforms meant better prisons. No longer were all convicts, regardless of age or sex, locked in one cell where they were left to their own devices to secure food. Prison reforms—starting in 1790 with the Walnut Street Prison in Philadelphia—segregated the sexes, banned liquor, fed the inmates, and required them to work. An experiment was tried at the New York prison at Auburn, starting in the 1820s, of locking inmates in their own cells at night. Reforms reduced flogging and proposed more subtle punishments such as diets of bread and water and solitary confinement. The fewer executions that took place usually occurred within prison walls. Imprisonment for debt became less popular, particularly because, in a sup-posedly rational society, nobody could explain how such prisoners could raise the money to pay even small debts while incarcerated. But the practice died slowly, perhaps because it represented a way to control people of little means, and was not outlawed in most states until the late 1840s.

Laws subjugating women to their husbands were also eased. American law repli-cated the English common law principle of "coverture" in which married women became legally subsumed by their husbands at marriage, symbolized by their loss of name. Gradually, however, in the face of the growing practice of fathers leaving equal estates to all of their children, female and male, and rising female literacy, women were allowed to control the property that they had brought into the mar-riage and to assign such property to heirs of their choice. A few states even allowed women to divorce their husbands for adultery and in such cases to retain custody of their children. These were small, but significant, gains that not only distin-guished American women from European women, but also fueled later demands for full female equality.

A New American Prospect

By 1820 Americans had made great strides with their experiment in nation building. Borrowing heavily from European experiences, especially England's, Americans adapted willy-nilly, ideas, political structures, cultures, and traditional religions to fit their own needs; if they served, they were kept; if they did not, they were discarded. The experiment was on a grand scale, continental in scope, involv-ing the destinies and fortunes of millions of people, and full of dangerous para-doxes. A commitment to individual freedom with strong tendencies toward political centralization, a state-aided laissez-faire, "free market" capitalism with state aid, a democracy of the well-born and rich, slave-ownership in a nation of equals, reverence for the rights of property and ownership of people, political ideals indelibly engraved in a written Constitution in a country that worshipped change—all these might have torn the fledgling republic apart had they not been muted in the face of hostile outside threats. Washington, Adams, Hamilton, Jeffer-son, and other early political leaders had read their classical history; they knew that many great ancient civilizations had fallen because of internal conflicts when con-fronted by hostile powers. They understood that the great domestic disagreements that threatened American unity, differences over constitutional interpretation, states' rights, sectional jealousies, class antagonisms, commercial rivalries, and political feuding were less important than national self-preservation. The crucial question by 1820 was whether this American experiment could endure, not just in the face of the classical political concerns expressed in the founders' political writings, but in the wake of unprecedented change. In the half century between the War of 1812 and the Civil War, American society underwent more fundamental change than in the previous 250 years combined. On the foundation of the young republic emerged a quite different and new American society, far beyond anything that the founders could have imagined.

Historical Potpourri

Americans of the late 18th and early 19th centuries were afflicted with every ill known to humankind. While the medical profession in the new nation was probably no better or worse than elsewhere, most Americans when ill resorted to time-tested home remedies, many of which were popularized in yearly almanacs. The selection below gives you some taste for the trials and tribulations of the afflicted; the authors of this volume warn their readers, however, that these recipes may be hazardous to your health:

> "Hic-cough" - A single drop of chymical oil of cinnamon drops on a piece of treble refined sugar, let it dissolve in the mouth leisurely.

> "Bleeding at the nose" - Rub your nostrils with juice of nettles, or young nettles bruised.

> "Indolent tumours" - Take the common plaster, four pounds; gum ammoniac and galbanum strained of each half a pound. Melt them together, and add, of Venice turpentine, six ounces. This plaster is used as a as a digestive.

> "To stench a bleeding wound" - Lay Hog's Dung (hot from the hog) to the Bleeding Wound.

> "Curing the Earach" - Rub the Ear hard for a Quarter of an Hour: Or, apply to it a hot roll: Or, put in a roasted Fig, as hot as may be: Or, blow the smoke of Tobacco strongly into it: Or, drop in Juice of Goose-Grease.

> "Worms in Children" - take 6, 8, or 10 red Earth-Worms, and let them purge in Bay Salt, then slit them open and wash them in fair Water, then dry them in an Earthen Dish and beat them to a Powder, and give them to the Child in the Morning fasting, for 3 or 4 Mornings, but let them eat nothing for an hour after.

"To purge the head - a drench" - Take white Dogs-Turd in Powder, and a handful of Rue beat small, boil them in Sallet-oil till thick, then spread it on a Cloath Plaster-wise and apply it to the Sore from Ear to Ear.

"For the Cough in Horses" - Take Garlick and Gun-Powder, pound them well together with Vinegar, and pour it down his Throat: Or use sharp Vinegar alone.

Almanacs often offered advice to their readers on how to stay healthy. The 1797 sage words reprinted below seem appropriate even today.

"To the GENTLEMEN SMOAKERS, whether of Pipes or Segars"

1st. It was smoak; so are all the vanities of this world.

2nd. It delighteth them who take it;
so do all the pleasures of the world.

3rd. It maketh men drunken, and light in the head;
so do all the vanities.

4th. He that taketh tobacco, saith he cannot leave it, it doth bewitch him; even so the pleasures of the world . . . And farther, besides all this, it is like hell in the very substance of it, for it is a stinking loathsome thing; and so is hell.

Source: Marian Barber Stowell, *Early American Almanacs: The Colonial Weekday Bible* (New York, Burt Franklin & Co., 1977).

Good Books

Highly readable surveys of the Federalist Era are Marcus Cunliffe, *The Nation Takes Shape* (1959), John C. Miller, *The Federalist Era* (1960); and Joyce Appleby, *Inventing the Revolution* (2000). Forrest McDonald illustrates the manifold difficulties in creating a new country in *The Presidency of George Washington* (1974), while Russell B. Nye details the problems of creating *The Cultural Life of the New Nation* (1963) and traces the course of *American Literary History, 1607-1830* (1970). Daniel Boorstin, *The Americans: The National Experience* (1965) also broadly covers American Cultural vistas in an entertaining manner.

Adams' troubled administration is fully explained in Stephan G. Kurtz', *The Presidency of John Adams* (1957) and Page Smith's sterling's two-volume biography, *John Adams* (1962). Biographies contain important information on the period. John C. Miller, *Alexander Hamilton: A Portrait in Paradox* (1959) and Broadus Mitchell *Alexander Hamilton*, 2 vols. (1962) investigate the secretary of the treasury thoroughly. Jefferson seems almost impossible to squeeze between the covers of one volume; Dumas Malone has worked for years on his multi-volume *Jefferson and His Time* (19481974). Merrill Peterson, *Thomas Jefferson and the New Nation* (1970) remains the best over-all biography of Jefferson. Annette Gordon-Reed lays out the case for a close relation between *Thomas Jefferson and Sally Hemmings* (1997). James Simon's *What Kind of Nation?* (2002) explores the crucial relationship between John Marshall and Thomas Jefferson. Madison, too, fills volumes, the most notable being Irving Brant's six, James *Madison* (1948-1961). Burr remains always the enigmatic character. Thomas P. Abernethy, *The Burr Conspiracy* (1954) paints the man as a rogue, while Milton Lomask's, *Aaren Burr: The Years from Princeton to Vice President, 1756-1805* (1979) is a more evenhanded treatment of the man. Joseph Ellis looks at leading political figures in the *Founding Brothers* (2000) and Drew McCoy's *The Last of the Fathers and the Republican Legacy* (1989) is the best study of Madison.

Shaw Livermore has written a delightful account of *The Twilight of Federalism* (1962) and Donald Sisson explains Adams' defeat in *The American Revolution of 1800* (1974). Albert H. Bowman, with a distinctly Jeffersonian bias, examines Franco-American diplomacy through 1800 in the aptly named, *The Struggle for Neutrality* (1974). Noble E. Cunningham has an excellent account of *The Jeffersonian Republicans in Power* (1958) and Adrienne Koch recounts the politics of *Jefferson and Madison: The Great Collaboration* (1964). J.C.A. Stagg, *Mr Madison's War* (1983) is a recent reinterpretation of the War of 1812; Harry L. Coles has written the best one-volume history of *The War of 1812* (1965).

Two books have significantly deepened our knowledge of the economic changes that occurred after the war of 1812—Douglas North's stunning work, *The Economic Growth of* the United States 1790-1860 (1961) and Charles Sellers', *The Market Revolution: Jacksonian America: 1815-1846* (1991). Curtis P. Nettles provides a good overview of *The Emergence of A National Economy, 1775-1815* (1962). David B. Davis, in an excellent book, examines *The Problem of Slavery in an Age of Revolution 1770-1823* (1975). Alan Taylor, *William Cooper's Town* (1995) is in an interesting study of an upstate New York town in this era. Robert E. Riegel treats women in a wide context in his book *American Woman: A Story of Social Change* (1970), Charles W. Akers takes a closer look at women in *Abigail Adams* (1980), and Nancy Cott details the history of marriage in *Public Views: A History of Marriage and the Nation* (2000). Laurel Thatcher Ulrich's *A Midwife's Tale* (1991) clarifies the tension between professional and traditional medicine over obstetrics. Alvin M. Josephy treats native Americans in *The Indian Heritage of America* (1958).

CHAPTER FOUR

JACKSONIAN DEMOCRACY

1816	James Monroe fifth president
1819	Depression *McCulloch vs. Maryland* United States gained Florida by treaty
1820	Missouri Compromise
1823	Monroe Doctrine
1824	John Quincy Adams sixth president; "corrupt bargain"
1827	Cherokees established nation
1828	Andrew Jackson seventh president Construction of Baltimore and Ohio Railroad
1830	Webster-Hayne Debate *Cherokee Nation vs. Georgia*
1832	Jackson reelected Jackson vetoed Second Bank of the United States Black Hawk War
1834	Whig Party Cyrus McCormick patented reaper
1836	Martin Van Buren eighth president Texas won independence
1837	Financial panic Forced Indian removals
1839	Depression
1840	William Henry Harrison ninth president and died; John Tyler became tenth president
1841	Brook Farm Phalanx
1844	James K. Polk eleventh president

1846	Mexican War
1848	Zachary Taylor twelfth president
1852	Massachusetts passed first state compulsory school attendance law
1854	Henry David Thoreau, *Walden*

Jacksonian Democracy

A ndrew Jackson was the dominant force in American politics between 1814 and the Civil War. The great problems created by the nation's feverish growth swirled around Jackson. He and his generation professed their loyalty to the Jeffersonian ideas of individualism, laissez-faire government, and equal opportunity. Their task was not an easy one. The cotton revolution and the emergence of the factory system boosted the nation's economy but brought with them a host of new problems. Infant businesses had to be nurtured with federal and state aid without endangering free trade and the union of states. The rise of wealthy industrialists directly challenged earlier elites whose wealth derived from land and mercantile pursuits. The rapidly growing wage-earning classes clamored for political and economic rights; the revolution in transportation realigned sectional affiliations and regional wealth while it opened up new markets and increased demand for new products.

Acquiring wealth seemed the obsession of the age. At no other time in American history did greater opportunity exist for individuals to improve their standing in life. Andrew Jackson's own rise from a penniless orphan, born in a log cabin on the Carolina frontier, to a wealthy planter and president of the United States exemplified the dreams of thousands of Americans. They believed that amid the wealth of untapped abundance, anyone who worked hard could advance themselves, and in a truly free society, merit determined an individual's wealth, not heredity or privilege. But a free and intensely competitive society created enormous discord and disorder. Foremost was the growing sectional conflict between slave states and free states. Jacksonian ideals threatened southern values since freedom was incompatible with chattel slavery. Defenders of slavery fully understood the threat they faced. And yet, the expansion of the market economy undergirded the prosperity of southern slavery that depended on an ever-increasing demand for cotton. In the face of economic abundance, however, Jacksonian Americans avoided the issue of slavery by turning their attention to economic and territorial growth. In the short-term the strategy worked. Every census reported dramatic economic expansion, increased population, and a geographically larger federal union. By 1845, however, Americans were forced to confront the fundamental contradiction of a nation with slavery, committed to all humans' right to freely pursue their happiness, to secure a full claim to the fruit of their labor, and the liberty to use their wealth and earnings freely. Until then, the Jacksonians, like the republic's founders, employed the country's significant political resources to divert attention from slavery and continue to forge unstable compromises among the Declaration of Independence's assertion of the equality and freedom of all men, the Christian affirmation of the brotherhood of humankind, and the Constitution's unequivocal recognition of black men as the property of white men.

Author of the Monroe Doctrine, Virginian James Monroe was president of the United States from 1817 to 1825 (1938).

Era of Good Feelings

James Monroe served as president during the "Era of Good Feelings," the period of single-party dominance. The least talented of Jefferson's political heirs, Monroe was well-suited for the transitional period in which government control shifted from the revolutionary generation to men not yet born when General Gage marched his redcoats out to Concord. Monroe had studied law under Jefferson and was the last president to have served in the Continental Army. He had negotiated the Louisiana Purchase, had served as Jefferson's minister to Great Britain and Madison's secretaries of state and war. Monroe possessed neither brilliance nor eloquence. He was plodding, colorless, uninspiring, but dependable. He also had a keen eye for talent and appointed one of the ablest cabinets of any president: the brilliant John Q. Adams, as secretary of state, the able and ambitious William Crawford of Georgia as secretary of treasury, the intelligent and aspiring John C. Calhoun of South Carolina as secretary of war, and William Wirt of Maryland as attorney general. These men gave Monroe's troubled administrations a string of successes that overshadowed the president's own lack of ability. Thanks to them, Monroe left office more popular than when he entered.

The president enjoyed the fruits of the postwar boom until 1819 when a financial panic brought it to an abrupt end. Westward expansion had been accompanied by widespread land speculation fueled by more than 300 new state and local banks that issued more than 100 million dollars in paper money to help speculators buy land. These small banks, short on specie, long on mortgages, and unstable at best, survived only as long as the land boom continued. A combination of events undermined it. Congress passed an act in 1817 that required banks to convert their paper to specie on demand. Overseas markets for American agricultural products disappeared as European farmers renewed full production for the first time since the Napoleonic wars. Glutted textile markets injured both manufacturers and cotton producers, and the Bank of the United States, after pursuing inflationary policies during its first year of existence, in 1818 reverted to a deflationary policy that dried up the country's money supply. Low crop prices discouraged land sales, constriction of credit and the specie order wrecked small southern and western banks, and the slump in the textile market damaged the economy. As a result the United States suffered a financial panic, followed by a depression. The South and West were particularly hurt as these regions blamed the depression on the misguided policies of the Bank of the United States. For the rest of its chartered life, the bank faced increasingly stiff political resistance from southern and western politicians.

"McCulloch vs. Maryland"

The states' hostility toward the federal government intensified after an important supreme court case reasserted the primacy of the federal government over the states. Maryland levied a tax on the Baltimore branch of the Bank of the United States, but the bank's cashier, James McCulloch, refused to pay the tax. The state sued him. John Marshall's March 1819 opinion in the case of *McCulloch vs. Maryland* accepted Hamilton's doctrine of implied powers and held that as long as the means used by the federal government to achieve a constitutional end were within "the letter and spirit" of the constitution, then both the process and the bank were constitutional. Adding the memorable phrase that "the power to tax involves the power to destroy," Marshall averred that no state had the right to tax an agency of the federal government.

Marshall's decision touched off a nationwide controversy about rights of the states vis-a-vis the federal government. The debate had started with a February decision in the *Dartmouth College* case in which Marshall ruled that Dartmouth College's private charter represented a contract protected by the constitution from any

Daniel Webster, lawyer, politician, and famed orator from Massachusetts, argued the famous Dartmouth College case, partially because it was his alma mater. "It is a small college," he told the supreme court, "but there are those who love it." (1969)

interference by state legislatures. In these two cases, Marshall buttressed the power of the federal government over the states, placing a legal capstone on the Federalist programs enacted during the republic's first decade. The chief justice contrived to implement Hamilton's dream of a strong, centralized nation.

The Missouri Compromise

Marshall, though, was out of step with the national mood. Nationalistic sentiments, heightened by the War of 1812 and the postwar euphoria, had waned by 1819. The country faced no external enemies and Americans wanted to be left alone to pursue their fortunes. Politics became increasingly local. The trend toward localism and sectionalism became pronounced in 1818 when Missouri applied to congress for admission as a state. Already twenty-two states belonged to the union, eleven slave and eleven free. Since 1802 voting equality in the senate had been maintained by alternatively admitting slave and free states. In the house, however, the free states had a twenty-four-vote edge. Although surrounded on three sides by free areas, Missouri had been settled by slave holders from Kentucky and Virginia, although the territory still had less than three thousand slaves. Antagonisms surfaced in February, 1819, when New York Representative James Tallmadge offered an amendment to the Missouri bill that prohibited slaves from entering the state and provided that all slave children who had been born in Missouri should be freed at age twenty-five. Southern slave holders were shocked. For the first time slavery had been challenged in congress. Tallmadge's amendment passed the House, but failed in the Senate. The question was brought up again in the winter session of Congress when Senator Ruffis King of New York argued that Congress possessed the authority to prohibit slavery in Missouri. Senator William Pinkney of Maryland answered that the United States was a union of equal states and that the federal government could not deny the right of citizens to own property in one of those states. On a practical level the debate was over the same federal-state conflict on which Marshall had already ruled.

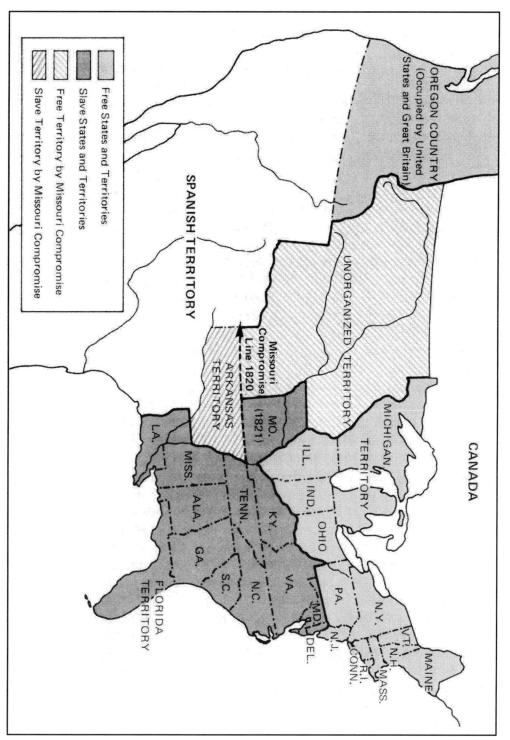

The Missouri Compromise, 1820

Just as the second round of the Missouri confrontation began, Maine applied for statehood. Maine's petition presented the congressional moderates with a chance for compromise—admit both Maine and Missouri and satisfy both sections. Speaker of the House Henry Clay warned that if northerners did not support Missouri's admission as a slave state, southerners would block the entry of Maine. The final compromise proscribed slavery in the rest of the Louisiana Purchase territory north of 36°30′ latitude, Missouri's southern boundary. Maine entered as a free state and Missouri became a slave state. The Missouri Compromise, however, hardened sectional lines all across the nation, particularly in the South. Jefferson described the debate over Missouri's admission "as a firebell in the night" that someday might drive the South to secession. To most, however, the Missouri Compromise solved the immediate problem. The sectional balance in the senate was preserved and congress had implicitly authorized the expansion of slavery south of 36°30′. For the next three decades the Missouri Compromise served as a virtual amendment to the Constitution that limited the expansion of slavery to the territories below Missouri's southern boundary.

Monroe Doctrine

The discord of the slave debates almost obscured Monroe's major diplomatic triumphs. In 1819 the president signed the Adams-Onis Treaty in which Spain ceded East and West Florida to the United States after it dropped its claims to Texas and agreed to pay American claims against Spain amounting to about five million dollars. Moreover, Spain's cession of the Floridas ended the border warfare in the South and left the Florida Indians to the mercy of the United States. The treaty rounded out the nation's boundaries east of the Mississippi River, except for northern Maine's, which remained unsettled until 1842 when the Webster-Ashburton Treaty with Great Britain resolved the Canadian boundary dispute.

Secretary of state Adams' most serious foreign policy problem arose when Spain's Latin American colonies declared their independence. The revolts began in 1810, and although Madison and Monroe were sympathetic, they refused to recognize the new Latin American republics for fear of antagonizing Spain while negotiations for Florida continued. The Holy Alliance, a consortium of monarchial European powers, sought to recapture Spain's lost empire. Alarmed at the prospect of European intrusion into the affairs of the Western Hemisphere, Adams realized that the United States' interests lay in having a multitude of small weak powers to the south instead of one or two strong European ones. Great Britain, which had opened profitable trade relations with the newly independent countries, shared these sentiments. When British Foreign Minister George Canning asked Adams to consider a joint declaration against outside intervention in the Western Hemisphere, Adams was intrigued but suspicious. He knew that Britain and the United States had vastly different interests in Latin America. Unlike America, Britain expressed no sympathy for the republican principles espoused in the emerging countries. Adams, ever the realist and sensitive to New England trading interests, also sought commercial rights for the United States in South America. Moreover, Adams feared that the British wanted to limit the future growth and power of the United States. Under Canning's proposal, the United States could not annex Cuba, Texas, or California. Believing that the territories, some above the 36°30' line and some below it, might later join the United States, Adams opposed Channing's agreement.

President Monroe sent copies of the British proposal to Madison and Jefferson asking their advice. Both favored accepting Canning's offer. A series of long, stormy cabinet meetings followed. Adams finally prevailed with his argument that the United States should brook no interference in the Western Hemisphere. With little fanfare, Monroe included the statement in his annual message to congress on December 2, 1823. He declared that "the American continents, by the free and independent condition which they have assumed and maintain, are henceforth not to be considered as subjects for future colonization by any European powers." Monroe reassured all colonial powers, however, that America would not interfere with their existing colonies nor intervene in European affairs.

The Monroe Doctrine was deceptively simple and wholly in America's interest. The United States insisted on absolute security in the Western Hemisphere, not relative security as in Europe. The New World became an American sphere of influence with the United States the only great resident power. Adams rejected any notion of a balance of power in the hemisphere. Moreover, the Monroe Doctrine reserved the new world for republics. Such a bold position required a much larger navy than the United States could muster, but Adams cleverly and accurately calculated that the British would enforce the doctrine for their own national reasons. The Monroe Doctrine had no legal standing until ratified by the senate 117 years later in the Act of Havana, but since its pronouncement it has served as the cornerstone of the United States' Latin American policy.

The Rise of Jacksonian Democracy

Monroe won reelection in 1820 with only one dissenting electoral vote. Despite his personal popularity, he failed to hold the various contending and ambitious factions of his party together. By the end of his second term, the "Era of Good Feelings" had come to an end. Five men, three of them in his own administration, openly jockeyed for Monroe's office. The president, who appeared disposed to pass his mantle to his secretary of state, Adams, confronted a rising popular antagonism against the congressional party caucus action as the presidential nominating body. To many it smacked of intrigue, secrecy, and corruption, at odds with popular democratic processes. Still, in 1824, the presidential hopefuls endorsed by state legislatures carried with them distinct sectional baggage. Massachusetts sponsored John Quincy Adams; Tennessee, Andrew Jackson; Kentucky, Henry Clay; and a poorly attended caucus nominated treasury secretary William Crawford of Georgia. With two southern candidates in the field, Calhoun, who had announced his own availability, withdrew and ran for the vice presidency on both the Jackson and Adams tickets.

Such intra-party squabbling produced predictable results—no candidate received a majority of the electoral votes. The hero of the Battle of New Orleans, Jackson led with ninety-nine; Adams was second with eighty-four; Crawford, who suffered a stroke during the campaign, was third; and Clay followed a poor fourth. The election went into the house where furious bargaining among the candidates ensued. Clay occupied center stage because he controlled the votes of three states, yet as the fourth candidate he could not be considered for the presidency. Jackson shunned a bargain with his western competitor, but Adams was amenable. The Clay and Adams men held several private meetings, the details of which never became public. Afterward Clay threw his support to Adams. Crawford, his health wrecked, never had a real chance. On the first ballot Adams received the votes of the needed thirteen states and named Clay as secretary of state, the traditional stepping stone to the presidency. Immediately Jackson called foul. His supporters charged Clay and Adams with making a "corrupt bargain." Both heatedly denied the allegation, but to no avail. The court of public opinion believed they had. More importantly, Andrew Jackson believed that they had conspired to steal the election.

John Quincy Adams

Adams had received only one-third of the popular vote and with Jackson already out campaigning for 1828, the Adams administration was doomed from the start.

The new president's personality did nothing to rally public support for his policies. Perceived as austere and aloof, Adams was a lonely figure in political Washington. He never sought, nor did he apparently enjoy, a high level of popularity. The last president who openly considered himself apart from, and above, the people, Adams preferred being right to being popular. Intelligent and widely read, he relied on the force of his intellect rather than a pleasing personality or meaningless polite chatter to persuade others. He worked long hours, rising before five A.M. to read his Bible and often retiring long after midnight. For recreation he enjoyed being alone. Unless his doctor counseled otherwise, Adams often took solitary nude swims in the Potomac early in the morning. Haunted with tragedy, he married a hypochondriac while one of his sons committed suicide and another died from overwork.

Adams' presidential years were the low point of his public career. A vigorous nationalist, he refused to acknowledge the growing divisions between the slave and free states. Similarly, he would not stoop to use patronage to build up a personal political following; in four years he removed only twelve officials, all for incompetence. His first annual message to congress indicated just how far he misread the mood of the country. Praising European progress, at the moment Americans were searching for a distinct national identity, he asked for legislation to enable the federal government to expand the navy, to build a national system of roads and canals, to fund scientific explorations, and to establish a national university and observatory. The latter he called "the lighthouse of the sky," a phrase that produced peals of laughter in congress. Adams accomplished none of his objectives. During his last two years in office, he faced a hostile pro-Jackson majority in both houses of congress that relentlessly badgered him. When Adams suggested founding a naval academy in 1827, the congressional opposition charged that, among other things, it would turn out homosexuals.

Andrew Jackson and 1828 Election

At the end of four years Adams could not claim a single major accomplishment, not even in foreign affairs, his area of expertise. His failure was due to the constant opposition from Jackson and his allies in congress. The wealthy war hero from Tennessee rode a crest of popularity created by the broadening of democracy throughout the nation. By 1828 eight states had removed all property-holding requirements for voting to allow wage laborers to vote. Almost all religious qualifications had been removed, and in 1828 the presidential electors, in all but two states, were chosen directly by the voters rather than by state legislatures. Successful candidates had to attract broad public support, not just curry favor with political

Depicting military heroes Andrew Jackson, who won the Battle of New Orleans after the Treaty of Ghent ended the War of 1812, and Winfield Scott, who made his reputation in the Mexican War and for a brief period commanded Union forces during the Civil War. (1936)

elites. The colonial pattern of deferential politics, in which voters had yielded to their social betters had fallen into disfavor by the 1820s, replaced by a boisterous, new and overtly democratic politics in which candidates openly campaigned for office by promising voters to look after their interests.

Andrew Jackson thrived in this new political environment. Born on the Carolina frontier, he moved to the raw Tennessee country as a young man. Without the benefit of family connections or a formal education, Jackson amassed a large fortune as a country lawyer, land speculator, slave and plantation owner, and consummate politician. Adams described him as "a barbarian who could not write a sentence of grammar and hardly could spell his own name." Cursed with an uncontrollable temper and a finely honed sense of personal honor, Jackson fought numerous duels and was considered the most dangerous hand-to-hand fighter in the West. Like many slave owners and military men, he projected a sense of command. He served as congressman and senator from Tennessee, held a seat on the Tennessee supreme court, and received an appointment as a major-general in the army during the War of 1812. Over the years he made and lost several fortunes, at least one of them disappearing in a bank failure. Politically, he appealed strongly to the less fortunate, perhaps because he offered living proof that any American born in a log cabin had the opportunity to become rich and president. He was a living embodiment of Americans' belief in meritocracy.

The 1828 presidential election was the dirtiest ever. Adams' supporters accused Jackson of bigamy because he had married his beloved, pipe-smoking Rachel before she had secured a divorce from her former husband. The ungrounded charges enraged Jackson, whose widowed mother had also been accused of sexual impropriety. Rachel died before his inauguration, and Jackson brooded that her death had resulted from Adams' mean-spirited, class-ridden campaign tactics. The new president seemed unbothered by other accusations that he was a murderer and an assassin. In turn, Jackson's supporters whispered that Adams had pimped for Czar

Alexander I while minister to Russia from 1809 to 1814. Titillated by the various charges, voters loved the campaign, giving Jackson and his running mate, Calhoun, an overwhelming victory. The expansion of the franchise produced a voter turnout in 1828 almost four times larger than the 1824 total. Popular participation continued to grow in subsequent elections, making politics the country's foremost pastime and mudslinging an admired virtue.

Jacksonian Democracy

Jackson symbolized the new political changes popularly called "Jacksonian Democracy." A new generation of enfranchised voters rejected the older idea that government, rooted in English aristocratic politics, should be conducted by the "best men." Like Jackson, most American voters believed that anyone with a modicum of common sense could adequately discharge public duties. This attitude was grounded in economic prosperity and in a rising sense of material expectation on the part of average Americans. Jacksonians spurned the idea that political and social preferment belonged naturally to a small permanent elite of wealth and talent. They envisioned instead an open and fluid society in which those at the bottom had a fair chance to rise and, just as importantly, those at the top could fall. For that reason many delighted in Adams' defeat.

Jacksonian Democracy harbored a number of inherent contradictions that mirrored larger American inconsistencies. It grew into a national party in the sense that Jackson put together a political coalition composed of his own West, New York Governor Martin Van Buren's Northeast, and Calhoun's slaveholding South. Most Jacksonians, while viscerally committed to the federal union, accepted Jefferson's concept of states' rights and minimal government. Jackson's followers opposed Henry Clay's "American System," which called for tariffs to protect domestic manufacturers and a federal transportation system to promote economic growth. In his famous Maysville Road veto in 1830, Jackson contended that if the nation wanted federally subsidized transportation, it should amend the Constitution. "Equal rights for all, special privileges for none," a favorite slogan of Democrats meant that no economic group should benefit at the expense of another. Widespread prosperity became a key theme in Jacksonian Democracy. Most Americans expected the government to maintain equal economic opportunity for all through an open, unfettered market place. Jacksonians professed a profound belief in equality, but like Jefferson, that meant white equality. They treated African Americans and Indians more harshly than their elitist predecessors. Lastly, thanks to Adams' snobbish supporters, Jackson and his followers became popularly associated with rough lower class ways. Paid cartoonists lampooned Jackson's supposed ignorance by using the jackass to symbolize his political faction. Alexis de Tocqueville, the French noble-man who toured the United States in the early 1830s, summed up the differences between Jacksonians and their Republican predecessors when he observed that with the disappearance of the old political elite "is lost the tradition of cultivated man-ners. The people become educated, knowledge extends, a middling ability becomes common. Outstanding talents and great characters are more rare. Society is less bril-liant and more prosperous."

The Controversial Jackson

The contrast between Jackson's and Adams' administrations was striking from the first. Earlier inaugural celebrations had been sedate affairs, but Jackson invited the nation to attend—and many did. Barrels of whisky stood on the front lawn and the drunks swarmed into the White House, cut up the curtains and furniture for souvenirs, carved their initials on the walls, and nearly destroyed the place. The president, almost crushed by the mob, fled out a back window and spent the night with a friend. Adams had disdained political patronage, Jackson perfected the polit-ical spoils system at the national level. The acid test for officeholding became, not ability but political loyalty. The new president also downgraded the cabinet. For his first three years in office it held no regular meetings. Instead Jackson relied on a cir-cle of his personal confidantes, his "kitchen cabinet," Amos Kendall, Isaac Hill, Duff Green, and others, for advice. As the people's president, Jackson also became the country's first strong president, who governed more like a king; Washington had been "first among equals." Faced with a challenge from South Carolina slavehold-ers, Jackson used his carefully nurtured power to thwart all efforts to weaken the federal union.

The Whig Party

Jackson's loyal opposition, the supporters of Adams and Clay, first coalesced into the National Republican Party. Declaring the president, "King Andrew," in 1834, the opposition took the name Whigs, named after the English party that traditionally opposed the monarchy. United by their hatred of Jackson, the Whigs represented an uneasy alliance of wealthy southern slave holders, led by Calhoun after 1831, pow-erful northern commercial, banking, and manufacturing interests, and those Amer-icans who favored an extensive system of federal internal improvements. Whigs rallied around Clay's "American System." Although the substantive differences between the two parties were few, for two decades they furiously fought each other for control of state and federal governments.

The forces that pulled the political parties and the sections apart accelerated during Jackson's first term. In congress, a bitter debate between Daniel Webster and Robert Hayne of South Carolina raged for eight days in January 1830 over the nature of the Constitution. Webster argued that the federal government was sovereign while Hayne contended that the federal government was a compact among the states which could disobey federal laws. Behind the national debate lurked the fear that South Carolina would nullify the 1828 tariff. Four years later, when South Carolina directly challenged the authority of the federal government to collect the tariff, Jackson threatened to use the army to force South Carolina into compliance with federal law. Cooler heads prevailed, after Congress passed a compromise lower tariff, and South Carolina rescinded its nullification ordinance but approved another nullifying the Force Bill. While the nullification crisis failed to answer the long-standing questions about states' rights, it bolstered the authority of the federal government and the power of the presidency. In many northerners' minds, it also linked southern slave holders with treason.

Even within Jackson's Democratic Party, infighting was intense. Early in 1830, Crawford, ever the disappointed candidate and Calhoun's implacable foe, heard that Calhoun had recommended censuring Jackson for his invasion of Florida in the Seminole War in 1818. Vice President Calhoun's explanation failed to convince Jackson. For the last two years of his first term, Jackson shunned Calhoun. A more serious scandal, however, broke up his cabinet. In 1829, Jackson's secretary of war, John Eaton, had married a barmaid of uncertain reputation. Led by Calhoun's wife, the wives of the other cabinet members refused to entertain Mrs. Eaton. Jackson, remembering the accusations against his own wife and mother, raised the issue at a cabinet meeting. Only Van Buren, a bachelor, supported Mrs. Eaton. In April 1831, five members of the cabinet resigned rather than treat Peggy Eaton courteously. Floride Calhoun, the vice president's wife, led the shunning of Peggy Eaton, pushing her husband further into political limbo and opening the door for Martin Van Buren to replace Calhoun as Jackson's heir apparent.

War on the Bank

Jackson further aggravated sectional antagonisms when he declared war on the Second Bank of the United States. The bank's charter was due to expire in 1836, but its worried president, Nicholas Biddle, applied for a charter renewal early in 1832 to throw the issue into the election campaign of that year. Many southerners and westerners believed the bank unconstitutional. Biddle's tight money policy and his favoritism toward eastern bankers, angered those who desired easier credit. Moreover, state and local bankers resented the United States Bank's dominance. To its detractors, the national bank symbolized unfair monopoly, special privilege, corporate greed, and Eastern wealth. They believed that the bank hindered economic freedom and fostered unearned, government-derived privilege as had the East India Tea Company in 1773.

Jackson found the bank issue made to order. Not only did he portray the bank as anti-democratic, he also turned the campaign into a personal attack on Biddle. When the rechartering bill passed congress, in July 1832, Jackson delivered a ringing veto insisting that the bank was unconstitutional, undemocratic, and un-American. Easily reelected in 1832, Jackson continued his attack on "The Monster" bank. Biddle, who played politics throughout the conflict, tightened credit, almost causing a depression in late 1833, and tried to force the administration to come to his support. Jackson countered by removing government deposits from the bank and spreading them among state banks quickly labeled "pet banks," although Jackson had to fire two secretaries of the treasury before he found one willing to do his bidding.

Congressional Whigs, led by Clay, engineered a bill through the senate in 1834 that censured Jackson for his bank policy, but a similar effort in the house failed. The confrontation continued until the end of Jackson's second term. The senate finally removed its censure in 1837, and the bank, already weakened by the removal of the government's deposits, declined, even though it secured a state charter from Pennsylvania. With congressional passage of the 1836 Deposit Act, which required the secretary of the treasury to designate at least one bank in each state and territory to hold government funds, Jackson decentralized American banking, anticipating some aspects of the later Federal Reserve System. At the same time, he opened many old wounds that involved sectional interests, class antagonisms, constitutional interpretations, and the power of the federal government. Of more immediate consequence, the death of the bank led to a relaxation of currency restraints and a rampant inflation fueled by widespread land speculation that led to a financial panic in 1837 and the worst depression the nation had yet experienced.

Indian Affairs

One of the few areas of agreement during Jackson's administrations was the government's Indian policy. Almost all whites, regardless of their political persuasion or geographical loyalty, agreed that strong measures were needed to end the bloody conflict on all of America's borders and open new lands for white settlement. The easy distribution of those lands at low cost—a major demand of western politicians and their worker allies in the East—promised rich rewards for all white Americans. After 225 years of steadily pressing against tribal lands, however, the United States had not yet evolved a humane Indian policy. Instead, Americans worried about the Indians only when they proved troublesome. As long as vast tracts of unsettled eastern land remained onto which the Indians could move, the nation's Indian policy was dispossession and expulsion. By the 1820s as eastern wilderness areas continued to shrink, however, the Indians became less disposed to move and Americans talked seriously about removal of all eastern Indians west of the Mississippi River.

Sequoyah, a Cherokee Indian who was illiterate but a genius, developed a language for his people with 85 characters; his language enabled the tribal group to publish a newspaper (*Cherokee Phoenix*), write a constitution, and engage in missionary activities. (1980)

By 1830 whites had driven Indian groups out of the Northwest Territory; but the Five Civilized Tribes of the southeast—the Choctaw, Cherokee, Creek, Seminole, and Chickasaw—refused to budge. Americans found it difficult to rationalize evicting these people because they had adopted Christianity and European ways. Among the most civilized people in the South, they had become settled agriculturalists who improved their property, immune to the usual white charges that Indians should forfeit their lands because they failed to work them. In 1827 Cherokee leaders even drafted a constitution modeled after that of the federal constitution, set up an elected representative government, and declared themselves a sovereign nation. The Cherokee nation adopted a written language developed by the Georgian Sequoyah and published a newspaper and parts of the Bible in English and Cherokee.

As American westward expansion reached boom proportions, pressure on the Indians increased. A major problem involved differing concepts of land ownership. Most Indians found individual ownership of land incomprehensible. To them the land was sacred and tribal. Personal possession of land was as impossible as claiming ownership of the air or sky. Indians often thought that when they signed a treaty they had simply allowed whites to share the land. When whites settled the land, fenced, farmed, and claimed it as their exclusive property, the Indians became confused and angry. The misunderstanding continued on both sides, leading to innumerable conflicts and tragedies throughout the nineteenth century.

In 1827, when the Cherokees ratified their constitution, Georgia state authorities protested, claiming that it violated the nation's basic law, that the Cherokee's land belonged to Georgia, and that the Indians were simple tenants on the land. The state occupied the Cherokee's land, divided it into counties, and voided all Cherokee laws and customs. The Cherokees appealed to President Adams, who concluded that the Cherokee constitution was not unconstitutional because the Indians had not been parties to the Philadelphia constitutional compact and that their tribal laws rested on quite explicit treaty rights. In the meantime, gold was discovered on Cherokee land in Georgia. The state posted guards inside the Cherokee territory to "protect" the gold deposits. The Cherokees sued in the United States Supreme Court for an injunction against the state. The venerable Marshall, although sympathetic to the Indians' cause and dedicated to strengthening federal control over the states, dodged the thorny question. In *Cherokee Nation vs. Georgia* (1830), Marshall declared that the court had no jurisdiction, asserting that the Cherokees were a "domestic dependent" rather than a sovereign state as they claimed.

Not willing to let Marshall have the last word, congress passed the Indian Removal Act of 1830. Under the terms of this act, Jackson could set aside as much land outside the states and territories for the Indians as he desired, but before they could be removed their claims to their old lands had to be settled. The act guaranteed the Indians that their new lands would be theirs forever; the government promised to provide the Indians with agricultural tools to help them farm in the West, and to pay their migration expenses. Despite the fact that the Indians' new western lands lay squarely in the middle of what most whites called the "great American desert," the Indians were expected to farm them.

Congress appropriated $500,000 for Indian removal, and pressure on the Indians mounted. Georgia was particularly anxious to be rid of the tribes and moved to assert the state's authority over the disputed land, but in 1832 the supreme court in *Worcester vs. Georgia* confirmed that the federal government had exclusive jurisdiction in Cherokee territory and ruled that Georgia had acted unconstitutionally. Georgia, however, defied the supreme court, and when the Cherokees appealed to Adams' successor to enforce the court's decision, President Jackson is supposed to have bellowed, "John Marshall has made his decision, now let him enforce it!"

Indian Removal

The Indians, now helplessly caught between Marshall, Jackson, and Georgia authorities, had no recourse but to move. Between 1832 and 1834, Creeks, Choctaws, Cherokees, and Chickasaws moved, more or less voluntarily, to what later became North Texas and Oklahoma. Many Cherokees resisted until 1835, when they finally signed their lands away in the Treaty of Echota and agreed to leave within two years. When by 1837 almost 18,000 still had not surrendered, Jackson sent the army in to round up the remainder and move them out by force. Confined to stockades, many Indians started drinking heavily and tribal morale deteriorated. Forced to move at gunpoint in the middle of winter, thousands of Cherokee died on the "Trail of Tears." Corrupt contractors hired to stock supplies along the way cheated the government and, ultimately the Indians, with poor or nonexistent food, shelter, and clothing. The death rate was appalling. Of the 11,500 Indians herded onto the trail, an estimated 4,000 died of old age, dysentery, malnutrition, exposure, and in childbirth.

Jackson's Indian removal policy was institutionalized in the 1830 Indian Removal Act and the Indian Intercourse Act of 1834, which governed tribal relations for over half a century. The intercourse act defined Indian territory as all land outside the states and organized territories. Indian relations were delegated to the Indian Bureau, an office within the war department, which licensed all whites who entered Indian lands. The act prohibited manufacturing or selling liquor in Indian territory, although Indian agents could take liquor in for their own use. Agents' per capita consumption rose astronomically. The legislation further stipulated that any disputes between Indians and whites were to be decided in American courts. On the frontier, where sentiment against the Indians ran high, few Native Americans received an impartial hearing. In practice, the laws proved impossible to enforce. Indian territory was too large to patrol, and there were few Indian agents. In many cases they were too corrupt to do an adequate job. Pressure for better communications with the West Coast, especially after the discovery of gold in California in 1849, destroyed the possibility of an isolated, untouchable Indian preserve in the West. In truth, the acts showed no real concern for the Indians, other than to segregate them for the good of whites. When isolation was no longer possible the next logical step was annihilation.

Jacksonian Americans appeared satisfied with their short-term solution to the Indian problem. Indian removal multiplied the opportunities for whites. As long as the United States continued to expand, the Jacksonian belief in an equal chance for all whites proved viable. Moreover, the opening of new lands and the tide of westward migration promoted the extension of the market economy and market values into rural, republican America, an America, more than ever, for whites only.

Growth and Industrialization

On July 4 in the year of Jackson's first election, Charles Carroll of Carrollton, Maryland, the last surviving signer of the Declaration of Independence, laid the cornerstone on the Baltimore and Ohio Railroad, the first railway chartered in the nation. The magic of the steam locomotive transformed the United States. Capitalists in the great eastern cities smarted under the rapid growth of New York City that dominated the growing Ohio valley trade after construction of the Erie Canal. Other eastern cities seized on the new railroad technology to compete with New York's colossus. Urban promoters planned, organized, and heavily financed the early railroads to tap inland trade areas and to prevent other port cities from stealing their business. The Boston and Worcester Railroad and later the Western Railroad of Massachusetts linked Boston with the Hudson River and New York's Erie Canal. With the New York and Erie and the New York Central railroads, New York City entrepreneurs acted to protect their established markets. In the 1830s, the Pennsylvania State Works, a clumsy system of railroads and canals financed by the state, connected Philadelphia and Pittsburgh. The Erie and New York Central, were the largest, most technologically efficient, and best operated private enterprises in the world. The Baltimore and Ohio linked the Chesapeake city with the Midwest while Charleston chartered the nation's second railroad company in 1828, the Charleston and Hamburg, that connected the southern port with the cotton upcountry. In Georgia, Savannah bankers financed the Central of Georgia, and Augusta interests pushed the Georgia Railroad across the northern part of the state that intersected, in 1845, in Atlanta, the South's only true rail head.

Enthusiasm for Railroads

The railroad mania of the 1830s spread quickly to the West, where inland towns and cities sought constructed railroads to secure their commercial positions in the country's hinterland. River and lake cities early recognized the advantages of railways and subsidized local companies. With the railroad, Pittsburgh, Cleveland, Cincinnati, Louisville, and St. Louis grew into regional economic centers. In Chicago, which in 1830 had forty families, fifteen railroads in 1860 intersected at the Lake Michigan city, with about one hundred daily trains, making it the largest railroad city in the country and the gateway to the West. All goods destined to western markets passed through Chicago and western raw materials and food were shipped to Chicago for national distribution. As a consequence, Chicago not only became the nation's most important transportation hub, it also pioneered mail order marketing. By the end of the century, lonely farm families in the Dakota Territory, the Mississippi Delta, and the Texas hill country, factory work-

Railroads, first built in the United States in the mid 1820s, had a profound affect on American life, ranging from moving goods and people quickly to putting towns on the map and to standardizing the concept of time. (1975)

ers in Pittsburgh and Lowell, and day laborers in Philadelphia and St. Louis all eagerly awaited the annual arrival from Chicago of their Sears and Roebuck and Montgomery Ward catalogs.

Urban domination of the railroads left a distinctive imprint on the nation's transportation system. As late as the Civil War, many important rivers were not yet bridged because cities fiercely defended their geographical monopolies. In 1860 four railways served Richmond, but none physically touched. The legally enforced separation provided business for a city's teamsters, hotels, saloons, and retail districts, but hampered regional economic development. Worse, railroads' different gauges plagued travelers and shippers. By 1860 the 4' 8 ½" gauge prevailed in the North and West but the slave South generally used the broader 5' gauge, sealing its borders from the uninterrupted flow of national commerce. There were exceptions to these patterns, however; the New York and Erie used a 6' gauge to prevent other rail companies from interchanging with it, and one southern railroad began construction of its line using a different gauge at each end.

Early railroads were dangerous because of the primitive technology and the inability of many undercapitalized companies to afford substantial, well-built equipment and roadbeds. Boilers exploded with regularity and trains wandered off their tracks, which at first amounted to nothing more than thin strips of cast iron nailed to the top of wooden rails. These strips frequently gave way in cold weather when trains ran over them, snapping upward like snakes to puncture car bottoms and injure passengers. Working for a railroad was also dangerous. Employees walked over the tops of pitching cars and turned down the handbrakes to stop the trains. Managers often refused to employ brakemen who still had all their fingers—a ten-fingered prospective employee was considered either inexperienced or lazy.

Despite its disadvantages, the new mode of transport brought great changes to the nation. The cost of shipping goods fell drastically. Freight rates on turnpikes averaged fifteen cents to ship one ton one mile, on the canals 10 cents, and on the railroad three cents. Railroads also greatly reduced travel time. In 1817 a traveler from Cincinnati to New York city was on the road for fifty-two days. Thirty-five years later a traveler could make the same trip by rail in seven days. A passenger train lurched along at only fifteen to twenty miles per hour, but to Americans of the Jacksonian generation, that approached the speed of light. Frontiersman Davy Crockett once told of trying to judge the speed of such a fast train "by putting my head out to spit, which I did, and overtook it so quick, that it hit me smack."

Railroads standardized time. Before the railroad, time in the United States was, at best, approximate. Theoretically tied to Greenwich Standard Time, it in fact varied from a few minutes to an hour even in places sometimes only a few miles apart. It might be 11:06 in New York City, 10:31 in Cleveland, and 10:53 in Chicago at the same moment. Telegraph lines, which paralleled most rail lines, enabled railroads to coordinate traffic and set schedules. They also used the telegraph to synchronize the nation's clocks. To standardize time, railroads installed large clocks in their depots set to "company time." Whole cities quickly followed suit, installing "railroad" clocks in central locations to insure that everyone adhered to the same time and punctually kept their appointments. In this manner railroads fundamentally altered Americans' notions of time, distance, and speed, thereby undercutting traditional conceptions of reality. The slave South's failure to adopt the railroad's new, more exact and measured outlook, only reinforced the nation's growing divergent values.

Railroad mileage increased phenomenally before the Civil War. In 1830 the country had only about seventy-five miles of track, a decade later 3,323; in 1850, 8,879; and at the outbreak of the Civil War, 30,636. A railroad map of 1860 showed that almost all the roads ran East-West, flattening the traditional Appalachian Mountain barrier that separated the sections. Ironically, the expanding railway network strengthened regional political and economic alliances. As the West became economically connected to the East, the two also became politically allied. The South found itself increasingly isolated from the rest of the country. By the 1850s, in part due to the railroad, the three traditional regions had merged into two, North and South. By 1860, virtually every western and northern line was connected to an emerging national network while southern railroad companies struggled to catch up. Only in Atlanta did the South have a semblance of a true rail network. At the time of the Civil War, railroads in the free states touched lines in the slave states only at Bowling Green, Kentucky.

The Rise of Manufacturing

The railroads also enlarged internal markets and introduced a chain reaction that touched the lives of practically every American. Prior to the construction of a national transportation system, America's merchants bought their products from local artisans or from overseas and resold them in small, local markets. Most manufacturing took place in the home or in small shops for local distribution, hence the term "cottage industries." The artisans who handcrafted shoes, candles, tinware, harnesses, clothes, bricks, or other necessary goods were respected, self-employed members of the middle class, free to set their own hours of work, contract their goods, and determine the quantity and quality of their output.

Western expansion, lower shipping costs, and faster, more reliable transportation, swelled consumer demand, and expanded entrepreneurial opportunity. Businessmen discovered that the old ways no longer sufficed. They could not depend on the production of numerous independent artisans to meet growing consumer demands. Merchants employed the once-independent artisans, furnished them with needed raw materials and told them what to make, how many, of what quality, and when to deliver the merchandise. Frequently, the merchant-capitalist purchased machinery, installed it in the former artisans' homes, supplied the raw materials, and picked up the finished products. The "putting out" system was used in the production of shoes, textiles, and wearing apparel. Such merchant-capitalism reduced the formerly independent artisan class to the status of a wage earner.

Impatient with this decentralized system, other entrepreneurs brought workers to the machines. Factories had existed in the United States before the War of 1812, but until the 1840s, with the exception of iron and textiles, consumer demand remained too low to make large capital investments worthwhile. By 1840, however, steam was economical and reliable, although most factories at the eve of the Civil War still used water power. The competition from European manufactured products that had long retarded domestic manufacturing lessened as United States markets surged and consumer demand intensified.

American mechanical ingenuity also fostered the spread of the factory system. Labor in the United States was expensive, so American capitalists had a great inducement to develop labor-saving devices. The increase in American inventions was mirrored in the rise in the number of patents. In 1790 the United States Patent

Office issued only three patents, but in 1860 it processed almost 4,500 new ideas. The enormous demand for new and better tools resulted in an American tool industry, which by 1860 was more advanced than its European counterpart. Americans pioneered the development of the milling machine, the turret lathe, the slide lathe, gear cutters, the circular saw, and the vernier calipers that enabled tool makers to make more dependable and more efficient machines.

To raise the large amounts of capital necessary to purchase these new machines, American businessmen increasingly resorted to the use of the joint-stock company. Prior to widespread adoption of the factory system in the 1840s, most companies in the United States were single proprietor or simple partnerships with all the capital raised from the owners' private means. When such private companies went bankrupt, debtors could legally hold the owners personally responsible for all business debts. The public joint-stock company, on the other hand, raised capital more easily by selling its stock in public sales to investors. Shareholders in such corporations were only responsible for the company's debts equal to the amount they had invested. Such public corporations broadened investor opportunity while curtailing risk. They allowed small investors to share in the profits of the new, large corporations, and they enabled American entrepreneurs to raise enormous sums of capital at low rates of interest to underwrite their capital investments. In Andrew Carnegie's words, in America, the road to wealth was paved with "other people's money." Jacksonian entrepreneurs believed that the joint-stock company had brought democracy to the business world.

With the emergence of large public corporations, the factory and rail system, the national output of goods rose astronomically. To protect manufacturers from foreign competition, the federal government levied tariffs, especially on cotton and woolen goods and iron, the country's basic industries. The value of all manufactured goods in 1810 had been only about 200 million dollars. But by 1850 it had risen to one billion dollars. In the next decade it doubled again. Prices fell just as dramatically—cotton sheeting dropped from eighteen cents a yard in 1815 to two cents in 1860, iron by almost fifty percent between 1830 and 1860, cotton yarn from ninety-two cents per pound in 1805 to nineteen cents in 1845 and other goods in like proportion. The combination of rising demand and declining costs created enormous wealth for the nation's upper and middle classes. Prosperity also attracted millions of impoverished Europeans to northern cities.

The United States did not immediately become a nation of smokestacks and factories. Until 1860, older handcraft or cottage industries and putting out systems worked side by side with the new factories. But by the war the days of the merchant capitalists and the craft guilds of skilled artisans were numbered. The future belonged to the rising class of industrial capitalists who owned the facilities that produced the machine-made goods for the new mass markets. American manufacturers specialized in inexpensive, crudely made goods, leaving the high priced, luxury goods to European manufacturers. Poor farmers and slaves did not require finely made goods. Some new shirts scratched so much that buyers paid people to break them in for them, and slaves were notorious for walking around in the winter bare-foot, carrying their ill-fitting shoes in their hands.

Changing American Life

American industrialization also set in motion a social revolution that broadened the gap between the very rich and the mass of Americans. The destruction of the artisan middle class marked the most noticeable change. Already in decline by the 1830s because of the encroaching factory system and mechanization, most traditional crafts had become obsolete by the 1850s. The process, however, was gradual. Artisans, who faced falling demand for their hand-wrought projects and a declining income, did not immediately give up and seek factory employment. Instead, they worked longer hours, lowered their prices, and pressed their families into service in a futile attempt to preserve their way of life. Hatters, tailors, shoemakers, handloom weavers, felt workers, lace makers, and other artisans struggled to retain their independence, but they slipped slowly and surely into the factory system. But, except in rare cases of artisans patronized by wealthy customers, the "carriage trade," their efforts were doomed as, year by year, their life gave way to the factory system, much as Native Americans had fallen victim to commercial farming.

Factory Laborers

The early workers, especially in the textile mills that pioneered the factory system, included single women from the countryside, not displaced artisans. These "factory girls" expected to work only long enough to accumulate a dowry so they could return to the farm and get married. Factory operators felt an obligation to oversee their morals. Owners of the huge Lowell and Lawrence textile mills in Massachusetts built clean, well-lighted dormitories, enforced curfews, furnished wholesome reading materials, sponsored weekly discussion groups, and of course required church attendance every Sunday. In the late 1830s, the factory girls in the Lowell Mills earned between $2.00 and $3.50 a week, out of which they repaid the company about $1.50 for their keep. European observers invariably commented favorably. An Englishman who visited Lowell testified that "the whole discipline, ventilation, and other arrangements appeared to be excellent, of which the best proof was the healthy and cheerful look of the girls."

Such factories offered wholesome employment. But the paternalistic Lowell system was exceptional and short lived. By the 1830s, farmers in the northeastern part of the country, where most of the mills were located along the falls line, found themselves competing with the rich virgin soils of the West opened up by canals and railroads. Farming in the Northeast became increasingly unprofitable. Factory girls discovered there was no farm to go home to, no young farmer to marry. They had to stay where they were. Moreover, when children fled the farm they often ended up in the factory towns and cities looking for work. Mill owners, who had earlier dispatched agents to recruit farm girls, now hired the men and women begging for work at their gates.

This labor surplus degraded working conditions inside the mills. Expensive amenities to protect the operatives' morals disappeared. With nowhere else to go, the workers accepted increasingly harsh factory discipline or lost their jobs, forcing many into prostitution. If workers complained and tried to organize, they found themselves placed on a blacklist that mill owners circulated among one another to prevent the hiring of troublemakers. Conditions in the mills disintegrated even further with the flood of Irish and French Canadians into the Northeast in the 1830s and 1840s. Work hours increased, typically from dawn to dark, or about thirteen hours a day, six days a week. Sharp competition within the textile industry after the late 1840s, as well as falling textile prices, led to the hated "speed-up" that required operatives to tend more machines for the same or even less pay. Some factory owners, squeezed the last ounce of work out of their employees, including an increasing number of children, sometimes even modifying factory clocks to run faster at night and more slowly during the day. The operatives accepted these worsening conditions because few had a second occupation or a farm to fall back upon. During depressions workers simply went hungry. By the 1840s economic conditions had placed American workers at the mercy of industrial taskmasters and economic fluctuations. By 1860 the United States had developed a rapidly growing and permanent class of industrial operatives who lived at bare levels of subsistence, including many skilled artisans.

The loss of dignity and independence bothered workers. They saw themselves as little more than "wage slaves," their worth measured by their incomes. Gone was the dignity accorded by the quality of their work or their promptness. Instead, to make a living wage, entire families toiled in the mills. Working class families no longer ate together, played together, or even worked together. The factory system undermined the traditional family as fathers lost their authority at home. Males could not maintain their authority, when everyone in the family was a breadwinner and few spent their waking hours in the home. The driving force of the relentless, unforgiving, factory clock destroyed the easier paced life of the preindustrial, self-employed artisan and farmer.

Labor Organizations

Because industrialization increased conflicts between employers and employees, some workers organized themselves into unions. The fortunes of antebellum unions rose and fell. They prospered during good economic times when employment levels were high, but in hard times, as in the depressions of 1837, 1843, 1848, 1853–1854, and 1857–1859, unions disappeared in the face of a labor surplus. Most successful unions consisted entirely of skilled workers with like interests and complaints. They tended to be local, or at most statewide, because they lacked the connections and ties to build national unions. Refusing to accept their status as members of a permanent working class, factory operatives dreamed of becoming employers themselves, or at least being self-employed. Such residual proprietary values inhibited working-class identity and presented a stumbling block to unions. The absense of unity also bedeviled unions. Jacksonian unions scattered their energies fighting for reforms as diverse as a ten-hour work day, free public schools, abolition of imprisonment for debt, an end to militia duty, the direct election of public officials, and opposition to banks.

Such unions fit the tone of Jacksonian Democracy as unions grew rapidly during the prosperous early years of the 1830s. Nationwide, union membership stood at about 300,000. Between 1834 and 1837 unions called 175 strikes. In some areas these skilled organizations attained political success. In Philadelphia and New York City, workingmen's political parties held the balance of power between the Democrats and the Whigs and elected representatives to the state legislatures. They achieved a ten-hour day in Philadelphia, and in 1840 persuaded President Martin Van Buren to require the shorter day on all government contracts. Labor support helped to achieve early public education in Pennsylvania, New York, and Massachusetts, backed Jackson's attack on the Second Bank of the United States, and won a number of specific gains for skilled workers. Unskilled workers and factory operatives failed to unionize and suffered accordingly.

The 1837 financial panic destroyed most of the labor unions. When they regrouped in the 1840s, they became more concerned with the workers' loss of dignity than with specific economic and political goals. Factory workers wanted to return to the older craft ways, rather than challenge the factory system itself. Middle class in outlook, skilled workers were drawn to such panaceas as communism, agrarianism, land reform, cooperatives, abolition of slavery, temperance, feminism, and even vegetarianism. The ideas of French reformer Charles Fourier were especially attractive. Fourier believed that the ideal society, which he called a Phalanx, had exactly 1,620 souls, each performing the task for which he was most suited within the community. About 10,000 reformers experimented in forty phalanxes during the 1840s. Wage earners carefully watched such experiments, hoping that they might offer an alterative to competition and the wage system that ruined their lives. Laborers' search for small-scale, rural answers to urbanization and the factory system was doomed to failure, a fact brought home to workers in the early 1850s when California gold strikes drove up prices but not wages, luring thousands to the Golden West. The reality of declining living standards galvanized workers in the 1850s to again organize along trade lines and agitate for specific, achievable objectives. Strikes became more frequent, and labor violence mounted until the 1857 financial panic once more wiped out many unions.

One of organized labors' most serious weaknesses revolved around its ambiguous legal status. Employers regularly broke strikes, as they had been doing since 1806, by alleging in court that such walkouts were conspiracies in restraint of trade. English common law said that an individual could refuse to work to secure higher wages or better conditions, but when two persons agreed to act together it constituted a conspiracy. The notion reflected the free market view that prices and wages would regulate themselves through unfettered competition. Workers realized that the concept had less and less applicability to an industrial world where they never saw an employer, much less had the opportunity or the power to bargain freely. In 1842 the Massachusetts Supreme Court redefined "restraint of trade"

First American streetcar, New York City, 1832

Cities used street cars, originally pulled by horses as depicted here, to move people quickly and to expand their reach into larger geographical areas. Cars powered with electricity did not appear until nearly a decade after the Civil War. (1975)

in the pathbreaking case of the *Commonwealth v. Hunt*. The court ruled that unions were legal entities as long as they pursued lawful ends and recognized the legality of the closed shop that required all workers to join the union. Not until after the Civil War did employers find other legal means to legally thwart union activities.

Ante-bellum Cities

Industrialization in the United States was not tied exclusively to cities. Factories were often located near waterfalls to power their machinery as in the case of Lowell, Fall River, Worcester, Steubenville, Newburyport, Lawrence, and dozens of other mill towns scattered about the country. In the two decades prior to 1860, living conditions in factory towns everywhere worsened—in smaller towns because of the workers' declining standard of living and in large cities because of the massive influx of poor, unskilled immigrants. Congestion in many towns and cities was nearly indescribable as municipalities struggled to meet their needs with inadequate tax bases and antiquated forms of city government. To make matters worse, unskilled workers wandered about, floating city to city seeking work. During the winter, when seasonal work was unavailable, many relied on private charity for survival. By the 1850s, about ten percent of all American workers sought charity each year because their wages could not support a family.

The rapidly changing national economy radically altered urban residential patterns. Traditionally, artisans had worked and lived in neighborhoods near their customers. In pre-industrial cities residential districts were not, except for the very lowest classes, normally segregated economically. When artisans lost their independence, however, the interdependence of the old neighborhoods declined. The introduction of horse-drawn streetcars in the 1830s allowed wealthier residents to escape congested cities and still come downtown to work. The fleeing owners sold their commodious houses to landlords who divided them into flats and rented them to new workers desperate for housing. Living conditions in the neighborhoods deteriorated as landlords crammed as many tenants into their buildings as possible, segregating ante-bellum cities by social class. In Boston, a city inspector vividly described a building with a three-story basement, "one cellar, was reported by the police to be occupied nightly as a sleeping apartment for thirty-nine persons. In another, the tide had risen so high that it was necessary to approach the bedside of a patient by means of a plank which was laid from one stool to another; while the dead body of an infant was actually sailing about the room in its coffin." New York's chief of police estimated in 1850 that five percent of the city's inhabitants lived underground. In poorer sections of the city an average of six people occupied a single-room apartment, with up to twenty people per room in the most squalid sections. Amazingly, many of these families rented out sleeping space at night. Even smaller factory towns suffered. Lowell, once an industrial showcase, by 1840 had become a study in working class misery. A local investigator in 1847 found a building in Lowell that housed a store and twenty-five families, totaling 120 people. In one case, two large families shared one room.

Such human congestion overburdened already minimal city services. Masses of humanity crammed into old wooden buildings posed serious fire hazards when most cities depended upon volunteer fire departments and bucket brigades. In the larger cities the firebell rang virtually every night. Sanitation facilities, always primitive, posed serious health hazards. Many homes in large cities drew their water from backyard wells often located right next to their privies so that the sewage seeped into the water supply. In cities such as New York, where real estate dealers maximized profits by selling lots only twenty-five feet wide, there was no way to separate such facilities. Typhoid and typhus thrived. Even at best, the disposal of human and animal wastes, posed simple problems of comfort. One report in 1849 indicated that in Lowell "the numerous outhouses were of necessity near the windows, sometimes filling the whole neighborhood with noxious exhalations." Those who could afford it moved uptown.

By the 1840s crime also plagued American towns and cities. Where police forces existed, they were small, underpaid, and invariably corrupt. In New York City and Philadelphia the police did not wear uniforms. In the face of danger they could and did melt into the onlookers. Widespread dishonesty stemmed primarily from two sources: bars and brothels. Heavy taxes and expensive licenses were levied on saloons to discourage such enterprises, but the owners found it cheaper to pay off the local constabulary to escape such costs. Prostitution existed at least covertly in every city, usually with the connivance of the local police. Simply declaring it illegal did not make it disappear. A few cities tried to control the vice. New Orleans set aside a legal red light district, Storyville, and restricted prostitution to its borders. Because ante-bellum cities suffered a significant gender imbalance males greatly outnumbered females—prostitution, venereal disease, and abandoned children were rampant, especially in the crowded working class districts, making ante-bellum Americans cities comparable to the worst areas in London portrayed by English novelist Charles Dickens.

Even so, conditions in American ante-bellum cities improved slowly. Boston, New York City, and Philadelphia all solved their water supply problems prior to the Civil War—New York City by building the Croton Reservoir forty miles away and bringing the water down to the city through a covered aqueduct. Other cities laid pipes of hollowed-out logs to pump in water and carry away sewage, though the waste frequently ran into the same stream that supplied water. Lacking a disease theory, municipal authorities treated such problems as irremediable nuances rather than threats to public health. Street lighting improved once cities switched from oil lamps to coal gas. Cities began to pave their streets with either stones or bricks. Still, largely due the dependence of horses for conveyance, all aspects of Jacksonian city life took place amid unimaginable filth, stench, and congestion. When it rained, the powdered horse manure simply turned from dust into mud and slush.

On the Farms

The vast majority of the nation's citizens, however, continued to farm. More people in 1860 made their living from the land than from any other activity. As late as 1859, sixty-five percent of Americans in the North and West still lived in rural areas. Farmers tilled 165 million acres and earned a little over thirty percent of the total national income.

Farmers also suffered from the pre-Civil War economic changes; farm life, though, resisted most of the changes that affected city dwellers. The most noticeable agricultural change in the period was the decline of farming in the Northeast. Rocky soils and a short growing season severely limited northeastern farmers' ability to compete with their western counterparts who took advantage of cheap transportation and mechanization to break into eastern markets. New England farmers formed a mass exodus into the region's mill towns and to the Midwest while those left behind changed their old farming habits. Wheat and corn cultivation declined as New England farmers turned to dairying and sheep raising. By the 1840s, they also cultivated fruits and vegetables for urban buyers and hay for dairy cattle. Lumbering and the manufacture of maple sugar rounded out the section's rural economy. The staple crops, wheat and corn, moved relentlessly westward during the prewar years. By 1860 Illinois led the nation in the production of both. Most of the corn crop went to market on the hoof, as hogs for pork remained the favorite American meat.

Even though most farms continued as family enterprises, changing economic conditions slowly tied the farmers to urban markets and brought them into the cash economy. Farmers no longer grew and met all their families' needs, rather selling their surplus to buy small luxuries. They farmed more acreage and, with the help of machines, fertilizer, and hired help, produced food for millions of people in American and European cities, who had left the land and now depended on others to eat. The demand for American food had grown so large that after 1830, wheat replaced cotton as the nation's largest export commodity. Perhaps, not coincidentally, the 1830s also marked the beginning of the American anti-slavery movement.

Pressures on American farmers to increase production brought improvement in agricultural techniques. The number of hours needed to grow and harvest one acre of wheat fell from fifty-six in 1800 to thirty-five in 1840. For corn, the hours dropped from eighty-six to sixty-nine. Numerous improvements appeared: by the 1830s the cradle had replaced the sickle for reaping grain, and the cast iron plow superseded the wooden one. Soon after, John Deere's steel plow replaced its cast iron predecessor. Seed drills, mowers, and hay rakes reduced the work load further. In 1834 Cyrus McCormick, a Virginian, revolutionized wheat production when he patented a practical reaper that promised to cut harvesting time in half. McCormick moved to Chicago to produce his reaper, and by 1860 about 70,000 of his and imitators' machines were in use. The threshing machine, available by the 1840s, raised the efficiency of wheat culture even more by ending the need to flail grain by hand or with animals; soon Jerome Case's threshers were common sights in the midwestern wheat belt. Except for the cotton gin and steampowered balers, the South experienced little change in agricultural technology, continuing to rely on manual slave labor for most activities.

But even with these technological improvements, farmers' productivity increased only gradually. Each farmer in 1820 fed his family and 3.1 other people; forty years later he fed his family and 3.5 others. Wary of change, ante-bellum farmers resisted suggestions for betterment. Land remained cheap in relation to the cost of labor, and many farmers continued to wear out their soil and move on. Except in the East, they neither joined agricultural societies nor read scientific journals. Advice on how to fertilize, rotate crops, and contour plow passed largely unheeded. Soil depletion and erosion, both easily preventable, endured as chronic rural problems everywhere. Farmers showed a quickened interest in selective breeding of livestock, largely because it did not require a great expenditure of money nor energy. New strains of animals, such as the Spanish Merino sheep, came from abroad and farmers fenced in the superior animals to preserve the breed. Prior to the Civil War, emerging agricultural changes lagged behind the industrial innovations that were rapidly transforming the nation. Not until after the Civil War did American farming undergo the same process of mechanization and consolidation that had reshaped ante-bellum manufacturing.

Social and Cultural Ferment

The 1830s were a major watershed in American life. The canal systems had been built, the railroad appeared, cities began to grow rapidly, western expansion accelerated, and the factory system emerged. Antebellum Americans, more than ever, measured themselves and others with clocks and bank balances. In the East and West, anyone who paused to admire God's creations risked being trampled under by those eager to find their fortunes. Such change led a number of people to reexamine their lives and to restructure their society's moral order. Henry David Thoreau penned *Walden Pond*, hoping that readers would reconsider the "quiet desperation" of their lives, while Mother Anne Lee asked her followers to give up all carnal pleasures, especially sex, and form devout and puritanical communities of Shakers. John Humphey Noyes, in contrast, believed that without free and plentiful sex humans would never find happiness. In Oneida, New York Noyes formed a community of consenting adults, bound in a "complex marriage" in which adult members had to comply with requests by other adult members of the community for biblically sanctioned sex. Joseph Smith founded the Church of the Latter Day Saints, which believed in polygamy and the evolution of believers into gods. William Miller adopted a millennial form of Adventist Christianity that preached the immediate end of the world. The most far-reaching and influential of the antebellum social ferment occurred in the "Burned-Over District" of upstate New York that paralleled the Erie Canal.

Following the opening of the Erie Canal, upstate New York underwent rapid settlement. The canal changed western New York into a prosperous agricultural region with easy access to New York City. Moreover, the canal stimulated the growth of cities along its banks, including Albany, Utica, Syracuse, and Buffalo, and Rochester nearby on Lake Ontario. In the process, western New York replaced Pennsylvania as the gateway to the West. After 1825, New Englanders, seeking inexpensive farms in Ohio, Indiana, and Michigan traveled west by way of the Erie Canal. European immigrants, too, now embarked for New York City, rather than Philadelphia or Baltimore, traveled on a boat north up the Hudson to Albany, boarded a canal barge to Buffalo from where they headed to points west, either overland or on Lake Erie.

The net effect of all this activity made western New York a prosperous, rapidly growing, and confusing place. Towns sprouted up at every hand, newcomers came and went, fortunes were made over night, and from year to year almost nothing remained the same. A majority of the region's settlers were displaced Yankees from over-populated areas of New England, particularly Vermont, who retained their Puritan forbears' interest in radical religion and stable communities. Many such Yankees became so disoriented by the pace of change in western New York that they concluded it signified something momentous, perhaps cataclysmic, even millennial and apocalyptic.

Preachers responded to their congregants' concerns and fears in two ways. One group of revivalist ministers, influenced by Charles Finney, declared that God called all true Christians to action. A truly saved Christian should go out into the world and reform it consistent with Christian values. A saved Christian should "perfect" society, making it a Godly place. Finney's doctrine of "perfectionism" inspired thousands of Protestants in Western New York, Ohio, Indiana, and Michigan, especially those of New England backgrounds, to bring moral order to the social and moral chaos in which they found themselves.

Consequently, beginning in the 1830s, as this Second Great Awakening spread across the region, Finney-inspired evangelicals formed hundreds of reform societies to suppress the consumption of alcoholic beverages. They also organized Sunday Schools, missionary societies, and Bible societies, built orphanages, public schools, homes for wayward girls and poor houses, and formed women's rights groups and anti-slavery societies. They organized hundreds of organizations—national, state, and local—to reform the evils of their society, to make the United States a godly community. The overwhelming majority of individuals who joined this evangelical reform crusade were women, marking the entry of women into American public life. Such reformers sought a revitalized sense of community to replace one lost to rapid change, the market economy, and urbanization.

Such changes were paralleled similar trends in education. The Jacksonians' promise to extend political rights to all mature white males and to offer equal economic opportunities for all was self-defeating without an enlightened citizenry. The one point on which Hamilton, Jefferson, and Jackson all agreed was that the nation's destinies should be guided by a literate public. They disagreed, however, on the size and status of that public. As the Jacksonians labored to uplift the growing working class, they continued to send their children into the factories at an early age, making a mockery of participatory democracy. Moreover, growing businesses desperately needed workers who could think, read, write, and cipher, as well as literate workers to tend complicated and expensive machinery. Jacksonian Americans came to view literacy as a birthright because they identified personal success in the industrial world with the mastery of arithmetic, reading, and writing. And among those in the rapidly growing evangelical Protestant sects, schooling became imperative so that believers could read their Bibles.

Public Schools

The ideal of a public primary education for every child was not new, but until the 1830s public education had been limited to pauper schools for orphans and poor children. Prodded by numerous workingmen's associations, Pennsylvania led the way in 1834 with legislation that divided the state into school districts. Each district decided whether to levy taxes for public education. Most did so immediately, though the last rural district lagged behind until 1873. New Jersey passed a free school law in 1829, but it did not become permanent until 1838. Most Northeast and mid-Atlantic states followed suit by 1840. Public education developed much more slowly in the South, however, where the absence of a free working class and the relatively sparse population hindered its growth. Slave holders, who dominated southern state legislatures, saw little value in taxing themselves to educate other people's children, and they considered literacy inappropriate, even dangerous, for slaves. Some southern states aided private schools, and by the Civil War the percentage of white southern children enrolled in school was close to that in the rest of the country, but the educational quality was much lower.

Horace Mann, secretary of the Massachusetts State Board of Education from 1837 to 1849, did more than any other American to upgrade the quality of public education. Massachusetts also set an example for the rest of the nation. Acutely aware of the needs of the developing economy, he raised salaries, improved physical facilities, lengthened the school year, required schools to keep student records, investigated teaching methods, minimized corporal punishment, and encouraged teacher education. Nearly every state had its Horace Mann, but in the 1840s still less than one-half of the nation's free children attended any school. No compulsory school attendance laws existed before Massachusetts passed the first in 1852. Many working class families desperately needed their children's income to survive. Others lived in rural areas where no public schools existed. The agitation for public education also extended to secondary schools, but progress was slower. Boston formed the first public high school in 1821, and six years later the state required every town with over 500 people to maintain a public high school. Maine and New York picked up the idea, but it went little further. By 1860, most states offered secondary education only through private academies.

Except for primary school, educational opportunities for females were scant. Private secondary schools rarely admitted girls. Starting with Troy, in upstate New

York, in 1821, however, "female seminaries" began to offer girls a high school education. The curriculum of such schools emphasized household tasks, hygiene, religion, social duties, art, music, fiction, and poetry. On the college level, Oberlin became the nation's first coeducational college when it admitted women in 1833. Three years later, the first women's college, Mount Holyoke College, advertised its opening. But since college was seen as preparation for a profession-law, medicine, and the ministry-few women felt the need to attend.

At the college level, public education was meager. The demand for colleges freed from church control had resulted in the establishment of numerous state universities, especially in the slave South— including the University of Georgia, the University of Virginia, the University of North Carolina, and the College of South Carolina—so that the sons of planters would not have to endure education in the North. Outside the South, the Jacksonian era did not witness an expansion of state systems. Instead the new colleges begun in the last three decades before the war were usually private religious colleges spawned by the Second Great Awakening. By 1860 the United States had many colleges, but only a few worthy of the name. Large schools such as Harvard and Yale enrolled less than 500 students. Most, like Amherst and Kenyon, claimed student bodies of fewer than 200. Students rarely took elective courses. Instead most received the standard fare of Latin, Greek, mathematics, history, and philosophy—the traditional liberal arts program that led to an A.B. Harvard offered the first B.S. degree in 1850, differing from the A.B. only that it required no foreign language. Industrialization brought a few changes to higher education, notably in the establishment of the military academy at West Point, Rensselaer Polytechnic Institute, and Union College to train engineers to plan and construct internal improvements. Most students, however, still pursued the A.B. that conferred on the graduate the distinction of a gentleman and opened the door to professions. Such changes meant little, however, since only 3% of the male population attended college in the antebellum period—the lowest percentage of college attendance any time in American history and much lower than it was in the colonial period.

American Literature

With the increase in literacy and the rise of several major cities, the United States produced a host of native writers. Many hailed from New England, forming the "New England Renaissance." They included the poet and essayist Ralph Waldo Emerson. An American sage, Emerson penned essays on "Nature" and "Self-Reliance" and guided two generations of American intellectuals who formed a school of American thought called "transcendentalism." Emerson's emphasis on an indwelling and innate Spirit that gave man the capacity to comprehend all truths flowed naturally into a philosophy of self-reliance and individualism and was in harmony with older American religious and communal ideals. Emerson raised questions about the factory system that demeaned workers and destroyed all possibility of artful work. In the age of factories, slavery, and cities, Emerson's ideas questioned Americans' unbridled pursuit of wealth and contempt for the natural world.

Massachusettsian Henry David Thoreau (1817-62) was a counter-cultural figure who wrote of the glories of rural life but was most famous for his *Essay on Civil Disobedience*; he also supported radical abolitionism in the person of John Brown. (1967)

Emerson's close friend and protege, Henry David Thoreau, deeply influenced by Emerson's transcendentalism, rejected American's obsession with wealth and power. Instead he spent his time walking the woods and contemplating nature. As an experiment Thoreau built a small shack at Walden Pond where he observed nature and wrote. Thoreau published his notes as *Walden*, a carefully written essay that attacked Americans' empty pursuit of wealth that resulted in their lives of "quiet desperation." During the Mexican War, Thoreau spent one night in jail in 1846 for refusing to pay taxes that supported what he described as the imperialist Mexican War in pursuit of more land and slaves. Thoreau's essay "Civil Disobedience" justified his "marching to a different drumbeat" and became a central work in the growing ranks of American pacifists. An international classic, "Civil Disobedience," influenced the thought of future activists like Leo Tolstoi, Mahatma Gandhi, and Martin Luther King.

Other followers of Emerson formed a transcendental circle of writers and poets, established a commune at Brook Farm, and started a literary magazine, *The Dial*, edited by Margaret Fuller. The most published of the transcendentalists, Nathaniel Hawthorn wrote such American classics as, *The House of Seven Gables* and the *Scarlet Letter*. Other American writers, such as Herman Melville, read the transcendentalists, but drew more pessimistic conclusions. Melville's monumental seafaring allegory, *Moby Dick*, dealt with sin, love between men, and divine retribution. In a similar vein, but uninfluenced by the transcendentalists, New York poet Edgar Allen Poe, in his poetry and short-stories, wrote about death and self-destruction. In contrast, the South witnessed no such flowering, producing no significant writer. Its most read author, Charlestonian William Gilmore Sims, wrote romances as well as

Yamasee, a novel of the destruction of a Carolina Indian tribe in a similar vein to James Fenimore Cooper's *Leather Stocking Tales*.

Brooklyn poet Walt Whitman in his *Leaves of Grass*, broke with the genteel and religious concerns of New England writers and, instead, became the poet laureate of American democracy. Influenced by Quakers, Whitman believed in the perfectibility of humankind and wrote in a free style, unhindered by traditional literary notions of rhyme and meter. He supported the anti-slavery movement and during the Civil War served as a nurse in Union field hospitals. He considered democracy the salvation of humankind and believed that ultimately, if left to their own devices, people would behave humanely. Leaders simply had to have confidence in people and democracy and their inherent decency.

The End of National Unity

All these economic and literary developments served to mark off the Northeast and, increasingly, the West from the South to create the America that most Americans came to regard as the norm. The most important political change involved the alignment of the Northeast with the West against the South. This realignment took place slowly during the 1840s because the national politicians plainly feared its consequences, particularly on the two political parties.

In the North a new American democracy developed that Northerners increasingly regarded as the American norm, viewing the South and slavery as "peculiar." The most important political change involved the realignment of the free labor North and Midwest against the slave South. The country's politicians desperately fought to stave off the growing divisions and preserve the eighteenth-century federal union. The most effective of these antebellum compromisers was Martin Van Buren, Jackson's vice president and head of the New York Democratic Party. Of New York Dutch ancestry, the "Red Fox of Kinderhook" assembled a northern and southern coalition of voters. During the election of 1836, sectional concern surfaced over the black children of Van Buren's Kentucky running mate, Richard Johnson. The Whigs, however, could not agree on a single candidate, running Daniel Webster in New England, William Henry Harrison in the West, and Hugh White in the South. Van Buren received a majority of the electoral votes, but his vice president did not. For the first and only time the Senate chose the vice president, Richard M. Johnson.

Thanks to the financial Panic of 1837 and the ensuing depression, Van Buren's administration turned into a disaster. Widespread unemployment led to food riots in New York City in 1837. Banks across the country suspended payments, even Biddle's bank succumbed in 1841. Several states defaulted on their obligations, and federal land sales dried up. The seeds for the panic, planted during the 1830s boom, included speculation and inflation. Speculators gobbled up western lands, borrowed money from banks and used their local bank notes to pay the federal treasury. The number of such note issues increased after Jackson vetoed the Second Bank of the United States and placed its deposits in the state banks where the federal government deposited its income from land sales. The state banks treated the government funds as specie deposits and increased their loans so that inflation grew like a cancer. In 1836, however, it was checked when the government distributed surplus funds to the states based on their congressional representation. As the states spent these funds, they drew down bank reserves, particularly in rural areas. By 1836 Jackson had grown concerned about the rate of credit expansion and, to stabilize the situation, issued the Specie Circular that required payment for land in gold and silver. The circular cut land sales short and raised doubts about the value of all state bank notes. At the same time European banks, especially the Bank of London, reduced new advances to the United States and called in old loans, particularly those backed by futures in the unharvested 1836 cotton crop. Depositors removed specie from their bank accounts. Banks, in turn, responded by restricting loans and issuance of new currency. Then several New Orleans cotton houses failed, creating panic in New York City. In May 1837 banks suspended all specie payments. With the stabilizing hand of the Bank of the United States gone and the sudden contraction of European credit, the country's financial structure collapsed. Van Buren and the Democrats reaped the political storm.

The president tried to stabilize the shattered economy by strengthening the federal role with an "independent treasury," a plan he advanced in 1837 to avoid the political passions excited by a national bank. He proposed the government handle its own money at an independent treasury in Washington with "sub-treasuries" located around the country to receive funds and pay the government's bills—no "pet banks" and no Bank of the United States. The bill raised such a storm of protest in congress that it took three years to secure passage. A year later congress repealed the act.

In the 1840 presidential election the Whigs smelled victory. At their nominating convention, they passed over Clay and turned to Indiana's General William Henry Harrison, a "man on horseback," a military hero, to rescue them. For vice president, the Whigs tapped John Tyler of Virginia to balance the ticket. The Democrats unenthusiastically endorsed Van Buren. In the "log cabin and hard cider" campaign the Whigs portrayed the wealthy Harrison, hero of Tippecanoe, as a man of humble origins. They depicted Van Buren as a haughty eastern aristocrat who dined off gold spoons in the people's White House. The public fell in love with "Old Tippecanoe and Tyler too." The Whigs captured the White House and congress. The sixty-eight-year-old Harrison promptly caught pneumonia and died thirty days after taking office. Tyler became the first vice president to ascend to the presidency.

John Tyler, Whig

Like Van Buren, Tyler stumbled from one disaster to another. His opponents dubbed him "His Accidency.' More at home with conservative, southern states' rights Democrats than with members of his own party, Tyler opposed the formation of a new banking system similar to the old Bank of the United States, opting instead for a "states' rights national bank" with a central bank in Washington and branches only in those states that wanted them. Tyler's party stood for federally aided internal improvements, but the president regularly vetoed such bills. Finally, in September 1841, his entire cabinet, with the exception of secretary of state Webster, resigned in disgust. Later, congressional Whigs took the unusual step of repudiating Tyler. Without a political base, he had trouble getting anybody of note to serve in his administration. His cabinet officers resigned almost as soon as they took office.

The Webster-Ashburton Treaty, signed with Britain in 1842, was Tyler's only accomplishment. In the treaty, the United States finally gained an internationally recognized northern boundary from the Atlantic Ocean to the Rocky Mountains. Since 1783 the British had claimed 12,000 square miles along the northern boundary of Maine. In the Webster-Ashburton Treaty, the United States acquired about 7/12 of the disputed area and the federal government reimbursed Maine and Massachusetts, which had once controlled Maine, for lost land claim.

Political Factions

During the interval from Monroe to Tyler a political revolution had taken place. The old Jeffersonian Republican Party of the "Era of Good Feeling" split into two major parties. After 1840 the political divisions splintered even further into an assortment of "third parties" as the country's sectional divisions became more difficult to ignore. One of these, the Anti-Masonic Party, appeared after a former Mason, William Morgan, who had threatened to reveal the secrets of the order, disappeared, apparently the victim of foul play. Five years of investigations failed to solve the mystery and only fanned public fears of the Masons. Because Washington, Jefferson, and Jackson had been or were members of the order, public animosity quickly turned political. A semblance of a political party appeared in New York in 1830 dedicated to driving Masons from office. The party became an anti-Jackson party, and in 1832 ran a presidential ticket headed by William Wirt, who belonged to the secret order himself. Wirt garnered only seven electoral votes, and over the next four years the crusade lost much of its fervor. In 1836 the Anti Masons united with the Whigs in opposition to Jackson, Van Buren, and the Democrats.

To further complicate the scene, the Native American Party surfaced, an anti-Irish, anti-Catholic movement ignited by rising Irish immigration fueled by the Irish famine. On a state level in the Northeast, the new party joined with the Whigs and in 1844 elected the mayor of New York City. The same year anti-Irish, nativist feelings in Philadelphia provoked two riots that pitted Protestants against Catholics. Twenty-one people were killed. Such nativist sentiment continued strong wherever there were large numbers of Irish immigrants.

In 1840 the Liberty Party, another anti-Democratic Party, refocused the nation's attention on slavery. Ignoring Democratic and Whig efforts to address such a volatile issue, anti-slavery groups insisted that national political leaders confront the question. Dedicated to the gradual emancipation of slaves and opposed to the admission of Texas as a slave state, the Liberty Party determined the outcome of the presidential election of 1844.

The ability of a minor third party to affect a national election graphically illustrated the challenge that the two major parties faced in seeking to avoid any discussion of slavery. In the 1840s the Democrats and Whigs desperately sought to hold together their southern and northern wings. But no single, national party could bridge the differences that had developed between the two regions. The factory system, public education, urbanization, the Second Great Awakening, the westward movement, immigration, and changing attitudes toward women, children, the family, and slavery, prompted the formation of a new, urban-based middle class. In the North everything, it seemed, had changed. In the South, the world that had led to the great compromises over slavery at the federal convention and the Missouri debates remained intact. The two major parties adopted this compromise as the cornerstone of national unity, hoping that states' rights and Americans' pursuit of wealth would allow the federal republic to weather the winds of change. But by the 1840s, voters in both North and South increasingly viewed the earlier compromises as "corrupt bargains" that morally tainted the republic and threatened the future of their children.

By mid-century the dreams and aspirations of the nation's two regions had become vastly different. America's second generation of national leaders—Calhoun,

Webster, Clay, and Jackson—had overseen enormous, unprecedented change. In the South the cotton revolution had rescued slavey from almost certain extinction and insulated the slave South from most of the changes that had transformed the East and Midwest. In the free states the factory system, the railroad, urbanization, and Irish immigration had destroyed the older, agriculturally-based, rural world of the nation's founders. Having remade their world, both materially and morally, northerners, especially evangelical Protestants, found themselves unhappy with a constitutional order that placed state interests above national interests, thwarted economic development, and valued the property claims and political prerogatives of slave owners over universal freedom and Christian morality. By 1844 the differences between North and South had become too fundamental for the nation's political institutions to resolve peacefully. For the second time in a century, the American people moved irrevocably toward civil war and constitutional revolution. This time, there would be no compromise.

Historical Potpourri

In the mid 19th century American primary schools taught a heavy dose of Christian morality along with reading, writing, and arithmetic. One of the most popular schoolbooks of the period was *McGuffey's Reader* in which the author made it clear what type of book he was presenting:

> *The lessons are short, the language simple, the subjects interesting, and especially attractive to children. At the same time, it has been made an important object to append valuable instruction, and to exercise a healthy moral influence upon the mind of the learner. The readings in the book emphasized honesty, thrift, helpfulness, and kindness to animals.*

Below is a typical object lesson:

1. A boy was once sent from home to carry a basket.

2. The basket was so full, that it was very heavy.

3. His little brother was to go with him to help him.

4. They put a pole under the handle of the basket.

5. Each then took hold of an end of the pole, to carry the basket.

6. Now the boy thought, my brother does not know about this pole.

7. If the basket is in the middle of the pole, it will be as heavy for me as for him.

8. But if I slip the basket near him, his side will be heavy, and mine light.

9. He does not know this as I do. But I will not do it.

10. It would be wrong, and I will not do what is wrong.

11. Then he slipped the basket near his own side.

12. His load was now heavy, while that of his little brother was light.

13. Yet he was happy; for he felt he had done right.

14. We may be sure that we shall always be happy when we do right.

Frequently the morality tales were put into verse form although the rhymes were not always perfect:

> *Whatever brawls disturb the street, There should be peace at home;*
> *Where sisters dwell, and brothers meet, Quarrels should never come.*

Or, as in another example:

> *My mother, I know,*
> *Would sorrow so,*
> *Should I be stolen away;*
> *So I'll speak to the birds,*
> *In my softest words.*

Exhortations to Christian living was a major theme in *McGuffey's Reader* as the following verse indicates:

> *A LITTLE child who loves to pray;*
> *And read his Bible, too,*
> *Shall rise above the sky one day,*
> *And sing as angels do;*
>
> *Shall live in heaven, that world above,*
> *Where all is joy, and peace, and love.*
> *Look up, dear children, see that star,*
> *Which shines so brightly there;*
> *But you shall brighter shine by far,*
> *When in that world so fair;*
> *A harp of gold you each shall have,*
> *And sing the power of Christ to save.*

Source: *McGuffey's New Second Eclectic Reader* (New York: American Book Company, 1857). Reprinted by Henry Ford, 1930.

Good Books

George Dangerfield's *The Era of Good Feelings* (1952) is an excellent starting place for the period 1815 to 1828. Rush Welter's penetrating insights into *The Mind of America, 1820-1860* (1975) makes this a good companion volume. Charles M. Wiltse examines political theory in *The New Nation, 1800-1845* (1961). Richard Hofstader's *The Idea of the Party System (1969)*, not only establishes the importance of Martin Van Buren, but also the emergence of a new notion of "loyal opposition." See *The Birth of Modern America, 1820-1850* (1970) by Douglas T. Miller; Arthur M. Schlesinger, Jr., *The Age of Jackson* (1945), and John W. Ward, *Andrew Jackson: Symbol for an Age* (1962). A more recent survey of the period is Robert Remini's two excellent volumes, *Andrew Jackson and the Course of American Empire* (1977) and *Andrew Jackson and the Course of American Freedom* (1981) . Maurice Baxter has written a solid, short biography, *Henry Clay: The Lawyer* (2000).

Indian removal was at the center of Jacksonian politics. See Anthony F.C. Wallace, *The Long Bitter Trail: Andrew Jackson and the Indians* (1993). For additional insights to the Indian "problem," Grant Foreman's book, *Indian Removal* (1969) and Ronald Satz', *American Indian Policy in the Jacksonian Er*a (1975) are excellent. Also see Michael P. Rogin's *Fathers and Children: Andrew Jackson and the Subjugation of the American Indian* (1975).

Gray Hammond, *Banks and Politics in America from the Revolution to the Civil War* (1957) and Robert V. Remini, *Andrew Jackson and the Bank War* (1967) clarify Jackson's bank troubles as well as the general role of banks in the United States economy. A recent study of early banking is Howard Bodenhorn, *A History of Banking in Antebellum America* (2000). See Charles Sellers' *The Market Economy* (1992) and Peter Temin's *The Jacksonian Economy* (1969). George R. Taylor's, *The Transportation Revolution* (1951), captures the critical importance of transportation while John F. Stover's *American Railroads* (1961) and *Railroads Triumphant* (1992) are solid treatments of the railroad. Paul W. Gates describes *The Farmer's Age: Agriculture 1815-1860* (1968). Norman Ware treats *The Industrial Worker, 1840-1860* (1924). Russell B. Nye's *Society and Culture in America, 1830-1860* (1974) does a good job with popular culture. Also see Robert G. Albion's *The Rise of New York Port*, 1815-1860 (1939); Richard C. Wade's *The Urban Frontier: The Rise of Western Cities, 1790-1830* (1959); and Frederick Rudolph's *The American College and University* (1962).

The most important recent work on the Jacksonian period focuses on women and family. Start with Ann Douglas, *The Femininization of American Culture* (1977) which raises important questions about how middle class women shaped antebellum culture. Also see Mary Ryan's *Cradle of the Middle Class: The Family in Oneida County, New York,*

1790-1865 (1981). Gilman Ostander looks at *The Republic of Letters* (1999). An interesting perspective on working class culture is Sean Wilentz, *Chants Democratic* (1983). A. F. Tyler watches *Freedom's Ferment* (1944) as she describes phases of social history and reformers rising in the period.

CHAPTER FIVE

 A House Divided

1822	First land grant to Americans in Texas
1822	Denmark Vesey slave plot
1826	Thomas Jefferson and John Adams both died on Independence Day
1828	Tariff of Abominations South Carolina Exposition protested protective tariffs
1831	First issue of *The Liberator* Nat Turner slave insurrection in Virginia Debate in Virginia over compensated slave emancipation
1832	South Carolina nullified tariff Jackson's "Proclamation to the People of South Carolina"
1833	Force Bill
1835	Compromise tariff Charleston, South Carolina postmaster impounded abolitionist mail
1836	Americans in Texas adopted their Declaration of Independence Siege and fall of the Alamo House of Representatives adopted the "gag rule"
1839	Liberty party founded
1842	Dorr Rebellion
1845	Texas annexed
1846	Mexican War Bear Flag revolt in California Treaty with Great Britain set Oregon boundary
1848	Zachary Taylor twelfth president Gold discovered in California Treaty of Guadadalupe Hildago

1849	Taylor recommended admission of California to the Union
1850	Taylor died Millard Fillmore thirteenth president Compromise of 1850
1852	Franklin Pierce fourteenth president
1853	*Uncle Tom's Cabin* Gadsden Purchase

A House Divided

By the third decade of the nineteenth century, sectional differences dominated most public discussions. Hints of sectional divergences had occurred during debates over the colonial slave trade, regional antagonisms had surfaced again at the Constitutional Convention, and later Alexander Hamilton's economic program had convinced some southerners that they would bear a disproportionate share of its costs. Despite these differences, the successful experiment in nation building muted any continuing animosities between leaders from the various parts of the country. In view of later developments George Washington erred when he told Americans, "with slight shades of difference, you have the same religion, manners, habits, and political principles," but his view mirrored the hopes of most of his countrymen.

Southerners were no exception in the celebration of national unity. For one thing, the national government permitted them to enjoy a measure of political influence that enhanced their section's power. Save for the one term of John Adams, southerners had occupied the White House every year from its creation to 1837. Of the twenty supreme court justices appointed through 1822, thirteen had come from the South, and for most of these years southerners had dominated congress. As long as they conceived their interests—economic, political, and social—in basic harmony with those of the rest of the country, divisive sectionalism remained submerged in the national unity.

No one worked harder to advance his region' s prerogatives within the framework of the federal union than South Carolina's John Caldwell Calhoun. With bushy hair, bright flashing eyes, and what all conceded was a steel trap mind, he regularly championed southern interests. Yet, Calhoun consistently remained at heart a nationalist. As a symbol of the South he acted as an accurate barometer of the changes that convulsed his native region and the nation during the first half of the nineteenth century.

It was an era when simple expedients such as a protective tariff, a national road, and a stable currency could reduce and control what Calhoun liked to refer to as "selfish instincts of our nature." Calhoun and other southern leaders vigorously supported such legislation. Having already endorsed the bill establishing the Second National Bank, Calhoun called for a tariff law in 1816 to tax imports and to protect American manufacturers so as to "bind together our widely spread Republic." Former president Jefferson, who had once expressed qualms about such measures, smiled down on his disciple's efforts from Monticello.

South Carolina and Nullification

By the mid-1820s, however, the South found itself at the end of those happy days when its own immediate interests coincided with the desires of the rest of the nation. An incident involving an obscure free black house servant in Charleston, South Carolina, in conjunction with the advent of twelve-cent cotton together shook the region to its foundations and changed its relationship to the rest of the union. On May 30, 1822, a house slave in Charleston whispered to his master that another black man had tried to recruit him for an insurrection to seize control of the city. The plot was the brainchild of Denmark Vesey, whose reading of the Bible had convinced him he had a mission to liberate his benighted brothers. Two days before the date set for the revolt, Charleston authorities descended and summarily hanged thirty-seven alleged conspirators. The plot was scotched, but its memory lingered on all across the South. Every time a master looked directly at one of his servants he could well wonder what treacherous thoughts might lurk behind those downcast eyes.

The abortive Vesey revolt occurred during a prolonged depression that drove cotton prices relentlessly down from a high of thirty-three cents in 1819 to twelve cents a year later. The large profits in cotton cultivation right after 1815 encouraged planters across the South to expand their cotton production. They were soon wedded to the white fiber and correspondingly to the institution of slavery, which helped them produce it. The depression of 1819, however, brought an end to the postwar boom; banks became popular villains as they foreclosed mortgages and called in their debts. Simple folk faced with disabling losses paid little heed to those better off who advised, "let us turn from the wickedness of our ways, humble ourselves before the throne of Almighty God." It was not Almighty God, after all, who foreclosed.

By the late 1820s, South Carolina's low-country aristocrats were disquieted as they listened to the open attacks on slavery that continued after the Missouri statehood debate. Calhoun, vice president under—certainly not with—John Quincy Adams, found himself pressured by political forces in his home state to take a stand against any broad constitutional interpretations that would allow a future congress to interfere with slavery. If nationalists in Washington succeeded in reading the constitution as an unlimited grant of power, southerners thought that their "domestic and peculiar" slave institution was endangered.

The Tariff Question

The tariff provoked already edgy South Carolina slave holders to defy the federal government. Southerners claimed that protective duties represented a broad construction because the constitution authorized only a tariff for revenue. If congress granted the federal government the power to enact protective tariffs, there was nothing to stop it from using the interstate commerce clause to interfere with the domestic slave trades. Moreover, protection also meant high prices on manufactured items—woolens and shoes—and might also lead to retaliation from foreign countries against cotton. In 1827, Calhoun cast the deciding vote in the senate to defeat increased import duties on woolens, but the protectionist demands continued to mount. In 1825 a convention in Harrisburg, Pennsylvania, demanded across-the-board increases from congress. Thanks to the maneuvering of Jacksonians out to embarrass President Adams and to damage his reelection chances, the persuasive influence of a horde of industrial lobbyists, and the miscalculations of southerners, a bill increasing import duties from $33^1/_3$ percent to 50 percent *ad valorem* won congressional and presidential approval. Southerners labeled the tariff of 1828 the "Tariff of Abominations."

Nullification

The South Carolina legislature quickly adopted eight resolutions that described the tariff as unjust and unconstitutional while it circulated a document entitled the "South Carolina Exposition," secretly written by Calhoun, to justify its actions. The South Carolina Exposition sought to protect the rights of minority slave holders from majority freeholders. Drawing on the Kentucky and Virginia Resolves of a quarter century earlier, Calhoun claimed that the power to declare a law unconstitutional—to nullify it—rested with each state, because the states had called the central government into existence and state constituent assemblies had ratified it; the sovereign people, organized by states, predated the federal government. Acting as sovereigns, the people in the states had created the federal government and retained the authority to change the constitution. A nullifying ordinance, according to Calhoun, overrode any federal law with which it dealt, unless and until congress could secure a constitutional amendment, ratified by three quarters of the states meeting in constituent assemblies to authorize the nullified statute.

Most other opponents of protective tariffs, however, relied on political deals rather than constitutional arguments to resolve the dispute. After his inauguration, Jackson recommended a revision of the tariff, affirming the constitutionality of protection. Jackson might have played the political game, but he had not endorsed the nullifiers' position. On July 14, 1832, congress approved a new tariff with lower rates, but still affirmed the principle of protection; the nullifiers only waxed stronger. Putting Calhoun's theory to a practical test, the South Carolina legislature called a special election for representatives to a nullification convention to meet in November. The convention met to approve an ordinance pronouncing the tariffs of 1828 and 1832 "unauthorized by the Constitution of the United States and null and void, and no law, nor binding upon this State, its officers or citizens." The next move was up to Andrew Jackson.

The Union Rampant

Jackson wasted no time. On December 4, he asked congress to further lower tariff duties, and on December 10, he issued a ringing assertion of national authority in a proclamation to the people of South Carolina. The most important state paper since the Constitution, Jackson attacked head-on the theoretical basis of states' rights, nullification, and secession. Jackson affirmed that nullification was "incompatible with the existence of the Union, contradicted expressly by the letter of the Constitution, unauthorized by its spirit, inconsistent with every principle on which it was founded, and destructive of the great object for which it was formed." He described South Carolina's threatened secession as "a revolutionary act" that might be morally justified, but it was not a constitutional right and only deceived those who would embark on revolution. To back up Jackson's strong stand, congress passed the Force Bill on March I, 1833, that authorized the president to use troops, if necessary, to collect the lowered tariff duties. The South Carolina legislature mobilized the state guard, increasing the possibility of civil strife.

Jackson's proclamation in 1832 closed the government's case against nullification and secession. But for southerners committed to slavery, Jackson's words meant little. For these radicals, the president's words would have to be inscribed in blood. South Carolina slave holders' behavior during the nullification crisis reflected, not just their determination to defend slavery, but their belief that slavery represented a morally defensible institution, wholly consistent with liberty, Christianity, and honor.

The Old South

Since colonial times, the South had always been somewhat different than the remainder of the nation. Its warmer climate was conducive to large scale commercial agriculture that by eighteenth century had become based almost exclusively on chattel slavery. Apart from the distinctiveness of slavery itself, southern slaves were exclusively Africans in background, making the South the only truly multi-racial region in British North America. Moreover, slavery led to the concentration of great wealth in a relatively few families, who used their wealth to control southern politics. At the time of the American Revolution the region was dominated by wealthy Chesapeake tobacco planters and Carolina and Georgia rice barons. Compared to the middle states and New England, southern politics was highly elitist. Finally, even in the colonial era, the South lacked any significant urbanization. At 8,000 residents, Charleston was the only city in the southern colonies at the time of the Revolution. Otherwise, it was a region of large plantations and small subsistence backcountry farms with an occasional farm-to-market town.

The cotton revolution accentuated the differences that had developed during the colonial era between the southern slave states and the northern free states. By expanding slavery, cotton dispersed slavery, African-Americans, and tidewater elitism across the South, giving the region an identity and definition it had heretofore lacked. In the Northeast and Midwest, ambitious young men looked to commerce, banking, transportation, manufacturing, and the professions to make their mark. In the South, virtually all white males dreamed of becoming a planter. Through ownership of slaves, ambitious men believed that they could enter the planter elite. Indeed, hundreds of hard-driving, ruthless whites did manage to acquire enough slaves and cotton land to join the planter class, particularly beyond the tidewater in upcountry South Carolina, Georgia, Alabama, Mississippi, and Louisiana.

Outside the Plantation South

A vast gap separated white slaveholders from white dirt farmers. In 1860 only 385,000 whites possessed even a single slave; the remaining whites, better than 7.5 million, could only dream of obtaining a slave. Such hopes were usually dashed, for the slave master in the big house owned the best, most fertile land, the rich soil along the coast and river bottoms that enabled him to remain at the top of his society. Small farmers, however, often related by blood to the planter aristocracy, identified their own interests with those of the slave holders. Neither rich nor poor, they worked their farms, and raised much of the grains and corn the South produced. They were intensely democratic, but usually voted for the planters or their supporters, and elected them to offices in Nashville, Montgomery, and Washington. Most attended Baptist, Methodist, or Presbyterian churches and made those democratic denominations dominant in the South. They faced a lifetime of hard toil with but little chance of lifting their families' fortunes.

Most whites, however, had little reason to aspire to such heights, for they were almost beyond the pale of what passed for civilized living. "Po whites," as they were called by all, including the slaves who looked down on them, lived on the edges of the plantations, in one-room shacks, stuck away in the piney woods, hidden back in the mountain hollows, and condemned to an existence of picking at their rocky soil in the hope of raising enough corn for their daily needs. The women worked hard, married young, and died early, often while bringing yet another child into the world. Most gave little thought to their impoverished condition, for they expected little from life—it had always been that way. And besides, they could at least proclaim they were white and free, neither black nor enslaved.

As the sectional conflict intensified, southern whites muted their class antagonisms and sought strength in white unity. Southern leaders stifled any dissent that bore the remotest threat to the established order; in 1835, for example, a botany teacher in Washington spent eight months in jail charged with intending to circulate incendiary, anti-slavery publications. Whereas before 1830, opposition to slavery flourished in the South, especially among Quakers and hill country people, by the time of the Civil War most of these groups had been forced to leave or had their power sharply reduced. Planters knew their survival depended on tightening their grip on the South; as with all societies, the institutions of the region below the Potomac swung around to reflect the values and interests of the dominant groups.

Cotton perpetuated the rural character of the South. Cotton was grown in the South, ginned in the South, and then transported outside the region to be processed in New England and Europe. While cotton earned money for its producers, it created relatively few other jobs in the South. Like tobacco and rice in the colonial era, cotton stimulated urbanization and manufacturing outside the region. The South underwent modest urbanization after 1800 in cities that included Richmond, Atlanta, Baltimore, Raleigh, Columbia, Chattanooga, Mobile, and New

Orleans. But as in the colonial period, southern cities were primarily ports of entry or distribution points—not industrial cities dominated by an innovative and dynamic middle class. It is revealing that the two largest and most important cities in the South (New Orleans and Baltimore) were large and important because they served regions outside the South. The introduction of steamboats after 1820 and railroads after 1840 made it easier for the South to depend on cities outside the region for its urban needs. In contrast to the North and Midwest, cotton did not stimulate southern urbanization or industrialization. The South remained very much a colonial economy, a prisoner of slavery.

Nat Turner

Between Whitney's invention of the cotton gin and the Civil War, only one slave state seriously debated whether or not to abolish slavery. In 1832, Virginia, in the wake of Nat Turner's slave insurrection, addressed the abolition of slavery. The year before, southern slave holders had been shaken by William Lloyd Garrison's publication of the *Liberator*. They were genuinely outraged that the northern public had not suppressed its publication and believed that northern politicians were engaged in a conspiracy to destroy slavery. When news of Nat Turner's rebellion spread across the South, many concluded that Turner was the beginning of an organized attack on slavery.

The rebellion, itself, took place in August 1831 in Southampton, Virginia, just north of the Dismal Swamp, near the border with North Carolina. Turner had grown up in Southeastern Virginia. An extremely religious man, he had taught himself to read and write so that he could study the Bible. His owners held him in highest trust, allowing him to go about Southampton pretty much as he wished. A mystic, Turner received visions from heaven at numerous times in his life. His literacy and vivid accounts of divine revelations made him an awesome figure among Southampton slaves. Turner formed a church and preached regularly every Sunday. He even had a limited following among whites and is known to have baptized at least one white man. Despite Turner's good treatment by his master, including privileges normally denied a slave, he developed an intense hatred for all whites. He interpreted the Old Testament as if God were speaking to him, as God had spoken to Moses, commanding Turner to lead his people out of bondage. He believed that God wanted him to kill whites in atonement for the suffering of his fellow black slaves.

In the summer of 1831 Turner gathered about him half a dozen trusted friends who met weekly to roast a pig, drink rum, and listen to Turner interpret the Holy Scripture and recount his latest vision. On August 13th Turner saw what he believed was a heavenly sign from God to act, perhaps an eclipse. Turner and his friends started to plot their insurrection in earnest. On the morning of August 22, Turner and his band of followers embarked on a systematic effort to annihilate every white person in Southampton. They stole up to isolated farmsteads, slipped inside and murdered the inhabitants in their sleep. Before noon, they had killed 57 men, women, and children. At each farmstead they picked up recruits among the household slaves until the revolt numbered almost 80 armed insurrectionists, mostly men but also about a dozen women. After killing the residents of the surrounding farms, Turner tried to capture the town's arsenal. By then, however, the whites of Southampton had become aware of Turner's insurrection and managed to drive him off. Facing a disciplined and well-armed white force, the slaves retreated, heading south to hide in the Dismal Swamp. They were overtaken and nearly every participating slave was captured or killed. Turner, himself, eluded capture the longest. Six weeks after the insurrection, a hunter and his dog located Turner, hiding in a shallow cave about 2 miles from Southampton. The Southampton court tried and convicted Turner, ordering his execution. His head was chopped off and mounted at the town's cross roads, then his body was skinned, and finally, the flesh boiled off his bones as a lesson to any other like-minded slave.

The Nat Turner rebellion was the largest and bloodiest slave revolt in American history. Fifty-seven whites had been killed and as many blacks. From all available evidence, it was an entirely local affair. Turner seemed to have been the immediate cause, and he provided the inspiration as well as the leadership of the rebellion. It did not lead to other insurrections, but it scared southern slaveholders badly. Previous to Turner's rebellion, slave holders had comforted themselves with the unfounded belief that their slaves loved them and indeed enjoyed being slaves. No longer. Afterward, no one could tell which one of those outwardly pleasant black faces hid another Nat Turner, patiently waiting for a chance to murder their white master. Turner's revolt especially scared South Carolina planters and in part triggered the nullification crisis of 1832. In Virginia, itself, it led to the first and only serious public debate over whether or not to abolish slavery.

Virginia Slave Debates

Following the Turner insurrection, for two weeks, beginning on January 11, 1832, the Virginia legislature debated and voted on measures to abolish slavery in Virginia. The advocates of abolition argued that natural rights and simple humanity demanded that slavery be ended. Others supported ending slavery on the more pragmatic grounds that blacks and whites could not live together and that more

Turner insurrections were inevitable unless Virginia ended slavery and provided for the removal of freed blacks from the Old Dominion. The defenders of slavery argued that slavery was essential to Virginia's continued prosperity and genteel ways. Furthermore, abolition of slavery violated slave owner's property rights.

In series of votes, the legislature defeated all motions to abolish slavery, but the vote was close, 73 to sustain slavery, 58 to abolish it. A change of eight votes would have resulted in abolition. Tellingly, virtually all the votes to sustain slavery came from the predominantly slaveholding regions of the Tidewater and Piedmont; those in opposition lived in the Blue Ridge Mountain counties that in 1861 refused to secede from the Union and formed the loyal state of West Virginia. Had representation to the Virginia legislature been based on the free, white population, rather than on the combined population of free and slave, it is possible abolition of slavery would have prevailed in the Old Dominion.

Southern Honor

Southern education in the antebellum period reinforced this commitment to a provincial, rural culture. Prior to the revolution, William and Mary had been the only college in the South. As a result, southern students had traveled either North or to England for their college educations. As a consequence, the revolutionary generation of southern leaders was remarkably cosmopolitan. By 1820, however, over twenty additional colleges were built in the South, but even so, the total student population in all of them in 1820 was less than 1000! After 1820, collegiate education in the South experienced a boom that reflected the wealth generated by the cotton boom. By 1850 there were 113 colleges in the South out of a national total of 239. In 1850 nearly half of the students enrolled in colleges in the United States attended southern colleges while twice the percentage of southern whites attended college as in the remainder of the nation. Moreover, southern colleges often boasted the best scientific, classical, and foreign language faculties in the United States.

In other ways, however, southern colleges were quite traditional as they emphasized classical study, history, and political philosophy. Furthermore, even as northern schools became more secular and even co-educational, southern colleges became increasingly dominated by religious groups—particularly Presbyterians. Even the public universities became bastions of religious orthodoxy as only the University of Virginia, the College of Charleston, and South Carolina College remained secular institutions. Southern education served the needs of the planter elite, not the general public.

While the South led the nation in higher learning, it trailed in all other areas of education. No southern state operated anything more than a rudimentary and completely inadequate public school system. In 1830, the best estimates place illiteracy of the white population of the South at about one third, nearly twice the level of any other region in the United States. This uneven record in education had a significant impact on southern regionalism. Because very few southern youth traveled outside the region to be educated, the southern elite became increasingly parochial and regional in outlook. Very likely, a southern student's professor was a southerner, his classmates were southerners, and in his classes he was exposed only to subjects deemed safe and acceptable. A typical southern college education was anything but a liberating experience; rather, it became four years of intense regional indoctrination. A southern male learned in college what it was to be a southerner and why slavery made the South superior to all other societies.

The planter class received a good, if provincial and traditional education, but the middle and lower classes received almost no education. This accentuated differences between social classes as education reinforced economic differences. Because poorly educated and inarticulate persons were far less likely to challenge authority, lack of education encouraged poorer Southerners to defer to their social and economic betters on all matters of public policy. Nineteenth-century southern education strengthened the elitist class structure of southern society at the same time that it fostered parochialism among its elite. Education had precisely the opposite effect on the South that it had on the remainder of the country.

Nothing, however, was more important in forging southern self-consciousness than religion. Outside the South, in the antebellum period, religion became more diversified and less Calvinistic with many of the new immigrants adhering to Catholicism. The Protestant denominations, challenged by the changes northern society faced, absorbed evangelist Charles Finney's ideas of human perfectionism. In contrast, in the South, the more conservative and evangelical Calvinist churches thrived as never before. Baptists, Methodists, and Presbyterians converted the back country, the slaves, and completely dominated the religious life of the lower South except for Catholic southern Louisiana. Calvinists defended traditional social values and looked with suspicion on the freer, more egalitarian behavior of northerners, and especially the freer behavior of northern women. Southern religion fostered among its adherents a sense of moral superiority to the most promiscuous and secular North. By Calvinist standards, the North had succumbed to corruption, decadence, and immorality—little better than Babylon or Sodom and Gomorrah. Calvinists rejected all notions of progress or the possibility of human perfection. As a result, Calvinism immunized most southerners against many of the utopian and reformist fads that had swept the North. Calvinism lent religious sanction and support to white southerners' belief in their regional superiority; it accepted slavery as a necessary and immutable institution; and it encouraged white southerners to see themselves as God's anointed and chosen people.

In the face of northern criticism, southern whites saw themselves as a distinct people, threatened by a hostile world. All change seemed ominous, causing them to turn more strongly to traditional values. This can even be seen in southern antebellum architecture. Under Jefferson's influence, southern planters became infatuated with Greek and Roman architecture. Public buildings were built to resemble Greek and Roman temples, and all across the South Doric, Ionic, and Corinthian columns were erected in front of public buildings and many private homes. Even modest farm houses sprouted two-story piazzas whose roofs were propped up with white-washed wooden columns. The appeal of the classical went beyond architecture, however, as antebellum southerners viewed themselves as the cultural and intellectual heirs of Greece and Rome. Southerners took great comfort in the fact that classical civilization had been based on slavery, a view lending support to their own parochialism. Southerners read the classics, encouraged classical studys in southern colleges, and graced their children with such names as Cassius, Penelope, Cicero, Claudius and Claudia, Cato, Plato, and Socrates. Georgia went further than most, gracing its cities and towns with names such as Rome, Atlanta, Alexandria, Augusta, Sparta, and Athens.

The southern planter class was equally fascinated by the Middle Ages. Sir Walter Scott's romantic novels were read by all educated southern youth. Southern novelists and poets drew on the feudal period for literary allusions and symbols while dueling became the accepted mode to settle disputes of "honor" between gentlemen. Southern leaders' attraction to the classical and medieval pasts was an apparent rejection of modern society and all notions of progress. The North embodied everything that southerners considered new and modern—cities, irreligion, foreigners, and feminism. In contrast, Greece, Rome, and medieval Europe appeared to white southerners as roughly analogous to their own rural, traditional slave society. In white southern minds, each was hierarchical, authoritarian, patriarchal, servile, and therefore, virtuous.

Northerners frequently criticized the South for its backwardness. In response, the southern planter elite charged that northerners were but crass, materialistic, money grubbers, a people completely devoid of honor. The cult of southern honor became the South's answer to northern accusations of southern backwardness. Southerners insisted that honor, not intelligence, wealth, or even education, determined an individual's worth. And honor rested on an individual's reputation among his peers. All else was unimportant, and any male, when called upon, had to defend his own and his family's honor at the risk of death. Upper class southerners defended their honor in duels while poorer southerners resorted to knife fights or guns. Whether a highly ritualized duel or a no-holds-barred street brawl, white southerners became an extraordinarily violent people, suffering ten times the murder rate of the North. The code of southern honor, combined with southern propensity to violence, seeped into southern politics. By the 1850s white southerners quite willingly resorted to violence to defend their regional as well as their personal honor. Any honorable southern white much preferred death to humiliation. The southern defense of slavery became itself a badge of southern honor.

John C. Calhoun did not regard himself as living in a slave society, despite the fact that slavery was all around him and that he himself owned slaves. On the contrary, he thought he lived in the "freest" society in the world, one whose freedom rested on human slavery. Most southerners generally held a pessimistic view of human nature; they believed people had a natural tendency to do evil, to use their fellows for their own ends, and saw slavery imposing mutual responsibilities, obligations, and duties. It permitted the existence of a stable social order. Slaveholders had little use for Thomas Jefferson and his prating about equality. Calhoun spoke for most slaveholders when he remarked about the Declaration of Independence's reference to equality, "there is not a word of truth in it." Other spokesmen for the peculiar institution explained that blacks had been created as inferiors, destined by nature and the Bible to be hewers of wood and drawers of water. The popular "mudsill theory" taught that in every society one group occupied the lower ranks and made it possible for the rest to devote themselves to higher pursuits as a mudsill rested on the ground and supported a bridge or building. Defensive southerners cited the apostle Paul's description of the church to justify the kind of structured society they had created; the ideal society was one in which every person had an assigned role—the eye and the hand doing its necessary job.

The Peculiar Institution

Honorable or not, the peculiar institution did not vest all power in slave masters. In point of fact the real power of masters was never as great as their legal power. Masters who mutilated their slaves or killed them for something other than self-defense were subject to legal punishment. There are documented examples of masters occasionally being jailed and fined for abusing their slaves. A man could legally whip or enchain his slaves, just as he could his wife and children, but he could not intentionally mutilate his human property. Public opinion also checked, somewhat, a master's despotic power. White Southerners were sensitive to critics' charges that slaves were physically abused, and a notoriously cruel slave master became a social outcast. Simon Legree was antithetical to white southerners' image of themselves as a genteel and humane society, even though Stowe's fictional character was based on a historical figure. Finally, planters, like most people, wanted to be loved and respected and did not like to be thought of as cruel, inhuman tyrants, thus moderating some of the system's inherent cruelty.

Economic self-interest also acted as a restraint on a master's power. When a master maimed or killed his slave, he lost $70,000 to $100,000 in present-day money. To the frontiersman the only good Indian might have been a dead Indian, but to the southern planter the only good slave was a healthy slave. If owners expected their slaves to live long enough to pay off their initial investment, they had to feed them wholesome rations, provide clean and weather-proof housing, and good, warm clothing. Compared to our own standards, however, the lot of southern slaves was grim. They generally lived in a single room cabin, sometimes with a floor and fire place. They usually received 2 sets of summer clothing, two sets of shoes, two blankets, and one set of woolen winter clothing per year. Their weekly food ration averaged three-quarters of a bushel of dried corn, two to three pounds of salted bacon, and a quart of molasses per adult worker. Children received similar but smaller rations. This was supplemented by garden vegetables, chickens, eggs, and pigs that slaves raised themselves. On holidays and Sundays slaves might receive something extra such as liquor, candy, cheese, or fresh meat.

Although meager, it was a steady diet, comparable to the living standards of eastern European peasants of the time. It was superior to what Caribbean and South American slaves received where the importation of new slaves barely kept up with the death rate. The southern slave system was the only slave system that did not require continuous importations to maintain its numbers. The life-spans of southern slaves, their fertility rates, and child mortality rates were somewhat worse than American farmers and factory workers, but they were comparable to poor whites in the South, free blacks in the North and South, and European industrial workers and peasants. Life was harsh for all working class people in the West during the nineteenth century and southern slaves shared in the deprivation. Nonetheless, slaves were King Cotton's most important subjects, and with the end of the slave trade in 1808, slave holders realized that these were the only slaves they were ever going to get, so they treated them with the same care that they provided valuable livestock.

Unquestionably, however, slaves placed the most important limitations on the power of southern slave masters. Many a master confided to his friends that he never knew whether he controlled his slaves or his slaves controlled him. George Washington called his slaves "a most troublesome property." Slaves had one powerful weapon that their masters could not take from them: they could withhold their labor. If slaves refused to work or if they worked slowly or inefficiently, the planter would quickly go broke. If a master beat his slaves excessively or otherwise humiliated them, the next morning his entire crew might claim to be sick and refuse to work. Or disgruntled slaves might hoe down the cotton instead of the weeds, or they might fill up their cotton sacks with rocks instead of cotton and ruin the cotton gin, or they might put sand in the wheel bearings or burn down the tobacco barn in the middle of the night, or they might run away. In the last resort they might kill their tormentor. All of these things occurred in the South, but they happened most frequently on those plantations that mistreated their slaves. On well-run, profitable plantations, such things happened less often because the slaves and masters had reached certain, often unverbalized understandings on work-load and working conditions.

The key person in this management-labor give-and-take was the "gang boss." A gang boss was a slave who directed other slaves. Some persons have viewed the gang boss as a pawn of the master, who for small favors helped the master make the slave system work at the expense of his fellow slaves. In practice, the gang boss acted as the go-between. Instead of individual slaves confronting the master or overseer face to face, trying to explain their grievances, slaves frequently took their complaints to the gang boss. The gang boss would then go to the overseer and "make suggestions" that might make the work go better. If the overseer knew his business, he would bargain with the gang boss, and they would arrive at an acceptable agreement. In a primitive way, the gang boss performed the function of a union shop steward. This prevented direct confrontations between angry slaves and the defensive master, reducing the chances for violence. At the same time it gave the slaves an articulate and experienced spokesmen. Southern slaves seldom acted as individuals, rather they banded together and responded collectively to the power of the master, and the key to this collective response often was the gang boss. Slaves who acted on their own by running away or by murdering their masters were exceptional and usually lived on poorly run and unprofitable plantations.

The banding together and refusal to be mistreated resulted in concrete benefits for the slaves. On nearly every plantation informal understandings were reached which limited work to twelve hours a day and a maximum of 16 hours during the harvest. After the harvest most slaves were given several days off. Slaves were not worked on Sunday and they usually received half a day off on Saturday. Also masters allowed them to form their own churches, have parties and social gatherings on Saturday night, and often paid slaves cash incentives to work harder and more efficiently. The average slave might earn in a year anywhere from $15 to $30, and since they did not have to pay for their room and board, they could save it all. Also, most slaves were allowed to sell their surplus vegetables and chickens. This meant that slaves to a limited degree participated in the cash economy. They bought small luxuries, a new dress, or a hat, tobacco, liquor, or a gift for their spouse or lover. In almost every southern community there existed taverns run by free blacks that catered to the slave trade who were usually allowed to move around their neighborhood without restraint during their off hours.

All of this worked to the advantage of both parties. Masters could get their cotton produced with a minimum of coercion and a maximum of efficiency, and the slaves, in return, received reduced hours, better working conditions, and higher wages. One of the myths of southern slavery was that it was inefficient. Actually, it was remarkably efficient. Slaves were productive and skillful. Factory owners in the South often preferred slave labor to free, and there is no reason to believe that slavery could not have been successfully adapted to manufacturing. If it had not been profitable, slave owners would not have fought so strenuously at so great a sacrifice to defend it.

Southern slaves also gained a great deal of control over their personal lives. Slaves unhappy in their private lives were slaves who did not work well. This was particularly true of the field hands who lived clustered together in their slave cabins out of sight and hearing of the master and overseer. In their off-hours slaves established relationships with one another that made it possible for them to work together against the master. They taught each other songs, told stories to one another, partied and worshiped together. In the shadow of the plantation house, they created a culture distinctly their own, drawing on their West African roots, borrowing from southern white culture, and adapting both to their own experience. Much of African-American culture, especially its music, religion, food, and speech, originated in the small clustered cabins of the field hands. Such African ways permeated southern life, white and black, giving the region its distinctive character long after slavery, and later racial segregation, disappeared. In the slave South white plantation owners ruled unchallenged. But outside the corridors of power, in those areas that Tocqueville called "matters of the heart," African American slaves prevailed.

African-American slave culture also fostered family life. Slaves paired off as husbands and wives and raised children. Parents cared for their children with all the affection and concern of non-slave parents. Other slaves respected the marriages and few overseers or planters were foolish enough to sexually impose themselves on the wife of a male slave. Most of the murders of whites by slaves reported in southern newspapers were committed by the spouse of a slave who had been hurt or abused by the murdered white. If a master foolishly broke up a slave marriage, it had a negative impact on his people's morale. Most masters honored slave marriages and even encouraged them, and when they sold their slaves, smart masters went to great length to sell them as families, although, if this proved impossible, families were broken up. But no one wished to buy a slave who had been separated from his or her spouse since most runaways were slaves trying to reunite themselves with their mates or children. So strong were slave family ties that when the Civil War broke up many of the plantations and scattered slave families here and yon, for years afterward, ex-slaves roamed the South, looking for a lost wife, husband, child, or parent.

The religion of African-American slaves revealed the complexity and the paradoxes of southern slavery. At first, slave owners were reluctant to convert their slaves to Christianity for fear that conversion might guarantee freedom. But once state laws made it clear that Christians, as long as they were black, could also be slaves, most masters allowed their slaves to be converted. Protestant ministers encouraged this by pointing out that masters had a moral obligation to bring their slaves to God. Ministers argued that a Christian slave made a peaceful, respectful, and hard working slave. By 1860, partly out of concern for their slaves' souls and partly out of a belief that religion made a slave a better worker, most planters encouraged the conversion of their slaves. Most African-American slaves were ostensibly Protestant Christians, but their Christianity was infused with West African religion.

The effect of Christianity on slaves was complex. Christianity tended to make slaves better workers. They drank less, became more obedient, were less likely to sulk, and they internalized many of their masters' values. Nonetheless, Christianity also elevated slaves in their own eyes as well as in their masters'. A Christian slave possessed moral significance, and even southern courts accepted the testimony of a devout slave. Through Christianity, slaves shared in the dignity of humankind and on a spiritual level became equal to their masters. Christianity gave meaning to slaves' lives and, if slaves loved God and worshiped him, they could expect a life after death much better than that of a slave. Perhaps more importantly, Christianity offered slaves a higher source of authority than even their masters, an authority to which their masters were themselves accountable. While a person might only be a lowly slave, in the eyes of God, all people, including their masters, were slaves, and slaves had reason to believe that God loved them more than their masters with the Gospels' emphasis on the meek and the lowly.

At first, most masters tried to retain control over their slaves' religious lives by hiring a white minister and limiting worship to specified times and places. This proved futile. Slaves organized their own congregations, provided their own preachers, and shaped Christianity to their own ends and their own West African beliefs. They rejected the harsh, guilt-ridden, and highly formal Calvinism of their masters with its work ethic and, instead, preferred biblical stories in which God protected his chosen people and punished all who persecuted them. Drawing on West African religion, slave worship services were highly emotional. The congregation played as active a role as the preacher, and the service included music, shouting, and ring dancing. During the service the Holy Spirit possessed worshipers, causing them to go into trances and to speak in tongues. Slaves' African Christianity brought them together, provided them a common bond, gave them an authorized means to express their innermost feelings and emotions, and afforded them a vehicle in which to preserve important aspects of West African culture. The bond of humanity extended beyond the slaves themselves as Christianity forced masters to recognized their own bond in Christ with their slaves. Christian masters, no matter what their legal rights, could never treat Christian slaves as if they were no more than livestock. To do so would jeopardize their own souls.

Debate Over Slavery

By the early 1830s, the question of slavery dominated public consciousness. The anti-slavery cause had long been marked by a certain restraint and sedateness. Indeed, the oldest abolition society, the American Colonization Society, founded in 1817, counted men like James Monroe, John Marshall, and Daniel Webster among its leaders. So moderate was this group that it simply encouraged the freeing of slaves by persuasion and their re-colonization in Africa. By 1832, it had transported only about 1000 blacks to the new country of Liberia, where the immigrants were left to fend for themselves.

On January 1, 1831, in Boston, William Lloyd Garrison, a twenty-five-year-old journalist, shook the country out of its apathy with the publication of the *Liberator*. "I am in earnest," Garrison proclaimed, "I will not equivocate—I will not excuse—I will not retreat a single inch—and I will be heard." He founded two anti-slavery organizations that reflected his growing anti-government views. In 1834 the Massachusetts Anti-slavery Society resolved that the federal constitution which sanctioned slavery was "a covenant with death and an agreement with hell." Garrison aroused strong resentments, both North and South. In Boston, a mob dragged him through the streets while southern states put a price on his head and tried to prevent circulation of the *Liberator*.

Southern slaveholders faced increased hostility. In the Midwest, anti-slavery revivalists such as Charles G. Finney won converts both to Christianity and to the abolitionists' cause. Finney's most famous disciple was Theodore Dwight Weld, a one-time agent for the American Temperance Society. Weld proved a skillful organizer and, drawing primarily on seminary students, he enlisted a zealous cadre of abolitionist agitators. They stressed the inhumanity of slavery and the way it corrupted all concerned. Soon pious pamphlets and petitions to free the black man were clogging the mail. One black abolitionist, a freeborn North Carolinian named David Walker, issued a religiously worded *Appeal* addressed to his fellows that stressed justice, not charitable appeals to conscience. Will God, he asked, "not cause the very children of the oppressors to rise up against them, and oftimes put them to death?" Congress was a central focus of the abolitionist attack. Women's aid societies and anti-slavery groups unleashed a torrent of petitions praying that the national legislature abolish the slave trade and slavery in the District of Columbia, which it controlled. In 1836, in a gesture to the South, house Democrats pushed through a rules change that made it practically impossible to act on any slavery petitions put forward by house members. This "gag rule" elevated the slave issue into one of constitutional liberty. Each Monday morning, Massachusetts congressman and ex-president John Quincy Adams rose on the house floor to protest this violation of the right to petition. The gag rule worked to the abolitionists' advantage. It led seminary students and mission-minded women in Ohio, Indiana, and Vermont to vigorously applaud Adams' actions and redouble their efforts.

Southern leaders not only played into abolitionists' hands with the gag rule, but they also created martyrs. Garrison crowed whenever he had to make his way through a howling mob. In 1837 an outraged gang of southern sympathizers murdered the Reverend Elijah P. Lovejoy in Alton, Illinois, after he insisted on publishing his abolitionist newspaper. After 1831, southern postmasters refused to deliver abolitionist literature, like Weld's influential compendium *American Slavery as It Is*. Defenders of slavery consolidated their positions in the South and prevented dissemination of information detrimental to their interests, but their behavior only confirmed their critics' charges that the slave system threatened personal liberty everywhere. People who had no feel toward slavery or African Americans equated the North with "freedom" and the South with "slavery." Abolitionists succeeded in defining the struggle for millions of otherwise uncommitted citizens who were asked to choose between freedom and slavery.

At mid-century, southern politics appeared free and democratic on the surface. Universal white manhood suffrage existed everywhere, the South sustained a vigorous two-party system, and the majority of its citizens were small yoemen farmers. Except in the Appalachian and Ozark Mountains, southern farmers usually cast their ballots for members of the planter class or lawyers closely associated with the plantation economy. The planter class tied the South's interest and honor to slavery. If anyone openly challenged planters' leadership, as in 1856 did Hinton R. Helper, an anti-slavery white who published a bitter attack on slavery entitled *The Impending Crisis*, planters and their sympathizers depicted the individual as a traitor.

Slavery polarized southern and northern voters. The disagreements, however, masked the view of most white antebellum Americans that blacks were innately inferior to whites. In the North, liberty did not mean the civic or the social equality of African Americans. Blacks were freer in the North than in the South, but free blacks in the North found their lives hemmed in by the same kinds of restrictions that free blacks in the South faced. Slaves who had escaped to the North lived in daily fear that a southern slave catcher, backed by the Fugitive Slave Law, would capture and return them to slavery.

In the North, African Americans held only the most menial jobs, although they managed to carve out discrete communities in which they lived largely free of white harassment. In 1816 free blacks in Philadelphia seceded from the Methodist Church and formed the African Episcopal Methodist Church. In time black Baptist, Presbyterian, and Episcopal congregations

Frederick Douglass (1817-95), a slave who escaped from his Maryland owner, was a famous lecturer on abolition who published *A Narrative of the Life of Frederick Douglass* in 1845. It brought the message of antislavery into numerous households as did his newspaper, the *North Star*, which he published for 17 years. (1967)

formed, free of whites and racial prejudice. Black children were denied entry to white schools and were segregated at theaters, restaurants, hospitals, and on public conveyances. Except in Massachusetts, blacks could not sit on juries, and most northern states denied blacks the right to vote or hold public office. As late as 1818 Illinois allowed the use of slave labor, and Cincinnati barred blacks from living in the city limits. Such prejudice coincided with white egalitarianism that viewed every white man a king, superior to women and all non-whites. Increasing northern opposition to slavery failed to undercut Americans' pervasive racism. Northern politicians attacked slavery, not as racial egalitarians, but as white democrats morally offended by what they perceived as an immoral, arrogant, slaveholder aristocracy who wished to monopolize the western territories, denying to ambitious young whites an opportunity to acquire land and become freehold farmers. The future of the federal territories, not racial justice, fueled the anti-slavery movement.

Northern leaders used such hatred of slavery to rally support, particularly in the Midwest. The Great Lake and upper Mississippi Valley states, were the key to national political dominance. Whichever side gained the loyalty of the Midwest would control national politics. Ohio congressman Joshua R. Giddings, an abolitionist, explained to his constituents that pro-slavery advocates opposed a higher tariff, federal support for internal improvements, and the distribution to states of funds from public land sales. Slave owners, declared Giddings, "regard them as opposed to the interest of slavery." Giddings believed that destruction of the slave power would open the way for congressional approval of such measures. To Giddings and increasing numbers of northern leaders, the slave South stood in the way of economic progress. And opportunity. While most anti-slavery advocates saw slavery as the great national evil, others joined their ranks because they believed that southern planters blocked legislation critical for the national economic growth. They understood that the victorious section would shape the American future in accord with its own vision.

Antebellum Reform

In the decades following the War of 1812, Northern voters, whether Democrat or Whig, affirmed a belief in "Equal rights for all, special privileges for none." Most believed that given an equal chance, they could rise to any heights. With a special attraction for the young, the vigorous, the competitive, and the visionary, this ideology of upward mobility kept people scrambling after their main chance and the pot of gold at the end of the ever-beckoning, ever-retreating rainbow. Anyone who happened to fall by the wayside had only himself to blame.

Such reasoning bound northern society together, for it kept most failures from challenging the inequities of the political and economic system. Failures were seen as glaring exceptions. Such notions of freedom carried revolutionary overtones, igniting forces ever more difficult to suppress. Many opposed slavery because it denied black men the fruit of their labor and the opportunity to acquire land and form families of their own. Slavery gave a privileged class of men an unfair advantage over non-slave holders. Slaveholders, using their political connections, acquired the best land; outsiders made do with the rest. Thus, Abraham Lincoln, attributed his Kentucky father's failure to his inability to compete with slaveholders. Freeholders and aspiring freeholders viewed slavery as a conspiracy to monopolize the western territories, leaving the nation's landless and the young to make do with only marginal, unproductive land. If left unchecked, freeholders believed that slavery would reduce all farmers to the level of poor southern whites, an impoverished, illiterate, and disenfranchised class of "mud sills." In *The Impending Crisis*, a North Carolina farmer, Hinton R. Helper, declared that yeomen farmers could not survive in the face of slavery. In the East, skilled artisans compared their struggle against the factory system as similar to yeomen farmers' against the slavocracy. Labor radical William Legge demanded the right to organize and bargain collectively so that workers could free themselves from the wage slave system and gain a measure of control over their work. Legge proclaimed, "We are for leaving trade free; and the right to combine is an indispensable attribute of its freedom." By the 1850s, the slogan "free land, free labor, and free men" expressed these widely shared ideas that saw farmers, laborers, and slaves engaged in a common struggle to secure their autonomy and gain control over their lives.

Women activists would have changed the slogan to say "free men and women." Influenced by the Second Great Awakening, Elizabeth Cady Stanton, Lydia Chapman Child, and Angelina and Sarah Grimké, all demanded that freedom also be extended to women, especially over issues that affected the sanctity of the family. In the antebellum decades the northern middle classes

Two of the women shown here played lead roles in the Senaca Falls, N.Y., Women's Rights Convention of 1848: Lucretia Mott (1793-1880) and Lydia Cady Stanton (1815-1902) wrote the Declaration of Rights of Women, modeling it on the Declaration of Independence. Carrie Chapman Catt (1859-1947) labored a generation later for a constitutional amendment granting the vote to women, the famous 19th Amendment, ratified in 1920. (1948)

were drawn to a set of beliefs that idealized motherhood, a virtual "cult of domesticity." According to educator Catherine Beecher and others, Christian morality resided in women who God had charged to oversee their homes, insuring that children were raised in a safe and moral environment. On issues that related to the home and morality, husbands should defer to their wives, just as wives should defer to their husbands on public issues. For some, belief in the cult of domesticity dictated the liberation of women. If they were, indeed, morally superior to men, if women were charged with society's most important responsibility, the preservation of the home, they should possess the legal authority to protect themselves and their children from their husband's follies and immoralities. All too many women, they pointed out, through no fault of their own, had married drunkards, who squandered their families' resources, physically abused their wives and children, and even infected their wives with venereal diseases. To protect themselves and their families, women concluded that they should be legally and politically empowered.

In the 1830s, mobilized by the Second Great Awakening, urban middle class women, in the East and the Midwest, formed civic, religious, and charitable organizations by the thousands. In 1835, the city directory of Utica, New York, for example, listed nearly 100 such organizations, largely made up of middle class women and many led by women. These civic and charitable organizations represented the first examples of American women acting in a public capacity. Women justified their intrusion into the public, male sphere by insisting that these organizations were logical extensions of their domestic responsibilities as the overseers of their families' and their communities' moral lives. They described these reformist organizations as extensions of the home. And most of these organizations were primarily concerned with extending, to those denied a safe and affectionate home, the benefits of a Christian family with a nurturing mother. The appeal of the temperance societies, the Anti-Saloon League, the Sunday school movement, orphan asylums, homes for wayward girls, the Foreign Mission to Convert the Heathen, and the anti-slavery societies were based on extending the benefits of the middle class home to others. In this manner, no one could deny that these organizations were inherently female in their moral concerns.

Participation in such organizations had several consequences. It gave middle class women important public experience. Up until the 1830s, virtually no woman had ever addressed a public meeting in the United States nor had any worked formally with other women outside the home. Moreover, once out of their homes, many women found public life exciting. They met important people, traveled unaccompanied on railroads across the country to attend conferences and conventions, and a few even visited England; their ideas on public issues were taken seriously. Even more exhilarating, they believed their activities made a difference. As a consequence of their efforts, orphans, widows, and wayward girls were provided for; they offered food and lodging for the indigent; they organized public schools, libraries, drama societies, and literary and art guilds; they forced public officials to regulate bars and close bordellos, and to enforce public order on the streets, making their communities safe for women and children. As these women became sensitive to social problems, they realized that they, as women, were also subject to unjust treatment. Not surprisingly, the antebellum women's rights movement focused on those issues that most affected women as mothers—custody of their children in the cases of divorce or abandonment, the right of divorce due to a husband's physical abuse or adultery, and a woman's control over property free from either her husband's or her father's will. Feminists insisted on the abolition of the common law doctrine of coverture. The more radical feminists demanded the right to vote. Most of these demands were simply the basic rights of citizenship that even the most impoverished antebellum white male enjoyed. The women's rights movement first manifested itself in the 1830s in New York and Massachusetts. In these states women's rights advocates petitioned their respective legislatures, asking that married women be secured in their property and that mothers be given custodial rights over their children. In the next decade, one by one, state legislatures in the East and Midwest made modest gestures at female property and child custody reform, but the changes were token at best. Despairing that male-dominated legislatures, on their own, would ever make the necessary changes, in 1848, Elizabeth Cady Stanton, with the support of Lucretia Mott, called the first Women's Rights Convention. On July 19, 1848, 200 women and 40 men assembled at Seneca Falls, NY. In convening the Seneca Falls convention, Stanton declared, "I should feel exceedingly diffident to appear before you at this time, having never before spoken in public, were I not nerved by a sense of right and duty, did I not feel that the time had come for the question of women's wrongs to be laid before the public, did I not believe that woman herself must do this work." Unanimously the Seneca Falls convention resolved in the Declaration of Principles that women be granted 1) equal education, 2) equal opportunity for employment, 3) equality before the law, 4) equal right to speak in public, and 5) the right to vote. The Seneca Falls Declaration of Principle provided the agenda for women's rights for the remainder of the nineteenth century.

For the next ten years the women's rights convention met annually, serving as spring board for state reform. By 1860, 14 states had granted married women control over their property, and in 1860, New York granted women the right to keep their wages, giving women, if not a "room of their own," at least a "purse of their own." Moreover, by 1860, most northern and midwestern states had placed limits on home mortgages, prohibiting foreclosure on a home unless the wife had co-signed the mortgage. Following the Civil War, during Reconstruction, the Republican-dominated southern state legislatures wrote into nearly every southern state constitution women's basic rights to property and child custody.

Before Reconstruction, however, the South lagged far behind. A southern intellectual, like George Fitzhugh of Virginia, argued that freedom was a mixed blessing that fostered selfish individuals who threaten social well-being. In the 1850s Fitzhugh wrote a series of essays that attacked what he described as modern, democratic society, plagued with communists, feminists, free love advocates, and capitalists. Because free society was so individualistic and its members rarely cared about anything except their immediate needs. Fitzhugh argued that only slavery could protect the poor and the weak from the greed of the rich and powerful. "Slaves without masters," he said, would make "cannibals" of us all. Northerners found Fitzhugh's books perverse and unconvincing. Moreover, as the nation's population grew, each census ratified the power of the North. From an even congressional balance between North and South in 1789, northern states decade by decade gained the upperhand. In 1823, at the time of the constitutionally mandated reapportionment of house seats, the slave states did not receive a single new seat, the new southwestern states got nine while the Mid-Atlantic and Ohio Valley gained nineteen. Nullification having failed, the South, led by Calhoun, turned westward.

Southern Expansion

Calhoun believed that slavery and the South were both doomed unless the region expanded territorially. In December 1837 Calhoun addressed the senate. He denounced any attempt to prevent slave expansion as a threat to the union. He warned that efforts to abolish slavery or the slave trade in either the territories or the District of Columbia were a "direct and dangerous attack on the institutions of the slave-holding States," would effectively disfranchise the South, and lead to the breakup of the union. Calhoun's declaration on slavery defined the South's position for the next two decades, making clear that if southern demands were ignored, secession was the likely consequence.

Mississippi Senator Robert Walker observed that as slavery moved westward it declined in the East. He concluded that southerners could win northern support for slave expansion if they argued that territorial expansion drew slavery deeper into the South, into Mexico, and then the Caribbean, leaving the remainder of North

America open to freehold farming. Many northerners, however, had come to regard slavery as a threat to liberty and Christian morality. They saw southern expansion as a sinister conspiracy to extend slavery and to subvert northern notions of freedom.

Southern expansion dated back to 1822 when Stephen Austin, the "Father of Texas," received a grant from the Mexican government to bring 300 families, with their slaves, to settle the Mexican lands west of Louisiana. Although agreeing to take oaths of allegiance to Mexico and to embrace Roman Catholicism, the settlers considered themselves the vanguard of American and southern expansion. When the rapid influx of southerners threatened to overwhelm the Mexicans, the Mexican government abolished slavery in the Texas territory in the 1830s and prohibited further American immigration. In 1836, Anglo-Texans rebelled, declared their independence, and under Sam Houston, established the Lone Star Republic. Abolitionists blocked Texas' request for annexation by the United States, and neither Jackson nor Van Buren wanted to risk a war with Mexico. The annexation of Texas, which could be divided into several different states, became critical to the South after 1841. Reapportionment had reduced South Carolina's and Virginia's representation in congress while other southern states barely maintained theirs. With the addition of Texas, the South could recoup its loss of congressional seats and add two pro-slavery senators. Anxious to secure congressional allies, the South tied Texas annexation to the border dispute over the Oregon Territory.

The United States based its claim to Oregon on the vague wording of the Louisiana Purchase agreement and demanded that Great Britain recognize a line at 54°40′ north latitude, more than 600 miles north of the mouth of the Columbia River, which the British claimed as Canada's southern frontier. For both sides, the disagreement involved practical matters of real substance. English fur traders in the area believed that control of the Columbia River was vital for shipping their pelts. American settlers who were trickling in over the long Oregon trail wanted exclusive control of the high and fertile valleys.

Manifest Destiny

The southern push for expansion had become an integral part of a broader vision, "Manifest Destiny." Although John L. O'Sullivan coined the term in 1845, the vision itself went back to the Puritans who had hoped to build a "city on a hill" as a model Christian community for others to immolate. The revolutionary generation rephrased it as a "new star in heaven's firmament" and a "new empire." By the 1840s, Americans generally envisioned the day when the American flag would wave proudly "from sea to shining sea." For many, manifest destiny conjured images of bustling Pacific coast ports, lucrative trade with the Orient, bridging the Great American Desert, and extending the benefits of republicanism and Protestant Christianity to Mexicans and Indians. It meant rounding out the natural, divinely manifested borders of the United States. The editor of the *New York Morning News* declared, "We take from no man; the reverse rather—we give to man. This national policy, necessity or destiny, we know to be just and beneficent, and we can, therefore, afford to scorn the invective and imputations of rival nations."

National power, greatness and mission called Americans. In 1843, Mexican President Antonio Lopez de Santa Anna, however, warned that the annexation of his former province would lead to an "immediate proclamation of war." In 1844 President John Tyler appointed expansionist and southerner Calhoun as secretary of state. Within twelve days of his appointment, Calhoun signed an annexation treaty and dispatched a note to the British that heartily defended slavery. Leaked to the abolitionist press, Calhoun's confidential memo fed fears of a pro-southern plot. When the senate considered the treaty on June 18, even ardent expansionists voted "nay." Texas annexation was lost by a better than two-to-one vote.

The Campaign of 1844

In 1844, the principal Whig presidential candidate, Henry Clay, whose reputation for being right at whatever personal cost was about to lose him yet another election, issued his "Raleigh letter" to supporters there in April to warn that annexation of Texas would destroy the union. Although he later tried vainly to qualify such a bald assertion, the damage was done. He could not hope to win the votes of southerners, nor of northerners who thought his clarifications indicated a vagueness on the issue of slave expansion.

Before their convention, many Democrats had favored former president Van Buren, who had come more and more under the influence of an important and noisy faction of New York Democrats, the Loco-Focos—so named after they lit the newfangled matches (loco-focos) when their opponents turned off the gas lamps in a hall where they gathered. These labor activists represented a growing wing of the party that threatened southern influence among Democrats. They took the egalitarian side of the American tradition seriously. In boisterous rallies they championed such lost causes as a popular rebellion in Rhode Island led by Thomas Dorr who claimed to be governor. No longer a states' righter, Tyler suppressed the whole affair with federal troops. Van Buren's large bloc of votes at the Baltimore

A House Divided ★ 231

convention could not prevent the enactment of a permanent rule that required a two-thirds majority to nominate; this provision continued as a mainstay of the Democratic Party until 1936. Van Buren failed to secure the necessary margin, and the door was opened for a relative unknown.

Texas was annexed to the United States in 1845 after Polk's victory in the presidential campaign but before he took office. President John Tyler recommended a congressional joint resolution because he recognized that he could not win the necessary two-thirds Senate majority. (1945)

James K. "Young Hickory" Polk had been former President Jackson's choice from the beginning. Polk was also a Tennessean, and the first "dark horse," or unexpected victor, to win a presidential nomination. The Whigs ridiculed his selection by asking during the campaign, "Who is James K. Polk?" but they could not detract from his ardent expansionist stand, which proved popular with the electorate. Polk had no overwhelming desire to expand slavery. All he wanted, as the Democratic platform pledged, was the "reannexation of Texas" and the "reoccupation of Oregon," both of which were misleading terms. The Democrats shouted "54-40 or Fight" across the midwestern states in a successful effort to secure the votes of those willing to countenance expansion into Texas if all of Oregon were also acquired. When the balloting ended on December 4, Polk's popular margin was only 30,000 votes out of 3.3 million cast. He won only because the abolitionist Liberty party siphoned off enough votes in New York to prevent Clay from carrying that state.

Texas Annexation and War

After Polk's election, Tyler paved the way for Polk to carry out his campaign promises. When congress met in December, Tyler recommended to both houses the immediate annexation of Texas by joint resolution, which could be done without the two-thirds senate majority required of a treaty. The congressional resolution, which contained nothing to ease Mexican sensibilities or any reference to the need for Mexico's consent, squeezed through the senate on February 27 on a straight party vote and through the house the next day. On the last day of his term, Tyler proudly proclaimed that Texas was now a full-fledged member of the union.

Polk, on entering office, exhibited the vigor and expansionist purpose that characterized his tenure by proclaiming that settlement of the status of the former Lone

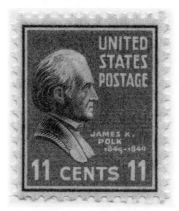

Tennesseean James K. Polk, president of the United States from 1845-49, was popularly known as "Young Hickory." Best known for his foreign policy that led to a war with Mexico in 1846, Polk's administration laid the foundation for subsequent sectional conflict over slavery. (1938)

Star Republic belonged "exclusively to the United States and Texas." To appease the Midwest he asserted that the United States had a "clear and unquestionable" right to Oregon. Nonetheless, the annexation of Texas made the split between South and Midwest almost unbridgeable.

On March 28 Mexico severed diplomatic relations with the United States and refused to recognize the Rio Grande as Texas' southern border. Mexico insisted that the Nueces River, about 150 miles farther north, had always been Texas' true boundary. To forestall American intrigue and clandestine activities in California, Mexico ordered the expulsion of all United States citizens from its California territory.

Polk wanted to avert military action against Mexico if possible, but as a precaution, he ordered General Zachary Taylor, a sixty-year-old veteran whose exploits as an Indian fighter had won him the nickname "Old Rough and Ready," to move his 3500 troops from Louisiana to the Rio Grande area. While Taylor's men set up camp near Corpus Christi, Polk dispatched a secret mission to Mexico led by special emissary John Slidell. Instructed to purchase California and New Mexico and to confirm the Rio Grande boundary, Slidell was authorized to spend up to $40 million. Mexico's foreign minister, however, claimed that Slidell did not have the backing of the United States senate and that Mexico only wanted to negotiate the Texas question. After a fruitless three months in Mexico City, shuffling from office to office as the government experienced a coup d'etat, Slidell left for Washington in a royal huff. Polk had long since ordered Taylor's army to defend American territorial claims on the Rio Grande.

Along the Rio Grande hostility mounted. Only a decision at the highest level in Washington or Mexico City could avert an armed confrontation, and both leaders refused to back down. Mexican and American forces anxiously faced each other across the Rio Grande. On April 24, 1846, 1600 Mexican calvary crossed the river and the Mexican commander notified Taylor that he considered hostilities had commenced. On April 25, an American scouting party skirmished with Mexican troops and eleven Americans were killed. Two weeks later on Saturday, May 9, word of the clash reached Washington, and on the following Monday Polk asked congress for a declaration of war. Mexico, the president said with a straight face, "has invaded our territory and shed American blood on American soil." War already existed, he claimed, "not withstanding all our efforts to avoid it." Opposition to war in the house came from northern representatives, particularly from the Whigs. In the senate the declaration passed nearly unanimously, although Calhoun abstained because he believed the president had unconstitutionally usurped congress' war-making power. Practically shouting, and with his thin hand pounding the desk in front of him, the South Carolinian referred to the conflict on the Rio Grande as a "border brawl" and proclaimed, "sooner than vote for that lying preamble, I would plunge a dagger through my heart."

In California, Captain John Fremont, son-in-law of the ardent expansionist from Missouri, Senator Thomas Hart Benton, established an army post in the Salinas Valley. On June 14, 1846, less than six months after Fremont's arrival, the 500 or so Americans raised a "Bear Flag" in Sonoma and proclaimed a new republic for themselves and the approximately 36,000 Mexican subjects in the area.

The war with Mexico continued for nearly two years marked by constant friction between Whig generals Zachary Taylor and Winfield Scott, and their Democratic commander-in-chief. A great deal of bumbling took place—at one point, for example, American forces allowed Santa Anna to pass through their lines on his way home from exile in Cuba. Instead of helping to end the fighting, he was elected president of Mexico and pushed the war effort more vigorously. Much of the military action took place in northern Mexico, where American volunteers, particularly those from Texas, wreaked bloody vengeance on the local inhabitants. Lieutenant U.S. Grant wrote from Matamoros that the soldiers thought they could murder civilians with impunity "where the act can be covered by dark." To the south General Winfield Scott embarked on an uphill campaign to capture Mexico City, which fell to American forces in mid-September 1847.

Meanwhile Polk's representative in Vera Cruz continued negotiations with Mexican authorities. Scott and diplomat Nicholas Trist ignored their instructions from Polk and signed a treaty on February 2, 1848, at Guadalupe Hidalgo. The United States achieved every one of its goals: recognition of the Rio Grande as Texas' southern boundary and acquisition of territory for the future states of California, Arizona, Nevada, Utah, New Mexico, as well as slices of Colorado and Wyoming. The United States agreed to pay Mexico 15 million dollars in what some war critics called conscience money, and to assume 3.2 million dollars in American claims against that government. With the exception of the Gadsden purchase of nearly 30,000 square miles of Mexican territory south of New Mexico and Arizona in 1853, the Mexican War rounded out the territorial limits of the continental United States.

American expansion cost Mexico more than a third of her richest territory, a fact underscored by the discovery of gold in California in January 1848. That discovery set off a land rush to the Pacific coast that soon resulted in passage of a law requiring local Mexican landowners to prove the validity of their California land titles. In the meantime, white squatters, with the connivance of local officials, wrested the disputed land from its Chicano owners. The land grab occurred despite specific provisions in the peace treaty guaranteeing the property rights of inhabitants at the time of annexation. Aside from Indians, the Hispanic residents were the only minority incorporated into the United States by conquest and protected by treaty. These special assurances, however, were largely ignored especially when Mexicans held property attractive to Anglo-Americans. Like the Native Americans, who also had no economic base, Mexican-Americans were left hapless before the onrush of English-speaking settlers.

Slavery Becomes the Central Key Issue

Polk's achievement added prestige to his administration, but his policies heightened the emotional level of the slave controversy, worsened the sectional split, and brought the Civil War a giant step closer. The peaceful settlement of the Oregon boundary dispute exacerbated sectional tensions, partially because Polk had promised more than he could deliver short of a full-scale war. Despite his sword-rattling over Oregon, Polk accepted a compromise proposal that had floated around for years. In mid-June 1846 just after the outbreak of the Mexican War, the senate ratified a treaty with Great Britain extending the boundary between Canada and the United States along the forty-ninth parallel to the Pacific Ocean but leaving Vancouver Island under British control.

Midwestern senators complained that Polk had reneged on his campaign promise to acquire all of the Oregon Territory. They accused Polk of surrendering more land to the British than he had acquired. Sectional controversies mounted as the Democratic congress approved the Walker tariff in July. That measure, which slipped through the senate only with the tie-breaking vote of the vice president, led an Ohio congressman to denounce the tax on coffee and tea because free workers and farmers enjoyed these imports while the "three million slave laborers" in the South drank only tax-free water. This pro-southern administration, he concluded, gave away northern territory, reduced tariff protection for northern manufactures, and levied taxes on essentials to support war to acquire new slave territories. Calhoun referred to Mexico as the "forbidden fruit," luring southerners with the last, absolutely the final territory that northerners would allow southern slave holders to control. If the continuation of southern slavery required territorial expansion, Calhoun contended, the South was doomed.

The Mexican War enabled abolitionists to make deeper inroads in the North. Henry David Thoreau, in his essay "Civil Disobedience," opposed cooperation with a government bent on immoral ends, while the Massachusetts legislature condemned the war as "unChristian," calling on loyal citizens of the Bay State to withhold supplies and to resist the government. A freshman Whig congressman from Illinois, Abraham Lincoln, introduced the "spot resolution" that asked Polk to designate "the spot on American soil" where American blood had first been shed. Lincoln did not stand for reelection, but his action highlighted Whig opposition to a conflict that territorially expanded slavery. The most dramatic expression of dissent, however, came from David Wilmot, a Democratic congressman from Pennsylvania. On August 8, 1846, Wilmot attached an anti-administration proviso to an appropriations bill that stipulated that any territory acquired as a result of the war should be closed to slavery. The Wilmot Proviso indicated the seriousness of northern opposition to slave expansion. The proviso passed the house, but failed in the senate where southern strength remained too powerful.

The Election of 1848

The election of 1848 revealed the growing divisiveness caused by the pursuit of manifest destiny. A group of New York anti-slavery Democrats, called Barnburners, an epithet acquired when their opponents compared them to the Dutch farmer who burned down his barn to rid it of rats, left the Democratic Party. They joined with dissident "conscience" Whigs to form the Free-Soil Party, a group dedicated to containing slavery where it already existed and reserving the remaining western territories for white, freehold farmers. Van Buren won the Free-Soil presidential nomination with Charles Francis Adams, the son and grandson of presidents, as his running mate. Even with its slogan "Free soil, free speech, free labor, and free men," the new party had little chance of winning the election. Its leaders knew, however, it could spoil the election for the Democrats by appealing to western and midwestern voters.

The Democrats faced growing evidence of voter discontent with Polk's policies when the Whigs racked up a narrow congressional margin in 1846 and made strong gains in state races. In 1848, the Democrats abandoned Polk and chose Lewis Cass of Michigan as their standard-bearer. Cass advocated "squatter sovereignty," later called "popular sovereignty," which authorized citizens of a territory to determine the status of slavery in the territory. This idea did not go as far as Calhoun and more extreme slave holders desired, but they found the concept attractive.

The Whigs, tasting victory, nominated another general, Louisiana slave holder Zachery "Old Rough and Ready" Taylor, with Millard Fillmore from New York as his running mate. The Whigs gingerly sidestepped the slavery issue with a stirring recital of Taylor's military exploits, a tactic that appealed to enough of the electorate to permit their candidate to eke out a narrow victory. Van Buren played the spoiler by winning enough votes in New York to deprive Cass of the state's electors, throwing the election to the Whig.

Constitutional Politics

Although a southerner would occupy the White House, southern leaders realized that the safety of the slave system depended on their ability to win political support outside their region. The South still enjoyed a parity with the North in the senate, but by 1849 southern representatives were outnumbered 168 to 118 in the house. Moreover, more than a dozen new free states could be carved from American territory north of the Missouri Compromise line of 36°30' but only one below it. Demography was running against the slave states. The surprising popularity of the Free-Soil party indicated that the slavery issue had galvanized large numbers of Americans to take a stand against the South. Aside from radicals such as William Lloyd Garrison who refused to vote altogether, many antislavery proponents opposed the institution because of the power that it gave slave holders. The overthrow of the slave power became the touchstone of the free-soil movement. One of its leaders wrote, "We must make the most of that word . . . . Let it appear that it is the *Slave Power* which we wish to restrict and curtail."

On the defensive, southern leaders raised the constitutional issue that would dominate the sectional dispute until the Civil War settled the matter. Put simply, southerners asserted that the Fifth Amendment gave them the right, despite the Missouri Compromise, to take their slave property anywhere they desired. The central government, they claimed, had a positive obligation to protect its citizens' right to enter any western territory without restriction. Jefferson Davis, a senator from Mississippi, summed it up: "If the existence of the slave as property be admitted, what power has congress to interfere with it? . . . Entering a territory with his property, the citizen has a right to its protection."

By 1850 both sides had well-developed arguments. Garrisonian abolitionists demanded "gradual emancipation immediately arrived at." This set a tone for the rest of the debate that made most anti-slavery proponents seem moderate by comparison and gave abolitionists an air of legitimacy. The majority of anti-slavery advocates were content to restrict slavery to where it existed, in the belief that it would eventually die out. They spoke aggressively of an evil southern power determined to destroy basic American freedoms wherever the slave system expanded—the freedom to work your own land, to rise by your own efforts, and to enjoy the fruits of your own labor. Southerners responded with the well-worn argument that the constitution protected slaveholders'. rights to carry their human chattel wherever they wished. By 1850, the debate over slavery had come down to the future of the territories. The slavery debates often soared into rhetorical abstractions, yet these rhetorical flourishes carried very concrete and practical implications. Each side saw its way of life threatened by the other.

The Compromise of 1850

In 1849, the thirty-first congress convened in an atmosphere heavy with suspicion and hostility. In the house, it took three weeks and sixty-three ballots for the majority Democrats to elect a speaker. In this volatile situation, President Taylor dropped a political bombshell by asking congress to admit California as a state. In the wake of discovery of gold, Anglo-American settlers had rushed to form a state government to protect themselves from the depredations of hordes of gold-hunting "forty-niners." Taylor

California's fate as the first state on the west coast was sealed with the discovery of gold there in January 1848 and the United States' victory in the Mexican war. Its admission in 1850 as a free state was one of the major provisions of the Compromise of 1850. (1950)

asked lawmakers to "abstain from the introduction of those exciting topics of sectional character which have hitherto produced painful apprehensions in the public mind." He need not have bothered. For eight months, through Taylor's death on July 9 and Fillmore's ascension, the bitter debate over slave expansion to California, the status of slavery in Washington, D.C., and the South's desire for a stronger fugitive slave law racked the nation.

Eighteen-fifty also marked a change of the guard. The political triumvirate that had led the country since 1812—Calhoun, Clay, and Webster—were at the end of their careers. All had died by October 1852. A generation of new leaders, less willing to compromise—William Seward of New York, Salmon P. Chase of Ohio,

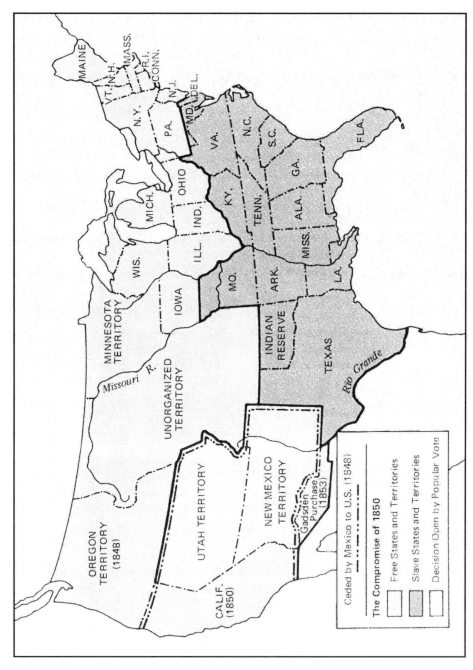

The United States in 1850

MAINE

VT. N.H. MASS.
R.I.
CONN.

N.Y.
N.J.

PA.
MD. DEL.

VA. N.C.
S.C.

OHIO FLA.
MICH. GA.
KY. ALA.
ILL. IND. TENN.
MISS.
WIS.

IOWA MO. ARK. LA.

MINNESOTA
TERRITORY

INDIAN
RESERVE TEXAS

UNORGANIZED
TERRITORY Rio Grande

Missouri R.

UTAH TERRITORY

NEW MEXICO
TERRITORY

OREGON Gadsden
TERRITORY Purchase
(1848) (1853)

CALIF.
(1850)

Ceded by Mexico to U.S. (1848)

The Compromise of 1850

Free States and Territories

Slave States and Territories

Decision Open by Popular Vote

Alexander Stephens and Robert Toombs of Georgia, and Jefferson Davis of Mississippi-were unabashed advocates for their regions, uninhibited by arguments on behalf of compromise and national unity.

The controversy surrounding California's admission produced the last compromise over slavery brokered by Clay, Webster, and Calhoun. On January 29, 1850, Henry Clay presented to congress a series of resolutions designed to give each section something. Living up to his reputation as the "Great Compromiser," Clay proposed to admit California as a free state, upsetting the delicate balance between North and South in the senate, to allow the remainder of the Mexican cession to be organized without restricting slavery, to adjust the disputed New Mexico-Texas boundary line, to assume the old Texas debts, to prohibit the slave trade in the District of Columbia but not to otherwise interfere with slavery there, and to enact a tougher federal fugitive slave law. Each section received something, Clay explained, so each should make a concession for the sake of national unity. But the debate raged. The dramatic high point came on March 4 when Calhoun, too weak to rise from his seat, asked a colleague to read his speech deploring the onward rush toward disunion that he attributed to northern attacks on slavery. Returning again and again to the Constitution, he pleaded for the restoration of a lost political "equilibrium" between the sections. In a posthumously published essay, *A Disquisition on Government*, he recognized the South's loss of power in congress and suggested that the country elect two presidents, one from the North, the other from the South, each with an absolute veto over legislation. Such a "constituent veto" would prevent powerful majorities from destroying the interests of vulnerable minorities.

Three days later, Daniel Webster gave the the most memorable speech of his career. Webster came before congress, as he declared, "not as a Massachusetts man, nor as a Northern man, but as an American, pleading for compromise." To those who wanted a Wilmot Proviso, he asked, why "reenact the law of God?" Climate and geography had already foreclosed the possibility of slavery in the territories. It made no sense to Webster to prohibit something that would not happen anyway. New York Senator William Seward's thunderous response echoed across the North and hounded the sixty-nine-year-old Webster

Daniel Webster (1782-1852) was one of the most famous orators of his day and sometimes called "the god-like Daniel." An ardent tariff protectionist after 1828, he was especially noted for his nationalism, a position that enabled him to support the Compromise of 1850, which also assured his defeat. (1932)

to his grave. "All legislative compromises," Seward asserted, were "radically wrong and essentially vicious," so he called upon a higher law, the law of God, which condemned slavery and made the Wilmot Proviso necessary. By such a moral standard, no opponent of slavery could compromise. Later speakers hurled taunts and challenges, making it clear that no compromise would ever pass as a single package. Led by the Democratic senator from Illinois, Stephen A. Douglas, supporters of compromise divided the issues into five parts and shepherded each through both houses in eleven intense days of bargaining.

The most controversial measure was the new fugitive slave law. Because the number of runaway slaves was small, the statute was little more than a symbolic gesture to appease the South; it raised fundamental questions about legal due process. The Fugitive Slave Act authorized federal commissioners to grant certificates ordering the return of escaped slaves conditional on the slave owners' oath of ownership. Commissioners received a fee of ten dollars if they authorized the certificate and only five dollars if they refused authorization. The testimony of alleged fugitives was not admissible as evidence. According to the Fugitive Slave law, a slave owner could enter a free state and on his own testimony accuse a black freedman, born in the North of free parents, of being a fugitive slave. The accused black, even though a free-born citizen of a free state, could not testify nor bring evidence in his behalf. Rarely has congress so flagrantly violated a class of citizens' first amendment rights or so disregarded states' rights.

The result was a fire storm throughout the North. Beginning with Vermont, northern states enacted "personal liberty laws" that interposed state authority between the runaways and the federal government. When slave holders on the federal bench overruled these laws, abolitionist mobs and other enraged citizens descended on jails to free all accused slaves awaiting shipment south, effectively nullifying the enforcement of the statute north of the Ohio River. Southern slave holders fumed about the northern public's thwarting of federal law and slave owners' rights of due process.

Other statutes in the compromise were less controversial. Congress admitted California as a free state, organized the New Mexico and Utah territories without any restriction on slavery, took over Texas' state debt, resolved its boundary dispute with the New Mexico territory, and abolished the slave trade in the District of Columbia. Except for the anti-slavery minority, the Compromise of 1850 worked, acceptable to most of the nation, which breathed easier. But angry anti-slavery forces in Massachusetts ousted Webster from the senate and replaced him with the fiery and determined abolitionist Charles Sumner.

Fruits of Compromise

The compromise, however, temporarily forestalled disunion. It did not affect most Americans' lives. The Ohioans and Indianans who floated their goods down the Ohio and Mississippi rivers to New Orleans marveled at the cotton plantations they passed as evidence of the nation's strength and majesty, giving little more than passing attention to the black slaves who toiled in the fields. Merchants and cotton dealers in Charleston, Savannah, and Mobile maintained their financial ties with New York and Philadelphia brokers and bankers with little thought that things might be different. A few even worked for even more territorial expansion, this time to the South-Puerto Rico, Santo Domingo, Cuba, and Brazil-areas with well established slave systems. Such heirs of manifest destiny formed a shadowy movement called Young America that promoted free trade, aid to republican groups in foreign countries, and southern territorial expansion. Citizens of both regions harbored vague notions that people were somehow different on the other side of Mason and Dixon's line, but their way of life, the things they knew and accepted without question, were bound up in keeping things as they were. Most expressed only casual interest in the status of the territories or expansion of slavery. By the early 1850s, Americans found more that unified than divided them. Still, the sinews that bound the body politic together had been stretched thin.

The Whig Party became the first major casualty of the Compromise of 1850. Upset with the legislation, several angry southern Whigs drifted into an association with the Democrats in a short-lived Union Rights Party. In the North moderate Whigs moved slowly toward the abolitionist position. Southern moderates seemed in firm control when they squelched South Carolina's fire-eating Robert Barnwell Rhett at a 1850 Nashville convention to discuss a southern strategy. In 1851 local elections southern voters repudiated extremists. But the center of the Whig party continued to erode. The economic issues that had traditionally bound it together, such as internal improvements, protective tariffs, and national banking gave way as anti-slavery Whigs insisted that the party oppose slavery.

In the election of 1852 most voters rejected the extreme anti-slavery position which many northern Whigs had adopted. By election day the Whigs had lost many of their southern adherents to the Democrats, who, in turn, became an increasingly southern party. The Democrats nominated a "doughface," a northern man with southern sympathies, Franklin Pierce from New Hampshire. The Whigs nominated another "man on horseback," General Winfield Scott of Mexican war fame. The Free-Soil Party refused to support the Compromise of 1850 and endorsed free homesteads for "landless settlers." Pierce rolled up a massive victory in the electoral college, carrying twenty-seven of thirty-one states, although he received only 200,000 more popular votes than Scott. Voters had opted for moderation and the status quo. Even so, the disintegration of the Whigs and the growing ranks of abolitionists indicated that the election represented only a brief respite from the country's ever growing sectional crisis.

Such political developments drove southerners to form a unified front against anti-slavery advocates. In 1844 both the Methodists and Baptists had divided along sectional lines; only the smaller Presbyterian and Episcopal churches remained intact until the war. Southerners, anxious to promote sectional institutions, sent their sons to colleges in the South while publishers preached the gospel of regional self-sufficiency. In the pages of his *Review*, J. D. B. DeBow, a New Orleans editor, advised southern farmers to grow their own wheat and make their own bread. DeBow also admonished southern authors to write textbooks to prevent the South's young minds from being poisoned by abolitionist writers. Others worked on expanding the southern rail system and pressed for government assistance for harbor and port facilities to forge direct trade links with Europe.

Such efforts undermined the broad popular support the Compromise of 1850 enjoyed. Similarly, the dynamic quality of southern slavery required constant infusions of new land and resulted in renewed demands for its extension into the West. The fragile balance created by the compromise was thus upset, and the will to compromise eroded, bit by bit, plantation by plantation. Southerners, who had once believed that the future of the national union depended on the mutual recognition by each section of the other's rights and interests, now refused to grant the necessary concessions to maintain the union unchanged. Calhoun sternly insisted on such recognition, but he had also refused to compromise. The Compromise of 1850 was the last great prewar accommodation based on such mutual give-and-take. Southern leaders, fire-eaters almost to a man, elevated their region's rights above those of the union. The South had evolved a constitutional sectionalism, whose proponents believed by 1852 that it embodied the only correct reading of the nation's past. On the other side, abolitionists had a position of moral superiority. Many approved when William Lloyd Garrison publicly burned a copy of the Constitution on July 4, 1854. The advocates of disunion simply awaited an issue explosive enough to tear the nation apart.

In 1852 Harriet Beecher Stowe provided that charge. In her novel, Stowe recounted the harrowing travail of a simple Kentucky slave family. Uncle Tom, his wife Chloe, his children and grandchildren lived a quiet, hardworking Christian life on the Shelby plantation. On first glance Mr. and Mrs. Shelby were ideal slave owners. They loved their slaves as their children and encouraged their religious faith. They treated them kindly and with respect, and they honored their marriages. But Mr. Shelby had fallen into debt due to gambling. Forced by his creditor to choose between selling his farm or some of his most loyal slaves, Shelby chose to sell Uncle Tom, his married daughter Eliza, and her nursing infant. A beautiful mulatto, Eliza feared being sold to a New Orleans brothel and her separation from her infant and husband. In consort with other slaves, she ran off ahead of the slave catchers, crossing the Ohio River in the height of winter, luckily finding refuge with a Quaker ferryman. As she and her baby set out on this "underground railroad," an Ohio senator's wife provided her shelter.

When the senator discovered that his wife, in violation of the Fugitive Slave law, which he had supported, harbored a fugitive, he insisted that the fugitives be turned over to the slave catchers. As the senator and his wife search their consciences, Eliza asked the wife, "Have you ever lost a child?" With that question, hundreds of thousands of Stowe's readers ceased their moral equivocations. Stowe forced northern readers to understand that slavery involved human beings, much like themselves, who married, bore children, worshipped God, and struggled with life. Slavery, even more than the factory system, denied hard working, god-fearing, moral family people the opportunity and the means to live decent lives. At any moment their master had the legal power to break up their marriages, take their children from them, sell them down river to a distant land, or to sexually molest them. As property, the Constitution denied them protection of the law, denied them opportunity to live a Christian life. Northern, middle class evangelical women, aroused by the Second Great Awakening, by their education, and by new notions of women's moral responsibilities, after reading *Uncle Tom's Cabin*, refused to countenance any compromise with slavery. Such women formed the core of the antislavery movement; they served as teachers in the new public school systems; they joined missionary societies, formed temperance unions, and they founded orphanages and homes for wayward girls. They also led their husbands into the Republican Party and supported its absolute refusal to allow the expansion of slavery into the territories. At most, they agreed to tolerate slavery where it existed under the belief that, denied the means to expand, it would soon die out. Only a handful of radicals, such as William Lloyd Garrison and John Brown, believed that slavery must be destroyed wherever it existed. But an increasing number of antebellum Americans understood that the nation could no longer stand divided between free and slave. Seventy-five years of compromises had come to an end.

Historical Potpourri

The most native of all American music was the spirituals that enlivened and expressed a slave's life. Black children heard these songs in the quarters, at praise meetings, and in the fields; with a well developed sense of harmony, they could pick up parts and improvise lyrics for the occasion. The words expressed the slaves' own longings, as well as how they viewed the world and their roles in it.

> *Ev'rybody who am living, Ev'rybody got to die.*
> *Ev'rybody who am living, Ev'rybody got to die.*
> *Rich an' poor, great an' small, Got to meet in Judgment Hall,*
> *Ev'rybody who am living, Ev'rybody got to die.*

The same theme ran though:
> *You got a right,*
> *I got a right,*
> *We all got a right, to the tree of life.*
> *Yes, tree of life.*

> *De very time I thought I was los'*
> *De dungeon shuck an' de chain fell off.*
> *You may hinder me here*
> *But you cannot dere, 'Cause God in de heav'n gwinter answer prayer.*

Unfortunately for the slaves, most rights were not recognized in the world they inhabited. To survive, slaves had to learn from one another about their roles in a hostile society:
> *Oh de ol'sheep done know de road, De ol'sheep done know de road,*
> *De ol'sheep done know de road, De young lam's mus' fin' de way.*
> *Oh, soon-a in the mornin' when I rise, De young lam's mus' fin' de way.*
> *Wid crosses an' trials on ev'ry side, De young lam's must' fin' de way.*

Often the advice was stoic in nature—bear up, carry on, keep the faith:
> *Keep a inchin' along, Keep a inchin' along*
> *Massa Jesus is comm' bye an' bye,*
> *Keep a inchin' along like a po' inch worm,*
> *Massa Jesus is comm' bye and bye.*

Sometimes physical troubles were spiritualized, but the meaning was clear:

O by an' by, by an' by
I'm gwinter lay down my heavy load.
O hell is deep an' a dark despair,
I'm gwiner lay down my heavy load
Stop po' sinner an 'dont' go dere.

Solving a slave's problems meant dealing with his master. Every slave and every master knew about stealing so when slaves sang about stealing away to Jesus, all who heard knew who would be losing something valuable:

Steal a-way, steal a-way, steal a-way to Jesus
Steal a-way, steal a-way home, I ain't got long to stay here.
My Lord, He calls me, He calls me by the thunder,
The trumpet sounds within-a my soul, I ain't got long to stay here.

Violent emotions lurked just beneath the surface:

Singin' wid a sword in my han'
Lord, Singin' wid a sword in my han'.

The most poignant, however, were those songs that expressed longings to recapture what slavery had rent asunder:

Oh, Peter, go ring dem bells,
Peter, go ring dem bells,
Peter, go ring dem bells,
I heard f'om heav'n today.
I wonder where my mother is gone,
I wonder where my mother is gone,
I wonder where my mother is gone
I heard f'rm heav'n today.
Peter go ring dem bells.

All spirituals except "Ev'rybody Who Am Living" is from James Weldon Johnson and J. Rosamond Johnson, eds., *The Books of American Negro Spirituals* (New York: The Viking Press, 1969). "Ev'rybody Who Am Living" is from *The Treasury of Negro Spirituals*, H. A. Chambers, ed., (New York: Emerson Books, 1963.

Good Books

The best overall study of the period is David Potter's posthumously published, *The Impending Crisis: 1848-1861* (1976). The good and brief introduction to John Calhoun is Richard Current, *John C. Calhoun (1963)*; the chapter on Calhoun, "The Marx of the Master Class," in Richard Hofstadter's *American Political Tradition* is most provocative. William Freehling, *Prelude to Civil War* (1966), expertly ties together Calhoun's South Carolina, nullification, and slave unrest. Olive Vernon Burton, *In My Father's House are Many Mansions: Family and Community in Edgefield County. South Carolina (1985)* provides a social context to Calhoun's and other slave holders' outlook. Wilbur J. Cash, *The Mind of the South* (1941) remains the most insightful and provocative comment on the South.

Slavery continues as one of the most lively areas of historical controversy. Several older studies still worth reading are Kenneth Stampp, *The Peculiar Institution* (1956); Eugene Genovese, *Roll, Jordan, Roll* (1974), Herbert Gutman, *The Black Family in Slavery and Freedom* (1976), and Alex Haley, in his imaginative *Roots* (1976). John W. Blassingame revisits *The Slave Community* (1972). James Oakes suggestively explores *The Ruling Race* (1982) while Peter Kolchin's *Unfree Labor: American Slavery and Russian Serfdom* (1987) places southern slavery in an international context. For southern honor see Bertram Wyatt-Brown's *Southern Honor* (1982); Kenneth Greenberg's *Masters and Statesmen* (1985); and Stephanie McCurry, *Masters of Small Worlds* (1995).

All future work on slavery will begin with Ira Berlin, *Many Thousands Gone: The First Two Centuries of Slavery in North America* (1998). Albert J. Raboteau's *Slave Religion* (1978) has transformed historians' understanding of African-American culture and its relationship to west Africa and slavery. Also see Robert Ferris Thompson, *Flash of the Spirit* (1983) for insight into the complexities of west African art and its transmission to the New World. Marie Jenkins Schwartz, *Born in Bondage* (2002), examines how slave children's lives were shaped. Also see Brenda Stevenson, *Life in Black and White: Family and Community in the Slave South* (1996). Bernard Powers, *Black Charlestonians: A Social History 1822-1885* is a complex and detailed study of African-American urban life. Stephen Oates' gripping study of Nat Turner, *The Fires of Jubilee* (1974), is a great read. Genovese, in *The World the Slaveholders Made* (1969), writes compellingly of southern apologist George Fitzhugh. A powerful account of slavery from the inside emerges in an exciting fashion from the *Narrative of the Life of Frederick Douglass* (originally 1844) and from William Feeley, *Frederick Douglas* (1991).

Eric Foner's *Free Soil, Free Labor, Free Men* (1970) changed the way historians have looked at anti-slavery advocates. Almost as much controversy still swirls around William Lloyd

Garrison, whose historical remains have been disinterred and raked over by Walter Merrill, *Against Wind and Tide* (1963) and John L. Thomas, *The Liberator* (1963). Aileen Kraditor joined the debate with *Means and Ends in American Abolitionism* (1969). Louis Filler has catalogued the abolitionist contribution in *The Crusade Against Slavery* (1960).

Frederick Merk's *Manifest Destiny and Mission in American History* (1963) is still of interest. For a newer version, see Reginald Horseman, *Race and Manifest Destiny* (1981). Otis Singletary's volume, *The Mexican War* (1963) is the best brief survey of that conflict. Avery Craven, measures the effect of the war and Polk's policies in *The Growth of Southern Nationalism* (1953), while Holman Hamilton explores *Prologue to Conflict* (1964), as he describes the conflict over the Compromise of 1850.

CHAPTER SIX

Civil War and Beyond

1854	Kansas-Nebraska Act
	Organization of Republican party
1855	Wakarusa War in Kansas
1856	James Buchanan fifteenth president
	John Brown's Pottawatomie Creek massacre
1857	Hinton Helper's *Impending Crisis*
1858	Lincoln-Douglas debates
1859	Southern convention proposed reopening of slave trade
	John Brown's Harpers Ferry raid
1860	Abraham Lincoln sixteenth president
1861	Confederate government
	Morrill tariff
	Lincoln announced naval blockade
1863	Emancipation Proclamation
	New York City draft riots
	National Banking Act
	Battle of Gettysburg
	Lincoln's reconstruction plan
1864	Wade-Davis Bill
1865	Appomattox
	Lincoln assassinated
	Andrew Johnson seventeenth president
	Freedman's Bureau
	Johnson's restoration policies
	Thirteenth Amendment
1866	Republicans won decisive control of Congress
	Ku Klux Klan founded at Pulaski, Tennessee
1867	Congressional Reconstruction

1868	Ulysses S. Grant eighteenth president
	Fourteenth Amendment
	Ominibus Act readmitted seven southern states to the Union
1871	Tweed ring broken in New York City
1872	Credit Mobilier
1876	Rutherford B. Hayes nineteenth president
1877	End of Reconstruction

Civil War and Beyond

Congress hoped that the Compromise of 1850 would lay to rest the issue of the expansion of slavery. The 1820 Missouri Compromise had closed the territory north of 36°30′ in Louisiana Territory to slavery while congress had applied the doctrine of popular sovereignty to the New Mexico and Utah territories and California and Oregon had been declared free. Politicians from the North, had ignored, however, the reality that slavery was a dynamic labor system. Beginning in colonial Virginia, where slavery had first been legalized, and later in South Carolina and Louisiana, masters had taken their slaves wherever fertile land, climate, and the law enabled plantations to thrive. After Eli Whitney developed his cotton gin in 1793, short-fiber cotton production expanded into the rich bottom lands of the deep South, the Gulf coastal plain, and up the Mississippi and Missouri river valleys, wherever there were 200 or more frost-free days a year. Slaves labored on the Louisiana sugar plantations, Carolina rice lands, and in Kentucky hemp fields. Many southerners believed slave labor could be applied to western mining or the rapidly spreading wheat fields. And throughout the South, during the antebellum period, southern manufactures used slaves in their factories and forges. In the slave South, wealth, power, and status, all, depended on the territorial expansion of slavery.

Prior to the Civil War, slavery differentiated the South from the North. It marked two different ways of life, one aristocratic, rural, agricultural, and slave-based, the other a democratic, free labor, mixed economy of farming, manufacturing, banking, and commerce, dominated by large industrial cities. The South was a self-consciously hierarchal society that valued conformity, and it was ruled by men who believed they should command. The North encouraged upward mobility, fostered personal freedom, and shared political power among farmers, manufacturers, merchants, an expanding urban middle class, and urban laborers, including recent Irish immigrants. The presence of African Americans underlay southern notions of distinctiveness, leading southerners to reject the notion of human equality and economic liberalism espoused by Jefferson and enshrined in American law and the Constitution. All understood that the conflict between North and South rested on fundamental, moral and political principles.

The Compromise of 1850 did not resolve these differences. It did not even address them. The compromise only solved several practical problems that had arisen from the increasing sectional differences. It was landmark legislation only because most Americans wanted to believe that it had resolved the causes of sectional conflict. Events proved otherwise. At best, it was merely cosmetic, a desperate attempt to resolve specific issues between increasingly hostile sections to preserve the federal union. It amounted to only a temporary reprieve.

In the 50s each section clung ever more resolutely to its own basic self-definition, creating a host of new problems unaddressed by the mid-century compromise. In the course of the decade, political leaders on both sides lost the means and the will to solve the problems that drove the nation apart, largely because the differences were themselves irreconcilable. By 1861, each side was certain that it pursued a righteous cause and political leaders bowed to the inevitable war. Pitting kin against kin, the American Civil War killed more Americans than all of its other wars put together, altogether over a million casualties, including nearly one quarter of southern males between the age of 16 and 30 years. They did not, however, die in vain. The Civil War destroyed slavery and with it, the primary threat to disunion. Unlike most wars, the American Civil War resolved the fundamental questions of national unity and human slavery, not just for North Americans, but also for the world. In Lincoln's words, the Civil War tested whether the United States "or any nation dedicated to the proposition that all men are created equal can long endure." The destruction of southern slavery sounded the death knell to chattel slavery world-wide. By 1880, an institution older than civilization itself had been legally abolished everywhere, opening the way for constitutional democracy and new ideas of racial justice. Few events have borne such momentous consequences.

"Bleeding Kansas and the Threat of War"

In the early 1850s all this lay in the future. Events in Kansas made clear that the fundamental differences between South and North had not been resolved. On January 4, 1854, Illinois senator, Stephan A. Douglas, rose in the senate to introduce a bill designed to promote the national interest, that of his business associates, his hometown of Chicago, and his presidential ambitions. With no intention of unsettling the body politic, Douglas proposed to organize the territory west of Missouri and Iowa, to open the region to white settlement, and to construct a transcontinental railroad whose eastern terminus would be Chicago. Southerners were prepared. On January 16, Kentucky senator, Archibald Dixon, introduced an amendment to nullify the Missouri Compromise and to allow slave holders to take slaves into the new region that lay north of the Missouri Compromise line of 36°30'. On the following day, Massachusetts senator, Charles Sumner, responded with an amendment that reaffirmed the Missouri Compromise. Douglas modified his bill to provide for two territories, Kansas to the south and Nebraska to the north. The Kansas-Nebraska Bill, approved on May 30, repealed the 1820 Missouri Compromise and upheld the doctrine of popular sovereignty. Douglas assumed that Kansas would become a slave state and Nebraska would be free.

The Kansas-Nebraska Act reflected Douglas' hope that the principles of self-determination would allow white Americans to settle their problems amicably. Subsequent events demonstrated the emptiness of his hopes. Even before final passage of the bill, Eli Thayer, an educator and congressman from Massachusetts, organized an emigrant aid society to settle Kansas with free-soilers. In turn, Missouri slave holders formed secret societies that offered protection to slave holders who moved into the region. The two sides fought to settle the question of popular sovereignty. Armed bands of Missourians crossed the border, terrorized the free-soilers, and elected a pro-slavery legislature that met in July 1855 in Lawrence. Brooklyn New York's Plymouth Congregational Church supplied antislavery settlers with twenty-five Sharp's rifles, called "Beecher Bibles," after the church's minister, Henry Ward Beecher, an outspoken critic of slavery and brother of Harriet Beecher Stowe. Beecher exhorted Kansas free-soilers, "Inasmuch as ye do it unto the least of these, ye do it unto me." Free-soilers formed a rival territorial government in Topeka. The Topeka constitution prohibited blacks, whether slave or free, from settling in Kansas. The two rival governments each raised a military force to prepare for a decisive showdown.

Birth of the Republican Party

Meanwhile, throughout the Northeast and Midwest, anti-slavery advocates held mass rallies to protest the Kansas-Nebraska bill and its repeal of the Missouri Compromise. In Ripon, Wisconsin, in Jackson, Michigan, in upstate New York, in New England, and elsewhere these groups called themselves "Republicans." They believed that the Kansas and Nebraska Act represented only the latest effort of the "Slave Power" to expand. Republicans feared that all the western territories would be occupied by slave holders, squeezing out small farmers. The new party pledged to repeal the Kansas-Nebraska Act and to hammer away at the slave power until southern leaders agreed to halt the expansion of slavery in the federal territories-the last remaining unclaimed land available for freehold farming.

The Republican Party, in its early years fiercely opposed the expansion of slavery and attracted those fearful of the slave power. Republicans never specified what the slave power meant in concrete terms, but a manifesto written in Ostend, Belgium, by three pro-slavery diplomats, confirmed Republican fears. In 1854 the Ostend Manifesto urged the United States to purchase Cuba so that it could become another slave state and, if that failed, to wrest it by force from the Spanish, a course justified "by every law human and Divine." As the Whig party disintegrated, Republicans sought to attract its former members with little interest in slavery but who agreed with the party's Whiggish stand on economic issues such as the tariff, internal improvements, and national banking. Many former Whigs had affiliated with the "Know-Nothings," or the American Party, heir to anti-Catholic, anti-immigrant sentiment going back decades. The Know-Nothings served as a way station for many Whig moderates on their way to becoming Republicans.

As the political parties realigned, things went from bad to worse in Kansas. President Pierce aggravated the situation by siding openly with the pro-slavery Lawrence government forces against the free-soil Topeka government. By early 1856 violence in Kansas attracted increasing numbers of fanatics, including fifty-six-year-old John Brown, who with six companions, descended on a settlement of pro-slavery farmers on Pottawatomie Creek. Brown and his group massacred five unarmed settlers and mutilated their bodies. Shortly after, Brown slipped back East, where leading abolitionists eagerly supported his still obscure anti-slavery plots. With guerrilla warfare raging across Kansas, Charles Sumner of Massachusetts thundered in the senate about the "crime against Kansas," perpetuated by a "slave oligarchy." On May 22, in defense of a kinsman, whom Sumner had accused by name, Congressman Preston Brooks from South Carolina savagely beat Sumner into unconsciousness with a cane in the senate chamber. "Bleeding Sumner" and "Bleeding Kansas" became the rallying cries for the Republican presidential campaign in 1856.

The Election of 1856

The 1856 presidential election revealed a surprising support for the Republican ticket led by Californian John C. Fremont. The party's platform called for the admission of Kansas as a free state and argued that congress had the exclusive authority to determine the status of slavery in the territories. 'We deny," they declared, "that a territorial legislature, of any individual or association of individuals" can "give legal existence to slavery in any territory of the United States."

The Democrats chose another doughface, James Buchanan of Pennsylvania, an author of the Ostend Manifesto. Because Buchanan had just returned as American minister to Great Britain, he was untainted by the Kansas dispute, which Democrats hoped would make him more acceptable to northern voters. Buchanan's platform endorsed popular sovereignty and warned that further abolitionist agitation over slavery promised "dangerous consequences" for the nation.

The American party was wracked by violent internal dissensions. With the Republicans vigorously opposed to slave expansion, southern Know-Nothings flocked to the Democratic standard while northern Know-Nothings worried that a Republican victory might destroy the American Party. Buchanan won the electoral votes of New Jersey, Illinois, Indiana, and Pennsylvania as well as the slave South. He only managed, however, to win a plurality of the popular vote—1,838,169 to Fremont's 1,335,264, and 874,534 for the Know-Nothing's Millard Fillmore. As a party "untorn in former battles and unsullied by past errors," New York Senator William Seward declared the Republicans had done amazingly well. If they could just pick up the American Party's northern voters, in 1860, they would win the White House.

Increasing Sectionalism

Buchanan's victory did not end concerns on either side of the Mason and Dixon Line. With each passing day, the sectional dispute tore at the nation's unity with increasing ferocity. The South momentarily gained the upper hand on March 6, 1857, when the supreme court, for only the second time in history, overturned an act of Congress in *Dred Scott v. Sandford*. The case involved a Missouri slave whose owner, an army doctor, had taken him into territory declared free by the Missouri Compromise. Scott based his claim on his temporary residence in a free territory. Led by its slave holding majority, the supreme court denied that Scott, or any black person, could be an American citizen with access to the federal courts. Chief Justice Roger Taney went further by asserting that the 1820 Missouri Compromise was unconstitutional because it deprived a United States citizen the use of his property without due process. Although two northern justices dissented, the decision against Scott opened the legal door for slave holders to take their slaves into any territory. Southern slaveholders found the *Dred Scott* doctrine much more attractive than popular sovereignty, while anti-slavery advocates insisted that they would never obey the ruling. Moderate Illinois senator Stephen Douglas found himself in an impossible situation of appealing for moderation in a revolutionary situation as he prepared for a tough senatorial reelection campaign in 1858 with hopes of winning the Democratic presidential nomination in 1860.

In the summer of 1857, events in Kansas once more captured national attention. Without legal authority, pro-southern elements convened a constitutional convention in Lecompton and drew up a new territorial constitution. Through high-sounding phrases, they carefully wove into the document provisions that guaranteed the protection of slave property and submitted it to Kansas voters for their approval. Free-soilers, who comprised a majority of Kansas voters, boycotted the plebiscite. Pro-slavery voters ratified the Lecompton Constitution by better than ten to one. Ignoring inevitable protests, Buchanan accepted the Lecompton Constitution and submitted it to congress for approval. Northern voters were outraged at Buchanan's open support of pro-slavery elements and at the blatantly illegal efforts by slave holders to achieve their ends. Douglas split with Buchanan over the Lecompton Constitution, injuring himself in the South without gaining support in the North. After intense maneuvering, including the use of federal troops to patrol the polling places, Kansan free-soilers engineered another vote. On August 2, 1858, Kansas voters decisively rejected the Lecompton constitution. Kansas quieted down and entered the union as a free state in January 1861, just days after South Carolina seceded from the Union. Throughout it all, the Kansas slave population was exactly two.

Kansas left its mark on the nation. The bloodshed and violence had discredited the nation's political institutions and leaders. Northerners lost respect for the Democratic Party, the presidency, and the supreme court. Northern Democrats found it impossible to remain in a party which had become an instrument of slavery. Douglas, the most important Democratic moderate, suffered especially. After his break with Buchanan, the president withdrew patronage from the "Little Giant" and dismissed his supporters from public office. Some southern radicals, dubbed fire-eaters, considered

The seven debates between the incumbent Stephen A. Douglas and Abraham Lincoln in the 1858 Illinois senatorial campaign spread over seven weeks and first brought Lincoln to national attention. The major issue between them boiled down to whether congress had power to restrict the expansion of slavery into the western territories, a position the challenger championed. (1958)

Douglas more dangerous than the Republicans because as a moderate he might secure the presidency and deny slave holders the practical means to secure their slaves in the territories.

In the fall of 1858, following a debate with his Republican senatorial opponent, Abraham Lincoln, Douglas further alienated southern voters. At Freeport, Illinois, Douglas declared that the people of a territory might exclude or permit slavery as they wished. Although the "Freeport Doctrine" repeated Douglas' views on popular sovereignty and enabled him to defeat Lincoln, it publically acknowledged Douglas' disapproval of the *Dred Scott* decision. Although Lincoln lost the Illinois senatorial election, he gained stature with his unequivocal statement that slavery was "a moral, a social, and a political wrong," whose expansion must be stopped. New York Senator William Seward went further when he addressed a Rochester audience in October, declaring that the nation faced "an irrepressible conflict" between two contending forces, one devoted to free labor, one to slave holding. The American republic had become irrevocably divided, and as constituted, could no longer stand.

In 1859 controversy abated somewhat. Kansas was forgotten, the recession of 1857 had lifted, and congress busied itself with such mundane issues as railroads, homestead legislation, and tariffs. Then in October, the unbalanced fugitive John Brown descended like an avenging angel on the federal arsenal at Harper's Ferry, Virginia. Leading a band of twenty-one followers that included five African Americans, Brown hoped to provoke a slave uprising, arm the slaves, and establish a redoubt for freedmen in the Appalachian Mountains. After two days, no slaves had appeared. Under siege, with two of his sons dead, Brown surrendered to Marine Colonel Robert E. Lee. Less than six weeks later, federal authorities hanged Brown as a convicted traitor. As he faced the hangman Brown declared, "If I should forfeit my life for the furtherance of the ends of justice and mingle my blood with the blood of millions of slaves, I say let it be." In death Brown displayed a dignity and eloquence that had eluded him in life. In the North, church bells knelled Brown's death. He had done what no one else had dared to do, waged war on slavery, giving no mercy and asking for none. He did not debate, seek an accommodation, or equivocate. Instead, he acted with unbridled courage and died, knowing that the republic's complicity with human slavery could only be purged with blood.

The Election of 1860

As the election of 1860 drew near, sectional tensions heightened. Republicans circulated copies of Hinton Helper's *The Impending Crisis and How to Meet It* that used census figures to prove that slavery had retarded the South's growth in every conceivable area—wealth, population, political strength, newspapers and schools, but it had especially impoverished the region's small farmers, who could not compete with planters for choice land. Helper wrote on behalf of the 7.5 million non-slaveholding southern whites who outnumbered slave holders by twenty to one. In the deep South, politicians and state legislatures busied themselves with preparations for secession and war, if the election brought to power a "black Republican" such as Lincoln.

On April 23, the Democratic Party convened in Charleston. Southern fire eaters presented their "Alabama Platform" calling for congressional endorsement of the *Dred Scott* decision that authorized slavery in the territories. Douglas' supporters offered, instead, popular sovereignty and congressional non-interference with slavery in the territories. Though Douglas commanded a majority of the delegates, he failed to secure the two-thirds majority required for nomination. Eight southern states withdrew from the national Democratic convention, protesting adoption of Douglas' plank. In June, the national party reconvened in Baltimore and quickly nominated Douglas as its presidential candidate and Hershel V. Johnson of Georgia for vice president. In the interim, southern Democrats met separately and chose Buchanan's vice president, John C. Breckinridge of Kentucky, to run on their Alabama platform.

The rag-tag remnants of the Whig and American Parties formed the Constitutional Union Party. Its platform upheld "the Constitution of the country, the Union of the States, and the enforcement of the laws." Delegates selected John Bell of Tennessee for president and Edward Everett of Massachusetts for vice president. They hoped to win by appealing to moderates everywhere.

The Republicans met in Chicago. After a long debate, on the third ballot, they chose the least radical candidate, Abraham Lincoln. The Republican platform mirrored the diverse interests of those who made up the party. The document reaffirmed the principles of the Declaration of Independence, the non-interference of congress with domestic institutions within a state, and opposed polygamy. Appealing to former Whig voters, the Republicans endorsed internal improvements, a transcontinental railroad, a protective tariff, and a national banking system. They promised landless farmers homestead legislation, as they urged prospective farmers to "vote yourself a farm." Most critically, the Republicans resolutely opposed the expansion of slavery into the territories.

Southerners saw Abraham Lincoln as the embodiment of black Republicanism, a clear and present danger to slavery everywhere. Northerners considered a vote for Breckinridge unthinkable, even though he came from a border state and personally opposed the fire-eaters who championed him. Southerners hated Douglas almost as much as they hated Lincoln, even though he campaigned vigorously in the South. On election day, Republicans captured the electoral votes of twenty states, none from the South. Lincoln claimed a great victory, although he received only 35 percent of the 4.6 million votes cast. Douglas won twelve electoral votes, Breckinridge seventy-two, all in the South, and Bell garnered thirty-nine from three border states. Lincoln's support was confined to the free states. Many southern states refused to place his name on the ballot, and he did not bother to campaign in the South. Lincoln's election marked the triumph of the North. The North now controlled both houses of congress, the presidency, and in time the supreme court as well. Yet, the Republicans only had the presidency.

Ironically, southerners should have found Lincoln the most acceptable of all the Republicans who might have succeeded Buchanan. A lanky, loosejointed, rough-hewn man born in Kentucky, Lincoln was a self-educated lawyer whose political principles had drawn him to the Whig Party. He had served as an Illinois state legislator and one-term member of congress during the Mexican war. His ambition for political office led him into the Republican Party and senatorial campaign against the incumbent Stephen Douglas. Lincoln tempered his Whiggish views on the economy with a healthy dose of Jeffersonian egalitarianism. "I have always hated slavery," he said in 1858, and also like Jefferson, he opposed racial equality. Instead, to solve the "racial problem," he suggested transporting blacks out of the country. In his campaign, he promised that as president he would not interfere with slavery where it already existed, although he vehemently opposed its extension into the territories. Again, like Jefferson, Lincoln cast the nation's fate with its freehold farmers as he prepared for war against slave holders.

Secession and War

On hearing that Lincoln had won, South Carolina met in convention on December 20, 1860, to repeal its ratification of the federal constitution. The proposal passed unanimously. Six states of the lower South followed quickly. In the rush to secede and preserve slavery, they overlooked the fact that in leaving the union they left behind the very territories into which slavery might expand. Even Democratic control of the supreme court and congress failed to slow the onward rush. Secessionists shouted down strong unionist sentiment in Tennessee, North Carolina, Virginia, and among vocal and influential minorities in the other states with dire warnings that the new sectional president harbored "opinions and purposes hostile to slavery."

While the secession debate raged, border state moderates scurried about formulating compromises to forestall war. Faced with either peaceful secession or a forceful defense of the union, President Buchanan rejected the use of force to compel the return of the seceded states. Several compromise plans were proposed, but only Kentucky Senator John J. Crittenden's held much promise. Crittenden proposed a constitutional amendment that would extend the Missouri Compromise line of 36°30' to the Pacific and would protect slavery south of that line.

Lincoln squelched the idea when he let it be known that he could not approve any measure allowing the expansion of slavery. In February 1861 the seceded states met in Montgomery, Alabama, to write a Confederate constitution. It updated the federal constitution, providing for a president with a single six-year term and an item veto. While the federal constitution scrupulously avoided the term "slavery," the Confederate constitution explicitly protected slavery, although, it did prohibit the importation of new slaves. On February 18, 1861, the former senator from Mississippi, Jefferson Davis, became president of the Confederate States of America and Alexander H. Stephens, a Georgia Whig, became vice-president.

Lincoln's Response to Secession

The creation of a separate government did not necessarily mean war. Even Lincoln's inauguration address on March 4 promised no war. Lincoln considered himself president of all the American people, and he wanted to preserve the union without war, if possible. In his inaugural address, he declared that he would not, "directly or indirectly," interfere with slavery where it already existed, remaining silent on the expansion of slavery. However, the problem of what to do with federal property in the South, especially military installations, demanded action. The Confederacy stated that anything less than full evacuation of United States military installations and personnel would not be allowed. By early April all federal installations had been evacuated except Fort Sumter in Charleston harbor and Fort Pickens at Pensacola, Florida. The United States commander of Fort Sumter, Kentuckian Major Robert Anderson, informed his superiors in Washington that he would have to surrender by mid-April, without fresh supplies. Lincoln either had to evacuate the fort or to risk a war in an attempt to resupply the installation. Northern newspaper editors demanded that Lincoln stand firm. To withdraw Anderson's men would acknowledge the Confederacy's legitimacy, an admission that the American union was not permanent. Acceptance of secession would undermine the authority of the federal government.

On April 4, one month after his inauguration, Lincoln ordered that relief be sent to Fort Sumter and Fort Pickens. Lincoln informed South Carolina authorities that only provisions, not arms or men, were being forwarded to Fort Sumter. Lincoln had decided to resupply the fort peaceably, but if war came, he insisted that the Confederates fire the first shot. The Confederate government ordered General P.G.T. Beauregard to demand Anderson's surrender and to "reduce" the fort if he refused. At 4:30 A.M. on April 12, 1861, after Anderson refused to surrender, forty hours of artillery bombardment began. On April 14, Anderson surrendered and was taken north by the

The shots at Fort Sumter in April 1861 opened the Civil War. The sixty-seven year old Edmund Ruffin, a militant secessionist from Virginia, dressed in his student uniform from the Virginia Military Institute, fired the first shot; four years later he took his own life when Union forces marched into Richmond. (1961)

relief expedition. On April 15, Lincoln called for 75,000 enlistees, as one by one the states of the upper South seceded. The slave states of Missouri, Kentucky, Maryland and Delaware, as well as the western portion of Virginia, remained under federal control, although Kentucky proclaimed its neutrality. The Civil War had begun.

At first glance, it was difficult to imagine how the Confederacy could have possibly expected to win. The North contained almost 21 million people compared to only 9 million in the South of whom over one-third were slaves, people who, during wartime, were often more of a liability than an asset, since the war involved their status. In addition, the North enjoyed an overwhelming superiority over the South in such militarily vital areas as heavy manufacturing, armament making, and railroads. While the northern armies were well supplied, from the start the Confederate armies suffered shortages of such essential items as medicine, gunpowder, weapons, and uniforms. As the war dragged on, these shortages became critical and extended even to food which, although plentiful in the South, could not reach its armies due to breakdowns in the rail system. Finally, the North controlled a large and effective navy while the South boasted only a few armored river boats and half-a-dozen ocean cruisers.

Nonetheless, the South was not without advantages. It was on the defensive. Just by standing still the Confederacy could obtain its objective of independence. If an invasion took place Confederates would be highly motivated, defending their homes and institutions. Northern leaders, on the other hand, had to convince their people of the necessity of a war of aggression. It was much harder to convince people to fight for the abstract cause of national unity than it was to motivate them to repel an invader. If the Confederacy could hold on long enough and exact a high price from the North, there was good reason to believe that the northern public would tire of the war and concede to the Confederacy its independence. Moreover, although the North had an edge over the Confederacy in the number of West Point graduates, the Confederacy enjoyed a significant advantage in the number and quality of its junior officers. The Confederate armies, although smaller in size and more poorly equipped than their northern enemies, were better led troops. Nowhere was the superiority of Confederate military leadership more evident than at the very top. Not until the final year of the war did Lincoln find a general, Ulysses S. Grant, who was as capable as Robert E. Lee, the head of the biggest Confederate Army, one of the great military commanders of the nineteenth century, the equal of Grant himself.

Domestic Dissent

Since nullification southern politicians had blocked all efforts to increase the powers and functions of the national government. Slave holders believed that every increase in national power represented an additional threat to slavery. Southerners' control of the senate, the presidency, and the supreme court assured that their interpretation of the constitution as a federal union was the dominant one as represented in the supreme court's *Dred Scott* decision. But with the South's secession, in 1861, that restraint on national power no longer existed. The Republican Party took control of both houses of congress, the presidency, and with southern resignations, also the supreme court. At no other time in American history has a single group of individuals, representing such a narrow range of interests, exercised as much power as the Republican Party did during the Civil War.

Nonetheless, even after secession, northern Democrats remained a potent opposition. The Democrats opposed most Republican policies and, at several points, seemed on the verge of regaining national power. There were large numbers of Democrats in the border states that stayed in the Union—Maryland, Kentucky, Missouri, Delaware, and West Virginia. Additionally, the cities of New York, Philadelphia, Boston, and Baltimore, reflecting large Irish immigration, voted heavily Democratic. In the Midwest, the bastion of Republican strength during the Civil War, Democrats won several governorships and senate seats. Even Lincoln's home state of Illinois elected a Democratic governor during the war. Democrats were particularly strong in southern Illinois, southern Indiana, and southern Ohio, reflecting the southern origins of the residents of those areas.

On the whole, Democrats tended to be sympathetic to the Confederacy and supported a negotiated peace that would recognize it. During the entire war, Lincoln led a divided North. One of his most important tasks was to gain the loyalty of most non-Republicans and to silence the remainder. Had Lincoln failed, he would not have been able to execute the war effectively. Confederate leaders counted on this division to secure independence, and Confederate military strategy aimed at winning the war by influencing Northern public opinion.

Republicans used Democrats' anti-war position to tar them with the brush of secession. At times, Republicans implied that to be a Democrat was tantamount to being a secessionist. Democrats, in turn, accused Republicans of sacrificing the cream of northern manhood to free black slaves. Despite their disadvantages, Democrats did surprisingly well. In 1864, their presidential candidate, George B. McClellan, erst-while Union commander, made a strong showing against Lincoln, even though by election time the war seemed to be coming rapidly to a close in the North's favor. The Union general William Tecumseh Sherman's capture and burning of Atlanta just before the election probably secured Lincoln's victory over McClellan. McClellan also had to contend with the none too conscientious Republican vote counting. Much of Lincoln's vote came from absentee army ballots that were overwhelming in his favor. In truth, the army vote was a bogus vote as loyal Republican commanders insured that their men voted Republican or, at least, that their troops' were counted as if they had voted Republican. Lest the story seem too one sided, Democratic generals turned in counts fully as lopsided for McClellan. There were just more Republican generals than Democratic—a situation that Lincoln and his far-sighted secretary of war Edwin Stanton had guaranteed.

During the war Lincoln and the Republican Party exercised extraordinary powers beginning with the fall of Ft. Sumter when, without congressional authority he declared a state of war and ordered up the militia to put down the "rebellion." When congress finally met in July it confronted a fait accompli. Lincoln had denied to congress the opportunity to debate whether or not the U.S. would use force to bring the Confederacy back into the Union—a momentous decision—with which the Democrats, at least, did not concur. Nonetheless, the Republican-dominated congress dutifully ratified Lincoln's action, accepting the president's explanation that the Civil War was not technically a war but a "domestic insurrection," which the Constitution gave the president broad discretionary powers to put down. Lincoln's declaration of war by executive fiat was the first of a long-line of actions in which he avoided, as much as possible, congressional participation in policy making. In retrospect, it is clear that Lincoln made most of the major decisions of the war while congress was in recess. His declaration of war, suspension of the writ of habeas corpus, and Emancipation Proclamation were three conspicuous examples, but there were many more.

On the heels of his declaration of war, Lincoln declared martial law in Missouri, Kentucky, and Maryland, suspended the writ of habeas corpus and barred those state legislatures from assembling—all without congressional approval and without constitutional authority. Lincoln believed that secessionists in these three border states intended to push bills of secession though their state legislatures. He also ordered federal troops to occupy their state houses. Lincoln then directed the secret police to round up anyone whom military authorities suspected of disloyalty. Lincoln illegally threw in jail, without charges, somewhere between 13,000 and 38,000 persons. In many instances the only crime the unfortunate individuals had committed was being Democratic politicians who had spoken out against the war and in favor of a negotiated peace.

The most dramatic example of such an arrest was Clement L. Vallandigham's. An Ohio Democratic politician, Vallandigham made a speech in Mt. Vernon, Ohio, in which he asserted that the war could easily be concluded by negotiation. He charged that the Lincoln administration had refused to negotiate and needlessly prolonged the bloodshed. General Ambrose Burnside, then commander of the Ohio military district, ordered Vallandigham arrested, denied his petition of habeas corpus, and tried him in a military court for violation of a military order even though civil courts were in session in Ohio and no emergency existed—all these with Lincoln's knowledge. To avoid making a martyr out of Vallandigham, Lincoln commuted his sentence and ordered him transported to Confederate lines. Later Vallandigham traveled to Canada and back to Ohio to campaign against Lincoln in 1864. This time he went unmolested.

Lincoln's illegal assumption of the powers of congress, the states, and the courts are difficult to excuse. Throughout the entire war large segments of the North remained under martial law, several newspapers were censored, and due process was honored primarily in the breech. Lincoln violated the Constitution, and he admitted doing so. The sole mitigating factor was that he had done so during an unprecedented national emergency. In all cases Lincoln openly acknowledged that under "normal" circumstances his actions could not be justified. Even as he exercised extraordinary powers, he always understood them to be extraordinary, illegal, and temporary. He never pretended that they were justified under any other circumstances and asked that they be seen as exceptions, not precedents for future presidents.

The War

At first, neither side believed that the war would last more than one battle. Confederates thought that the North could be easily demoralized. The North saw southern secession as the product of only a handful of hot heads who would be overawed by a show of force. Likewise, Confederates underestimated the extent that northerners would go to preserve the Union as well as their intense hatred of slavery. And, northerners misjudged the determination of Confederates to secure their independence and the breadth of popular support for secession. Each side's initial preparations were limited to calling up volunteers, shoring up defenses, and preparing for the inevitable and quick victory. Both sides exuded a casual confidence, almost a holiday mood.

The Confederate plan was simply to defend the South while making northern invasion as costly as possible. The northern strategy was to blockade the South, then send one army directly south from Washington into Virginia to destroy the Confederate capital at Richmond, and at the same time, to send a western army down the Mississippi to open up the river, cutting Texas and Arkansas off from the remainder of the Confederacy—the Anaconda Plan.

The first full scale battle came in the East, about two months after the firing on Ft. Sumter. At Bull Run or Manassas Junction, Virginia, about forty miles southeast of Washington, D.C., a Union army of about 30,000, led by Gen. Irvin McDowell, met a Confederate army of roughly the same size, commanded by Gen. Pierre G. T. Beauregard. Neither side fought well and, at first, it appeared that the Union troops might prevail. But just as a Confederate rout seemed assured, General Thomas J. Jackson and his Virginia troops rushed in and forestalled the Confederate panic. Jackson's firm stand earned him the nickname "Stonewall" and his brigade's courageous stand turned the tide of battle, rallying the green Confederate troops who drove back the equally green Union troops. In the turn of fate, the Union army panicked and fled in disorder to Washington. The Confederate troops hardly knew how to respond and fell into equal disorder, unable to follow up their victory.

In purely military terms the first battle of Bull Run meant nothing. Few troops were lost and little important territory was gained. Neither side won or lost anything except its dignity. Both sides, however, now realized that the war would not be a holiday. It would be won only after long and determined fighting. Lincoln fired McDowell and appointed George B. McClellan as head of the Union armies, imposed a naval blockade on southern ports, and called for an additional 500,000 volunteers.

In the East for the rest of 1861 and the early months of 1862 nothing happened as McClellan contented himself with training and parading his troops, unwilling to commit himself to any decisive action. In the West, however, Grant won several significant battles for the Union, gained control of the Mississippi as far south as Memphis, Tennessee, and secured Kentucky and western Tennessee. Then, in April, at

Civil War Campaigns, 1860-65

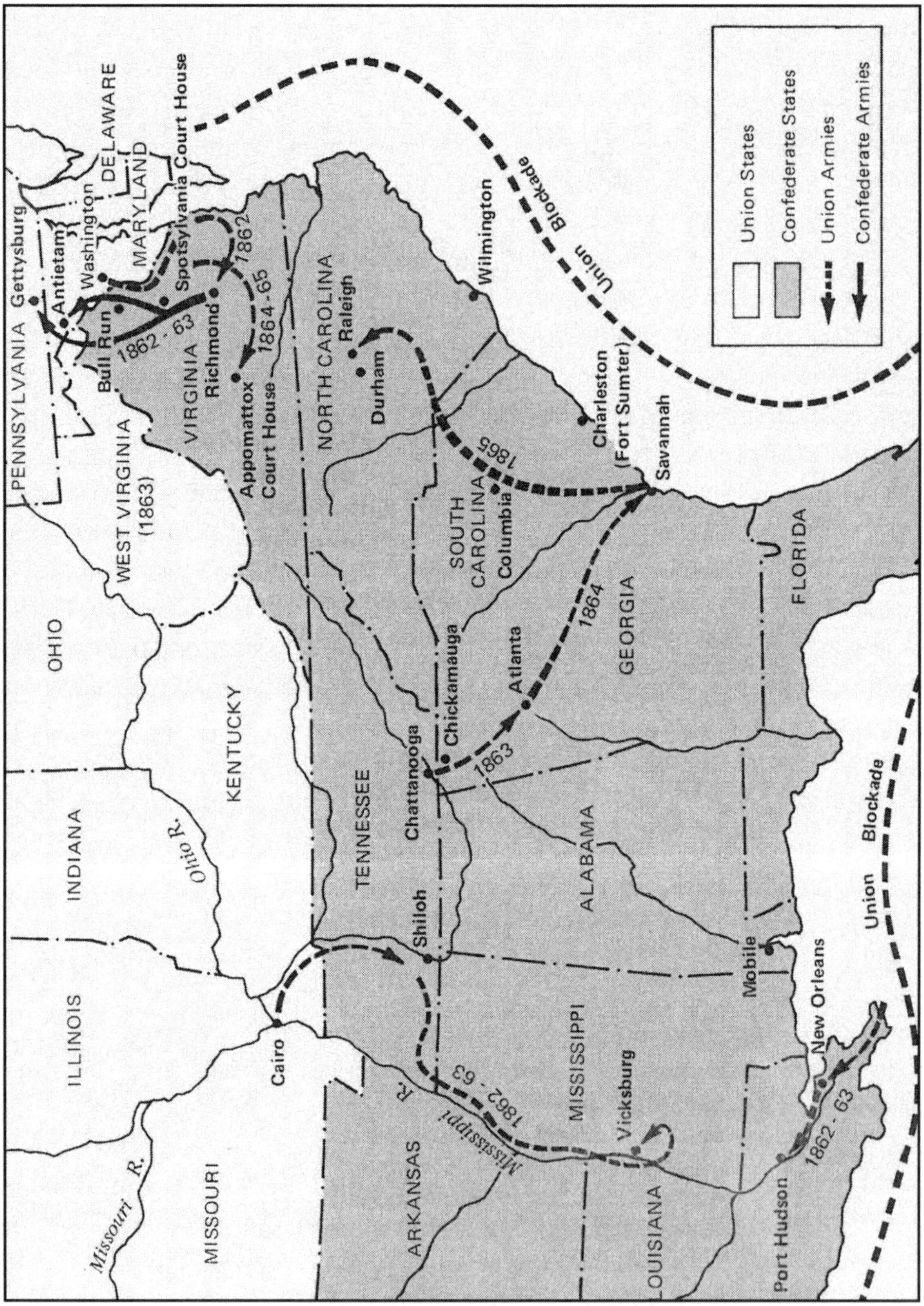

Shiloh, Tennessee, a Confederate counter-attack caught Grant by surprise. Grant's troops held, but his failure to destroy the opposing Confederate army led to his relief from command—a decision that brought a halt to Union advancement in the West.

Shiloh was the first major battle of the war. At the time, the casualties seemed astronomical. Over 13,000 Union soldiers and 10,000 Confederates died—more than had been killed in the revolution, the War of 1812, and the Mexican War put together. The casualties at Shiloh gave the Civil War a new and gruesome dimension, marking the beginning of modern warfare. Suddenly, war had lost its dash and romance; it had become unspeakably horrible.

Back in the East, McClellan finally decided to move. He transferred his 112,000 soldiers by sea to the York River near Norfolk, about 25 miles east of Richmond. In a series of battles, collectively called the Peninsula Campaign, the much smaller Confederate armies parried timid Union advances. By the first of July, 1862, McClellan had been pushed back to where he had started as he dug in. McClellan lost 50,000 soldiers with no gains to show. Lincoln ordered McClellan to withdraw and appointed General John Pope as head of the Union army in the East.

In the South, Lee had proven his mettle and was made commander of the Army of Virginia. McClellan's withdrawal freed Lee from the need to defend Richmond. He promptly marched north, and at Bull Run met and badly mauled Pope's army. Stung by his poor choice for general, Lincoln reappointed McClellan as head of the Eastern Army and ordered him to stop Lee at all costs. But Lee had other, grander plans. He had decided that to break Northern morale he must take the war to the North. Bypassing Washington, in September 1862, Lee marched north into Maryland. McClellan, after recovering a secret Confederate dispatch, followed Lee's army, catching him at

Robert E. Lee (1807-70), commander of the Army of Northern Virginia during the Civil War, was a brilliant tactician who used his dwindling forces to maximum advantage. He is shown here with Thomas J. ("Stonewall") Jackson (1824-63), who became a legend for his steadfastness at First Bull Run; he was accidentally shot by a Confederate picket and died of pneumonia. (1937)

Antietam Creek, Maryland, just south of the southern boundary of Pennsylvania. At Antietam the two armies clashed and fought to a stand off. Each side lost about 11,000 men, but Lee found himself in a precarious position, cut off from supplies and his troops exhausted. For an entire day, both armies confronted one another. If McClellan had struck, he might have destroyed Lee's army and ended the war because Lee was backed up to the swollen river and was low on ammunition. Characteristically, McClellan waited. Under cover of night, the river having fallen, Lee slipped away, leaving his camp fires burning to fool Union scouts. On learning of Lee's escape, Lincoln became furious, almost beyond words. He fired McClellan again, this time for good. Antietam had halted Lee's ambitious northern invasion and represented the first time in the East that a Union army had fought a Confederate army to a standstill. In retrospect, Antietam marked the turning point of the war.

Lee's leaving the field of battle to McClellan gave Lincoln the opportunity to declare it a great northern victory. In September, 1862, he used Antietam as the occasion to issue his long awaited Emancipation Proclamation. At first, in an effort to keep the border-slave states of Missouri, Kentucky, Delaware, and Maryland from seceding, Lincoln had intentionally not defined the Civil War as a war against slavery. But by the middle of 1862 these states were safely under the control of Union armies, and Lincoln feared that a war simply to save the Union was insufficient to motivate the northern public in the face of ever-mounting costs and casualties. A war to end slavery would infuse the northern war effort with a new, idealistic war aim that would directly punish those southerners whom northerners believed were responsible for the War—slaveholders. In the wake of Antietam, Lincoln issued a proclamation that declared all slaves free who lived in those areas still in rebellion after January 1, 1863.

Commemorating the 75th anniversary of the 13th Amendment ending slavery, this stamp depicts Abraham Lincoln with a freed slave at his feet, in a style that memorialized the president as "the Great Emancipator," something of an overstatement at best. (1940)

Lincoln's proclamation freed no slaves. Those still enslaved in the federal controlled areas of Missouri, Kentucky, and western Tennessee were not affected since those regions were not in rebellion, and Lincoln of course had no power over slaves still under Confederate control. But it did mean that every Union victory would result in the liberation of additional slaves. Following Antietam, Lincoln transformed the Union armies from aggressors into liberators. It gave the North an ideal for which to fight and made its sacrifices seem more worth while. The "Battle Hymn of the Republic," with its stirring stanzas of "Glory, Glory Halleluya the truth goes marching on," voiced the morale lifting crusade of emancipation. It gave the war a major new dimension.

After Antietam, Lincoln appointed Ambrose Burnside to head the army of the East. Burnside proceeded immediately to march on Richmond. But when he reached Fredericksburg, he found Lee in an almost impregnable defensive position. Foolishly, Burnside attacked. In his pig-headed attempt to dislodge Lee at any price, Burnside ordered wave after wave of infantry assaults only to see his soldiers annihilated. Horrified with the casualty figures, Lincoln immediately replaced Burnside with "Fighting" Joe Hooker. With a 2 to 1 advantage over Lee, Hooker marched north from Fredricksburg to Chancellorsville where Lee completely outmaneuvered Hooker, letting Jackson, in a flanking movement, maul Hooker's army. Humiliated, Hooker retreated to Fredericksburg, and forever after his name became a slang term for a prostitute. Lee's tactical movements at Chancellorsville were considered some of the most brilliantly conceived maneuvers in military history, but it remained a hollow victory. Lincoln immediately replaced Hooker's losses while Lee lost his best general, Stonewall Jackson in a freak accident.

Following Chancellorsville Lee realized that he could not hold out indefinitely. Every battle reduced his limited number of men and supplies. Victories were of small, long-run consequence. Once again, Lee decided he must win a major victory in the North in the hope of demoralizing northern public opinion and forcing Lincoln to sue for peace. With 75,000 troops Lee moved North into Pennsylvania. The Union army now under the command of George Meade caught up with Lee at Gettysburg, Pennsylvania. From July 2 to July 3, 1863, in the most important battle of the war, Lee ordered assault after assault against the Union positions in a desperate effort to break through. But the Union lines held. On July 4th fighting on both sides ceased and on the 5th Lee retreated, as he had at Antietam.

On the day of calm at Gettysburg, July 4th, 1863, in the West, at Vicksburg, Grant won another major victory, defeating a Confederate force there. Grant's victory at

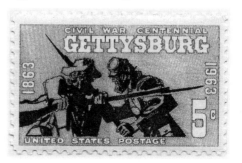

Vicksburg secured the Mississippi River and cut Texas and Arkansas off from the remainder of the Confederacy. Together, the twin victories of Vicksburg and Gettysburg signaled the beginning of the end for the Confederacy. Now, for the first time, Confederate victory seemed a remote possibility and defeat unavoidable. The Confederacy could no longer replace its losses, and at Gettysburg, it had lost some of its best fighting units. In the North, morale soared, and for the first time since secession, Lincoln's popularity climbed.

These three Union generals, Ulysses S. Grant (1822-85), best known as commander of American forces in the latter stages of the war, William Tecumseh Sherman (1820-91), who conquered Atlanta and proceeded to march to the sea leaving behind a scorched earth that made his name a byword in the South, and Phillip Sheridan (1831-88), who made his mark at Chattanooga and then commanded the army in the Shenandoah valley. (1937)

After Vicksburg Lincoln decided that Grant was the man he had been looking for to defeat Lee. Grant took over command of the American armies and settled on a simple two pronged plan. He would attack Lee from the North and with his superior numbers wear Lee down. At the same time, Grant ordered his friend William Tecumseh Sherman to strike out from the West through Chattanooga to Atlanta, cutting the Confederacy in half. Sherman carried out Grant's strategy with exacting efficiency. With over 100,000 troops, Sherman reached Atlanta in September, 1864, burned it, and then launched his famous "march to the sea." His army spread out and literally burned a sixty mile wide strip from Atlanta to Savannah and from there to Columbia, South Carolina, and then north to Raleigh, North Carolina. Sherman's "scorched earth" tactics completely demoralized the lower South as Sherman brought home to southerners the meaning of his famous statement, "War is Hell."

At the same time that Sherman marched through Georgia, Grant in a series of battles collectively called the Wilderness Campaign, from May 1864 to April 1865, mounted a relentless attack on Lee's army, forcing him slowly back to Richmond. At each encounter, Lee's army became smaller and smaller, less and less able to repel the next assault. Grant lost nearly 100,000 soldiers in this campaign, but they were quickly replaced. Finally, on April 9, 1865, with his army reduced to skeleton proportions and with almost no food, Lee surrendered to Grant at Appomattox Court House, ending the Civil War.

The Confederacy had lost, in part, because no European country would risk intervention on its behalf. Before the war, southerners had confidently predicted that the world's demand for cotton would force European governments to aid the South. Even with the blockade, the huge U.S. cotton crop of 1860 and increased British and French purchases of cotton from India and the Middle East kept the English textile industries humming. Early in the war British public opinion remained skeptical of the Union cause. British and French shipyards turned out sea raiders that Confederate commanders used against northern merchant vessels. Both Britain and France recognized the belligerency of the Confederacy and for a time inched toward a policy of full diplomatic recognition. But the diplomacy of the American minister to Britain, Charles Francis Adams, son of John Quincy, and the great Union victories in mid-1863 at Gettysburg and Vicksburg prevented it. The erratic French emperor, Napoleon III, irritated state department

Appomattox was the site of Lee's surrender to Grant's union army on April 9, 1865, and marked the effective end of the war. Surrender terms were generous and allowed Confederate troops to keep their horses and mules for spring plowing. (1965)

officials when he proposed to mediate between the two combatants, but he, too, drew back after Gettysburg. In the end, "King Cotton" proved a poor diplomat.

A More Perfect Union

The Civil War was not simply a war between the states, it had also been waged against the states. One of the most important results of the war was the permanent shift in power and authority from the various states to the federal government. The most significant shift occurred in military policy. Prior to the Civil War the U.S. did not have a standing federal army nor a centralized command. There was a federal army but it was, at best, a skeletal force designed for garrison duty and patrolling the Indian frontier. Even in times of war the federal government relied primarily on the states to raise troops and to organize regiments. At first, this is what Lincoln tried. But quickly state levies and state regiments proved unmanageable. Some states, like Republican Wisconsin, responded dramatically, but others such as Democratic New York, did not even try to meet their quotas. Consequently, under Lincoln's insistence, congress resorted to national conscription into a national army, under the centralized command of national officers, paid out of the national treasury. During the Civil War governors and state legislators lost almost all of their powers over military policy and the state militia was reduced to a police force. Lincoln's various financial innovations such as printing paper money, deficit financing, a national banking act, and a federal income tax were means by which he financed this new national army, freeing Lincoln from all state interference in military policy. His success in nationalizing military and financial policy stood in sharp contrast to the Confederate failure to centralize policy making—it represented one of the chief reasons that Lincoln succeeded as president and Jefferson Davis failed.

Lincoln also proved to be an effective party leader. The Republican Party was by no means a united party, but consisted of a loose coalition of radical anti-slavery advocates and other persons tied to manufacturing, financial, and commercial interests. Between them the Republican Party enacted legislation long advocated by the old Whig Party—internal improvements and high tariffs. The Republicans, in effect, negated the states' rights policies of Andrew Jackson, John C. Calhoun, and the Democratic Party and replaced them with the more nationalistic policies of the old Whig Party and its leaders, Henry Clay and Daniel Webster.

The Republican-controlled Civil War congress increased tariffs on manufactured goods to an average of 47 percent ad valorem; it enacted the Pacific Railroad Act that provided for the construction of a trans-continental railway, and in 1863, it passed the National Banking Act that gave the United States a uniform currency, overturning Jackson's veto of the national bank. To satisfy western Republicans and farmers, in 1862, Congress passed the Homestead Act and the Morrill Land Grant Act. The Homestead Act provided settlers 160 acres free if they lived on the land five years. The Morrill Land Grant gave each state 30,000 acres of land for each member of congress to be used to establish state agricultural colleges. The sale of the land from the Morrill Land Grant provided the endowment for a system of state universities, the beginning of a public commitment to an affordable college education for everyone. Together, these Republican sponsored and passed measures signified the acceptance of the proposition that the federal government should play an active role in economic and social development—a function prior to the Civil War that had been reserved almost exclusively to the states. Certainly, Alexander Hamilton would have been gratified, and even Thomas Jefferson received a sop with homestead legislation and the land grant colleges.

Reconstruction

The costs of the Civil War were enormous. Together the North and South suffered over 600,000 combat deaths and suffered another 400,000 deaths from sickness—most from gangrene and dysentery. The South had lost nearly a generation of white males in futile effort to defend slavery. As usual the losses were born disproportionately by the poor as both Union and Confederate governments allowed individuals with money to hire substitutes and avoid combat. The war left the South wrecked, its livestock lay dead and rotting, railroad rails had been twisted around trees, bushwackers roved the countryside, people lived in caves, fields lay fallow, widows and mothers grieved inconsolably in mourning. Most of the fighting had taken place in the South, leaving scars everywhere. A quarter of a million Confederate soldiers were killed, their loss accompanied by defeat, humiliation, shattered limbs, and famine that lingered for decades and created bitter memories. Areas captured by Union forces early in the war, such as New Orleans and Vicksburg suffered prolonged military occupation that placed enormous burdens on the population, especially women. Whether Union soldiers acted with greater honor than most other military occupation forces or southern women simply suffered in silence, few accusations of rape were made. Virtually all reported rapes of southern women by Union soldiers were committed against black women, an irony few noted at the time. Southern women, black and white, bore the enormous burdens of the home front that included nursing the injured, managing the farms and plantations, fending off marauders, and scrounging their fields and woods for food as well as finding substitutes for coffee, salt, sugar, and other scarce common necessities. Black men and women made the best of their opportunities, dropping their hoes and running off when Union troops neared. To slave owners their loss meant fewer mouths to feed and hands to watch, but they also represented a loss of labor and, more importantly, capital. The quiet of the empty slave quarters and the unplowed fields eloquently testified to slaves' thirst for freedom and their owners almost total dependence on their labor. Forced to fend for themselves, southern slave owners felt betrayed by the former slaves. Following the war, nothing exceeded the bitterness expressed by southern white women. The "lost cause" became their particular cross to bear.

"With Malice Towards None"

Even before the war ended, Lincoln and congress struggled over who would control post-war policy. The conflict involved more than simply restoring the constitutional balance between the president and congress. It also determined how the ex-Confederate states would be treated, the status of former slaves, and the future of the Republican Party once the ex-Confederate states returned to the Union—in short, the future of the nation. In late 1863 Lincoln issued a reconstruction proclamation based on his war powers as commander-in-chief. Lincoln promised amnesty to ex-Confederates who took an oath to uphold the Constitution. He specified that when 10 percent of the number of those voting in their state in 1860 had sworn their loyalty, he would recognize them to reorganize the state government. Although he required that ex-Confederate states abolish slavery, radicals detested the plan because it neither enfranchised the freedmen nor punished the rebels. These were vital considerations, for each free black now counted as a whole person for purposes of congressional representation, giving the vanquished ex-Confederate states two-fifths more congressmen than they had in 1860. Lincoln's plan actually enhanced ex-Confederates' power to thwart Republican policies since an unreconstructed South, with an all-white electorate, was unlikely to vote Republican. Under Lincoln's "ten percent" plan Arkansas, Louisiana, and Tennessee reorganized themselves and abolished slavery, but the Republican-dominated congress refused to seat their representatives, aborting Lincoln's restoration plan.

Distrustful of Lincoln's intentions, congressional radicals tried to deny him the Republican nomination in 1864. Confronting Lincoln's growing public popularity, radicals acquiesced in his candidacy and even accepted Lincoln's selection of Andrew Johnson, a Democrat from Tennessee, as his vice-presidential running mate. As a slap to congressional Republicans and as an expression of his determination to act without partisanship toward the former Confederacy, Lincoln ran as the "Union Party" candidate, not as a Republican. Begrudgingly, Republican radicals backed the ticket as the lesser of two evils after the Democrats named George B. McClellan on a platform that promised to end the war with a negotiated peace that left slavery intact. The president's vote was swelled by the army vote and by comfortable margins in the Republican rotten boroughs of Louisiana and Tennessee. He won by 400,000 votes out of 4 million cast.

Congress Takes Command

In the midst of the presidential campaign, Republicans passed the Wade-Davis Bill, named after its sponsors radical Republicans Benjamin Wade and Henry Winter Davis. The Wade-Davis bill stated that an ex-Confederate state would be readmitted only when the number of voters who took an "iron clad" oath of loyalty equaled half the number of votes cast by state voters in the 1860 presidential election. The "iron clad" oath disqualified from voting and office holding any individual who had held an office in the Confederacy, served as an officer in the Confederate army, or had volunteered to serve in the Confederate army. These provisions meant that for a state to secure the required 50 percent of loyal voters, it had to extend the franchise to poor whites and freedmen, insuring a pro-Republican electorate. Once reorganized, the ex-Confederate state had to abolish slavery and repudiate the state's war-time debt before congress would readmit it to the Union. With congress adjourned, Lincoln pocket-vetoed the bill. Ex-Confederate states, fearing harsher conditions once congress reconvened, rushed to accept Lincoln's lenient plan for southern restoration.

On April 14, 1865, John Wilkes Booth, a crazed Confederate die-hard and actor, shot and killed Lincoln in Ford's Theater. This shocking act—the first time a president had been assassinated—elevated Andrew Johnson to the presidency. With congress still in recess, the new president moved quickly to implement Lincoln's restoration plan, only modifying it to exclude from pardon all high ranking Confederate officials and those southerners worth more than $20,000. These additional provisions reflected Johnson's class hatred for the southern planter class who had snubbed him because of his humble background. Like Lincoln's, the Johnson program required that the southern provisional governments abolish slavery and repudiate the states' wartime debts. It failed to require that the new regimes enfranchise freedmen and forbid former Confederates from holding office. But the summer of 1865 found the new chief executive in a forgiving mood. Petitioned daily by planters pleading for pardon, Johnson approved virtually every request for a special presidential amnesty. When congress reconvened on December 4, 1865, every southern state, except Texas, had restored itself, and in many cases sent to congress former Confederates—a few proudly dressed in their worn grey uniforms.

Such behavior shocked northern voters who blamed ex-Confederates for the Civil War, the deaths of tens of thousands of northern youth, and the loss of billions of dollars in property. It seemed that these traitors had returned to the corridors of power and respectability without remorse or punishment for their treacherous conduct. Radical Republican congressman Thaddeus Stevens of Pennsylvania declared that the ex-Confederates must be treated as a "conquered people." Stevens insisted that the "property of the chief rebels" be seized and used to provide the loyal freedmen with a landed stake in the society, "forty acres and a mule." He echoed Jefferson's belief that a safe republic must be built on the firm foundation of small landowners. Only when small farmers, black and white, dominated southern life, would the republic be safe. Stevens also warned that he opposed "restoration" of the ex-Confederate states. Instead, they must be "reconstructed" in a manner that destroyed the plantation system, and the power of the old planter class, thus fostering freehold farming and including the freedman as full citizens. Otherwise, he prophesied that the "rebel states," under Johnson's governments, would send rebels to the capitol who would join northern Democrats to oust the "party of the Union" and regain control of the federal government, congress, and the White House. Having lost the war, declared Stevens, the Confederates should not be allowed to win the peace. To prevent such an eventuality, he demanded that congress seize control of Reconstruction and make basic changes in the defeated South, accepting restoration of the ex-Confederate states only after their reconstruction.

By the time congress reconvened, virtually all Republicans opposed the president's restoration plan of *status quo ante-bellum* minus slavery. Equally disturbing, southern restoration governments passed a series of "black codes" that had an uncanny resemblance, even in language, to their old slave codes. Replacing race with slavery, the black codes regularized slave marriages, allowed blacks to own property, and to sue and be sued. In some states, such as Alabama, the codes prohibited freedmen from testifying against whites and from owning firearms. Several states provided for black public education, but in all cases they required segregation. They also limited the trades open to African Americans. A few states demanded that blacks hold jobs by a certain date, and all of the states declared those who left their jobs without permission to be vagrants. Sheriffs were empowered to imprison any vagrant and judges to sentence them to hard labor usually for a private employer. Some of the sentences for vagrancy were for ten and twenty years. To Republican Radicals, such provisions smacked of slavery and demonstrated that ex-Confederates had not understood who had won the war.

Congressional Triumph

The northern public was also stunned by frequent newspaper reports of racial violence against ex-slaves, apparently sanctioned by white authorities. In New Orleans and Memphis white rioters attacked freedmen who had assembled for a political meeting, killing any who resisted, while all-white municipal officials looked on. Determined that such actions end, congressional Republicans established a joint house and senate committee, the fifteen-member Joint Committee on Reconstruction. Committee members refused to seat representatives and senators from the presidentially restored states. Congress then extended the Freedmen's Bureau, a relief agency that counteracted the black codes, made the former slaves "wards of the nation," and prepared them for citizenship. Johnson unwisely vetoed this popular and needed legislation, but congress immediately overrode his veto. Most northerners regarded the Freedmen's Bureau, administered by General Oliver O. Howard, as a necessary protection for former slaves making the difficult transition to freedom. In April, 1866 congress passed a Civil Rights bill that granted blacks minimal rights of citizenship, including the right to sue and be sued, to assemble, to marry, to own property, and to be tried by a jury of their peers. Johnson vetoed the 1866 Civil Rights Act, alienating almost all northerners. Using logic comprehensible only to extremist whites, Johnson declared that the Civil Rights Act favored "the colored and against the white race"; unmoved, congress overrode the veto. Still, Republicans realized that the 1866 Civil Rights Act was vulnerable to constitutional review. Its enforcement clause gave to congress the power to enforce in the various states the provisions of the act. Nowhere did the constitution define "American citizenship" and nowhere did it sanction congress' power over the states in such matters.

To remedy such concerns about constitutionality of the 1866 Civil Rights Act, congress drafted the Fourteenth Amendment and submitted it to the states for ratification. The Fourteenth Amendment broadly defined a citizen as any "Person born or naturalized in the US," and it prohibited states from abridging the "privileges and immunities" of any citizen or "deprive any person of life, liberty, or property without due process of the law." Interestingly, drafters of the Fourteenth Amendment used the "inclusive" language of "any person," rather than the more restrictive Jeffersonian language of "all men." For the first time, the Constitution specifically defined United States citizenship and in so doing made it national in character, asserting that American citizenship could not be denied to non-whites, thus overturning the *Dred Scott* decision. Not simply blacks, but Asians and all other persons born or naturalized in the United States became full citizens, even women. Radical Republicans insisted that no racial, religious, or ethnic limitations be placed on American citizenship. The Fourteenth Amendment provided the constitutional foundation for the multi-racial, multi-religious, and multi-ethnic character of post-Civil War America. It was the Magna Carta of modern America.

Although the Fourteenth Amendment did not enfranchise ex-slaves, section two specified that former slaves would be counted as whole persons and it provided for a reduction in a state's congressional representation if it denied blacks the right to vote. This provision was never enforced. Section three excluded former Confederates from office holding unless congress, not the president, removed their "disability." Section four repudiated Confederate war debts and declared as constitutional the obligation of the nation to pay "for services in suppressing insurrection or rebellion."

Finally, section five of the Fourteenth Amendment, the "enabling clause," stated that "Congress shall have the power to enforce by appropriate legislation, the provisions of this article." Section five was nothing less than a constitutional revolution, just as important as the ratification of the federal constitution and the annulment of the Articles of Confederation. For the first time, the Constitution explicitly granted to congress the power to enforce its laws over any state. The "enabling clause" became the constitutional basis of the supreme court's later nationalistic decisions that by the 1950s eroded away all states' rights. The Fourteenth Amendment legitimated Alexander Hamilton's, John Marshall's, and Abraham Lincoln's interpretation of the national union and nullified Thomas Jefferson's and John C. Calhoun's notion of states' rights. Constitutionally, the United States had become a nation, not simply a federal union of states. With the abolishment of slavery, this was the most important result of the Civil War. Tennessee, the only ex-Confederate state to ratify the Fourteenth Amendment immediately, approved the amendment on July 24, 1866, assuring that it escaped the brunt of congressional reconstruction.

Johnson, in a desperate attempt to shore up his deteriorating political position, decided to appeal to moderates in both parties. Determined to thwart congressional Radicals, he embarked on a speaking tour of crucial northern and midwestern states, urging election of moderates to congress in the 1866 elections. The campaign degenerated into shouting matches between Johnson and hecklers, organized by Republican Radicals, who hurled wild charges at the president, referring to him as an "insolent, drunken brute," and recounting atrocity tales of Confederates against blacks and Union soldiers, a tactic that became known as "waving the bloody shirt." A telling campaign slogan was "Vote the way you shot." Northern voters overwhelmingly repudiated Johnson and his lenient policy of southern restoration. Republicans gained their largest majority in congress ever, far in excess of the two-thirds needed in each house to override a presidential veto. With the president crippled, congress took control of southern reconstruction.

Radical Reconstruction

Shortly after the election, Thaddeus Stevens announced that before he had been a conservative, "but I mean to be a Radical henceforth." Although the new congress elected in 1866 was not scheduled to meet until December 1867, Republicans enacted legislation authorizing an additional session that would begin on March 4, ensuring that Johnson would not again be left alone in Washington free of house and senate watchdogs. Beginning on March 2, 1867, and continuing for over a year, Republicans enacted a series of laws that collectively constituted "Radical Reconstruction." Congressional reconstruction was complicated by the fact that congress had to work through a president who administered the laws that Congress had passed over his objections.

The most important 1867 reconstruction bill divided the South into five military districts and placed each under the command of a general appointed by Johnson. Congress required each ex-Confederate state to call a constitutional convention—elected by universal suffrage, but excluding former Confederates which would rewrite the state constitution in accordance with congressional instructions. When the new constitutions were ratified by a majority of registered voters, later modified to a majority of those voting, and the state had ratified the Fourteenth Amendment, it could apply for readmission to the Union. Johnson vetoed the bill, claiming it would "negroize" the South. Congress easily overrode the veto. To exercise some control over the president, congress enacted the Tenure of Office Act that prohibited Johnson from removing from office any official whom he had appointed who had received senate confirmation. Congress intended the Tenure of Office Act to prevent Johnson from firing either U.S. Grant as head of the armies or Edwin Stanton as secretary of war, both sympathetic to congressional reconstruction.

The South Under Radical Rule

The dismissal of Johnson's provisional governments altered southern politics. Ex-Confederate states now came under the control of those who had remained loyal Unionists during the war and were free to take the Iron Clad oath. Southern Republican governments consisted of three groups of voters. The largest and most important group of southern Republicans were ex-slaves. Across the South 703,000 African-Americans registered to vote compared 627,000 whites. With clear majorities in five southern states—South Carolina, Mississippi, Louisiana, Alabama, and Georgia—the newly enfranchised freemen cooperated willingly with whoever recognized their right to vote and hold public office. They paid particular attention to the establishment of public schools for their children and in expanding social services such as hospitals, orphanages, and asylums. Black voters elected a large number of black officeholders. African-Americans served in the southern judiciary, state legislatures, city and county governments, on school boards, and in the national house and senate. In several counties blacks were even elected sheriff, an especially sensitive office for whites. Mississippi elected two African-American senators, Hiram Revels and Blanche K. Bruce. Few African

Americans displayed vindictiveness toward whites, and across the South whites retained control of most offices, especially the highest in the state. And while blacks were involved in several highly publicized incidents of political corruption, on the whole, given their lack of previous experience, they served well, giving the South some of its most honest politicians. Even so, southern whites viewed them as incompetent and corrupt. Their very presence in public office offended ex-Confederates, who observed their every move, careful to note any impropriety.

Two groups of whites shared power during Reconstruction with blacks, one indigenous to the South, the others newcomers. Called "scallywags" by ex-Confederates, southern white Unionists and small farmers from hill country and mountain counties joined the Republican Party anxious to insure that state governments addressed their needs. Many from western Virginia, eastern Tennessee and Kentucky, the Ozarks of Missouri and Arkansas, and eastern and western North Carolina had served as volunteers in the Union Army during the Civil War Along with former Whigs and even an occasional former Confederate, such as General James A. Longstreet of Louisiana, these scallywags sought to democratize southern politics. They promoted state subsidies for the construction of roads, bridges, railroads, levees, and other public works designed to foster southern economic growth.

The third group of southern Republicans were not southerners at all, but "Carpetbaggers," who had come South after the war to seek their fortunes and to help remake the South. They included former Union soldiers, missionaries, teachers, ambitious business men as well as opportunists. In towns like Chattanooga, Atlanta, Charlotte, and Raleigh, former Whigs recognized the need for outside capital and enterprise, warmly welcoming these adopted southerners, many of whom quickly became pillars of their growing communities. Their economic interests, however, quickly drew them into the political arena where, with their natural allies, blacks and scallywags, they joined to organize the Republican or "Radical" Party. This natural evolution engendered hard feelings from native whites around election time, even if it did not prevent their integration into local economic life.

The biracial Republican coalitions were shaky arrangements, vulnerable to attacks from white Democrats or "Conservatives," as they styled themselves. Still, the Republicans faithfully followed congressionally mandated procedures to write and approve the new state constitutions. Only in the South Carolina constitutional convention did blacks constitute a majority of the delegates which reflected their proportion of the state's population. Virtually every constitution's preamble either quoted or paraphrased the assertion in the Declaration of Independence of the natural rights and equality of all men. Each southern constitution granted freed blacks their civil rights as well as mandated universal manhood suffrage-rights that African-Americans did not enjoy in most northern states. The constitutions also extended democratic procedures to local and county governments, provided for home rule, and established public school systems, although, in every state except Louisiana and South Carolina, public schools remained segregated by race. The new constitutions also included provisions that protected the rights of married women to their homes, their children, and their personal property.

Race-baiting Democrats unleashed an unprecedented barrage against these constitutions, concentrating their fire on the convention delegates rather than on the contents of the documents. They described black delegates as "monkeys," "mules," and "jailbirds." At the same time secret white societies, such as the Ku Klux Klan, used terror and violence to intimidate black voters and their white supporters. But the presence of federal troops enforced a semblance of order at polling places and public assemblies where voters overwhelmingly approved the constitutions. Some of the reconstruction constitutions remain in effect to this day. In June 1868, congress certified the readmission of Arkansas, Alabama, Florida, Georgia, Louisiana, and North and South Carolina to the Union.

Presidential Impeachment

Andrew Johnson futilely sought to resist congressional reconstruction. But his efforts only provoked congressional Radicals to remove him from office. In 1868 they charged Johnson with violating the Tenure of Office Act by firing his secretary of war, Radical favorite Edwin M. Stanton. On February 24 the house impeached Johnson on eleven counts of "high crimes and misdemeanors." Stevens, although near death's door, was determined to live long enough to see Johnson removed from the White House and agreed to serve, with General Benjamin Butler, as a House Manager before the senate on March 30. Butler acknowledged that Johnson had committed no crimes but insisted he had acted contrary to the "fundamental or essential principle of government." During the trial, congress admitted Nebraska and Colorado to the Union to secure four additional anti-Johnson votes in the senate. The president partially blocked this effort to stack the impeachment jury by vetoing Colorado's admission. On May 16, 1868, the senate voted for conviction by thirty-five to nineteen, one vote short of the two-thirds needed. Only seven Republicans joined senate Democrats who stood by Johnson. None was reelected. Though acquitted, Johnson served out his term, the lamest of lame ducks.

With the presidential election approaching, Johnson became a political liability for the Democrats so they ignored him. After twenty-two ballots, the Democrats chose Horatio Seymour, New York's effective wartime governor and critic of Lincoln's policies. Seymour ran on a platform that favored Johnson's restoration approach and the Pendleton Plan, a scheme to pay off the war debt with depreciated greenbacks rather than gold. The Republicans chose General Ulysses Grant. The outcome surprised no one. Grant's popular margin was 306,000 votes over Seymour, but the New Yorker received a majority of the white votes cast.

Economic Recovery

The post-war period was a time of unprecedented economic growth for the United States that made it the world's leading industrial power by the end of the century. Republican support of protective tariffs, its stabilization of the currency, its land subsidies to railroads, its opening the national domain to lumbering and ranching, all encouraged economic growth, although often at an enormous public cost. The government's military needs and wartime policies brought untold prosperity to the meat packing industry, fattened railroad profits—the Erie Railway's earnings doubled between 1860 and 1863—expanded agricultural production, created a constellation of new millionaires, and allowed the nation's financial resources to become concentrated in New York and Philadelphia. A flat rate income tax raised nearly 20 percent of wartime federal revenues, but did not weigh easily on the wealthy. The North could not have won the war without such innovations made possible by southern secession which removed their brake on federal economic intervention and led to the reconstruction of the American economy, an event fully as important as the reconstruction of southern politics.

New wealth flowed into capital investments that expanded the nation's rail mileage, from 35,085 in 1865 to 81,747 only thirteen years later, as well as into the rapidly changing coal and iron industries. Andrew Carnegie introduced the new Bessemer converter into his steel production and consolidated a variety of production tasks into a single, inter-related process housed under one roof in his new and efficient Edgar Thomson steel works in Pittsburgh. More startling was the rapid rise of the oil refining industry. The first oil well was drilled in western Pennsylvania in 1859. Six years later, John D. Rockefeller founded Standard Oil in Cleveland and made his name synonymous with wealth, power, and economic influence. Such dramatic changes did not extend to average laborers, however. Top workers in the North earned a meager twenty-five cents per hour for a ten-hour day, and until 1880 witnessed a decline in real income due to a short-term rise in the cost of living. Industrial leaders and their Republican spokesmen in Washington agreed that the power of the newly returned ex-Confederate states should be channeled in constructive directions when they returned to power, or they would obstruct national economic growth. National Republican movers and shakers understood that the newly enfranchised freedmen were critical to continued Republican control over national policy.

Political Corruption in the Grant Era

Corruption and malfeasance in office were not new to American politics. Indeed, the spoils system had been a feature of the national government since the days of John Adams. In the South both Democratic and Republican state governments cavalierly appropriated public funds for private purposes. South Carolina's Republican legislature lavished state funds on railroads, expensive cigars, fine whiskey, and brass cuspidors. Southern Democrats were even more aggressive in embezzling state funds to line their own and friends' pockets. In New York City, William Marcy Tweed, boss of the Tammany Hall Democratic machine, systematically defrauded the city treasury of more than $200 million through kickbacks and padded bills. Everywhere in post-war America corruption reigned. To many the war had unraveled the nation's moral fiber.

Grant got most of the blame. In permitting congress to assume national leadership, the president failed to assume his responsibility to oversee the conduct of administration appointments and federal officials. He allowed his associates, subordinates, and friends to enrich themselves at public expense without fear of presidential reprimand. Grant's brother-in-law participated in an abortive effort by two Wall Street financial manipulators, Jay Gould and James "Jubilee Jim" Fiske, to corner the nation's gold market and drive up the price of gold, making a fortune on their speculative holdings. Under Grant's unconcerned eye, a whisky ring, which included internal revenue officials, conspired with distillers to deprive the government of its tax revenues on liquor. Congress carried out a "salary grab" that doubled the president's salary to $50,000 and that of congress, making the raises retroactive. A ring in Washington drew up inflated contracts for local improvements to favorites of the city's mayor. The most publicized of the Grant administration's scandals involved the Credit Mobilier, a construction company founded by the Union Pacific Railroad to build that line on federal credit. Vice president Schuyler Colfax, representative James A. Garfield of Ohio, and others accepted shares of Credit Mobilier stock and used their influence to stifle an investigation of its enormous dividends. The most tragic and inexcusable scandal, however, implicated the Indian Bureau. Forcefully retained on government reservations and denied access to traditional hunting grounds, native Americans depended on the federal government for food, clothing, fuel, and education. Federal Indian agents frequently diverted funds appropriated for Indian subsistence into their own pockets, leaving tens of thousands of helpless people to starve and freeze to death on reservations that had become death camps. When such scandals became public, they angered voters and discredited the Grant Administration.

Grant simply ignored his critics. He continued to define the public interest in terms of his friends and supporters and their interests, many of the latter representatives of large business interests seeking public favors. The Republican congress colluded with the corruption of the Grant administration. For example, just prior to the 1870 and 1872 congressional elections, congress reduced tariff rates. With the balloting over, congress raised tariffs to please well-connected businesses. In 1869 the national debt stood at $2.5 billion. Large eastern financial interests, who loaned the government depreciated greenbacks, owned much of the debt, but they insisted that their bonds be redeemed in gold. Two weeks to the day after Grant's inauguration, congress approved the Public Credit Act that called for debt redemption in gold. In 1873 congress demonetized silver, making gold the sole monetary standard, deflating the currency to benefit bankers and other bond holders. Two years later congress agreed to redeem all outstanding greenbacks with gold.

Such practices plagued national and big city politics, but political commentators focused on the relatively modest corruption in southern, black-dominated governments. Indeed, many attributed the nation's postwar corruption directly to black participation in southern politics. National Republicans found that their southern cohorts had become political liabilities. Making common cause with "thinking and influential native Southerners," Republican leaders began to remove federal troops from the South. As the black southern governments collapsed, Republicans believed that white southerners, especially the business elite, would join the Republican effort to exploit southern labor, minerals, timber, land, and textiles, under the direction of northern capitalists. The Liberal Party's challenge to Grant in 1872 was the first effort to form a new national coalition that included the South's white elite. A hodgepodge of civil service reformers, free traders, anti-Grant Republican dissidents, and opponents of congressional reconstruction, the Liberal Party nominated the newspaper editor Horace Greeley, who also won the Democratic nomination. In 1872 Republican regulars had no trouble defeating this dissident Republican challenge. Grant's reputation as a war hero still commanded the affection and vote of white northerners and black southerners.

Two years later, however, the Democrats and small farmer-oriented independent parties, associated with the Patrons of Husbandry or Grange had a substantial impact on the 1874 congressional balloting, encouraging efforts for a full scale challenge to Republican dominance.

"Redeeming" the South

In the South, politics were reverting to the normal pattern of white dominance. The region's traditional leaders had assumed their accustomed positions of leadership. Such leaders, one by one, overthrew the unstable Radical regimes by skillfully using racial appeals to break up the tenuous black, "scalawag," and "carpetbag" alliances. As ex-Confederate states reentered the union, their legislatures excluded enough Republican members to give the Democrats working majorities. Republican corruption and electoral irregularities, trumped up or real, provided convenient excuses for local champions of public decency to regain political power and "redeem" their states. Moreover, the Freedmen's Bureau, whose schools and hospitals dotted the South, gradually reduced its operations as military authority gave way to civilian control. Year by year, blacks lost more and more federal protection. Hooded and robed Klansmen roamed the highways and byways, shooting into black homes, filling the night skies with the reddish glow of burning crosses, frightening Republicans away from the polls. The Klan and other groups, such as the White League and the Constitutional Union Guards, broke the back of the southern Republican parties. When Republicans fought back, as they did when North Carolina's Governor William Holden launched a full-scale military operation against the Klan in 1870, Democratic-dominated state courts thwarted them.

Even more important, northern Republicans had never taken seriously Stevens' and other agrarian radicals' pleas for land reform. Former slaves longing for their own land—"Forty Acres and a Mule"—had been dashed. Instead, many former slaves found themselves more vulnerable than ever to the white landowners. As sharecroppers and tenant farmers, toiling away on others' land, they were theoretically free to leave; but they did so at the risk of running afoul of the sheriff. Democratically dominated southern legislatures passed "crop lien" laws that gave creditors first claim to the production of their debtors. While legal, they resembled slavery, and were unjust. In addition, white landowners coerced the votes of their nominally free black tenants. Day-to-day life on the South's isolated farms required blacks to exhibit a subservient attitude toward their white overlords. Not even poor white farmers escaped this fate. Many planters sold their plantations to northern or absentee owners who cared little about the color of a sharecropper's skin.

Describing themselves as "redeemers," the South's new leaders resembled its old planter class. Redeemers opposed high taxes, public schools, and government aid for internal improvements, all of which they identified with Republican reconstruction. "Conservatives," as they called themselves, supported states' rights, the subordination of the freedmen, and the removal of federal troops. By 1876, every southern state except South Carolina, Louisiana, and Florida had been redeemed from Republican rule by Democrats. The South's restored white leadership hoped that the 1876 presidential election would end Reconstruction altogether.

1876

Democrats were optimistic about the election. Their 1874 congressional victories and their choice of Samuel J. Tilden, the popular reform governor of New York, augured well for their chances. Tilden had broken the infamous Boss Tweed and temporarily disrupted his machine, accomplishments that appealed to political independents and moderate Republicans alike. With most of the southern states now in Democratic hands, Tilden could expect to win a solid block of the South's electoral votes. In the wake of the scandals of Grant's administrations, the Republicans also assumed a reform posture by nominating Ohio's reform governor Rutherford B. Hayes, who campaigned for civil service reform.

When the votes were counted, Tilden had won an absolute majority of the popular vote, 4,284,265 to Hayes' 4,033,295. Republican strategists, however, noted that if the three southern states still under Republican control cast their electoral votes for Hayes, he would beat Tilden. Republican election boards in Louisiana, South Carolina, and Florida dutifully threw out enough Democratic votes to put their states electoral votes in the Hayes column. But in the same states, the newly elected Democratic legislatures certified that Tilden's electors had won. When congress counted the ballots in January 1877, it had to determine which candidate had won the twenty disputed electoral votes. Hayes needed all twenty to secure the 185 electoral votes needed to win. The Constitution had no provision on how to settle such a dispute. Democrats loudly threatened that they would not allow the Republicans to steal the election. In an effort to give an air of legitimacy to its decision, the Republican-controlled congress appointed a fifteen member electoral commission to recommend a course of action.

The commission, whose members were drawn equally from the house, the senate, and the supreme court, had a Republican majority of one. In each instance the electoral commission gave the disputed votes to Hayes by an eight to seven vote. Some Democrats talked of boycott and filibuster to forestall congressional action and prevent Hayes' election. By mid-February, with inauguration day looming ever closer, southern Democrats approached congressional Republicans with a compromise. The prime consideration was removal of the last federal troops from the South, an act that would lead to the collapse of the Republican Party in the South. Southern leaders also wanted congress to support construction of a transcontinental railroad with a southern terminus and Hayes to support internal improvements in the South. Finally, some southern leaders demanded a cabinet seat. By the end of February Hayes assented to the three demands. On inauguration day the country had its minority president. The South received a cabinet post when Hayes appointed David M. Key, a Chattanooga Whig, as Postmaster General, a post that controlled important federal patronage. In April, at Hayes order, federal troops in South Carolina and Louisiana returned to their barracks to prepare to depart those states. Florida's Republican government had already succumbed. Reconstruction had come to an end. But the newly elected congress refused to appropriate money for expensive, federal giveaways and to finance southern rail construction.

The "Compromise of 1877"

The "Compromise of 1877" was never written down, never formally publicized, and never officially ratified. In ending Reconstruction, it left free blacks to the mercies of the southern whites. It took another twenty-five years for southern whites to legally deprive African Americans of their Fourteenth and Fifteenth Amendment rights as citizens and electors, but by 1877 the process was well underway. Not until after World War II did the federal government begin to enforce African-Americans' constitutional rights. The principal obstacle to immediate white supremacy was the Fifteenth Amendment that prohibited states from denying adult males the right to vote based on their race. As long as African-Americans cast ballots, they played an important role in southern politics. They helped elect local officials, sent black representatives to state legislatures and to Washington, and swelled popular vote totals for Republican presidential candidates. Even Democratic politicians cultivated the black vote. This came to an end in the 1890s, in the wake of a severe agricultural depression that radicalized southern politics. Determined to remove blacks from southern politics, southern legislatures systematically disenfranchised them and imposed a rigid system of racial apartheid.

The Compromise of 1877 went well beyond Washington politics. It sealed the return of southern Democrats to power and marked the reconciliation of northern and southern whites. In the South whites also put their past differences behind them as the new conservative Democratic Party welcomed former Unionists and

Whigs, along with its traditional constituency of white southern farmers and planters. The new, white, southern Democratic Party ended the two-party system that had characterized southern politics since Andrew Jackson. As the "white man's party," southern Democrats dominated the region's political life until the late 1960s. Welcoming the much heralded "New South," Redeemer Democrats invited northern business interests South, where Democrats gave them a virtual free reign. Northern capital and enterprise flowed into the New South, exploiting southern mineral resources, organizing and updating its transportation systems, harvesting its stands of virgin timber, and exploiting its labor. After more than a decade and a half of Civil War and Reconstruction, the South had reverted to native white rule, but with a crucial difference. Unlike the Old South's slave holders, the "redeemers" allied themselves with northern business interests who treated the natural resources and people of the South as colonial possessions and southern economic and political leaders as hired-hands. The Civil War, fought to secure the Union, emancipate southern slaves, and secure federal territory for small farmers, ended up reconstructing the nation along lines favored by large business interests. The Compromise of 1877 ratified the control of the nation's business leaders over American government even as it sacrificed the citizenship of African-Americans on the altar of white, racial reconciliation. By the nation's centennial the United States had once again become a "white man's country," ruled by whites and divided as never before by social class. The quest for community, however, would continue.

Historical Potpourri

Americans on both sides of the Civil War sang songs that expressed the strong emotions that convulsed the nation and produced all the discord and death. The most famous of all northern songs was a stirring hymn whose haunting strains echoed across many a battlefield to offer a noble reason for dying:

> *Mine eyes have seen the glory of the coming of the Lord;*
> *He is trampling out the vintage where the grapes of wrath are stored;*
> *He hath loosed the fateful lightning of His terrible swift sword:*
> > *His truth is marching on.*
>
> *He has sounded forth the trumpet that shall never call retreat;*
> *He is sifting out the hearts of men before His judgment-seat;*
> *Oh, be swift, my soul to answer Him! be jubilant, my feet!*
> > *Our God is marching on.*
>
> *In the beauty of the lilies Christ was born across the sea,*
> *With a glory in His bosom that transfigures you and me:*
> *As He died to make men holy, let us die to make men free,*
> > *While God is marching on.*

Black regiments did not play a major role in the war until 1863, after which, even though they constituted only ten percent of the Union Army, they suffered over twenty-five percent of its casualties. Confederate commanders were so unnerved confronting black troops that to discourage further Union enlistments they refused to accept them as prisoners of war and instead summarily executed all black Union captives. More than anyone else, black soldiers sensed that their destiny would be determined by the outcome of the "Great Rebellion."

> *No more moaning, no more moaning,*
> *No more moaning, Lord, for me!*
> *And before I'd be a slave, I'd be buried in my grave,*
> *And go home to my Lord and be free.*
>
> *O freedom! Freedom! O freedom, Lord, for me!*
> *And before I'd be a slave, I'd be buried in my grave,*
> *And go home to my Lord and be free.*

The best known southern anthem was, of course, "Dixie," but the Iyrics that attracted the most composers, even in the North, was "Somebody's Darling":

> *Somebody's watching and waiting for him,*
> *Yearning to hold him again to her heart*
> *Yet there he lies with his blue eyes so dim,*
> *And purple child-like lips half apart.*
> *Tenderly bury the fair, unknown dead,*
> *Pausing to drop on his grave a tear;*
> *Carve on the wooden slab over his head,*
> *Somebody's darling is slumbering here.*

Chorus:

> *Somebody's darling, somebody's pride.*
> *Who'll tell his mother where her boy died?*

Few sang during the grim days of Reconstruction. Southerners who wanted to might choose "Oh, I'm a Good Old Rebel" and underscore what made reunion so difficult.

> *Oh, I'm a good old rebel, that's just what I am;*
> *For this "Fair Land of Freedom " I don't care a damn!*
> *I'm glad I fit against it, I only wish we'd won,*
> *And I don't want no pardon for anything I've done.*
>
> *I hates the Constitution, this great Republic too,*
> *I hates the Freedman's Buro in uniforms of blue;*
> *I hates the nasty eagle with all his brag and fuss,*
> *The lyin' thievin' Yankees, I hates them wuss and wuss!*
>
> *I hates the Yankee nation and everthing they do,*
> *I hates the Declaration of Independence, too;*
> *I hates the glorious Union—'tis dripping with our blood,*
> *I hates the striped banner, I fit it all I could.*
>
> *Three hundred thousand Yankees lie stiff in Southern dust;*
> *We got three hundred thousand before they conquered us!*
> *They died of Southern fever and Southern steel and shot,*
> *I wish they was three million instead of what we got!*

I can't take up my musket and fight 'em no no more,
But I ain't a-going to love 'em, now that is sartain sure;
And I don't want no pardon for what I was and am,
I won't be reconstructed, and I don't care a damn!

Finally, white males toasted one another with "Here's to the Great Bald Eagle."

Here's to the Great Bald Eagle,
That wondrous bird of prey;
Who furls its wings o'r northern soil,
But shits on southern clay.

Here's to the South land,
Whose soil so fertile and rich.
Who needs your turds? You God Damn Bird!
You Yankee son of a bitch!

The last two songs from Willard A. and Porter W. Heaps, *The Singing Sixties*, (Norman: University of Oklahoma Press, 1960).

Good Books

A brief, readable account of *The Death of Slavery* (1967) by Elbert Smith is a good place to begin. Eric Foner's influential book highlights the ideology of the Republican party in *Free Soil, Free Labor, Free Men* (1970). Two of many excellent biographies that deal with men involved in the sectional struggles are Stephen Oates' *To Purge this Land with Blood* (1970), a look at John Brown, and David Donald, *Charles Sumner and the Coming of the Civil War* (1960). A good study of Lincoln is Oates' *With Malice Toward None* (1977), and David Donald's *Lincoln* (1995). William McFeely writes movingly of *Grant* (1982).

The most readable retelling of the dramatic events surrounding secession is Kenneth Stampp, *And the War Came* (1950). James McPherson has written a good, short history of the war in his *Battle Cry of Freedom* (1988). More recent treatments of secession are William Freehling's *The Road to Disunion* (1990) and Bruce Levine, *Half Slave, Half Free* (1992). David Donald collaborated with Grady McWhiney to present a series of essays on *Why the North Won the War* (1960). Charles Roland, *The Confederacy* (1960) and George C. Rable, *The Confederate Republic* (1994) focus on the South. Two other works by James McPherson delineate the war's effect on blacks: *The Struggle for Equality* (1964) and *The Negro's Civil War* (1965). Charles Royster, *The Destructive War*, (1991) examines the scope of the war's violence.

The best and most up-to-date account of reconstruction is Leon Litwack, *Been the Storm Too Long* (1979). Two brief accounts of reconstruction are John Hope Franklin, *Reconstruction: After the Civil War* (1961) and Stampp, *The Era of Reconstruction* (1965). Two works by Vann Woodward are still important *Reunion and Reaction* (1956) and *Origins of the New South* (1951). Paul Gaston also underlines southern continuity in *The New South Creed* (1970). A fascinating local study is Willie Lee Rose, *Rehearsal for Reconstruction* (1964), which shows how the best laid plans of Yankee schoolmarms went awry. Tera W. Hunter, *To Joy My Freedom* (1997) looks at African-American women the last quarter of the nineteenth century. McKee Evans uncovers examples of black and white cooperation in *Ballots and Fence Rails* (1967). Woodward offers expert coverage of *The Strange Career of Jim Crow* (1974); for a moving contemporary analysis that has become a classic, see W. E. B. Dubois, *The Souls of Black Folk* (1901). Roger L. Ransom and Richard Sutch, *One Kind of Freedom* (1977) look at the economic consequences of the war.

The Declaration of Independence
of the Thirteen Colonies

In CONGRESS, July 4, 1776

The unanimous Declaration of the thirteen United States of America,

When in the Course of human events, it becomes necessary for one people to dissolve the political bands which have connected them with another, and to assume among the powers of the earth, the separate and equal station to which the Laws of Nature and of Nature's God entitle them, a decent respect to the opinions of mankind requires that they should declare the causes which impel them to the separation.

We hold these truths to be self-evident, that all men are created equal, that they are endowed by their Creator with certain unalienable Rights, that among these are Life, Liberty and the pursuit of Happiness. —That to secure these rights, Governments are instituted among Men, deriving their just powers from the consent of the governed, —That whenever any Form of Government becomes destructive of these ends, it is the Right of the People to alter or to abolish it, and to institute new Government, laying its foundation on such principles and organizing its powers in such form, as to them shall seem most likely to effect their Safety and Happiness. Prudence, indeed, will dictate that Governments long established should not be changed for light and transient causes; and accordingly all experience hath shewn, that mankind are more disposed to suffer, while evils are sufferable, than to right themselves by abolishing the forms to which they are accustomed. But when a long train of abuses and usurpations, pursuing invariably the same Object evinces a design to reduce them under absolute Despotism, it is their right, it is their duty, to throw off such Government, and to provide new Guards for their future security. —Such has been the patient sufferance of these Colonies; and such is now the necessity which constrains them to alter their former Systems of Government. The history of the present King of Great Britain [George III] is a history of repeated injuries and usurpations, all having in direct object the establishment of an absolute Tyranny over these States. To prove this, let Facts be submitted to a candid world.

He has refused his Assent to Laws, the most wholesome and necessary for the public good.

He has forbidden his Governors to pass Laws of immediate and pressing importance, unless suspended in their operation till his Assent should be obtained; and when so suspended, he has utterly neglected to attend to them.

He has refused to pass other Laws for the accommodation of large districts of people, unless those people would relinquish the right of Representation in the Legislature, a right inestimable to them and formidable to tyrants only.

He has called together legislative bodies at places unusual, uncomfortable, and distant from the depository of their public Records, for the sole purpose of fatiguing them into compliance with his measures.

He has dissolved Representative Houses repeatedly, for opposing with manly firmness his invasions on the rights of the people.

He has refused for a long time, after such dissolutions, to cause others to be elected; whereby the Legislative powers, incapable of Annihilation, have returned to the People at large for their exercise; the State remaining in the mean time exposed to all the dangers of invasion from without, and convulsions within.

He has endeavoured to prevent the population of these States; for that purpose obstructing the Laws for Naturalization of Foreigners; refusing to pass others to encourage their migrations hither, and raising the conditions of new Appropriations of Lands.

He has obstructed the Administration of Justice, by refusing his Assent to Laws for establishing Judiciary powers.

He has made Judges dependent on his Will alone, for the tenure of their offices, and the amount and payment of their salaries.

He has erected a multitude of New Offices, and sent hither swarms of Officers to harass our people, and eat out their substance.

He has kept among us, in times of peace, Standing Armies without the consent of our legislatures.

He has affected to render the Military independent of and superior to the Civil power.

He has combined with others to subject us to a jurisdiction foreign to our constitution and unacknowledged by our laws; giving his Assent to their Acts of pretended Legislation:

For Quartering large bodies of armed troops among us:

For protecting them, by a mock Trial, from punishment for any Murders which they should commit on the Inhabitants of these States:

For cutting off our Trade with all parts of the world:

For imposing Taxes on us without our Consent:

For depriving us, in many cases, of the benefits of Trial by Jury:

For transporting us beyond Seas to be tried for pretended offences:

For abolishing the free System of English Laws in a neighbouring Province, establishing therein an Arbitrary government, and enlarging its Boundaries so as to render it at once an example and fit instrument for introducing the same absolute rule into these Colonies:

For taking away our Charters, abolishing our most valuable Laws, and altering fundamentally the Forms of our Governments:

For suspending our own Legislatures, and declaring themselves invested with power to legislate for us in all cases whatsoever.

He has abdicated Government here, by declaring us out of his Protection and waging War against us.

He has plundered our seas, ravaged our Coasts, burnt our towns, and destroyed the lives of our people.

He is at this time transporting large Armies of foreign Mercenaries to compleat the works of death, desolation and tyranny, already begun with circumstances of Cruelty and perfidy scarcely paralleled in the most barbarous ages, and totally unworthy the Head of a civilized nation.

He has constrained our fellow Citizens taken Captive on the high Seas to bear Arms against their Country, to become the executioners of their friends and Brethren, or to fall themselves by their Hands.

He has excited domestic insurrections amongst us, and has endeavoured to bring on the inhabitants of our frontiers, the merciless Indian Savages, whose known rule of warfare, is an undistinguished destruction of all ages, sexes and conditions.

In every stage of these Oppressions We have Petitioned for Redress in the most humble terms: Our repeated Petitions have been answered only by repeated injury. A Prince whose character is thus marked by every act which may define a Tyrant, is unfit to be the ruler of a free people.

Nor have We been wanting in attentions to our British brethren. We have warned them from time to time of attempts by their legislature to extend an unwarrantable jurisdiction over us. We have reminded them of the circumstances of our emigration and settlement here. We have appealed to their native justice and magnanimity, and we have conjured them by the ties of our common kindred to disavow these usurpations, which, would inevitably interrupt our connections and correspondence. They too have been deaf to the voice of justice and of consanguinity. We must, therefore, acquiesce in the necessity, which denounces our Separation, and hold them, as we hold the rest of mankind, Enemies in War, in Peace Friends.

We, therefore, the Representatives of the united States of America, in General Congress, Assembled, appealing to the Supreme Judge of the world for the rectitude of our intentions, do, in the Name, and by the Authority of the good People of these Colonies, solemnly publish and declare, That these United Colonies are, and of Right ought to be Free and Independent States; that they are Absolved from all Allegiance to the British Crown, and that all political connection between them and the State of Great Britain, is and ought to be totally dissolved; and that as Free and Independent States, they have full Power to levy War, conclude Peace, contract Alliances, establish Commerce, and to do all other Acts and Things which Independent States may of right do. And for the support of this Declaration, with a firm reliance on the protection of divine Providence, we mutually pledge to each other our Lives, our Fortunes and our sacred Honor.

The United States Constitution

We the People of the United States, in Order to form a more perfect Union, establish Justice, insure domestic Tranquility, provide for the common defence, promote the general Welfare, and secure the Blessings of Liberty to ourselves and our Posterity, do ordain and establish this Constitution for the United States of America.

Article 1

Section 1

All legislative Powers herein granted shall be vested in a Congress of the United States, which shall consist of a Senate and House of Representatives.

Section 2

Clause 1: The House of Representatives shall be composed of Members chosen every second Year by the People of the several States, and the Electors in each State shall have the Qualifications requisite for Electors of the most numerous Branch of the State Legislature.

Clause 2: No Person shall be a Representative who shall not have attained to the Age of twenty five Years, and been seven Years a Citizen of the United States, and who shall not, when elected, be an Inhabitant of that State in which he shall be chosen.

Clause 3: Representatives and direct Taxes shall be apportioned among the several States which may be included within this Union, according to their respective

Numbers, which shall be determined by adding to the whole Number of free Persons, including those bound to Service for a Term of Years, and excluding Indians not taxed, three fifths of all other Persons. The actual Enumeration shall be made within three Years after the first Meeting of the Congress of the United States, and within every subsequent Term of ten Years, in such Manner as they shall by Law direct. The Number of Representatives shall not exceed one for every thirty Thousand, but each State shall have at Least one Representative; and until such enumeration shall be made, the State of New Hampshire shall be entitled to chuse three, Massachusetts eight, Rhode-Island and Providence Plantations one, Connecticut five, New-York six, New Jersey four, Pennsylvania eight, Delaware one, Maryland six, Virginia ten, North Carolina five, South Carolina five, and Georgia three.

Clause 4: When vacancies happen in the Representation from any State, the Executive Authority thereof shall issue Writs of Election to fill such Vacancies.

Clause 5: The House of Representatives shall chuse their Speaker and other Officers; and shall have the sole Power of Impeachment.

Section 3

Clause 1: The Senate of the United States shall be composed of two Senators from each State, chosen by the Legislature thereof, for six Years; and each Senator shall have one Vote.

Clause 2: Immediately after they shall be assembled in Consequence of the first Election, they shall be divided as equally as may be into three Classes. The Seats of the Senators of the first Class shall be vacated at the Expiration of the second Year, of the second Class at the Expiration of the fourth Year, and of the third Class at the Expiration of the sixth Year, so that one third may be chosen every second Year; and if Vacancies happen by Resignation, or otherwise, during the Recess of the Legislature of any State, the Executive thereof may make temporary Appointments until the next Meeting of the Legislature, which shall then fill such Vacancies.

Clause 3: No Person shall be a Senator who shall not have attained to the Age of thirty Years, and been nine Years a Citizen of the United States, and who shall not, when elected, be an Inhabitant of that State for which he shall be chosen.

Clause 4: The Vice President of the United States shall be President of the Senate, but shall have no Vote, unless they be equally divided.

Clause 5: The Senate shall chuse their other Officers, and also a President pro tempore, in the Absence of the Vice President, or when he shall exercise the Office of President of the United States.

Clause 6: The Senate shall have the sole Power to try all Impeachments. When sitting for that Purpose, they shall be on Oath or Affirmation. When the President of the United States is tried, the Chief Justice shall preside: And no Person shall be convicted without the Concurrence of two thirds of the Members present.

Clause 7: Judgment in Cases of Impeachment shall not extend further than to removal from Office, and disqualification to hold and enjoy any Office of honor, Trust or Profit under the United States: but the Party convicted shall nevertheless be liable and subject to Indictment, Trial, Judgment and Punishment, according to Law.

Section 4

Clause 1: The Times, Places and Manner of holding Elections for Senators and Representatives, shall be prescribed in each State by the Legislature thereof; but the Congress may at any time by Law make or alter such Regulations, except as to the Places of chusing Senators.

Clause 2: The Congress shall assemble at least once in every Year, and such Meeting shall be on the first Monday in December, unless they shall by Law appoint a different Day.

Section 5

Clause 1: Each House shall be the Judge of the Elections, Returns and Qualifications of its own Members, and a Majority of each shall constitute a Quorum to do Business; but a smaller Number may adjourn from day to day, and may be authorized to compel the Attendance of absent Members, in such Manner, and under such Penalties as each House may provide.

Clause 2: Each House may determine the Rules of its Proceedings, punish its Members for disorderly Behaviour, and, with the Concurrence of two thirds, expel a Member.

Clause 3: Each House shall keep a Journal of its Proceedings, and from time to time publish the same, excepting such Parts as may in their Judgment require Secrecy; and the Yeas and Nays of the Members of either House on any question shall, at the Desire of one fifth of those Present, be entered on the Journal.

Clause 4: Neither House, during the Session of Congress, shall, without the Consent of the other, adjourn for more than three days, nor to any other Place than that in which the two Houses shall be sitting.

Section 6

Clause 1: The Senators and Representatives shall receive a Compensation for their Services, to be ascertained by Law, and paid out of the Treasury of the United States. They shall in all Cases, except Treason, Felony and Breach of the Peace, be privileged from Arrest during their Attendance at the Session of their respective Houses, and in going to and returning from the same; and for any Speech or Debate in either House, they shall not be questioned in any other Place.

Clause 2: No Senator or Representative shall, during the Time for which he was elected, be appointed to any civil Office under the Authority of the United States, which shall have been created, or the Emoluments whereof shall have been encreased during such time; and no Person holding any Office under the United States, shall be a Member of either House during his Continuance in Office.

Section 7

Clause 1: All Bills for raising Revenue shall originate in the House of Representatives; but the Senate may propose or concur with Amendments as on other Bills.

Clause 2: Every Bill which shall have passed the House of Representatives and the Senate, shall, before it become a Law, be presented to the President of the United States; If he approve he shall sign it, but if not he shall return it, with his Objections to that House in which it shall have originated, who shall enter the Objections at large on their Journal, and proceed to reconsider it. If after such Reconsideration two thirds of that House shall agree to pass the Bill, it shall be sent, together with the Objections, to the other House, by which it shall likewise be reconsidered, and if approved by two thirds of that House, it shall become a Law. But in all such Cases the Votes of both Houses shall be determined by yeas and Nays, and the Names of the Persons voting for and against the Bill shall be entered on the Journal of each House respectively. If any Bill shall not be returned by the President within ten Days (Sundays excepted) after it shall have been presented to him, the Same shall be a Law, in like Manner as if he had signed it, unless the Congress by their Adjournment prevent its Return, in which Case it shall not be a Law.

Clause 3: Every Order, Resolution, or Vote to which the Concurrence of the Senate and House of Representatives may be necessary (except on a question of Adjournment) shall be presented to the President of the United States; and before the Same shall take Effect, shall be approved by him, or being disapproved by him, shall be repassed by two thirds of the Senate and House of Representatives, according to the Rules and Limitations prescribed in the Case of a Bill.

Section 8

Clause 1: The Congress shall have Power To lay and collect Taxes, Duties,

Imposts and Excises, to pay the Debts and provide for the common Defence and general Welfare of the United States; but all Duties, Imposts and Excises shall be uniform throughout the United States;

Clause 2: To borrow Money on the credit of the United States;

Clause 3: To regulate Commerce with foreign Nations, and among the several States, and with the Indian Tribes;

Clause 4: To establish an uniform Rule of Naturalization, and uniform Laws on the subject of Bankruptcies throughout the United States;

Clause 5: To coin Money, regulate the Value thereof, and of foreign Coin, and fix the Standard of Weights and Measures;

Clause 6: To provide for the Punishment of counterfeiting the Securities and current Coin of the United States;

Clause 7: To establish Post Offices and post Roads;

Clause 8: To promote the Progress of Science and useful Arts, by securing for limited Times to Authors and Inventors the exclusive Right to their respective Writings and Discoveries;

Clause 9: To constitute Tribunals inferior to the supreme Court;

Clause 10: To define and punish Piracies and Felonies committed on the high Seas, and Offences against the Law of Nations;

Clause 11: To declare War, grant Letters of Marque and Reprisal, and make Rules concerning Captures on Land and Water;

Clause 12: To raise and support Armies, but no Appropriation of Money to that Use shall be for a longer Term than two Years;

Clause 13: To provide and maintain a Navy;

Clause 14: To make Rules for the Government and Regulation of the land and naval Forces;

Clause 15: To provide for calling forth the Militia to execute the Laws of the Union, suppress Insurrections and repel Invasions;

Clause 16: To provide for organizing, arming, and disciplining, the Militia, and for governing such Part of them as may be employed in the Service of the United States, reserving to the States respectively, the Appointment of the Officers, and the Authority of training the Militia according to the discipline prescribed by Congress;

Clause 17: To exercise exclusive Legislation in all Cases whatsoever, over such District (not exceeding ten Miles square) as may, by Cession of particular States, and the Acceptance of Congress, become the Seat of the Government of the United States, and to exercise like Authority over all Places purchased by the Consent of the Legislature of the State in which the Same shall be, for the Erection of Forts,

Magazines, Arsenals, dock-Yards, and other needful Buildings;—And

Clause 18: To make all Laws which shall be necessary and proper for carrying into Execution the foregoing Powers, and all other Powers vested by this Constitution in the Government of the United States, or in any Department or Officer thereof.

Section 9

Clause 1: The Migration or Importation of such Persons as any of the States now existing shall think proper to admit, shall not be prohibited by the Congress prior to the Year one thousand eight hundred and eight, but a Tax or duty may be imposed on such Importation, not exceeding ten dollars for each Person.

Clause 2: The Privilege of the Writ of Habeas Corpus shall not be suspended, unless when in Cases of Rebellion or Invasion the public Safety may require it.

Clause 3: No Bill of Attainder or ex post facto Law shall be passed.

Clause 4: No Capitation, or other direct, Tax shall be laid, unless in Proportion to the Census or Enumeration herein before directed to be taken.

Clause 5: No Tax or Duty shall be laid on Articles exported from any State.

Clause 6: No Preference shall be given by any Regulation of Commerce or Revenue to the Ports of one State over those of another: nor shall Vessels bound to, or from, one State, be obliged to enter, clear, or pay Duties in another.

Clause 7: No Money shall be drawn from the Treasury, but in Consequence of Appropriations made by Law; and a regular Statement and Account of the Receipts and Expenditures of all public Money shall be published from time to time.

Clause 8: No Title of Nobility shall be granted by the United States: And no Person holding any Office of Profit or Trust under them, shall, without the Consent of the Congress, accept of any present, Emolument, Office, or Title, of any kind whatever, from any King, Prince, or foreign State.

Section 10

Clause 1: No State shall enter into any Treaty, Alliance, or Confederation; grant Letters of Marque and Reprisal; coin Money; emit Bills of Credit; make any Thing but gold and silver Coin a Tender in Payment of Debts; pass any Bill of Attainder, ex post facto Law, or Law impairing the Obligation of Contracts, or grant any Title of Nobility.

Clause 2: No State shall, without the Consent of the Congress, lay any Imposts or Duties on Imports or Exports, except what may be absolutely necessary for executing it's inspection Laws: and the net Produce of all Duties and Imposts, laid by any State on Imports or Exports, shall be for the Use of the Treasury of the United States; and all such Laws shall be subject to the Revision and Control of the Congress.

Clause 3: No State shall, without the Consent of Congress, lay any Duty of Tonnage, keep Troops, or Ships of War in time of Peace, enter into any Agreement or Compact with another State, or with a foreign Power, or engage in War, unless actually invaded, or in such imminent Danger as will not admit of delay.

Article 11

Section 1

Clause 1: The executive Power shall be vested in a President of the United States of America. He shall hold his Office during the Term of four Years, and, together with the Vice President, chosen for the same Term, be elected, as follows

Clause 2: Each State shall appoint, in such Manner as the Legislature thereof may direct, a Number of Electors, equal to the whole Number of Senators and Representatives to which the State may be entitled in the Congress: but no Senator or Representative, or Person holding an Office of Trust or Profit under the United States, shall be appointed an Elector.

Clause 3: The Electors shall meet in their respective States, and vote by Ballot for two Persons, of whom one at least shall not be an Inhabitant of the same State with themselves. And they shall make a List of all the Persons voted for, and of the Number of Votes for each; which List they shall sign and certify, and transmit sealed to the Seat of the Government of the United States, directed to the President of the Senate. The President of the Senate shall, in the Presence of the Senate and House of Representatives, open all the Certificates, and the Votes shall then be counted. The Person having the greatest Number of Votes shall be the President, if such Number be a Majority of the whole Number of Electors appointed; and if there be more than one who have such Majority, and have an equal Number of Votes, then the House of Representatives shall immediately chuse by Ballot one of them for President; and if no Person have a Majority, then from the five highest on the List the said House shall in like Manner chuse the President. But in chusing the President, the Votes shall be taken by States, the Representation from each State having one Vote; A quorum for this Purpose shall consist of a Member or Members from two thirds of the States, and a Majority of all the States shall be necessary to a Choice. In every Case, after the Choice of the President, the Person having the greatest Number of Votes of the Electors shall be the Vice President. But if there should remain two or more who have equal Votes, the Senate shall chuse from them by Ballot the Vice President.

Clause 4: The Congress may determine the Time of chusing the Electors, and the Day on which they shall give their Votes; which Day shall be the same throughout the United States.

Clause 5: No Person except a natural born Citizen, or a Citizen of the United States, at the time of the Adoption of this Constitution, shall be eligible to the Office of President; neither shall any Person be eligible to that Office who shall not have attained to the Age of thirty five Years, and been fourteen Years a Resident within the United States.

Clause 6: In Case of the Removal of the President from Office, or of his Death, Resignation, or Inability to discharge the Powers and Duties of the said Office, the Same shall devolve on the Vice President, and the Congress may by Law provide for the Case of Removal, Death, Resignation or Inability, both of the President and Vice President, declaring what Officer shall then act as President, and such Officer shall act accordingly, until the Disability be removed, or a President shall be elected.

Clause 7: The President shall, at stated Times, receive for his Services, a Compensation, which shall neither be encreased nor diminished during the Period for which he shall have been elected, and he shall not receive within that Period any other Emolument from the United States, or any of them.

Clause 8: Before he enter on the Execution of his Office, he shall take the following Oath or Affirmation:—"I do solemnly swear (or affirm) that I will faithfully execute the Office of President of the United States, and will to the best of my Ability, preserve, protect and defend the Constitution of the United States."

Section 2

Clause 1: The President shall be Commander in Chief of the Army and Navy of the United States, and of the Militia of the several States, when called into the actual Service of the United States; he may require the Opinion, in writing, of the principal Officer in each of the executive Departments, upon any Subject relating to the Duties of their respective Offices, and he shall have Power to grant Reprieves and Pardons for Offences against the United States, except in Cases of Impeachment.

Clause 2: He shall have Power, by and with the Advice and Consent of the Senate, to make Treaties, provided two thirds of the Senators present concur; and he shall nominate, and by and with the Advice and Consent of the Senate, shall appoint Ambassadors, other public Ministers and Consuls, Judges of the supreme Court, and all other Officers of the United States, whose Appointments are not herein otherwise provided for, and which shall be established by Law: but the Congress may by Law vest the Appointment of such inferior Officers, as they think proper, in the President alone, in the Courts of Law, or in the Heads of Departments.

Clause 3: The President shall have Power to fill up all Vacancies that may happen during the Recess of the Senate, by granting Commissions which shall expire at the End of their next Session.

Section 3

He shall from time to time give to the Congress Information of the State of the Union, and recommend to their Consideration such Measures as he shall judge necessary and expedient; he may, on extraordinary Occasions, convene both Houses, or either of them, and in Case of Disagreement between them, with Respect to the Time of Adjournment, he may adjourn them to such Time as he shall think proper; he shall receive Ambassadors and other public Ministers; he shall take Care that the Laws be faithfully executed, and shall Commission all the Officers of the United States.

Section 4

The President, Vice President and all civil Officers of the United States, shall be removed from Office on Impeachment for, and Conviction of, Treason, Bribery, or other high Crimes and Misdemeanors.

Article III

Section 1

The judicial Power of the United States, shall be vested in one supreme Court, and in such inferior Courts as the Congress may from time to time ordain and establish. The Judges, both of the supreme and inferior Courts, shall hold their Offices during good Behaviour, and shall, at stated Times, receive for their Services, a Compensation, which shall not be diminished during their Continuance in Office.

Section 2

Clause 1: The judicial Power shall extend to all Cases, in Law and Equity, arising under this Constitution, the Laws of the United States, and Treaties made, or which shall be made, under their Authority;—to all Cases affecting Ambassadors, other public Ministers and Consuls;—to all Cases of admiralty and maritime Jurisdiction;—to Controversies to which the United States shall be a Party;—to Controversies between two or more States;—between a State and Citizens of another State; — between Citizens of different States, —between Citizens of the same State claiming Lands under Grants of different States, and between a State, or the Citizens thereof, and foreign States, Citizens or Subjects.

Clause 2: In all Cases affecting Ambassadors, other public Ministers and Consuls, and those in which a State shall be Party, the supreme Court shall have original Jurisdiction. In all the other Cases before mentioned, the supreme Court shall have appellate Jurisdiction, both as to Law and Fact, with such Exceptions, and under such Regulations as the Congress shall make.

Clause 3: The Trial of all Crimes, except in Cases of Impeachment, shall be by Jury; and such Trial shall be held in the State where the said Crimes shall have been committed; but when not committed within any State, the Trial shall be at such Place or Places as the Congress may by Law have directed.

Section 3

Clause 1: Treason against the United States, shall consist only in levying War against them, or in adhering to their Enemies, giving them Aid and Comfort. No Person shall be convicted of Treason unless on the Testimony of two Witnesses to the same overt Act, or on Confession in open Court.

Clause 2: The Congress shall have Power to declare the Punishment of Treason, but no Attainder of Treason shall work Corruption of Blood, or Forfeiture except during the Life of the Person attainted.

Article IV

Section 1

Full Faith and Credit shall be given in each State to the public Acts, Records, and judicial Proceedings of every other State. And the Congress may by general Laws prescribe the Manner in which such Acts, Records and Proceedings shall be proved, and the Effect thereof.

Section 2

Clause 1: The Citizens of each State shall be entitled to all Privileges and Immunities of Citizens in the several States.

Clause 2: A Person charged in any State with Treason, Felony, or other Crime, who shall flee from Justice, and be found in another State, shall on Demand of the executive Authority of the State from which he fled, be delivered up, to be removed to the State having Jurisdiction of the Crime.

Clause 3: No Person held to Service or Labour in one State, under the Laws thereof, escaping into another, shall, in Consequence of any Law or Regulation therein, be discharged from such Service or Labour, but shall be delivered up on Claim of the Party to whom such Service or Labour may be due.

Section 3

Clause 1: New States may be admitted by the Congress into this Union; but no new State shall be formed or erected within the Jurisdiction of any other State; nor any State be formed by the Junction of two or more States, or Parts of States, without the Consent of the Legislatures of the States concerned as well as of the Congress.

Clause 2: The Congress shall have Power to dispose of and make all needful Rules and Regulations respecting the Territory or other Property belonging to the United States; and nothing in this Constitution shall be so construed as to Prejudice any Claims of the United States, or of any particular State.

Section 4

The United States shall guarantee to every State in this Union a Republican Form of Government, and shall protect each of them against Invasion; and on Application of the Legislature, or of the Executive (when the Legislature cannot be convened) against domestic Violence.

Article V

The Congress, whenever two thirds of both Houses shall deem it necessary, shall propose Amendments to this Constitution, or, on the Application of the Legislatures of two thirds of the several States, shall call a Convention for proposing Amendments, which, in either Case, shall be valid to all Intents and Purposes, as Part of this Constitution, when ratified by the Legislatures of three fourths of the several States, or by Conventions in three fourths thereof, as the one or the other Mode of Ratification may be proposed by the Congress; Provided that no Amendment which may be made prior to the Year One thousand eight hundred and eight shall in any Manner affect the first and fourth Clauses in the Ninth Section of the first Article; and that no State, without its Consent, shall be deprived of its equal Suffrage in the Senate.

Article VI

Clause 1: All Debts contracted and Engagements entered into, before the Adoption of this Constitution, shall be as valid against the United States under this Constitution, as under the Confederation.

Clause 2: This Constitution, and the Laws of the United States which shall be made in Pursuance thereof; and all Treaties made, or which shall be made, under the Authority of the United States, shall be the supreme Law of the Land; and the Judges in every State shall be bound thereby, any Thing in the Constitution or Laws of any State to the Contrary notwithstanding.

Clause 3: The Senators and Representatives before mentioned, and the Members of the several State Legislatures, and all executive and judicial Officers, both of the United States and of the several States, shall be bound by Oath or Affirmation, to support this Constitution; but no religious Test shall ever be required as a Qualification to any Office or public Trust under the United States.

Article VII

The Ratification of the Conventions of nine States, shall be sufficient for the Establishment of this Constitution between the States so ratifying the Same.

done in Convention by the Unanimous Consent of the States present the Seventeenth Day of September in the Year of our Lord one thousand seven hundred and Eighty seven and of the Independence of the United States of America the Twelfth In witness whereof We have hereunto subscribed our Names,

Amendment I

Congress shall make no law respecting an establishment of religion, or prohibiting the free exercise thereof; or abridging the freedom of speech, or of the press; or the right of the people peaceably to assemble, and to petition the government for a redress of grievances.

Amendment II

A well regulated militia, being necessary to the security of a free state, the right of the people to keep and bear arms, shall not be infringed.

Amendment III

No soldier shall, in time of peace be quartered in any house, without the consent of the owner, nor in time of war, but in a manner to be prescribed by law.

Amendment IV

The right of the people to be secure in their persons, houses, papers, and effects, against unreasonable searches and seizures, shall not be violated, and no warrants shall issue, but upon probable cause, supported by oath or affirmation, and particularly describing the place to be searched, and the persons or things to be seized.

Amendment V

No person shall be held to answer for a capital, or otherwise infamous crime, unless on a presentment or indictment of a grand jury, except in cases arising in the land or naval forces, or in the militia, when in actual service in time of war or public danger; nor shall any person be subject for the same offense to be twice put in jeopardy of life or limb; nor shall be compelled in any criminal case to be a witness against himself, nor be deprived of life, liberty, or property, without due process of law; nor shall private property be taken for public use, without just compensation.

Amendment VI

In all criminal prosecutions, the accused shall enjoy the right to a speedy and public trial, by an impartial jury of the state and district wherein the crime shall have been committed, which district shall have been previously ascertained by law, and to be informed of the nature and cause of the accusation; to be confronted with the witnesses against him; to have compulsory process for obtaining witnesses in his favor, and to have the assistance of counsel for his defense.

Amendment VII

In suits at common law, where the value in controversy shall exceed twenty dollars, the right of trial by jury shall be preserved, and no fact tried by a jury, shall be otherwise reexamined in any court of the United States, than according to the rules of the common law.

Amendment VIII

Excessive bail shall not be required, nor excessive fines imposed, nor cruel and unusual punishments inflicted.

Amendment IX

The enumeration in the Constitution, of certain rights, shall not be construed to deny or disparage others retained by the people.

Amendment X

The powers not delegated to the United States by the Constitution, nor prohibited by it to the states, are reserved to the states respectively, or to the people.

Amendment XI

The judicial power of the United States shall not be construed to extend to any suit in law or equity, commenced or prosecuted against one of the United States by citizens of another state, or by citizens or subjects of any foreign state.

Amendment XII

The electors shall meet in their respective states and vote by ballot for President and Vice-President, one of whom, at least, shall not be an inhabitant of the same state with themselves; they shall name in their ballots the person voted for as President, and in distinct ballots the person voted for as Vice-President, and they shall make distinct lists of all persons voted for as President, and of all persons voted for as Vice-President, and of the number of votes for each, which lists they shall sign and certify, and transmit sealed to the seat of the government of the United States, directed to the President of the Senate;—The President of the Senate shall, in the presence of the Senate and House of Representatives, open all the certificates and the votes shall then be counted;—the person having the greatest number of votes for President, shall be the President, if such number be a majority of the whole number of electors appointed; and if no person have such majority, then from the persons having the highest numbers not exceeding three on the list of those voted for as President, the House of Representatives shall choose immediately, by ballot, the President. But in choosing the President, the votes shall be taken by states, the representation from each state having one vote; a quorum for this purpose shall consist of a member or members from two-thirds of the states, and a majority of all the states shall be necessary to a choice. *And if the House of Representatives shall not choose a President whenever the right of choice shall devolve upon them, before the fourth day of March next following, then the Vice-President shall act as President, as in the case of the death or other constitutional disability of the President.* The person having the greatest number of votes as Vice-President, shall be the Vice-President, if such number be a majority of the whole number of electors appointed, and if no person have a majority, then from the two highest numbers on the list, the Senate shall choose the Vice-President; a quorum for the purpose shall consist of two-thirds of the whole number of Senators, and a majority of the whole number shall be necessary to a choice. But no person constitutionally ineligible to the office of President shall be eligible to that of Vice-President of the United States.

Amendment **XIII**

Section 1

Neither slavery nor involuntary servitude, except as a punishment for crime whereof the party shall have been duly convicted, shall exist within the United States, or any place subject to their jurisdiction.

Section 2

Congress shall have power to enforce this article by appropriate legislation.

Amendment **XIV**

Section 1

All persons born or naturalized in the United States, and subject to the jurisdiction thereof, are citizens of the United States and of the state wherein they reside. No state shall make or enforce any law which shall abridge the privileges or immunities of citizens of the United States; nor shall any state deprive any person of life, liberty, or property, without due process of law; nor deny to any person within its jurisdiction the equal protection of the laws.

Section 2

Representatives shall be apportioned among the several states according to their respective numbers, counting the whole number of persons in each state, excluding Indians not taxed. But when the right to vote at any election for the choice of electors for President and Vice President of the United States, Representatives in Congress, the executive and judicial officers of a state, or the members of the legislature thereof, is denied to any of the male inhabitants of such state, *being twenty-one years of age,* and citizens of the United States, or in any way abridged, except for participation in rebellion, or other crime, the basis of representation therein shall be reduced in the proportion which the number of such male citizens shall bear to the whole number of male citizens twenty-one years of age in such state.

Section 3

No person shall be a Senator or Representative in Congress, or elector of President and Vice President, or hold any office, civil or military, under the United States, or under any state, who, having previously taken an oath, as a member of Congress, or as an officer of the United States, or as a member of any state legislature, or as an executive or judicial officer of any state, to support the Constitution of the United States, shall have engaged in insurrection or rebellion against the same, or given aid or comfort to the enemies thereof. But Congress may by a vote of two-thirds of each House, remove such disability.

Section 4

The validity of the public debt of the United States, authorized by law, including debts incurred for payment of pensions and bounties for services in suppressing insurrection or rebellion, shall not be questioned. But neither the United States nor any state shall assume or pay any debt or obligation incurred in aid of insurrection or rebellion against the United States, or any claim for the loss or emancipation of any slave; but all such debts, obligations and claims shall be held illegal and void.

Section 5

The Congress shall have power to enforce, by appropriate legislation, the provisions of this article.

Amendment XV

Section 1
The right of citizens of the United States to vote shall not be denied or abridged by the United States or by any state on account of race, color, or previous condition of servitude.

Section 2
The Congress shall have power to enforce this article by appropriate legislation.

Amendment XVI

The Congress shall have power to lay and collect taxes on incomes, from whatever source derived, without apportionment among the several states, and without regard to any census or enumeration.

Amendment XVII

The Senate of the United States shall be composed of two Senators from each state, elected by the people thereof, for six years; and each Senator shall have one vote. The electors in each state shall have the qualifications requisite for electors of the most numerous branch of the state legislatures.

When vacancies happen in the representation of any state in the Senate, the executive authority of such state shall issue writs of election to fill such vacancies: Provided, that the legislature of any state may empower the executive thereof to make temporary appointments until the people fill the vacancies by election as the legislature may direct.

This amendment shall not be so construed as to affect the election or term of any Senator chosen before it becomes valid as part of the Constitution.

Amendment XVIII

Section 1
After one year from the ratification of this article the manufacture, sale, or

transportation of intoxicating liquors within, the importation thereof into, or the exportation thereof from the United States and all territory subject to the jurisdiction thereof for beverage purposes is hereby prohibited.

Section 2

The Congress and the several states shall have concurrent power to enforce this article by appropriate legislation.

Section 3

This article shall be inoperative unless it shall have been ratified as an amendment to the Constitution by the legislatures of the several states, as provided in the Constitution, within seven years from the date of the submission hereof to the states by the Congress.

Amendment XIX

The right of citizens of the United States to vote shall not be denied or abridged by the United States or by any state on account of sex.

Congress shall have power to enforce this article by appropriate legislation.

Amendment XX

Section 1

The terms of the President and Vice President shall end at noon on the 20th day of January, and the terms of Senators and Representatives at noon on the 3d day of January, of the years in which such terms would have ended if this article had not been ratified; and the terms of their successors shall then begin.

Section 2

The Congress shall assemble at least once in every year, and such meeting shall begin at noon on the 3d day of January, unless they shall by law appoint a different day.

Section 3

If, at the time fixed for the beginning of the term of the President, the President elect shall have died, the Vice President elect shall become President. If a President shall not have been chosen before the time fixed for the beginning of his term, or if the President elect shall have failed to qualify, then the Vice President elect shall act as President until a President shall have qualified; and the Congress may by law provide for the case wherein neither a President elect nor a Vice President elect shall have qualified, declaring who shall then act as President, or the manner in which one who is to act shall be selected, and such person shall act accordingly until a President or Vice President shall have qualified.

Section 4

The Congress may by law provide for the case of the death of any of the persons from whom the House of Representatives may choose a President whenever the right of choice shall have devolved upon them, and for the case of the death of any of the persons from whom the Senate may choose a Vice President whenever the right of choice shall have devolved upon them.

Section 5

Sections 1 and 2 shall take effect on the 15th day of October following the ratification of this article.

Section 6

This article shall be inoperative unless it shall have been ratified as an amendment to the Constitution by the legislatures of three-fourths of the several states within seven years from the date of its submission.

Amendment XXI

Section 1

The eighteenth article of amendment to the Constitution of the United States is hereby repealed.

Section 2

The transportation or importation into any state, territory, or possession of the United States for delivery or use therein of intoxicating liquors, in violation of the laws thereof, is hereby prohibited.

Section 3

This article shall be inoperative unless it shall have been ratified as an amendment to the Constitution by conventions in the several states, as provided in the Constitution, within seven years from the date of the submission hereof to the states by the Congress.

Amendment XXII

Section 1
No person shall be elected to the office of the President more than twice, and no person who has held the office of President, or acted as President, for more than two years of a term to which some other person was elected President shall be elected to the office of the President more than once. But this article shall not apply to any person holding the office of President when this article was proposed by the Congress, and shall not prevent any person who may be holding the office of President, or acting as President, during the term within which this article becomes operative from holding the office of President or acting as President during the remainder of such term.

Section 2
This article shall be inoperative unless it shall have been ratified as an amendment to the Constitution by the legislatures of three-fourths of the several states within seven years from the date of its submission to the states by the Congress.

Amendment XXIII

Section 1
The District constituting the seat of government of the United States shall appoint in such manner as the Congress may direct:

A number of electors of President and Vice President equal to the whole number of Senators and Representatives in Congress to which the District would be entitled if it were a state, but in no event more than the least populous state; they shall be in addition to those appointed by the states, but they shall be considered, for the purposes of the election of President and Vice President, to be electors appointed by a state; and they shall meet in the District and perform such duties as provided by the twelfth article of amendment.

Section 2

The Congress shall have power to enforce this article by appropriate legislation.

Amendment XXIV

Section 1

The right of citizens of the United States to vote in any primary or other election for President or Vice President, for electors for President or Vice President, or for Senator or Representative in Congress, shall not be denied or abridged by the United States or any state by reason of failure to pay any poll tax or other tax.

Section 2

The Congress shall have power to enforce this article by appropriate legislation.

Amendment XXV

Section 1

In case of the removal of the President from office or of his death or resignation, the Vice President shall become President.

Section 2

Whenever there is a vacancy in the office of the Vice President, the President shall nominate a Vice President who shall take office upon confirmation by a majority vote of both Houses of Congress.

Section 3

Whenever the President transmits to the President pro tempore of the Senate and the Speaker of the House of Representatives his written declaration that he is unable to discharge the powers and duties of his office, and until he transmits to them a written declaration to the contrary, such powers and duties shall be discharged by the Vice President as Acting President.

Section 4

Whenever the Vice President and a majority of either the principal officers of the executive departments or of such other body as Congress may by law provide, transmit to the President pro tempore of the Senate and the Speaker of the House of Representatives their written declaration that the President is unable to discharge the powers and duties of his office, the Vice President shall immediately assume the powers and duties of the office as Acting President.

Thereafter, when the President transmits to the President pro tempore of the Senate and the Speaker of the House of Representatives his written declaration that no inability exists, he shall resume the powers and duties of his office unless the Vice President and a majority of either the principal officers of the executive department or of such other body as Congress may by law provide, transmit within four days to the President pro tempore of the Senate and the Speaker of the House of Representatives their written declaration that the President is unable to discharge the powers and duties of his office. Thereupon Congress shall decide the issue, assembling within forty-eight hours for that purpose if not in session. If the Congress, within twenty-one days after receipt of the latter written declaration, or, if Congress is not in session, within twenty-one days after Congress is required to assemble, determines by two-thirds vote of both Houses that the President is unable to discharge the powers and duties of his office, the Vice President shall continue to discharge the same as Acting President; otherwise, the President shall resume the powers and duties of his office.

Amendment XXVI

Section 1

The right of citizens of the United States, who are 18 years of age or older, to vote, shall not be denied or abridged by the United States or any state on account of age.

Section 2

The Congress shall have the power to enforce this article by appropriate legislation.

Amendment XXVII

No law, varying the compensation for the services of the Senators and Representatives, shall take effect, until an election of Representatives shall have intervened.

Admission of States

Delaware	Dec. 7, 1787	Michigan	Jan. 26., 1837
Pennsylvania	Dec. 12, 1787	Florida	March 3, 1845
New Jersey	Dec. 18, 1787	Texas	Dec. 29, 1845
Georgia	Jan. 2, 1788	Iowa	Dec. 28, 1846
Connecticut	Jan. 9, 1788	Wisconsin	May 29, 1848
Massachusetts	Feb. 6, 1788	California	Sept. 9, 1850
Maryland	April 28, 1788	Minnesota	May 11, 1858
South Carolina	May 23, 1788	Oregon	Feb. 14, 1859
New Hampshire	June 21, 1788	Kansas	Jan. 29, 1861
Virginia	June 25, 1788	West Virginia	June 20, 1863
New York	July 26, 1788	Nevada	Oct. 31, 1864
North Carolina	Nov. 21, 1789	Nebraska	March 1, 1867
Rhode Island	May 29, 1790	Colorado	Aug. 1, 1876
Vermont	March 4, 1791	North Dakota	Nov. 2, 1889
Kentucky	June 1, 1792	South Dakota	Nov. 2, 1889
Tennessee	June 1, 1796	Montana	Nov. 8, 1889
Ohio	March 1, 1803	Washington	Nov. 11, 1889
Louisiana	April 30, 1812	Idaho	July 3, 1890
Indiana	Dec. 11, 1816	Wyoming	July 10, 1890
Mississippi	Dec. 10, 1817	Utah	Jan. 4, 1896
Illinois	Dec. 3, 1818	Oklahoma	Nov. 16, 1907
Alabama	Dec. 14, 1819	New Mexico	Jan. 6, 1912
Maine	March 15, 1820	Arizona	Feb. 14, 1912
Missouri	Aug. 10, 1821	Alaska	Jan. 3, 1959
Arkansas	June 15, 1836	Hawaii	Aug. 21, 1959

Presidential Elections: 1789~2001

George Washington, 1789–1797

John Adams, 1797–1801

Thomas Jefferson, 1801–1809

James Madison, 1809–1817

James Monroe, 1817–1825

John Quincy Adams, 1825–1829

Andrew Jackson, 1829–1837

Martin Van Buren, 1837–1841

William Henry Harrison, 1841

John Tyler, 1841–1845

James Knox Polk, 1845–1849

Zachary Taylor, 1849–1850

Millard Fillmore, 1850–1853

Franklin Pierce, 1853–1857

James Buchanan, 1857–1861

Abraham Lincoln, 1861–1865

Andrew Johnson, 1865–1869

Ulysses Simpson Grant, 1869–1877

Rutherford Birchard Hayes, 1877–1881

James Abram Garfield, 1881

Chester Alan Arthur, 1881–1885

Grover Cleveland, 1885–1889

Benjamin Harrison, 1889–1893

Grover Cleveland, 1893–1897

William McKinley, 1897–1901

Theodore Roosevelt, 1901–1909

William Howard Taft, 1909–1913

Woodrow Wilson, 1913–1921

Warren Gamaliel Harding, 1921–1923

Calvin Coolidge, 1923–1929

Herbert Clark Hoover, 1929–1933

Franklin Delano Roosevelt, 1933–1945

Harry S. Truman, 1945–1953

Dwight David Eisenhower, 1953–1961

John Fitzgerald Kennedy, 1961–1963

Lyndon Baines Johnson, 1963–1969

Richard Milhous Nixon, 1969–1974

Gerald Rudolph Ford, 1974–1977

James Earl Carter, Jr., 1977–1981

Ronald Wilson Reagan, 1981–1989

George Herbert Walker Bush, 1989–1993

William Jefferson Clinton, 1993–2001

George Walker Bush, 2001–

Index

~A~

abolitionists
  anti-slavery movement by, 243
  arguments of, 235–237
  attack by, 222–223
  debate by, 211
  re-colonization of slaves to Africa
    by, 221
Act of Havana, 165
activism, literary, 193
Adams, Abigail Smith, 79, 100–101,
  121
Adams, Charles Francis, 235
Adams, John
  as author of Massachusetts
    Constitution, 121
  character of, 64
  defense of British soldiers by, 71
  differences between Hamilton
    and, 124
  diplomacy by, 85
  justification of revolution by,
    77–78
  nomination for second term for,
    121
  presidency of, 122–124
  prominence in resistance
    movements by, 70
  support of Suffolk Resolves by, 74
  vice presidency by, 109
Adams, John Quincy
  character of, 166–167
  diplomacy by, 140
  protests as congressman by, 222

Adams, Samuel
  Boston Massacre and, 70
  character of, 64
  leadership by, 75
  letter by, 70
  role in Boston Tea Party by, 72
  support of Suffolk Resolves by, 74
Adams-Onis Treaty, 164
African Americans. *See also*
    abolitionists
  conditions for, after
      Reconstruction, 287–288
  culture of, 43
  loss of citizenship rights by, 288
  privileges of, 223–224
  Reconstruction for, 279–281
  social transformation of, 86,
    219–220
agriculture. *See also* farming
  crops for, 7
  improvements in, 188
Alien and Sedition Acts, 123, 126
Allen, Ethan, 80
American Colonization Society, 221
American dream, 159, 168, 224
American Party, 254–255
American Revolution
  aid by foreign soldiers during, 86
  aid by French for, 80, 82
  causes of, 66
  identification of Americans with,
    48
  lack of English enthusiasm for, 76
  legality of, 87

~Q~

~R~